BUTCHERY ON
BOND STREET

Spectators at 31 Bond Street after Dr. Burdell's body was discovered

BUTCHERY ON BOND STREET

SEXUAL POLITICS
AND THE BURDELL-CUNNINGHAM
CASE IN ANTE-BELLUM NEW YORK

BY

Benjamin Feldman

———◆✦◆———

THE GREEN-WOOD CEMETERY HISTORIC FUND
in association with
THE NEW YORK WANDERER PRESS
2007

ISBN   0-9795175-0-8

ISBN-13   978-0-9795175-0-1

For Frances, Tova, and Clara,
my precious ones

CONTENTS

INTRODUCTION

NEAR THE CREST of the Gowanus hills in Brooklyn's Green-Wood Cemetery, an unmarked murder victim's grave lies under scruffy evergreens, just a stone's throw from Horace Greeley's magnificent monument. The memory of the revered editor of *The New York Tribune* lives on today, in stark contrast to that of his anonymous neighbor. Dr. Harvey Burdell's gruesome death was front-page news in the *Tribune* for weeks on end in 1857, when the libertine dentist's life was snuffed out in his clinic at the end of January.

My first visit to Green-Wood in May 2000 began in a very ordinary way when I attended the recently re-instituted annual Memorial Day concert. Though the cemetery's massive brownstone portals made an instant impression as I strolled through them to the grassy seating area, I had no inkling of what waited for me inside. I stepped away from my picnic blanket during an intermission in the musical program and followed a trail downhill to a tent erected for the occasion by the Green-Wood Historic Fund. Among the promotional literature and refreshments offered for sale in the tent were copies of an elaborate coffee-table book about the cemetery, complete with a map of its many paths, roads and best-known gravesites. I glanced through the volume and on impulse, bought a copy.

One story above all others riveted my attention. I read with disbelief a tale completely unknown to me. The sordid, tragic personal histories of Dr. Harvey Burdell and Emma Augusta Hempstead Cunningham were on the lips of all of New York through most of 1857. The lovers' fierce uncoupling dominated the press from the beginning of February through August of that year, eclipsing news of great national and international importance in many morning editions. The pair lies buried in separate Green-Wood plots a few hundred yards apart, their long-forgotten names unmarked.

Though Dr. Burdell's courtship of Emma Cunningham began in a conventional manner, the couple's relations grew bizarre and violent as the months wore on. The mother of five young children eventually moved into her bachelor lover's townhouse, underwent an abortion at his insistence, and exchanged marriage vows before a local minister with a man pretending to be her wealthy suitor. Scarcely three months later, Emma stood accused of Dr. Burdell's grisly death. Her desperate attempts to wring a marriage commitment from the well-to-do dentist were to no avail, and Emma struggled to control his sizable estate through two separate incarcerations, while also claiming to be carrying the decedent's unborn child.

Despite the seemingly unusual circumstances of the Burdell-Cunningham case, I learned through my several-year journey rebuilding the couple's personal histories that their horrific experiences were, in fact, not extraordinary. The public attention given the murder trial and estate proceedings and the daily participation of New York's most prominent politicians and attorneys belied the fact that the pair's woeful interaction was all too commonplace. Although its violent end was rare, the battle between Dr. Harvey Burdell and Emma Cunningham epitomized widespread gender conflict in mid-nineteenth century urban America.

The Burdell murder case instantly became a political football, with Albany Republicans and various New York City Democratic factions vying furiously for advantage. Elected municipal officials may well have conducted a desperate cover-up when another suspect in Burdell's death threatened to publicize their private misbehavior. Prosecutor A. "Elegant" Oakey Hall and defense attorney Henry Lauren Clinton's bitter battles at Emma Cunningham's murder trial and the involvement of Samuel J. Tilden in the wrangling over Burdell's estate form an important but overlooked chapter in the history of New York City politics. The confrontation between Hall and Clinton at Emma's murder trial presaged the rematch of these two legal titans a decade and a half later in the criminal trials of New York's infamous Boss Tweed and his henchmen.

The clash of wills between Harvey Burdell and Emma

Cunningham first captivated the public's attention when Dr. Burdell was found strangled and stabbed to death in his lower Manhattan office on January 31, 1857. His live-in lover, Emma Hempstead Cunningham, was immediately accused of the crime. The violent death of a philandering member of the professional class in the sanctity of his own home was a virtually unknown event. In mid-century America, men in Burdell's position were free to seduce and abandon single women without recrimination or consequences. Dr. Burdell's death shook the foundations of respectable patriarchal urban homes across America. The dentist's violent end also became a focal point of debate and an emotional flash point for men and women all over the country as the details of longing, lust, greed and deceit became widely known.

Fear abounded in New York on a broader front as news of the murder spread. Dr. Burdell's death rode the crest of a wave of violent crime that was sweeping over the city. New York experienced an epidemic of stranger-perpetrated brutality in the months preceding the dentist's death. His murder symbolized precarious urban conditions, where crime and corruption were rife. Until Dr. Burdell's death, civic outcry demanding effective police action and reform had not produced results. This shocking case demanded action, with the futures of several elected officials riding on its outcome. Emma Cunningham's guilt or innocence soon became a celebrated cause in both city and state political circles, propelling upward the careers of many involved in the defense and the prosecution.

The murder story and accounts of subsequent legal proceedings filled newspapers and magazines across America in 1857. The publications consumed by the public provided a bill of fare, albeit prurient and sensationalist, quite different from that served up in similar circumstances today. Early nineteenth century American newspaper and pamphlet reporting of murder provided few details of the crimes themselves, focusing instead on the spiritual and moral issues of damnation and salvation that were echoed in execution sermons preached at the hangings of convicted perpetrators and transcribed for popular consumption. By mid-century, a murder story, be it fact or fiction, was common fodder for the public imagination in a very different way. By 1850, reporting focused on the grisly details of the crime and the unexpected nature of the violence, especially when it occurred within the confines of a family home.

Press coverage of Burdell's murder included few, if any, interviews with acquaintances of the deceased or of Emma Cunningham, police officials, attorneys, or neighborhood residents. Instead, reporters focused on the physical horridness of the crime itself. News articles and editorials were obsessed with the possible guilt of Mrs. Cunningham and her deceptive behavior. Speculation about motives and psychology was by and large confined to occasional character assassinations of Dr. Burdell and his former lover.

Since 1857, the Burdell murder has been the subject of chapters in several collections of famous New York crime stories, a novel published in the early 1980s, and a modern recapitulation of the *New York Times* coverage of the crime. No one has looked at basic archival sources to answer the questions that journalists would address today. Harvey Burdell's and Emma Hempstead Cunningham's birth families, formative years, and personalities, and the progress of their acquaintance, all in the cultural and political contexts of their times, have never been examined. What Harvey and Emma were like as young adults, and how and why they became obsessed with each other were almost totally ignored by the journalism of the day. In this book I have attempted to rectify those omissions.

Here, then, is their story.

PROLOGUE

THE ROOMS customarily occupied by the New York County Marine and Circuit Courts, located next to Manhattan's City Hall, fell silent on the morning of Tuesday, May 5, 1857. Judge Henry E. Davies presided over the Court of Oyer and Terminer, which, due to the immense public interest in the murder trial at hand, had been moved to the more spacious accomodations. Judge Davies, who within ten years would become the most powerful judge in all of New York State, cut a swarthy, handsome figure at the bench.[1] An elegantly upholstered backdrop framed his clean-shaven, chiseled face. The responsibility thrust upon him was immense: public outcry over the death of Dr. Harvey Burdell, allegedly at the hands of his lover, Emma Cunningham, was greater than any case heard in the city for the past twenty years. The political consequences for Democrats and Republicans alike could be disastrous if the defendant managed to escape the gallows.

The judge's bench glowed from the light cast by matching double-globed lamps. Natural light also flooded the room from tall windows, supplemented by wall sconces and the shine from an elaborate oil-lamp chandelier. Looking out, Judge Davies surveyed the tense scene before him. To his left sat the defense, to his right the prosecution, poised for the start of the morning's proceedings.

Outside on Chambers Street, a veritable circus prevailed. Ever since the discovery of Burdell's bloodied corpse on the morning of January 31, crowds had gathered where there was action, seeking admission to the coroner's inquest, peering through the windows of the house where the murder took place, trying to see and touch the core of gruesome reality that the crime embodied. New York newspapers provided front-page coverage of the case from day one.

Transcripts of the testimony before Coroner Connery's jurors, character sketches, editorials, and letters to the editor signed with pen names
such as "Justice," fed readers' appetites to know the circumstances of
Burdell's death and the role played by Emma Cunningham. During
her pre-trial incarceration, the defendant was bedeviled by curious
strangers traipsing through the open corridors in the Tombs, depriv-
ing her of any privacy or rest for most of three months. Legions of the
men and women peered shamelessly into Emma's jail cell, eager to
bear witness to what many considered the incarnation of evil.

Out of a need to maintain decorum, only jurors, witnesses, and
journalists were allowed by Judge Davies beyond the bar. The view
through the folding doors of the Marine Court afforded the mass of
excited curiosity-seekers limited views of the proceedings. Necks
strained forward and tip-toes arched to facilitate glimpses of the protagonists: the trial of Emma Augusta Cunningham for the premeditat-
ed capital murder of her lover struck at the city's psychic core in a manner as yet unknown in nineteenth century New York. Husbands and
wives, lovers and friends, parents and children: many took opposing
sides in the case, their allegiances frequently divided by gender.
Though unspoken in popular media, rapidly changing sexual mores
and the fierce fight for women's equality in American society
ineluctably guided the public's perception of right and wrong and colored the weighing of evidence in a case based almost wholly on circumstantial proof.

Condemned with thinly veiled misogyny from church pulpits and
in the popular press, Emma Cunningham was convicted in the court of
public opinion long before her case was brought to trial. Women's
rights activists organized several energetic and controversial public
gatherings during the preceding months, and Emma's indictment provided ample fodder for prominent critics of the feminist credo. The
Seventh Annual Women's Rights Convention was held in New York City
in November, 1856, and a strike by female garment workers on March
8, 1857, produced a street melee in lower Manhattan. A torrent of editorial complaint in the *Times* and other mainstream dailies poured
forth against the protesters, while endless articles passed judgment on
Emma: guilty as charged. Despite the outcry of establishment journal-

ism against her, Emma's skillful defense counsel, Henry Lauren Clinton, created a groundswell of popular support for her exoneration. While the major New York papers ridiculed women's rights activism, the facts of deceit, desertion and desperation in the murder case soon became known to the entire nation.

Emotions ran high in the courtroom on the day before opening speeches were delivered. The defendant entered her plea of not guilty, and the legally required all male jury was selected from a panel of hundreds of prospective candidates. Women were barred by law from serving on the jury, but formed an unusually large proportion of gallery spectators at the trial. Juror after juror was disqualified on the grounds of having formed a prior opinion about the guilt of the accused. It would have been hard for any person in control of his senses not to have formed one. The January 30 crime and the ensuing politically-motivated spectacles masquerading as legal proceedings had been the talk of New York for the past three months in saloons and salons, across breakfast tables and around the punch bowls at church socials. Despite these difficulties, a jury was finally seated in the courtroom Tuesday morning, awaiting the prosecutor's opening speech.

The reporter for Horace Greeley's *Tribune* wondered aloud at the highly charged atmosphere that prevailed in the normally staid and sometimes sparsely attended rooms of justice: "The room of the Marine Court was filled early this morning; people stood in all imaginable positions and places, and looked wistfully through the folding doors. The commands of officers were frequently necessary to prevent them from ruining the new furniture of the court-room." [2]

Shortly after 10:00 A.M., the district attorney rose in the hushed chamber. Thirty–year-old Abraham "Elegant" Oakey Hall faced the court in his frock coat and silk cravat. Across the room sat the veiled defendant, dressed in widow's weeds of black silk bombazine. Emma was flanked by two of her teen-age daughters. Nearby sat her defense counsel, Henry Lauren Clinton and Gilbert Dean.[3]

Young and handsome, Hall had already developed an impressive reputation in New York. After reading law at Harvard for only one term in 1844, the novice attorney practiced in New Orleans for a short time. Upon returning to his home state in 1848, Hall joined Nathaniel

Bowditch Blunt in the New York County prosecutor's office. A good nose for politics and keen legal skills quickly garnered attention for the new assistant district attorney from Mayor Fernando Wood. Although a member of the city's minority Republican Party, Hall was elected to head the office a few months after Blunt's death in 1853.[4]

Ten weeks before Emma's murder trial began, the district attorney endorsed his florid signature at the bottom of the two-page grand jury indictment, tolling the solemn accusations that he repeated in the courtroom. The grand jurors acted swiftly after the exhaustive, albeit irregular, proceedings conducted in the deceased's home by Coroner Connery while Burdell's corpse lay in its coffin in a room adjacent to the makeshift hearing chamber. Burdell's lacerated body was discovered in the second-floor examining room that the dentist maintained in his home at 31 Bond Street. The victim shared the Bond Street house with the defendant, her several children, and her various boarders. Emma Augusta Cunningham was formally charged with the willful and felonious murder of Dr. Harvey Burdell. According to the charges, malice aforethought guided the murderess's right hand, as she held a knife that "did strike, stab, cut and thrust . . . giving . . . him . . . one mortal wound, of the breadth of two inches and the depth of two inches of which . . . the said Harvey Burdell . . . did die." [5]

Perceiving Emma's sex and its proclivity for non-violence to be a significant hurdle to overcome in his quest for a capital murder conviction, Hall confronted the natural prejudices of the trial jury head-on. With scarlet rhetoric, the district attorney manipulated maudlin sentiment into a powerful tool used against the accused as he confronted the issues of gender. Keenly aware that the jury would instinctively consider a female defendant, particularly one of Emma Cunningham's seeming gentility, incapable of even the conception much less the execution of such a dastardly act, Hall cautioned the group to be even-handed: ". . .[A]t every step of this testimony," the D.A. warned, "the thought will be forced upon your minds . . . 'Remember, gentlemen, you are trying a woman.'" Common sense and modern jurisprudence were urged upon the twelve judges. Hall reminded them, "Crime has no sex; crime has no peculiar attribute of its own; no differences, when it settles, in the one breast of the man, or the other breast of the woman." Notions of sexual purity and innocence were parried aside by the prosecutor as he anticipated the psychological stance that Emma's counsel would use in her defense.

Hall displayed to the courtroom an assumed feminine canvas that he painted over masterfully, while sympathizing with the jury's dilemma of being asked to administer blind justice with unnatural and seemingly unchivalrous strokes: "When we remember the mother of our prayers, when we remember the sister of our household adoration, when we remember the wife of our life until death, when we remember the children who are to be the future women of the world, that sit upon our knee, and we feel as we look upon young girlhood and growing maidenhood, we say, can it ever be that this being, upon whom God Almighty has put his own seal of purity, should ever live to be the perpetrator of crime, the midnight assassin, to cherish hate, revenge and jealousy?"

Rising as if from a thirteenth seat in the box he faced, still tortured by his conflict supposedly shared with the jurors, Hall linked Emma Cunningham to a succession of the most violent harridans ever to walk the earth. Among them were Fulvia (of imperial Rome) whom, "when the head of Cicero was brought to her, she spat upon it, drew from her bosom, which had nourished children, a bodkin, and drove it though the tongue until it quivered; and . . . Agnes, Queen of Hungary, who bathed her feet in the blood of sixty-three knights, and said 'It seems as if I were wading in May dew'" [6]

The district attorney's keen sensibility for employing popular imagination would have to be matched by Messrs. Clinton and Dean if their client were to walk free. By the time Prosecutor Hall seated himself, Clinton and his partner were not only representing a distiller's widow. The defense table was encumbered with Lady Macbeth and several other harpies, both historical and fictional.

Harvey Burdell

CHAPTER 1

---◆·▸✕◂·◆---

"Murder!" on Bond Street

SLEET AND HAIL poured from the sky onto throngs of thickly cloaked curiosity seekers milling about a house on Manhattan's Bond Street on the last day of January 1857. Chilly temperatures and a harsh winter storm did little to dampen the excitement throughout the city early that Saturday: the corpse of a prominent neighborhood dentist, Dr. Harvey Burdell, had been found slumped on the floor of his home office, riddled with knife wounds. Garish bruises produced by a tightened garrote were splayed around the victim's pale neck.

Word of Dr. Burdell's bloody end attracted enormous attention from public authorities and the press. The murder of a well-to-do citizen was a rare event in mid-century New York, and the overall level of violent lawlessness and street crime in the months preceding the murder had become a matter of severe concern to the citizenry.[7]

Dr. Burdell left home about 5:00 P.M. the day before he died, planning to dine at his cousin's house in Brooklyn. Months of violent conflict with his landlady and ex-lover, Emma Cunningham, caused the wealthy bachelor to take pains to be secretive about his comings and goings. The 46-year-old dentist thought he had managed to escape attention from Emma's desperate eyes upon his return home that night.

Several months before, Harvey Burdell ceased eating at Emma's boarding table and began taking his meals at the nearby Lafarge House Hotel. The miserly bachelor could not longer bear dining with a woman whose marital desires were so painfully centered on him. Dr. Burdell's estrangement from nearly everyone in his house, boarders and servants alike, had become intense after a particularly severe explosion with Emma in mid-October. Whether or not he ever reached Brooklyn that late January evening, and what stops the dentist made on his way home are unknown. Rumor had it that Burdell was last seen in the company of a notoriously violent faro player. Supposedly the two argued over a rigged game in a gambling den near the Bowery. The possibility that the dispute had spilled over into the streets and perhaps even into the doctor's quarters kept several of police captain George Dilks' officers busy hunting for the missing gambler. The man was rumored to be well-acquainted with officers from the Mercer Street stationhouse.

At 7:00 A.M. on that Saturday, Dr. Burdell's office boy, John Burchell, arrived at the house, ready to rekindle the coal grates and go about his usual chores. Bringing scuttles of coal up from the cellar to provide a fire in Dr. Burdell's second-floor operatory was the boy's first task for a winter morning. Young John had worked for his master only three weeks, but was already well acquainted with the landlady of the premises, a frequently forlorn 36-year-old widow. Mrs. Cunningham seemed unusually sad at her breakfast table Saturday morning as John went about his business. Emma had good reason to be especially sad: the family had stayed up late Friday night marking clothing and packing trunks for Emma's younger daughter Helen. Reverend Luther Beecher was to call for Helen at 10:30 the next morning and escort her to the Hudson River Railroad Depot on West Broadway for their trip together to Saratoga Springs. Now that their mother was satisfied with the quality of instruction, Helen was to join her older sister there for winter-term studies at Beecher's Temple Grove Female Seminary.[8]

John Burchell trod up and down the winding stairway, stopping to leave a blackened pail outside one of the hall doors of Dr. Burdell's suite. After delivering yet another bucket to Mrs. Cunningham's third-floor rooms, the boy went back down to the second floor to inquire whether his master wished the hail and snow be cleaned off the sidewalks. As he approached the clinic entrance, John realized that something was amiss: a key inexplicably hung in the lock on the *outside* of the Doctor's door. The boy nudged open the latch and nearly swooned at the gruesome sight.

Harvey Burdell's mangled form lay on its left side "face downward; in a perfect pool of blood," as the *Herald's* reporter wrote.[9] A crimson trail led from Dr. Burdell's office chair and dentistry tool chest to a table in the center of the room, and then over to the hall door. One of many puncture wounds had severed Burdell's carotid artery as he struggled fiercely to escape his assassin's final thrusts. Blood had spurted violently from the victim's chest and neck. Smears were found more than five feet up the walls. The scene beggared description in what the *Herald* labeled "one of the most atrocious crimes ever committed in this city." The paper's Monday morning lead article spared no detail in informing the reading public of the horrific nature of Burdell's last moments on earth:

> *The condition of the room wherein the bloody scene was enacted bore evident traces of a long and desperate struggle having been made by the deceased ere he yielded to the knife of the assassin. The walls were smeared with gore, while the entire floor of the neighborhood of the spot where the body was found was one sea of blood. The mutilated condition of the body, and the number of wounds upon the corpse would lead one to think that there must have been more than one hand in the horrid butchery. Twice the steel had pierced the heart, twice the lungs had been reached with the deadly point of the stiletto, while the jugular vein and the carotid artery were both severed, and life's blood oozed from the gaping wounds . . . Any one [of] the six wounds alluded to would have been sufficient to cause almost instant death; so we were led to infer that the foul deed was the work of more persons than one.*[10]

After regaining his balance, John Burchell ran down to the basement and yelled to the cook, Hannah Conlan. Upstairs on the third floor, the breakfast trays had scarcely been cleared away. Emma's children and a few family friends were gathered in her bedroom to say farewell to 16-year-old Helen. The tearful goodbyes were aborted, though, as the cook raced up the two flights to Dr. Burdell's door, looked in on the awful scene, and screamed for help.

Houseguest George Snodgrass was distraught that Saturday morning, even before the alarm was sounded. December and January in the Cunningham home had been filled with a delightful romance, one that the minister's son knew would soon be sundered by Helen's departure for Saratoga. Young Snodgrass was the son of a Presbyterian clergyman of Emma's acquaintance, and had come from his father's home in Goshen, New York, in mid-November to board at 31 Bond while he worked in a brush warehouse near the South Street wharves. A poet and banjo-player, George had pleaded soulfully with Helen

Cunningham to delay her enrollment a few more days so that he might accompany her on her trip upstate.

One usual breakfast diner was missing from the tearful scene in Emma's rooms. Boarder John Eckel was absent. A note arrived at 31 Bond the previous day from a business acquaintance of Eckel's, requesting an early Saturday meeting at the boarder's Stanton Street tallow and hide dealership. Eckel hurried off that morning without eating.

As Emma sat on her bed with daughters Augusta and Helen, George Snodgrass rushed in, shouting out the discovery of Harvey Burdell's lifeless body. The two young women promptly fainted. Emma fell senseless, too, and George's swiftly extended arm around her waist was the only thing that prevented her from collapsing onto the floor. The quality of Emma Cunningham's swoon seemed curious to Snodgrass, though. Instead of lying still and gradually regaining consciousness, Emma rose from her bed quickly and commenced raving and tearing her hair with apparent grief.

Pandemonium raged through the house as John Burchell ran to summon Dr. J.W. Francis from across the street, and then hurried to the Fifteenth Ward stationhouse on nearby Mercer Street. Hannah Conlan and George Snodgrass attended to the grief-stricken family as best they could, hoping against hope that some sign of life would be found by Dr. Francis in Harvey Burdell's already cold corpse.

Captain George Dilks was away from the stationhouse when word of the crime first reached the desk officers. The coroner's and district attorney's offices were telegraphed immediately. Upon receiving the news, Dilks rushed over to Bond Street. A bevy of police officers was stationed to guard the front door. Word of the events had instantly drawn an enormous number of the area's residents to the broad-stooped house, as well as attracting hundreds of the transients who frequented the busy nearby commercial blocks. Members of the press connived to gain admission to the crime scene, wheedling unsuccessfully with Captain Dilks' men. By 9:00 A.M. the coroner's physicians were summoned. The men rushed upstairs, and peered into the room where Burdell's corpse lay. The *Herald* reported that despite Burdell's prominence in New York's medical community and his notoriety in lower Manhattan society, "[T]hey could not tell from the appearance of his face who the murdered man was, it was so disfigured and clotted with blood; there was nothing about him that looked like Dr. Burdell–his clothes were soaked and matted with gore." The decedent's professional colleagues went about their grim task with somber and respectful efficiency: "They cut his clothes off of him and washed the body; then examined the wounds; there were fifteen deeply incised cuts on the body, which penetrated into the heart, lungs and neck."[11]

Despite having noticed the papers askew on Burdell's desk, the *Herald*'s reporter jumped to a conclusion about the murderer's motive, one that soon proved to be deceptively simple and wrong-headed. The initial crime story noted that the victim's gold watch and pocketbook were found on his body and peremptorily concluded that the crime could not have been committed by burglars.[12]

Coroner Edward Downes Connery hurried to the scene late Saturday morning after hearing of the savagery. While Emma Cunningham sat upstairs in her rooms, weeping disconsolately at her sudden loss, the house was searched from top to bottom for the murder weapon. Bloodstains were found in a trail leading all the way to the top floor. The wooden flooring in an unoccupied bedroom was stained with spots of sperm oil and blood, and a fire grate held the remains of partially burned fabric.

Saturday morning's ice and sleet had turned to rain by 2:00 P.M. as the twelve neighborhood men summoned to serve as jurors assembled for an inquest into the circumstances of Dr. Burdell's demise. The few women admitted to the first-floor parlor were legally barred from serving, and remained as spectators in the makeshift hearing room. With the exception of testimony given by female witnesses, neither a woman's voice nor a feminine viewpoint was heard throughout the entire two-week-long inquest. After the initial inspection by Connery's physicians, Burdell's corpse was moved to his former second-floor sleeping quarters in the front of the house. The elegantly decorated adjacent rear room that had served as Dr. Burdell's clinic was searched for evidence, samples of blood stains were taken, and the dentistry patients' chair removed to the first floor parlor, where it was converted into the Coroner's witness stand.[13]

In his rush to take control of the situation, Connery questioned his first witness even before the jurors were officially impaneled. Dentist Allen T. Smith settled himself in Dr. Burdell's treatment chair, and his brief testimony instantly provided the officials and jurors with reason to suspect that the grief-stricken widow sitting two flights up had done in Harvey Burdell. Dr. Smith last saw Burdell at mid-day on Friday. They had met almost every day in recent months while Smith maintained a workroom behind the house for the fabrication of the "artificial work" that he produced in partnership with the deceased. Although not a confidante of Dr. Burdell's, Smith told the audience of overhearing angry encounters between Emma Cunningham and Harvey Burdell over the past several weeks. Burdell had accused her of stealing the key to his desk-safe and purloining an unpaid $600 promissory note that she had given to him in December 1855. Several days passed in the stifling room before the complicated sources of Burdell's geyser of anger and the circumstances of Emma's having signed the note were to come to light.

Over the next fourteen days, several municipal officials and District Attorney Hall joined with Coroner Connery and the twelve jurors in questioning witnesses. A parade of professional and personal acquaintances of the both the deceased and the landlady of the house, neighborhood shopkeepers, and passersby on the night of the murder were summoned to try and piece together the last twenty-four hours of the victim's life as well as the behavior of the suspect in the days before Burdell's death.

Coroner Connery's deputies and Captain Dilks' officers continued to comb the house in the waning light for further clues. Just before cook Hannah Conlan took the stand, a bloody shirt with the name "Charles J. Ketchum" inked on the sleeve and a bloody towel were retrieved from a garret room on the fourth floor. Speculation about the identity of Ketchum and the source of the bloodstains buzzed through the room as Hannah mounted the dentist's chair.

Conlan had been in Emma Cunningham's employ at 31 Bond Street almost from the start of Emma's tenure as boardinghouse landlady on May 1, 1856. The voluble Irishwoman surprised no one with the wealth of knowledge garnered from her co-workers about the goings-on in the house in recent months. Hannah's testimony not only corroborated earlier evidence of the previous autumn's friction between Emma and Harvey over the missing promissory note; she also described Emma's initial presence in the house as a boarder under the previous landlady, Mrs. Jones, who ran the operation with Dr. Burdell's permission for many months during 1855 and early 1856 before Emma replaced her.

Conlan's testimony gave the coroner and his jury their first inkling of the complexity of the relationship between the murder victim and Emma Cunningham, and the vortex of desperate parental fear, sexual longing, greed, and deceit that led to Burdell's violent death. With Conlan's simple words, Emma Cunningham's nearly hopeless personal circumstances and her battle to secure a stable future for herself and her children took shape in the minds of the press and public as well as the inquest jury. The details of her entanglement in Harvey Burdell's web of personal intrigue were woeful to hear.

The highlight of Hannah's testimony must have brought murmurs of astonishment from the many spectators packed into the room. Emma had suffered grievously at Burdell's hands in the year before his death; a broken heart was only one of several injuries. According to Conlan, Emma had lain bedridden in the house at Thanksgiving 1855, violently ill. Impregnated by Dr. Burdell, perhaps during their stay together at the Congress Hall Hotel in Saratoga Springs at the end of the previous summer, Emma either miscarried or unwillingly underwent an abortion over the autumn holiday. She remained confined to her bed for weeks thereafter.

The pleas Harvey Burdell heard repeatedly from Emma earlier that fall to marry her and make a name for her unborn child must have terrified the mercurial dentist. While recuperating in early December, Emma also nursed a bloody face wound that she had suffered under unexplained circumstances around the time her pregnancy ended. According to witness Conlan, the tragic results of Emma's pregnancy sent the lovers on a fifteen-month descent into violent recrimination and mutual accusations of infidelity. In an attempt to divert the jury's expected sympathy for Emma Cunningham, the coroner snidely attempted to force an admission of intemperance from Conlan, but it was to no avail.

Emma Cunningham appeared on the witness stand late that Saturday afternoon, and provided the raptly attentive audience with a few details of her recent life with the murder victim. Shedding copious tears, Emma revealed only a bare outline of the sordid personal intrigues in which Harvey Burdell had involved her. Dr. Burdell's character was first revealed in Emma's account of her lover's relationship with two of his brothers, also resident in New York City. The eldest, John Burdell, had become a prominent dentist and mentor to Harvey during the 1830s. John's separation from his wife, Margaret Alburtis, in 1843, provided an opportunity for Harvey and William Burdell to take opposing sides in John's affairs with a variety of bitter results.

William Burdell first sided with his sister-in-law in the couple's marital disputes, and at Margaret's request, hired attorney Edwards Pierrepont to represent her in a divorce action. The case dragged on for several years, and when Pierrepont's fees went unpaid, he obtained a judgment against William Burdell which was never satisfied. Despite William having initially sided with his sister-in-law, he and brother Harvey also fought after John's separation over who would provide shelter and financial assistance to their beleaguered sibling. One might have expected this battle to end when John died in 1850, but the fraternal hatred was deeper.

Some years after John's death, Harvey Burdell arranged to acquire attorney Pierrepont's still-outstanding judgment for legal fees against his brother William. Wishing to remain anonymous in his attempt to harass his surviving brother, Harvey enlisted the aid of his lover, Emma Cunningham, and arranged for her to acquire the judgment from Pierrepont in her own name in December 1855.[14] Sexual intimacy and trust were quite separate in Harvey's psychic makeup, though. After securing the favor from his lover, Burdell presented a promissory note for Emma to sign, made out in the exact amount of the assigned judgment. Despite their emotional and sexual relationship, money was still money, and Burdell took pains first and foremost to protect his pocketbook.

The second revelation about the murder victim Emma presented to the jurors was darker than the first, and concerned the presence in the house in the springtime 1856 of Harvey's young female first cousin, Dimis Hubbard, who sought shelter as her marriage foundered. Though the jurors would have to wait for full details to be furnished by other witnesses, it was clear from the scant mention made by Emma that the true nature of Burdell's generosity towards his attractive relative was inappropriate, at best. Her lover's disingenuousness inflamed Emma, and ultimately resulted in Burdell vacating his place at Emma's boarding table. Matters between Harvey and Emma were brought to a boil in October, 1856, when Harvey discovered the key to his desk safe missing, along with the promissory note that Emma had given him. Accusations of theft and slander on Emma's part and of Harvey's infidelity flew back and forth.

Emma's initial inquest testimony closed with another explosive revelation. Not only had Burdell tried to breach his promise to marry her; Emma then testified that Harvey in fact *had* married her one evening in late October, 1856, at the Greenwich Street parsonage of Reverend Uriah Marvine. With the jurors staring on incredulously, Emma backed up her claim by pulling a single sheet of paper from the folds of her dress. A primitive engraving heads the cheap printed form that survives to this day: a simple marriage scene shows a robed minister pronouncing the marriage ceremony. Troths are pledged by a waistcoat-clad groom and a modestly gowned bride. Above the ornate text announcing relevant details to "All whom it may concern," a bridesmaid and best man attend the new couple in a simple ceremonial room while four female onlookers stand demurely nearby. Reverend Marvine's uniform handwriting fills the blanks on the certificate, his only error being the misspelling of the groom's name.[15] If the document proved genuine, Emma Cunningham would be entitled to claim a major share of the deceased's sizeable estate.

Emma was escorted back upstairs for the night after her astounding claims were made public, and the first day's hearing came to a close. Coroner Connery dismissed his jurors until 2:30 the following afternoon. Meanwhile, he was taking no chances. The *Herald* reported: "Captain Dilks, with a posse of 15th Ward police, were *ordered to* stop in the premises all night, and had especial orders not to allow any of the inmates to leave the building."[16]

* * *

During the interlude, the press was permitted to closely examine the condition of the room where the murder took place. Motive was on

Certificate of Marriage of Emma Cunningham and Harvey Burdell

1856 Oct 28	Harvey Burdell	3.	New York		44			W.	732 Green
8 10	Augusta Emma Cunningham	W.	New York City	35	31	Bond st.		W.	wich st.
Witness Margaret Swalls	a Cunningham 31 Bond st, daughter of the bride								

Rev. Uriah Marvine marriage register entry for Emma Cunningham and Harvey Burdell

everyone's mind. Whatever urges impelled the murderer to strike must have been extreme, for a struggle of giant proportion had ensued, resulting in what one reporter described as "a perfect stream of gore upon the wall" in the corner of the room where Burdell's body was found.[17] Already identified as a suspect, Emma Cunningham was boxed into a corner in her first appearance on the witness stand. A matrix of shame and public embarrassment surrounded her with the disclosure of her abortion at Dr. Burdell's hands. Despite being the victim of an involuntary termination of her pregnancy, one urged upon her by a faithless lover, Emma realized that contemporary attitudes would automatically transform her from a victim of sexual misdeeds into a double murderer. The public would damn her for the killing of her unborn child, and then adjudge her guilty in its father's violent death.

The resumption of proceedings Sunday afternoon, February 1, was marked by the attendance of District Attorney Hall as well as Henry Lauren Clinton, Esq., a prominent Manhattan lawyer retained by Emma Cunningham. The jury was re-impaneled at 3:00 P.M., even as Coroner Connery's search of the house continued. A five-and-a-half-inch-long knife was promptly recovered, and despite assertions by several physicians present that the blade was incapable of inflicting the wounds suffered by the deceased, Connery insisted that he had found the murder weapon.

The coroner wasted no time in summoning Reverend Marvine to the inquest after Emma identified him as the officiant at her marriage to Burdell. First to stand witness that Sunday afternoon, Marvine was asked by Prosecutor Hall if he could identify either the bride or the groom from among the faces in the parlor or the corpse lying in the dental office upstairs. Reverend Marvine studied Emma's tear-streaked cheeks and then climbed to the second floor to view the victim's body. Upon his return, the witness declared that he could not identify Emma at all. In Marvine's opinion, Burdell's trimly bearded face merely bore some resemblance to the gentleman who arrived late one evening the previous October at 732 Greenwich Street, with his white-gloved bride-to-be on his arm and future step-daughter at their side.

With the mention of a third member of the bridal party, the district attorney then ordered Emma's oldest daughter, Margaret Augusta, to be brought downstairs. Reverend Marvine positively identified Margaret as the young woman present at the nuptials, noting also that the whiskers worn by the groom may have been false ones that would have enhanced a resemblance to the real Dr. Harvey Burdell. Marvine's only other recollection from that autumn night was that the groom had paid the Reverend's fee with a ten-dollar banknote, and then asked, oddly, that news of the marriage remain unpublished.

The next witness of significance was Sarah McManinien, a young servant in Reverend Marvine's household. Sarah was frequently permitted to look on from the adjoining room when marriages were performed in the rectory parlor. According to the girl, not only did Burdell's corpse resemble the groom; she was absolutely certain that Emma and Margaret Augusta were the same two women who had showed up at her employer's home that October evening.

Emma Cunningham's testimony about her relations with Burdell had, so far, been confined to the period after she recovered from her aborted pregnancy at Thanksgiving-time 1855. More details concerning Emma's and Harvey Burdell's relationship and their individual backgrounds were offered to the jury by Mrs. Margaret Jones. As was the custom of many bachelor homeowners, Burdell had leased most of 31 Bond Street to Mrs. Jones to operate a boarding house in the building. Upon their return from Saratoga in the fall of 1855, the ever-cautious Dr. Burdell arranged for Emma to move into his home. The anxious dentist insisted that Emma be admitted not as his mistress, but merely as Mrs. Jones' paying boarder.

Jones took the stand after Sarah McManinien, and gave an another account of the goings-on in the house after Emma and Harvey returned from their upstate tryst. The landlady claimed to have observed neither any particular intimacy nor any strife between the couple during her management of 31 Bond. Although she stoutly protested ignorance of Emma having undergone an abortion at the house, Jones did admit to her boarder having lain sick in bed for two weeks later that autumn. Emma confided in Jones at some length about her troubles with Harvey Burdell, and her dislike of the appearance and behavior of several women who frequently called upon the dentist. Among the unrefined callers Emma complained of, *"[t]here was one lady who came often, and not for the purpose of having her teeth fixed."* [18]

*   *   *

By Tuesday morning, February 3, excitement about the case reached a fevered pitch. The *Herald*'s front-page headlines blared the latest developments in the case:

INTENSE EXCITEMENT THROUGHOUT THE CITY
STARTLING DEVELOPMENTS
THOUSANDS VISIT THE SCENE OF THE TRAGEDY

According to the paper's reporters, the current frenzy exceeded even the tumults during the past two decades that followed the notorious murder of courtesan Helen Jewett and one carried out by the ghoul John Colt.[19] Comment in the major New York dailies about the identity of the perpetrator of the crime continued restrained through the first days of the inquest. Without an eyewitness or any other chain of conclusive evidence pointing to a likely suspect in Dr. Burdell's death, editors held forth instead on the social conditions that had precipitated a general wave of lawlessness and ineffective police administration. The *Herald* pointed out that London employed more than twice as many patrol officers as New York City on its police force, and suggested that the larger English patrol force was responsible for the relative safety of London's streets. Refusing to blame the police for the occurrence of such a dastardly act, James Gordon Bennett's editorials turned instead to an indictment of the morals of New Yorkers. Emma Cunningham was inculpated with a decidedly misogynist undertone:

> *"It may indeed serve as the text, or rather as the illustration to the sermon on the moral character of New York society. For, making every allowance for the numbers of moral and pious families in this city, both rich and poor, from Fifth [a]venue to [a]venue A, it is doubtful whether any place in the world contains as many houses where such crimes as this murder could be planned, and executed as this metropolis of ours. Whether any other city contains an equal number of women, in what is called society, with a certain kind of manners, and a certain kind of education, but utterly devoid of principle and virtue. Whether any other city, large or small, is ruled socially by a more wretched and vile clique-in the shape of society—and more used to worship whatever is contemptible and loathsome . . ."* [20]

Speculation in the early days of the inquest also extended to the moral character of the deceased. Alleged details of Dr. Burdell's life were investigated and published piecemeal. Various articles printed in the *Herald, Tribune, Times* and other dailies alluded to a previous marriage, broken engagements, and a sizeable estate that could be the subject of much post-mortem in-fighting among Burdell's many survivors. The Herald's February 2 sketch of the murder victim's personal history claimed that he had been granted an M.D. degree by Philadelphia's Jefferson Medical College, and that he was a member of the New York County Medical Society as well as an honorary member of the Philadelphia Medical Society. The truth about Burdell's credentials was far different.

Edward Downes Connery

John Eckel

Emma Cunningham

George Snodgrass

Margaret Augusta Cunningham

Georgiana Cunningham

Abraham Oakey Hall, Esq.   *Henry Clinton, Esq.*

Coroner Connery's assistants had lost no time in pursuing many leads available to them; even on Sunday night, one of the deputies busied himself calling on acquaintances of the murder victim, among them Cyrenius and Josephine Stevens of 87 Mercer Street. In their testimony on Monday, the couple implicated prisoner John Eckel in Dr. Burdell's death. According to Mrs. Stevens, Eckel appeared at their home several weeks before the murder and solicited their assistance in creating a row between Emma and the murder victim. When taken to view Eckel in his cell in the Tombs, the Stevenses both remarked that although the prisoner looked like the same man who had requested their help, he seemed much balder than when they first met. Further inspection of Eckel's cell turned up a wig secreted in his nightcap, which, after a moment of confusion, the prisoner claimed he had forgotten to don that morning.

Before testimony commenced Monday morning on the third day of the inquest, a disturbance broke out in the third floor of 31 Bond. Coroner Connery was summoned upstairs. Despite the coroner's orders, Henry Clinton and an associate had made their way past the police guards and entered Emma Cunningham's rooms. Connery sent the pair down to the second floor, where they and the delinquent police guards were upbraided. Clinton was left pondering just how he could gain access to his client before she made any more damaging admissions to the jury.

When the proceedings resumed, 18-year-old George Vail Snodgrass was the first to be summoned. The room was crammed with spectators eager to hear the youth's account of the hours immediately before and after the crime occurred. Snodgrass testified that his suspicions were aroused when John Eckel left the house unusually early that morning and that he had caught Emma in his arms as she swooned at the news of Dr. Burdell's death. When pressed for the nature of Emma and Harvey's relationship, Snodgrass offered little information other than Burdell's dissatisfaction with the noise and crowding in the house on the night of January 14 when Emma gave a party. Dr. Burdell had declined her invitation.

Snodgrass's room was searched prior to his giving testimony; in it were found the banjo that the carefree-seeming youngster occasionally strummed, as well as plaster statuettes of the quixotic Rolando and Gil Blas. When the coroner attempted to elicit an admission from George concerning his alleged intimacy with Emma's second-oldest daughter, Helen, the young man turned evasive. A search of Helen's room and dresser drawers would prove far more informative on the subject than George's simple protestation that he had not yet proposed marriage to the teenage girl. Snodgrass's testimony ended as he avowed ignorance of any intimacy between Emma and John Eckel, mentioning only that Emma had seemed complacent at the breakfast table on the morning of the murder, albeit curious as to the missing Eckel's whereabouts.

After displaying the note sent on the morning of Burdell's murder by a business acquaintance to John Eckel requesting a meeting to settle accounts, Coroner Connery assented to the demand placed upon him by one of his jurors to have Dr. Burdell's retinae examined. A recently popularized theory in France held that the retinae of a corpse retained an image of the last scene viewed before death; if the theory were true, then images in the eyes of Burdell's body might yield valuable evidence as to the identity of his murderer. Connery offered no resistance to the suggestion, and an examination of Burdell's motionless eyeballs was ordered to proceed.

* * *

During the break in Monday's testimony, Coroner Connery escorted the jury and press upstairs to Burdell's dentistry suite to examine his desk and safe. The contents of the furniture consisted of various deeds and leases for property that Burdell owned in Herkimer County, New York; Elizabethtown, New Jersey; and the houses at 2 and 31 Bond Street. Checkbooks for the dentist's accounts at the Artizan's Bank, where he had served as a director, and the Broadway Bank, showed various drafts drawn to the order of Emma Cunningham at the end of November, 1855, for $100; in May, 1856, totaling $97.14; and in November and December, 1856, amounting to another $275. The final check made to Emma's order dated January 8, 1857, for $356.32 was uncashed. Marginal notes in the ledger pages mentioned a settlement of disputed matters between her and Harvey reached in June of 1856, but no explanation was given for the other sums that Dr. Burdell had paid Emma since the end of her pregnancy in the fall of 1855.

Among the other items of interest to the jury were a response to a newspaper advertisement Burdell had placed seeking a wife, and the orders of arrest and release on bail from mid-October, 1856, which had resulted when the couple's disagreements erupted into two suits brought by Emma against Harvey for breach of promise to marry and for slander. The second action resulted from Burdell having accused Emma in September, 1856, of stealing the key to his safe and purloining the promissory note she had given him ten months prior to secure her collection of the judgment proceeds against William Burdell. Tucked in with these legal papers was the attachment for $1,056 obtained against William Burdell by Margaret Burdell's divorce lawyer, Edwards Pierrepont, purchased by Emma in her own name at Harvey's request.

It would be several days until the jury was presented with eyewitness testimony of a fight that had broken out in 31 Bond over these same papers in September of 1856. Policeman John Littell of the Fifteenth Ward stationhouse testified that he was summoned by a servant boy to join officer Davis at the home. Upon climbing the stairs, Littell found Harvey and Emma in the parlor arguing in front of Davis over the doctor's accusations of theft. Emma was enraged, and after venting her anger at the man she described as her husband, she struck Dr. Burdell. Rather than retaliate physically, Harvey countered with a brutality even more hurtful to his ex-lover. The policemen were told that the complainant was frequently seen in houses of assignation in the neighborhood, accompanied by a variety of gentlemen.

The *Herald* reported a startling discovery made by the coroner's group when it completed its examination of Burdell's desk and headed downstairs to resume examining witnesses. Readers were told of a cache of the doctor's private papers inexplicably found secreted in Eckel's bedroom. Suddenly an accusing finger pointed toward Eckel as complicit in the murder. The folder holding Burdell's personal documents bore a strange label: "Private Papers / John J. Eckel / 171 Stanton str. / Also Miss Augusta Cunningham / 31 Bond str." One of the officials present declared the label alone sufficient to convict Eckel and Emma of Burdell's murder.[21]

Eckel had apparently taken possession of an instrument that had played a key role in the conflict that had ended in Burdell's death. In the first of a pair of settlement agreements drafted between Emma and her lover, the outraged widow agreed to discontinue her lawsuits brought in October, 1856, only if Dr. Burdell met several conditions. The document read as if Dr. Burdell himself, and not his regular attorney, F.S. Sanxay, did the drafting, and left many matters open to argument:

> *In consideration of settling the two suits now pending between Mrs. E.A. Cunningham I agree as follows:—*
> *First, I agree to extend to Mrs. E.A. Cunningham and family my friendship through life.*
> *Second, I agree never to do or act in any manner to the disadvantage of Mrs. E.A. Cunningham.*
> *Third, I now do (erasures) I will rent to Mrs. E.A. Cunningham the suite of rooms she now occupies at the rate of $800 a year.* [22]

* * *

Police officials neglected the most basic forensic tools as documents and other physical evidence were sought in the house's many rooms. What reasons, if any, the authorities had to delay a physical examination of John Eckel, George Snodgrass and Emma Cunningham until Monday morning, February 2, are unclear. Several days after Burdell's corpse was found, Connery requested that Dr. George Woodward examine the suspects' bodies. Needless to say, Dr. Woodward found no marks of blood on any of the individuals after such a long interval had elapsed.

When the proceedings resumed on Monday, another potentially valuable witness was sworn in, Emma Cunningham's servant, Mary Donahoe.[23] Mary had lived with Emma at 31 Bond for the past two months, but had taken ill the Wednesday before Burdell's death, and had not yet returned to work in the home. After testifying from her limited first-hand knowledge about Burdell's apparent celibacy within the confines of 31 Bond, Donahoe informed the audience of a fight that she had witnessed on the previous October 24. Dr. Burdell had become enraged with the cook, whom he suspected of siding with Emma in her attempt to retain valuable documents that he felt had unjustly been taken from him.[24]

Mary's further testimony about the relationship between Emma Cunningham and John Eckel was the strongest evidence offered during the entire inquest about the nature of their alliance. Coroner Connery asked point-blank whether Eckel was in Emma's bedroom every night. Mary acknowledged such visits, informing the listeners that Eckel was in the habit of bringing with him caged birds that he kept in his room. After wisecracking to his audience about Eckel's own avian appearance and voice, Connery attempted to induce Mary to recall specifics of the conversations she had overheard between the two confidantes. When his initial attempts were rebuffed, Connery brandished a Bible in front of Mary's frightened face, admonishing the girl to avoid blemishing her eternal soul, and to adhere to her sworn oath. The imprecations apparently roused Mary's memory. When asked whether she had ever seen Eckel kiss Emma, Mary replied: "I did not, sir; but they seemed very intimate, and I'll speak plain-I did not like the way they acted; I thought she didn't act prudent for a woman that had grown-up daughters." [25] After attesting to Burdell's gentlemanly conduct toward Emma as well as Eckel's expressions of malice toward the master of the house, the young servant was then excused as the last witness of the day.

Appended to the transcript of Mary's testimony in the *Herald* were the first comprehensive physical descriptions of the three murder suspects, Emma Cunningham, John Eckel and George Snodgrass, as well as glimpses of Emma's two daughters:

As regards personal appearance Mrs. Cunningham is a woman of medi-um height. She looks about forty years of age, but is very well preserved for that time of life, her bust showing considerable fullness." The article then remarked upon Emma's dark complexion and almost-black eyes set in an oval and remarkably determined face. Although the reporter was not favorably impressed with her appearance, Emma was understood to have been a prepossessing beauty in days gone by. Older daughter Augusta was singled out as a 22-year-old *"lady of extreme hauteur and decision of character.*

John Eckel languished meanwhile in a holding cell in the Fifteenth Ward stationhouse on Mercer Street, where the *Herald's* reporter paid him a visit. Five feet, eight or nine inches in height, and near thirty-six years of age, the prisoner wore a heavy beard and moustache, his light-grey eyes overset with heavy brows. Eckel displayed a nervous twitch about the eyes, and had trouble looking at the reporter directly.

George Snodgrass's family background was detailed by the *Herald* with a sympathetic portrait of his appearance. The boy was said to be "a rather good looking young fellow, apparently about nineteen years of age, and slightly above average height. He has no tendency to either beard or moustache, and might be taken as a very fair sample of bud-ding young New York when that youthful specimen is only just begin-ning his career. . ." Snodgrass inquired callowly of his visitor "how long the Coroner's investigation would last, but evinced no fear or nervous-ness as to the result. Compared to his companion, Snodgrass was exceedingly easy, and chatted freely with his visitors."[26]

*   *   *

Breakfast tables in genteel homes in the city were abuzz with the day's headlines once again on Wednesday morning, February 4. The *Herald's* front page offered readers a smorgasbord of information about the case beneath bold face headlines.

THE BOND STREET TRAGEDY–DESCRIPTION OF SCENES
AT THE HOUSE OF DEATH-THE NEIGHBORS HEAR
THE CRY OF MURDER AND FIX THE EXACT HOUR
OF THE DEED

The paper's lead article insisted that even the diabolical murder and dismemberment of Dr. Parkman in Boston a few years back at the hands of a medical school colleague had created less excitement than the present spectacle. The picture of Bond Street as it existed in the 1850s painted by the correspondent added yet another macabre dimension to the scene described by the paper's reporters and editorial writers over recent days:

> *The locality of the murder is the Fifteenth ward, on the edge of the most aristocratic part of the city. Bond street was, until within a few years, one of the most fashionable in the city. The uptown movement has robbed it of some of its ultra aristocratic residents, whose former habitations are now occupied chiefly for boarding houses of the better class and by dentists. Some few of the old habitués yet remain, and the rents are kept fully up to the 'best street' standard . . . At present the street, which was one of the quietest in the city, is now invaded by a never-ceasing crowd from early morning till late at night . . . From one of the parlor windows the writer narrowly inspected this crowd. There was a knot of servant girls loitering on their errands, and earnestly canvassing such of the evidence as they had picked up from the conversation of their employers. There a bevy of little children, impressed with a vague idea that something terrible had been done, and gazing open mouthed at the locale of the tragedy. Further away was a coterie of rowdies, and perhaps thieves, their faces hardened by crime and bloated by indulgence, expressing that indefinable sympathy that draws all scoundrels to the theatre of a great crime. They would laugh and pass coarse jests upon the women, look uneasily at the police, and then stagger off to booze in some of the foul dens beyond the Bowery. Then the eye would rest upon a number of well dressed loungers, picking their teeth, looking at their boots, laughing, chatting, and apparently glad to have a sensation of any kind. Again, you would observe uneasy, solitary men pacing up and down with an uneasy, unsatisfied air, reluctant to go away, and still aware that they could learn nothing by remaining. The carmen leaned on their whips and talked learnedly of the probabilities. The postman's trot diminished to a saunter as he approached the house of death.*[27]

The setting inside the first-floor parlor where Connery opened the fourth day of hearings was one of shabby gentility. The press of attendees necessitated opening the doors separating the front and rear rooms on the first floor that had until recently served as reception areas both for Dr. Burdell's patients as well as other callers at 31 Bond. The furniture, which Emma claimed to have brought from her Brooklyn home after the death of her first husband, was showy but insubstantial, an ostentatious but uncomfortable sort that filled boarding houses in the city. A mangy appearance pervaded the quarters, which were lit by a single dusty chandelier. The only adornments consisted of some chipped girandoles and a single broken vase sitting on the mantelpiece. A bevy of shorthand reporters gathered in front of the dentistry chair that had been appropriated for use as a makeshift witness stand, while their relay-replacements waited in tow. Every word of testimony was scribbled down. Fresh clerks filled vacated seats as harried journalists rushed out of the room to transcribe their notes.

Among the first witnesses called on the fourth day of the inquest was Mercer Street resident Cyrenius Stevens, who had already briefly appeared with his wife Josephine. Mr. and Mrs. Stevens had been acquainted with Dr. Burdell for the past eight years, principally as dental patients. The husband's second round of testimony shed thorough light on the depth of Emma Cunningham's desperate state of mind as she struggled to force a marriage commitment from her lover while their relationship deteriorated.

Late in December, 1856, months after the autumn litigation between Emma and Harvey had supposedly been settled, Stevens was summoned from his home to 31 Bond Street by a messenger who claimed to be sent by Dr. Burdell. When Stevens arrived at the Bond Street house, he was greeted instead by Emma Cunningham, who then treated her guest to a lurid tale of his own wife's recent infidelities with Dr. Burdell. Cyrenius was advised to check his accounts and his pocketbook; Emma informed him that his wife, Josephine, and Harvey Burdell had been allied together in a scheme to steal money from Mr. Stevens for some time. Two days later, an individual named Van Dolen, who claimed to be Emma Cunningham's attorney, called upon Mr. Stevens at home. Van Dolen urged Stevens to accompany him to Bond Street to investigate the matter further, emphasizing that Emma had control of sizeable funds as well as an irresistible charm with many men, and an invincible determination to achieve her somewhat undefined goals in the matters at hand. Stevens demurred for the time being, but when he went to confer privately the next day at the 118 Chambers Street address Van Dolen gave as his office address, no trace of the lawyer could be found.

Cyrenius Stevens knew that his friend Harvey Burdell was out of town even at the beginning of the attempted subterfuge, and he and his wife confronted Emma Cunningham at her home a few days later. Emma admitted being behind the ruse played by Dr. Burdell's "messenger" that drew Cyrenius to her home to hear about his wife's supposed misconduct. Given these events in late December, Stevens well understood the urgent pleas that Burdell addressed to him early the next month to assist in getting Emma out of his house. The witness's conclusion about Emma was, at the end, a simple one, soon to be shared almost unanimously by those present at the inquest and throughout New York City: "I thought her design on Dr. Burdell was to ruin his character and get his money." [28]

Emma Cunningham's fortunes fared poorly as the inquest continued. Just as Cyrenius Stevens was stepping out of the witness chair, the coroner announced to the audience that a revolver had been found in Mrs. Cunningham's bedroom dresser. After this disclosure was made, Brooklyn resident John Hildreth mounted the stand, and proceeded to excoriate Emma and her first husband, distiller George Cunningham. The witness claimed to have known Emma Hempstead as a young woman in the Vinegar Hill neighborhood, where her parents, Christopher and Sarah Hempstead, were active members in the Sands Street Wesleyan Methodist Congregation. Hildreth's portrait of Emma hardly fit the eldest daughter of devout parents. He swore to her having been a prostitute as a young adult "when it was said she was married" to Cunningham. Emma's first husband was characterized as a "manufacturer of liquid death."

Many days would pass before Emma was given the opportunity to impugn Hildreth's credibility. Even with disclosure of her parents' role in having Hildreth barred from their strict Methodist community, the witness's lurid testimony about a supposed attempt on Emma's part to blackmail one of her assignation customers cannot have been ignored by the jury. Most powerful of all was Hildreth's charge about the circumstances of the death of Emma's first husband in 1854: "I heard he died very suddenly," the witness advised, "and I hope they will take up the body, because I believe she murdered [him]; as far as I know, she was a bad character, and hadn't a good example set her by her own mother." [29]

Over the next several days, the jurors were presented with a series of Bond Street neighbors who testified as to their observations late Friday night and early Saturday morning on the weekend of the murder. Emma's boarder, the prominent politician Daniel Ullman, returned home in the early morning hours on Saturday, but was too late to hear the anguished cries emanating from 31 Bond noticed by others late Friday evening. Dr. Stephen Main and his wife Susan, who resided directly across from 31 Bond, returned to their home around 1:00 A.M. Saturday morning. Mrs. Main noticed the smell of burning leather or cloth coming through the windows, which the investigating officials tried to link to the charred material found on the first day of the inquest in a fireplace on the fourth floor. No connection was ever established between the ashes and any of the suspects, although it occurred to many an observer that the successful assassin had run upstairs and attempted to burn his bloodied clothing immediately after Dr. Burdell was slain.

Dr. Main was also one of the first on the scene after Burdell's corpse was found. Rushing upstairs, Main found Emma and her two distraught daughters in the mother's room, and offered his assistance: "I took the youngest one by the arms and laid her on the bed; loosened her dress; she appeared to be in great agony; and the old lady (Mrs. Cunningham) exclaimed 'He is dead, and I always liked him;'" Like George Snodgrass, though, Dr. Main found Emma's behavior peculiar: he "thought hers a different kind of fainting from the others." [30] The physician's account was the last offered in the jury room on Tuesday, and Coroner Connery adjourned the proceedings until 9:00 A.M. the following morning.

*   *   *

Loathe to permit interment of the murder victim's corpse while physical evidence might yet be found, Connery employed four physicians to examine Burdell's body. The group's official report was published on

Wednesday, February 4. Drs. James Wood, George Woodward, David Uhl and William Knight measured each of the fifteen separate wounds in the corpse. Depth, breadth, and angle of penetration were noted in a catalog of lethal butchery that Dr. Burdell had suffered. Samples of blood taken from all over the house were also analyzed, and a hematology report was issued the same day by three other physicians. To the surprise of many, the red stains on pieces of linen found as part of the scorched remains in the fourth floor grate proved to be menstrual blood, quite dissimilar to the stains found in the room where Burdell met his death and in the hallway outside. A dagger and scabbard found in Emma's apartments were also examined closely, but no trace of blood was found. These reports, published in the *Herald* on February 4, were accompanied by a medical lesson for readers, completed with drawings demonstrating the difference between the stains made by menstrual blood "and the vital fluid flowing in the arteries and the veins."

Distinctly unflattering character sketches of Emma, John Eckel, and George Snodgrass also appeared in Wednesday's *Herald*. After reading of Emma's having bamboozled her neighborhood confectioner, Mr. Petelier, into providing refreshments for a party at 31 Bond on the night of January 14 last, the newspaper's audience was told that "Everything, so far, bears against this person . . ." The *Herald's* reporter also cast a long shadow on Eckel, giving credence to one witness's description of an unidentified woman having met Eckel at the tanner's Stanton Street shop on the morning Burdell's corpse was discovered, and there accepting a large roll of bills before departing in her carriage. Although the witness in question did not identify Emma as the occupant of the carriage, the paper nonetheless fingered her as present at the suspicious scene.[31]

George Vail Snodgrass, although not treated kindly by the *Herald*, was largely exculpated in Wednesday morning's article. The tongue-in-cheek appraisal of the youth's character matched the engraved portrait of the puerile 18-year-old published later that month by *Frank Leslie's Illustrated Magazine*:

> *This young man seems to have been sort of a cavalier ser[v]einte to the Demoiselles Cunningham. He has been pretty well known about the saloons in the Fifteenth ward, and has generally borne the reputation of*

a harmless, good-natured, gentlemanly young man. In his room – the northeast room of the attic – his clothes were hanging upon the wall, and a couple of bronze statuettes stood upon the drawers. There was no wash bowl. The bed was in a very topsy-turvy state – bolster and pillows being mixed up with feminine under clothes in the greatest confusion. The drawers – all but one – were filled with all sorts of knick knacks – articles of feminine wearing apparel. A dozen or so replies to invitations to the party given on the 14th , were mixed up with the rest. On a piece of paper were these lines, traced in a delicate hand:

> *What would the rose with all her pride be worth,*
> *Were there no sun to call her brightness forth?*
> *Maidens unloved, like flowers in darkness thrown.*
> *Want but that light which comes from love alone.'*

A little book entitled 'The Boat Builder' . . . was found on the piano in the front parlor. 'Miss Georgena A. Cunningham, 10 years old and 3900 days' was written on the fly leaf in a child's hand.

Blood smeared the edges of the volume's pages where other leaves had been excised. Everything pointed to Helen as the owner of the chemises found among George's bedclothes as well as having inscribed the pages of poetry found in the boy's dresser.[32]

The final sketch offered to the *Herald*'s readership in its February 4 issue was of the decedent himself. Painting a portrait of Dr. Harvey Burdell was a difficult task for the reporter, deluged, as he must have been, by the storms of rumor and innuendo. The preface to Burdell's biography in the article clarifies the paper's severely circumscribed compassion for the victim. What had begun several days before as full-fledged shock over the murder of an upright member of New York's upper-middle class ended up quite differently in the correspondent's preface: "To write the life of a good and great man is one of the most agreeable tasks that devolves upon the character of public events, but to perform the same service to a man of bad moral or doubtful character, is an unenviable task."

With this flourish, the *Herald* offered its first comprehensive description of Dr. Burdell's background. A tale of orphanage and dis-ownment at a young age by his widowed mother unfolded in the paper's authoritative style. Harvey's tempestuous relations with two of his brothers, John and William, was spelled out in some detail, with the reporter taking pains to characterize the murder victim as a man of licentious yet penurious habits. Rumors of broken nuptial engagements, extortion practiced on would be fathers-in-law, and a notorious career in gambling dens visited by greedy policemen were woven into a tawdry tale. Burdell was depicted as a man utterly possessed by his own desires, engrossed with sexual and financial swindlery, unfettered by ties of family, profession or simple humanity.

Not satisfied with the product of its reporter's shorthand taken during the official proceedings at 31 Bond, the *Herald* sent out other staff members to corral neighbors who might add information concerning the events on the block on Friday night, January 30. Charles Brooks of 44 Bond Street was interviewed and provided a vivid account of hearing cries of "Murder! Murder" at precisely 10:45 that evening, as he readied himself for bed. Rushing to the window, Brooks had looked up and down the street. A hush had quickly fallen, though, and knowing that drunks reeled through the block on their way from Bowery dives to Broadway pleasure palaces at all hours, Burdell's neighbor deemed the outburst a hoax and turned in for the night.

The *Herald's* investigator also privately interviewed New York County Deputy Sheriff Hugh Crombie, who had appeared earlier in the inquest, and had served writs against Harvey Burdell in the breach of promise and slander suits that Emma instigated in mid-October, 1856. The basic details of the suits and the terms of "settlement" document found in 31 Bond during the first days of the coroner's proceedings were confirmed by Crombie, but in the following exchange, the deputy offered his visitor much greater insight into the situation than had come to light on the record so far:

> *Reporter – You think the Doctor had not a very friendly feeling towards Mrs. Cunningham. Do you believe he ever thought of marrying her?*
>
> *Deputy – Marry her! Why he'd sooner have committed suicide first. He admitted to me that he had some times taken her to improper houses . . . It seems very strange to me that the marriage should occur just about the time these proceedings were being carried on against him.*[33]

Crombie was unable to provide copies of the lawsuit pleadings when visited by the reporter, however, and claimed that they had been stolen from his office.[34]

Attorney Levi Chatfield, who had been retained to draft the papers in the breach of promise suit against Dr. Burdell by Emma's lead counsel, B.C. Thayer, provided key details of the couple's fractious beginnings. According to the statements turned over to him by Thayer and from his interviews with Emma, Chatfield learned that Emma and Harvey Burdell had become engaged in the summer or fall of 1855. [35] Chatfield told of two individuals vying to increase their wealth and social positions through a long betrothal. Emma told Chatfield that on or about June 18, 1855, Burdell invited her to accompany him to Elizabethtown, New Jersey to visit an investment property that he owned in the village across from Staten Island's north shore. Somehow the pair missed the last train back that evening, and Harvey Burdell's courtship dance ended brutally. During their overnight stay in a local hotel, Burdell forced himself on his unwilling quarry. Some weeks later Emma told her suitor that she was pregnant. Chatfield and Thayer were informed by their client that after insisting on examining Emma himself, Dr. Burdell "produced an abortion" with his own hands. Two unintended pregnancies with disastrous results, as well as a slew of swindlery and manipulation finally brought Emma to the boiling point, and at her direction, Chatfield produced the affidavits and other pleadings which caused the Sheriff's office to arrest Dr. Burdell and hold him until a bond totaling $12,000 was posted to secure his release.[36]

The *Herald*'s crime coverage published the day after Deputy Sheriff Crombie's testimony ended with its correspondent's latest impressions of Emma Cunningham, John Eckel and George Snodgrass, culled from visits to 31 Bond and the Tombs late Tuesday evening. Conversations with the jail guards were printed, depicting Eckel as having "more than an ordinary predilection for the other sex" and a tendency on the prisoner's part to get into scrapes on account of his "amatory proclivities". The contemporary intellectual fad for explaining psychopathology via the size and shape of an individual's skull was readily applied to Eckel's physiognomy. The suspected murderer was said to have a "very peculiar shaped forehead, and a phrenological development of an exceedingly animal cast." [37]

John Eckel's neighbor in the Tombs, George Snodgrass, appeared carefree on a previous visit by the *Herald*'s correspondent, but now seemed circumspect in the cell. Apparently young George had been warned by Oakey Hall and City Judge Russell to come clean with everything he knew. Emma Cunningham's servants Mary Donahoe and Hannah Conlan were also incarcerated at the Tombs; the maids shared a cell adjacent to Eckel and Snodgrass.

One of Eckel's most recent liaisons, conducted simultaneously with his relationship with Emma Cunningham, was with Caroline Weathington. Ms. Weathington testified a few days later, telling the jurors of her year-long relationship with the prisoner. Their intimacy had ended recently, just as Burdell's bloodied corpse was discovered a short distance uptown. Eckel had informed Ms. Weathington that same morning that their sexual and economic relationship was over. The wronged mistress minced no words before the coroner's jury, despite the fact that her conduct might draw whispers of derision from spectators: "He told me not to come to him for any more money; he had previously told me that I must get another gentleman to take care of me, he couldn't take care of me any longer; he said if I could find out a reasonable boarding place he would be willing to pay my board till I could . . . He had said that I was too extravagant for him, and he could not take care of me." [38]

* * *

Only three of the twelve jurors showed up on time when the fifth day of Connery's hearing started, just past 9:00 A.M. on Wednesday morning, February 4. Access to the house continued to be strictly guarded by the police because of the ever-present throngs of curiosity seekers pressing for admission. The day's testimony was scattered among some fifteen witnesses, ranging from Burdell's co-director in the Artizan's Bank, Alexander Frazer, to Horace Laddin, a long-time business agent for Emma and her first husband, George Cunningham. Toward the end of the day, one of the strangest figures in the entire proceeding appeared on the stand, professional clairvoyant Elizabeth Jane Seymour. Coroner Connery had jailed Mrs. Seymour on Tuesday for having illicitly visited Emma upstairs at 31 Bond.

Mrs. Seymour lived with her unemployed husband at 110 Spring Street, not far from Burdell's home. The witness responded evasively to questioning about her husband George's daily activities, his working life, and their Boston abodes from years past. A garbled tale about the case at hand spilled out at great length, though: apparently Emma Cunningham had involved George Seymour in her attempt to trick Cyrenius and Josephine Stevens into embarrassing Dr. Burdell four weeks before the dentist's death. According to Mrs. Seymour, Emma had confided to her that the Stevenses had rented a room to Dr. Burdell for assignations with various lovers. Emma sought the clairvoyant's services and her husband's detective legwork in obtaining proof of Burdell's infidelities. The newspapers' portraits of the well-known fortune-teller from the lower Broadway demi-monde were most uncomplimentary, and several weeks later, the witness filed a slander action. Elizabeth Seymour vehemently resented published reports of her having been arrested by the police, instead of having merely been detained pending her appearance at the inquest.[39]

Mrs. Seymour's account of her life in Boston and New York, her various aliases and age, and her personal history described in the New York newspapers bore an uncanny resemblance to another 28-year-old woman named Eliza Jane Seymour, who pursued a career of petty thievery in Boston, New York City, and Hudson, New York in the 1840s and 50s, while suffering domestic violence at the hands of her husband, a brigand sometimes known as Lewis Lefferts. Whether by design or chance, the names of Eliza Jane Seymour and her spouse remained unknown throughout the Burdell case, while a gentleman with the exact same name as Eliza's husband served as one of Coroner Connery's inquest jurors. Lefferts is listed on the inquest verdict as residing at 105 Wooster Street in New York, a short distance from the homes of Elizabeth Seymour and Josephine Stevens. Even thirty-three years later, when the *Herald* published an article directly accusing Eliza Seymour's one-time husband of the unsolved Burdell murder, no mention was made of the strange coincidence in addresses and surnames.[40]

With Mrs. Seymour among the last witnesses to appear, the day's proceedings came to an end. Emma Cunningham remained upstairs in the house with her children at her side, as she had since their arrest days before. Without the chores and distractions of everyday life, there was little to do besides bemoan her fate and dream of revenge.

CHAPTER 2

The Genesis of Obsession

A FOG of desperation enveloped Emma Cunningham as the inquest continued. Held incommunicado on the third floor, with only her distraught children to keep her company, Emma wiled away the hours in her curtained bedroom, afraid of the decisions that were being reached in her absence, wrathful but virtually helpless to alter the course of events. Thanks to Harvey Burdell's financial and emotional parsimony, Emma and her children had never been allowed a comfortable or secure existence in the bachelor's home. Now even that scant shelter was being destroyed. Barely treading water since the death of her first husband, Emma knew that without a propitious marriage, she and her children could at any moment sink beneath the waves. Her lover's courtship had been ardent through the first summer of their acquaintance, even past her initial sexual acquiescence. But Burdell quickly demonstrated his mercurial nature, and as the true state of Emma's finances became clear to him, Dimis Hubbard was not the only young female to distract Harvey's attentions. Tearful entreaties, threats, even rage: nothing seemed to sway the recalcitrant schemer. Emma could take Burdell on his terms, or not at all. The doctor's confidantes knew his preference: the sooner Emma packed her bags, the better. Women were a pox on humankind, if the truth be known. Intimate relations with members of this essentially untruthful and dangerous sex were to be avoided at all costs.

In her dimly lit bedroom Emma carefully weighed her priorities while waiting for her lawyer to pay his first visit. First and foremost came her children: Margaret Augusta, Helen, and Georgiana had enjoyed the fruit of their mother's marriage to George Cunningham. The family had, for a short time, even been able to live in a fashionable Manhattan neighborhood. Two little boys, William and George Jr., had come along after Emma and her first husband were forced by business setbacks to move back to a series of more modest dwellings in Brooklyn. The boys were too young to know of the desires that glowed and dimmed like hearth embers in their sisters' and mother's imaginations. Dreams of recapturing a solid middle-class life together with promising matches for the girls were not easily renounced. Since their father's death in June, 1854, Emma had tried to make the best of a dismal situation. Keeping up appearances had been a lifelong habit for the young mother, even in her lower-middle-class Wesleyan Methodist family. Their mother's arrest threw all five of Emma's offspring into shock.

With her husband ill and his business dwindling since the late 1840s, it must have been nigh impossible for Emma to hide from the older girls the reality of the family's decline and its potential impact on their futures. Even the modest South Brooklyn home they shared during their father's last years had to be given up when George passed away. Devoid of family support and with only a modest estate to rely upon for their needs, Emma and her brood had only recently found some semblance of stability at 31 Bond, after months of overstayed welcomes in strange boardinghouses and with acquaintances in lower Manhattan. Now, though, the glass had shattered. At any moment the children might be separated and their mother hauled off to prison. Being turned over to court- appointed guardians was a terror too horrible for the children to imagine.

The sorry road traveled by Emma Hempstead Cunningham from her parents' modest and devoutly religious home in waterfront Brooklyn to the false-front society of 31 Bond Street had taken a seemingly final and bitter turn. Unlike previous detours from her intended climb, though, this fork in the road showed every sign of leading Emma on a one-way trip up the steps of the Tombs' courtyard gallows.[41] Many women would have dissolved in despair in such circumstances, but this suspect would prove an exception to the rule. From her bedroom windows Emma heard the raucous cries from the crowds outside, demanding a noose of swift justice be fitted to her damnable neck. Common sentiment had it that Burdell's murderess had transgressed every boundary of the genteel social order. Women were expected to submit, silently and willingly, to depredations far worse than Emma had claimed to suffer at the hands of her one-time suitor. Common sentiment held that female rebels were to be punished harshly and made an example of, while gentlemen like Dr. Harvey Burdell slipped away to their next conquests. Not this time, though, and not with this woman: Emma Hempstead Cunningham had suffered too much to think of folding her tent and stumbling off like some modern-day Hagar.

*   *   *

A sober and orderly life had filled Emma's parents' modest house during her childhood in the 1820s and 30s. Performance of one's earthly duties to God was measured daily by rope-maker Christopher Hempstead and his wife, Sarah. The Hempsteads were completely devoted to their faith, and each of their children was thoroughly instructed in the Wesleyan code. Piety, thrift and abstemiousness were only three of the many precepts of daily life that John Wesley had codified for his followers in 1743 along with a special guide to Sabbath behavior. The charismatic theologian's edicts included prohibitions against self-enrichment, swearing, "buying or selling spirituous liquors, or drinking them, . . . fighting . . . Uncharitable- or unprofitable conversation ; particularly speaking evil of Magistrates or of Ministers," and a host of other precepts that in large part mirrored the Old Testament commandments, ratcheted up to a fierce level of compliance.[42]

The Hempsteads moved across the East River to waterfront Brooklyn Village after starting their married life together in Corlear's Hook in Manhattan early in the century. Their eldest daughter, Emma Augusta, was expected to strictly heed the family's profession of faith and to set a worthy example for her younger siblings. Though Emma learned the lessons well, she fell short in practical application. Little could Christopher and Sarah have imagined how far their eldest would stray from the path of righteousness.

Wesley's proscriptions were but one of many forms of religious fundamentalism that swept through England and America during the later half of the eighteenth and the early nineteenth centuries, providing spiritual anchorage during the massive disruption of family structures and values that accompanied contemporary economic upheavals.

During those decades, legions of Americans were impelled by the failure of small-scale agriculture to turn from farming to other means of survival. Emigration of many families as well as single young men and women to the rapidly developing cities fueled the urban growth of strict Protestant denominations. Earnest revivalism and an aversion to intertwined governmental and religious authority were central features of the Wesleyan faith, and its practice among mechanics and tradesmen was well established in New York and England by the beginning of the nineteenth century as one of the alternative denominations challenging the contemporary Episcopalian establishment.

Emma Hempstead's earliest childhood years were spent in a Manhattan neighborhood that epitomized these developments. During the first two decades of the nineteenth century, visitors to the banks of the East River near Emma's father's loft in Corlear's Hook encountered a landscape undergoing rapid change, not only in physical appearance, but in the uses to which the river's banks were being put. Known in earlier decades for its sandy bathing beach and Baptist immersion ceremonies, by the start of the nineteenth century, shipyards had opened at the eastern dock ends of many streets in the area, bounded roughly by Delancey Street on the north, Montgomery Street on the south, and East Broadway to the west.

The blocks that protruded into the East River in a sharp shoreline curve were improved with docking facilities early in the century after wharves on downtown South Street became congested. Sail-makers, coopers, joiners, chandlers, rope-makers and other maritime tradesmen and artisans who operated in close proximity to the wharves flocked to the area.[43] Legions of working-class men filled the saloons, oyster-houses, and brothels that sprang up to serve the Hook's bustling commercial hub. Both the Hook itself as well the famous Bowery nearby became gruesome centers of public prostitution. Anonymity reigned in a densely packed, rowdy grid of slips and lanes. The streets swarmed with sailors newly ashore with freshly filled wallets and local residents visiting for an evening's adventure. The eponymous idiom "hookers" remains, today, a reminder of this area's dingy past.

Born on August 15, 1818, Emma was the eldest of her parents' three daughters. Emma's father worked at rope-making in Manhattan at least since 1809 on Stanton Street and other addresses in or adjacent to the Corlear's Hook and Bowery districts. [44] As one might expect of a devout Wesleyan Methodist, his personal fortune was modest. The craftsman was born in April, 1787, in New London, Connecticut, to Nathaniel Hempstead and Elizabeth Manwaring Hempstead, and was descended from a family residing there during the seventeenth and eighteenth centuries. The Hempstead men intermarried with women from the Booth, Hallam and Bayley families from New London and Southhold, New York.[45] Christopher Hempstead's father and mother probably lived in Brooklyn when Christopher was a child: a directory for the Village of Brooklyn for 1796 lists " ___ *Hamstead, ropemaker near New Ferry.* "[46]

Though he was likely raised in Brooklyn, Christopher's trade took him to Manhattan's far busier docks near the start of the nineteenth century.[47] Emma's parents' devout faith made the couple recoil, though, from the constant scenes of drunkenness, gambling and pandering in the Corlear's Hook streets. The rapid growth of the shipping trade in waterfront Brooklyn in the first quarter of the century, particularly near the Wallabout Navy Yard, provided the rope maker a healthy prospect of continuous employment as he and his wife prayed over how and where to best raise their brood in God's service.

In contrast to the Manhattan residential enclaves adjacent to commercial waterfront areas, Brooklyn's Vinegar Hill and Fulton Ferry were still relatively quiet communities. Industry grew there slowly but steadily through the first quarter of the nineteenth century. As late as 1834, the majority of Brooklyn residents lived within a three-quarter mile radius of the Fulton Street ferry crossing to Manhattan. Tree-lined, peaceful residential streets were the rule, whether lined with the mansions of the wealthy that stood on the heights south of the ferry slip, or spread out on the thoroughfares to the north and east of the hub.

Emma's father moved his rope-making business and his family's home to what was then still the village of Brooklyn by 1822, living and working in various locations east of Fulton Ferry in High, Sands, and Front Streets, during the 1820s and 30s. The family ended up at Classon Avenue near the Wallabout Road in the northern part of today's Fort Greene neighborhood.[48] These Brooklyn streets (other than the family's final home) were densely populated, and their tranquility deteriorated with the growth of the shipping and manufacturing industries during Emma's adolescent years. Regardless of such growth, the number of transients passing through the streets, and the quantity of immoral public behavior in the immediate vicinity of the Hempstead family's Brooklyn residences was far less than the layers of human degradation left behind them on the Lower East Side of Manhattan. Although garbage littered many streets and pigs roamed freely in all sections of Brooklyn village, the moral climate in the everydays across the East River was far preferable to that of Emma's native Manhattan.

Although the village of Brooklyn was well settled in the first quarter of the nineteenth century, it formed only a small part of a predominantly agricultural county whose population during Emma's childhood approximated one person for every two acres. The village was included in the Town of Brooklyn, one of six Kings County towns whose total 1820 population numbered 11,187, including Caucasian males and females, African-Americans of both sexes, and some 366 residents of the Navy Yard at Wallabout Bay.[49] In 1820, Kings County as a whole presented an overwhelmingly rural landscape: vegetable farming, swine breeding and dairy operations occupied over 22,000 acres.[50] The stench of animal waste and the squealing of swine pervaded many areas hard by residential enclaves. Crowded lanes in well-populated blocks were besmirched with horse manure and beteemed with wild pigs, scavenging for scraps.

Brooklyn's growth was steady, but slow in comparison with the population explosion in neighboring Manhattan. Even by the time of Emma's first marriage at the end of the 1830s, the population totaled only 36,233 in all twelve Brooklyn City Wards, with the balance of Kings County adding 11,000. Though explosive growth occurred over the ensuing fifteen years, Kings County, with a land mass far greater than New York County, had less than half the population of New York City in 1855. Coal yards, shipyards, breweries, slaughterhouses, metal smelting and other heavy industries were concentrated in the waterfront areas of Brooklyn village, which, together with a number of adjacent areas, was incorporated in 1834 as the City of Brooklyn. Particularly concentrated in blocks adjacent to the all-important harbor access, noxious industrial uses were randomly intermixed with residential structures, churches and a few school buildings.

After her family moved across the East River, Emma Hempstead and her sister, Cordelia Pease Hempstead, were baptized in the Sands Street Methodist Episcopal Church (also known as the First Methodist Episcopal Church of Brooklyn) on May 11, 1823.[51] Their father was a devoted churchgoer for years before moving to Brooklyn, and was prominent in Manhattan's growing Methodist movement. A third sister, Anna, was born to Christopher and Sarah Hempstead after the baptism of their two older daughters.[52]

The Hempstead family joined the Sands Street church soon after their move to Brooklyn, where the church's original frame structure was erected in 1794 on the block between Fulton and Washington Streets.[53] Working-class Methodism had grown rapidly among the population of waterfront Brooklyn village in the years before Emma's family joined the young congregation. The first, modest-sized sanctuary was replaced in about 1811 with one holding 1200 congregants. Even that expansion could not accommodate the popularity of the fundamentalist Wesleyans. Two other branches of the church were established in 1824 and 1832 to serve the burgeoning Wallabout Navy Yard population.[54]

Strict adherence to Wesleyan doctrine and its prescribed behaviors surely occupied center stage in Emma's childhood home while her father played an important role in the development of the family's worship group and the overall growth of Wesleyan Methodism in Brooklyn. Emma's parents practiced their faith with intense commitment for many years: in May 1833 church ledgers, Christopher Hempstead is listed as a trustee and leader, and also as a member of a 9:00 A.M. Sunday Class meeting at Adams Street under the direction of Jeremiah Wells. [55] Ledgers probably dating from 1835 list Emma's mother as a member of the "Preacher's Class" in York Street, meeting on Wednesday afternoons at 3:00 P.M. Mary Hempstead (Emma's aunt, and widow of Emma's uncle Nathaniel B. Hempstead, Jr.) also appears in these ledgers as a Wednesday afternoon Class member. Emma's father's removal from the congregations after relocating the family to the far eastern reaches of the Wallabout area is also noted.[56]

Over the course of the 1830s, the residential Brooklyn blocks inhabited by the Hempstead family changed radically. Wood-frame and masonry single-family homes were demolished on a wholesale basis and replaced by tenements and commercial structures. To escape this decline in living conditions, Christopher, Sarah and their children moved to the upland edges of wharf-lined Wallabout Bay in the late 1830s. Land in this area had, until the 1820s, been used almost entirely for agriculture, and was controlled by a small number of well-established patroons. Gradually, the large holdings were split up, some portions being sold to small-time dairymen and others for single-family home development. Several Brooklyn Methodists who elected to move to the then still remote Wallabout area in the 1830s organized a Methodist meeting in the home of one of the faithful. Road access to the established congregations was too difficult, so a new worship and study group was organized which Christopher Hempstead Sr. joined upon moving to his final home at 94 Classon Avenue.[57]

Determined efforts made by the Hempsteads and their co-parishioners were necessary to insure the unbroken practice of their faith in

94 Classon Avenue

the Wallabout community. Its distance from the established congregations and the difficulty of traveling between the areas on the primitive roads that linked central Brooklyn to outlying communities made intense devotion to their faith necessary for maintaining spiritual equanimity. The parents were constantly distracted from their children's needs, joining with their neighbors to build yet another temple of Wesleyan practice. Demands were undoubtedly placed upon Emma to care for her younger brothers and sisters that made her eager to leave home by any means possible.

Despite her parents' devout faith and ardent attempts to keep their daughter within their fold, extant records are devoid of evidence of Emma's participation as a youngster in any formal religious activities. Parental demands for puritanical behavior and complete modesty in dress and demeanor have taxed young women's patience since time immemorial, and life in the mid-1830s in Vinegar Hill and Wallabout was no different. The dour and pious single men in her parent's congregation suggested by her parents as suitable matches more than likely caused a headstrong young girl with independent aspirations to double over with disgust. Young Emma rejected Wesleyanism, with its decreed abstemiousness and rigid daily congregation activities. Rebellion against her parents' strict child-rearing practices as well as exposure to the tempting and variegated experiences available to a youngster in Brooklyn village incited the teenager like a moth to flame. Activities other than psalm reading and public religious testimony beckoned, but vicarious enjoyment would have to suffice for a few years.

Religious strictures were only one impetus for Emma Hempstead to find a way out of her immediate social surroundings. Emma realized that marrying well and moving to a clean and breeze-blown neighborhood would be far better for her health than breathing the noxious stew that wafted through the air around her childhood home and poisoned the surrounding streets. When hung out to dry, the Hempstead family's freshly laundered bed-clothes quickly became stained with the daily effusions of the nearby white lead works, foundries, and coal yards. Respiratory, neurological, and alimentary ailments were rife among the general population. The incidence of disease among the Hempsteads' neighbors was exacerbated by living in close proximity to the filth and chemicals spilling out of the neighborhood's stone yards, whiting factories, stables and turpentine distilleries. Emma's face must have curled in disgust walking about in her Sunday morning finest, having to side-step the detritus and endure the reek emanating from buildings that held the boilers and warehouses of several sperm oil and candle manufactories.[58]

Neighborhoods older and more developed than Vinegar Hill and Wallabout lacked adequate storm water drainage and sewage collection facilities during Emma's childhood. As late as 1844, street cleaning and night soil collection was contracted out to private scavengers throughout the City of Brooklyn. Sidewalks, if they existed at all, were a revolting experience, particularly for women. The *Brooklyn Daily Eagle* expressed considerable sympathy for the city's female pedestrians on a mid-winter day in 1843 when an editorial writer took note of the damage done to finely-turned ankles forced to plunge deep in mud and tred on discarded cabbage stalks in the ubiquitous intervals in curbside pedestrian paving. Gutter mire clung to ladies' boots and legwear as parasol-toting damsels went "'sposhing' through the thickest of it, to the utter ruin of their hose and morocco" [59]

Though she may have read in the popular press of the finery of Bond Street and the delights of Manhattan society, young Emma Hempstead had little opportunity within her parents' circumscribed society to experience first-hand the pleasures that young women of wealthier and more liberal Brooklyn families enjoyed in the village's streets and shops. The daughters of successful Kings County businessmen and artisans dressed in fine clothes, and adopted postures, speech, and patterns of social intercourse considered sinful in Methodist practice. Young female Presbyterians and Episcopalians could aspire to riches and social betterment; in most families they could sing non-religious songs and dance–perhaps even develop a genteel taste for weak alcoholic beverages, all the while maintaining respectability within their churches and family homes. Young women of English, Scotch and Irish heritage dreamt of leaping social barriers, perhaps marrying into one of Brooklyn's elite families of Dutch ancestry. These prospects were foreclosed for Emma unless she risked disownment by her parents and their entire community. [60] Improving her lot was impossible unless Emma struck out on her own.

A clever and ardent young woman made her Sabbath-morning journey past the neighborhood's quiet factories and over the muddied streets on many Sundays in the mid 1830s. Seated in the family pew, Emma pretended to listen respectfully to the pastor's harsh sermons on piety, duty and sobriety. Looking about the lackluster room filled with stern, uncompromising faces, Emma Hempstead could picture the marriage and poverty that adherence to her parents' strict Wesleyan Methodism would provide. Raising her voice with "How Firm a Foundation," and hewing to her parents' devout faith must have seemed neither a likely nor prompt means of acquiring some of the finer things in life, nor a practical means to escape the stench and noise pervading the adjacent blocks. Much better was in store for a resolute and handsome girl, and Emma Hempstead hadn't far to search when she went looking for a way out.

CHAPTER 3

———◆•><•◆———

The Road Out of Wallabout

CROSS ALL FAITHS and in every denomination, an oldest sibling is charged with a special filial obligation to set an example for the younger ones. Emma Hempstead may well have done her parents' bidding when it came to domestic chores, but her example failed miserably when it came to religious devotion.[61] Cordelia, Ann, and even young Christopher, Jr. could admire their older sister's facile fingers darting over her needlework hoop, her studious diligence with letters, and her energy at the washboard. Emma's private thoughts wandered far away, though, from John Wesley's ordered field of piety while she attended to the tasks at hand. Lucky for her: the family's modest finances, in part resulting from Christopher and Sarah Hempstead's strict tithing, precluded extensive employment of servants to meet and deal with the tradesmen and other neighborhood acquaintances who engaged the young woman's attention so differently than the stern Methodists. Whether out in the streets doing the daily marketing or merely sweeping the stoop, Emma became known in her teenage years as a feisty local beauty, attracting the eye of many potential suitors.

Nature took a predictable course, and Christopher and Sarah Hempstead were horrified when their oldest daughter became intimate with a man outside of the Wesleyan circle. Emma's lover was their neighbor, George D. Cunningham, a Presbyterian twenty-two years older than she. George had watched Emma blossom over a decade and a half from a plain deacon's daughter into a comely vision. It was bad enough for Emma's parents that the unwelcome caller was from a different faith. To make matters worse, George was the son of a well-known liquor maker, an evil trade according to the Wesleyan canon. The

Hempstead's potential in-law, William Cunningham, Sr., operated a sizeable distillery along the Vinegar Hill waterfront, and was prominent in civic affairs. Even absent Emma and George being romantically involved, the two families could never have melded smoothly. Divergent attitudes towards strong drink and very different religious beliefs made social intercourse impossible. Wesleyan Methodism strictly forbade the consumption or sale of any alcoholic beverages, while in contrast, although devout Presbyterians also eschewed the drinking of spirits, making one's living from their manufacture was permitted.

Differences over alcohol were not the only gulf between the two clans: the Hempstead family's modest economic status, consistent with their Wesleyan aversion to the accretion of excessive temporal wealth, also separated Emma's parents from their daughter's suitor and his family. The Yankee Hempsteads were certainly not destitute during Emma's childhood, but their focus on spiritual matters prevented the family from attaining upper-middle class status. Presbyterians, on the other hand, were Calvinists, and divine intervention or predestination was often measured by the accretion of personal wealth and the survival of the fittest. George Cunningham's father was a Scotch immigrant who began operating a distillery on the Brooklyn waterfront on the north side of Water Street between Old Ferry Road and Dock Street sometime after 1816, moving it to a newly erected structure on the corner of Front and Washington Streets before 1821.[62] The Cunningham patriarch successfully invested in distilling and real estate ventures in Brooklyn for over twenty years by the time Emma made her first acquaintance with his son George, and the family attained considerable prominence in the narrowly circumscribed Brooklyn village. The elder Cunningham amassed a fortune during the early decades of the nineteenth century while the distilling field was uncrowded. [63] As he built his firm, William Cunningham, Sr. also started a family, fathering George, his brother William, Jr. and their three sisters Mary, Margaret, and Eliza. The elder Cunningham's wealth and business savvy provided a solid foundation for his first son's future: George Cunningham was numbered in his own right among the wealthiest 200 taxpayers on Brooklyn's 1841 assessment roles. [64] By comparison, the Hempstead family business dealings were quite limited. The name Hempstead is not mentioned in this 1841 ranking. Recorded property transactions in Brooklyn to which Emma's father and brother were parties in the first half of the nineteenth century were modest in size and value.

Though they certainly knew each other by sight by the time Emma reached mid-adolescence, the exact circumstances of how Emma Hempstead and George Cunningham became acquainted, betrothed, and then married never made it to the pages of the New York dailies. In a community as small as Brooklyn village in the late 1830s, members of the Hempstead and Cunningham families undoubtedly knew each other by reputation as well as through chance encounter, despite their different religious circles and economic circumstances. The two families' businesses, places of worship, and residences were frequently located within a block or two of each other, sometimes even sharing the same street. As likely as not, George kept his eye on Emma through the open door of his father's Front Street distillery long after the day he first spotted her lithe little body skipping down the block. Emma probably showed up on the waterfront many a day; generosity with the leftovers from her grandfather Nathaniel's rope-making shop in all likelihood made the youngster a favorite among her gamin playmates as they twirled and dodged among the dairy farmers' carts taking on stinking still slops at the Cunningham loading dock.[65]

Years later, questions about pre-marital chastity and the legitimacy of her own children dogged Emma Cunningham, long after her first husband lay cold in his grave. Unconcealed merriment must have spread across Coroner Edward Connery's face as witnesses at the inquest into Harvey Burdell's death described a Vinegar Hill girl of dubious morals who, desperate for freedom and cash, formed alliances with well-to-do older gentlemen. Rumor had it that Emma was lured into common-law bigamy by the older and more sophisticated heir to William Cunningham's estate. Extant marriage records from the area's Methodist churches do not show the couple's wedding, nor would they be likely to record the union: George was from a Presbyterian family, and his marriage to Emma in a Wesleyan congregation would have been impossible without the groom first formally professing Wesleyan beliefs. Likewise, no record survives of George being active in his family's local Presbyterian church, much less his being married there. A union with Emma, if officially solemnized, probably took place outside of the Cunningham family's regular house of worship. Stories also abounded in 1857 (albeit aired in organs no more respected for their truthfulness than *The National Enquirer* is today), that Emma and George's marriage was never consecrated. Emma was said to have been kept as his mistress for many years while the distiller was married to another woman. Scandal-mongering journalism aside, it is likely that the pair was probably joined together in a religious ceremony at some point: officials of Brooklyn's Second Presbyterian Church were sufficiently satisfied with the legitimacy of the union to permit Emma's admission to that congregation in 1846. George followed her in 1849.[66]

Uniting with George Cunningham, who was twenty-one years Emma's senior, provided an escape route from more than her parents' fanatic fundamentalism. If brocades and servants were to come her way, they would be acquired far from John Wesley's followers. Independent economic security for young women of any faith was unknown throughout the century. Within the realm of the feasible, Emma's future would best brighten with marriage to a modestly well off merchant. Only a foolish girl would limit her choices to men of her parent's faith.

Ever a careful reckoner when it came to money and family politics, the wisdom of Emma's choosing to marry was borne out within a few years of her union with George Cunningham: during that time, her brother became insolvent and her father passed away, leaving her only a modest inheritance. Christopher, Jr. had never shown a particular talent for making money, and the Hempstead family suffered significant misfortune when he failed in business. Emma's only brother transferred his real and personal property to their father in a liquidating trust in 1838 with the alleged purpose of attempting to divide the proceeds equitably among his creditors. Other judgments haunted his assets for years thereafter, and he would never be in a position to assist his older sister, whether or not he was so inclined.[67]

Emma's dubious view of her father's estate as a sinecure proved accurate. Curses quickly formed on her pursed lips when the legatees gathered for the reading of the will. Not only were the total assets modest: Emma's share was less than that of a favored sister. Christopher

Hempstead, Sr. *"being weak & sick in body but of sound mind"* had dictated his last wishes eleven days before expiring on March 14, 1839.[68] How the decedent viewed his several daughters' independence is curious: two of the young women are said to be minors, even though Emma is also stated to be married to *"Henry* [sic] *Cunningham."* Three other offspring had been sired by Emma's father since the baptisms of Emma and Cordelia recorded in the Sands Street Church register: their father's will mentions another daughter, Sarah Covel, (married to Emmerson Covel)[69], an only son (Emma's brother, Christopher M. Hempstead Jr.), and a fifth child, Anna Maria Barnes, the wife of James Barnes.

Emma Hempstead may have expected the sad reward she reaped, but far worse could have befallen a daughter considered by her father to be unrepentant profligate. The unequal treatment accorded her devolved naturally from a family fractured by the stress of intensely held religious beliefs. Christopher Hempstead's probate documents give clues of family-wide pathologies; obsession and desperation were not unique to the eldest Hempstead daughter. The probate petition, presumably entrusted to an individual close to the family, oddly misstates the given name of the testator's son-in-law (Emma's husband) as Henry Cunningham. It also relates that the petitioner could not locate Mr. Cunningham, (although he was believed to reside in Richmond, Virginia), nor the whereabouts of Emma's brother-in-law, Emmerson Covel. Dysfunctional relations likewise show their face in the documents filed at the outset of the administration of Emma's paternal grandfather's will. Inexplicably, that will was probated close to the date her father's will was proven, despite the fact that the grandfather had predeceased Emma's father by five years.

One can only imagine the rancor that must have existed as Nathaniel Van Winkle (Emma's first cousin) succeeded in February 1840 in personally serving probate papers upon his cousin Anna Maria Barnes and her husband James, and Anna's and Emma's widowed mother Sarah S. Hempstead. Nathaniel was unable or unwilling, though, to take the time to serve Emma and her sister Sarah Covel except by leaving the documents with an African-American servant at their Mulberry Street dwelling. In a family with reasonably happy relations, one would assume that the cousins would have sat down over tea and exchanged whatever documents and signatures were necessary to move the legal process along smoothly. Not the case with the Hempsteads, though. Clueless as to his cousins' whereabouts, Van Winkle's affidavit recites that the way he knew that Emma and Sarah Covel (who boarded with Emma) lived at the Mulberry Street address was through information given him by a neighborhood stranger. The young man seems to have wandered the general area in which he believed his cousins resided, ultimately finding their home through the advice of a neighbor. His reception upon knocking on Emma's and Sarah's door completes the picture: when Nathaniel called at 219 Mulberry Street, a servant answered, and Van Winkle was informed that *"Sara Covel was out, and that Emma was ill and would not see him."* [70]

Many months before the completion of probate of her grandfather's will, Emma's aunt, Hannah Powers, filed an affidavit in the case demonstrating a striking depth of emotional distance among these close blood relations. Powers averred that she was unaware of the whereabouts of her nephew James Van Winkle (a potentially interested party in the estate) after his tour of duty with the U.S. Army from January, 1830 through January, 1832. Hannah also told the judge that she was quite uncertain about her niece Emma's whereabouts or those of her husband, misidentified as Henry Cunningham.

The supporting affidavits and service petitions do not survive in the Surrogate's Court probate files for Christopher Hempstead, Sr., but one can assume that service of the requisite citations in that proceeding was just as difficult as in his father Nathaniel's case. Given the not insignificant (although hardly plentiful) amount of property in the two estates, the disinformation among Emma's blood relatives indicates more than an ordinary lack of cordiality. Sibling rivalries and other contending loyalties, some of them infused with issues of religious observance, may well have created various inequalities in the planned disposition of estate assets. The foreknowledge of these disparate distributions and the ensuing anger are consistent with family members being unaware of each other's whereabouts.

Despite having abjured her parent's religious preferences, Emma was not singled out in her father's final will for miserly treatment. A special share was, however, granted to Emma's younger sister, Sarah

Covel, whose in-laws were, in all likelihood, members of her parent's beloved Methodist community. Sarah Covel was bequeathed all of her father's interest in five lots in Brooklyn which he acquired in 1834, together with all of his personalty already in her possession at the date of the making of the will: "to wit one Piano Forte, one claw-foot tea table, one Dozen curled maple chairs, one french bedstead, and one wardrobe and my largest looking glass," plus $180. Sarah's siblings, Emma, Cordelia, and Christopher Jr. each received only the unspecified personalty of their father already in their respective possessions plus the same cash allowance. Christopher's widow Sarah was granted *"in lieu of her dower and thirds,"* miscellaneous household furniture and the sum of $300, (apparently annually) to be paid out of the rents, issues and profits of the estate. This annuity was to cease, though, if Sarah remarried. The residual estate was divided equally among Christopher's five children; thus Anna M. Barnes fared the worst of all five of Christopher's offspring, as she was not entitled to any bequest of specific property. The estate's income from undistributed assets was first reserved, though, to pay Emma's mother's annuity, and then to pay debt service on a mortgage on real property owned by the testator, which he inherited from his father Nathaniel.

With the angel of death staring him in the face in mid-March, 1839, Christopher Hempstead, Sr. found it in his failing powers to execute a codicil which dealt with his children in a slightly more generous fashion. The day before he passed away, the pious rope-maker made one final gesture of wishful thinking about his children's faith. In the codicil, Cordelia is left *"one bed & bedstead & bedding, one Beaureau [sic] one Trunk one Mahogany Table 8 Curled Maple chairs,"* Sarah Covel is left one set of *"Adam Clark's Commentary",* (a Biblical reference work still in use today) and Christopher, two volumes of *"McGoun's Protestant."* Emma was provided an extensive added bequest: one bedstead, one bed and bedding, one bureau, twelve curled maple chairs, two trunks, one mahogany table, one ingrained carpet, and *"one new family Bible (to be purchased for and given to her by my Executors of my last will as soon as conveniently may be after my decease) and also all of my books not hereinbefore disposed of."* Perhaps with specific bequests of their father's personal copies of spiritual writings, Emma and her brother and sisters would hew to the Wesleyan line.

Christopher Hempstead's will also provides one of the two bits of evidence as to the timing of Emma's marriage to George Cunningham, as it refers to Emma as being married, albeit to a man with a different given name. Emma was only twenty years old when her father passed away, and likely already a mother. Emma's parents were doubtless unhappy over her romance with a non-Wesleyan, and it is more than probable that the marriage created a deep rift between parents and daughter. Remorse may have overcome Christopher on his deathbed, though; the added bequests to Emma, who is acknowledged to be married, are typical of such a resolution. Christopher Hempstead may also have become a grandfather shortly before his death. According to press reports published during the Burdell murder trial, Emma and George Cunningham's first child, Margaret Augusta, was born in 1839.

Unwilling to pay the cost of maintaining her advantage as eldest daughter in the race for parental affection, Emma Hempstead found recompense in her marriage to George Cunningham. George had gained legal control of his father's distillery via a 21-year lease in 1835, after the father and son had shared a number of business addresses through the previous decade. The scion of the Cunningham clan also became politically active in the years surrounding their marriage.[71] Commercial success for George, and Emma's dream of achieving a solid a middle-class existence were soon to dwindle away, though. By the end of the decade, an unfortunate investment with William Cornell and George's brother-in-law, William Harris, brought disaster.

George Cunningham sued William Cornell in New York County Chancery Court in September 1840, demanding an accounting of their distilling partnership, which had started as a two-man business in August, 1836. According to Cunningham's pleadings, Cornell borrowed $4,000 from Cunningham to invest as part of Cornell's share in what was stated to be an equal partnership, with each to contribute $10,000 in capital. The complaint alleges Cornell's failure to furnish requisite biennial accountings, diversion of partnership funds by the defendant for personal land purchases in the village of Bedford (a settlement in Kings County) and in Trumbull, Connecticut (Cornell's birthplace). George also complained of Cornell's failure to devote full time to the partnership's distilling business. Cornell's answer attached

a thorough accounting and denied all of George Cunningham's allegations of wrongdoing. Cornell pled that his partnership with
Cunningham had ended with its reconstitution as a new three member
partnership with William Harris, ongoing at the time of the suit.
George Cunningham was painted as a devious liar: the $4000 loan
which the plaintiff alleged to be payable upon demand was said by
Cornell to in fact have been a loan with a term of one year that had, in
any event, been repaid. Other insights into the mercenary traits that
bound Emma and George together also appear in the pleadings:
Cornell averred that the risk-laden loan was made not from George's
personal funds, but rather with monies George controlled as executor
and/or trustee of his brother William Cunningham Jr.'s estate, as well
as William, Jr.'s children. Without addressing the prudence of investing
the funds of a legal ward in a liquor business in which a guardian also
had a personal stake, the Chancery Court judge denied all of his
requested relief in mid-July 1841.[72]

Nine months thereafter, a Brooklyn grand jury petitioned the
Brooklyn Common Council to order the closing of the Cunningham
and Harris distillery on the grounds that it was obstructing traffic and
causing a public nuisance by the continuous loading of swill-carts in the
adjacent street. [73] The brothers-in-law and their wives were relieved
when the Council's Police Committee inspected the works and declined
to take action. No blockage of Front Street traffic was found by the
authorities; the gentlemen also rejected the grand jury's assertion that
the distillery's presence impaired the general populace's enjoyment of
the streets. The hand of fundamentalist temperance forces guiding the
grand jury was swept aside by the unsympathetic Police Committee.
Apparently Presbyterians and allied forces had greater sway over the
Common Council and that committee; their adopted report protected
Cunningham and Harris' operations from legal interference, at least
temporarily, as it rejected the strict religionists' recommendations:

*It is likewise presented by the Grand Jury, "That the distillery is a serious
obstruction to the enjoyment of the people." This will depend upon what
they themselves estimate as "enjoyment." If they are in possession of a con-
scientious belief that the distilling of spirituous liquors is a moral wrong,
then their enjoyment may be obstructed thereby; but this, in our opinion,*

is not a sufficient reason for the adoption of summary measures to remove the obstructions, even were it legal to do so. The firing of cannon, ringing of church bells, and the sound of the mechanic's hammer are all serious obstructions to some people, yet they must be tolerated.[74]

Marrying George Cunningham was a gift from heaven, or so it had seemed to an eager young Emma Hempstead when the wealthy young heir to a well-known local fortune pledged his troth. Emma's hopes of achieving upward mobility seemed all but assured after the pair set up house together, and these expectations were in part borne out when her father-in-law passed away a few years later. William Cunningham, Sr.'s will, probated one month after his death in June 1844, called for his estate to be distributed among his surviving son, George, and three daughters, Eliza, Margaret, and Mary but only Eliza remained unmarried and living on Front Street with her father at his death. A fifth child, William Cunningham, Jr., who would likely have shared in his father's estate, predeceased his father after having been the subject of a guardianship proceeding in Kings County Surrogate's Court in the late 1830s.[75]

George Cunningham was clearly favored over his siblings in the disposition of his father's estate. Even before his marriage to Emma, George's father granted him a long-term lease of the distillery at an annual rent of $1,850. George and his unmarried sister, Eliza Cunningham, were named co-executors in their father's will, and were instructed to collect the lease rents in trust for the payment of modest annual sums to George's three sisters, with small stipends also provided to the testator's grandchildren. The executors were given authority to dispose of the family distillery at auction if necessary to satisfy estate debts, but otherwise, George was to take total control. The Cunningham patriarch intended his daughters be protected with trust income only for the 21-year term of the 1835 lease, with all remaining property value to then vest in his favored son George's hands. George was also named as the legatee of his father's other real property, with the household effects going to sister Eliza.[76]

For a period of a few years after her father-in-law's death, Emma saw herself on the threshold of membership in contemporary novelist George Foster's famous "Upper Tendom." Her standing in the circle of New York's ten thousand wealthiest citizens was earned the hard way, for sure. With a limited education and few, if any, decent alternatives, Emma had seized upon the first realistic opportunity to free herself from the ropes of home-bound Methodist duty. Only with extraordinary grit and determination could a girl rise from working-class Methodism to a genteel life in the midst of the cult of domesticity that swept urban America in the 1840s [77]

Despite the reversals suffered at William Cornell's hands, George Cunningham enjoyed a modest amount of success with his brother-in-law as his remaining partner. These gains enabled George and Emma to briefly enter upper-middle class society in Manhattan. During 1844-5, the couple lived in a recently constructed townhouse at 26 Irving Place, in the heart of one of Manhattan's finest residential areas. While their luck held out, Emma and her family must have enjoyed living among the upscale precincts of Union Square, Gramercy Park and Rutherford Square that surrounded their Irving Place home. By the 1840s, these areas, developed with single-family homes by Gramercy Park's builder, Samuel Ruggles, as well as others, had replaced the Bond Street blocks less than a mile south as the most fashionable residential addresses. Much of the activity was driven by the city's designation of Union Square as a civic space in 1832 and its opening as a public park in 1839. The greensward west of Fourth Avenue and north of Fourteenth Street was regularized into a parallelogram modeled after Paris' Rue de la Paix and Place Vendome. Land acquisition was completed in 1832, the site graded in 1834, and an ornamental iron fence and other improvements added in 1835 and 1836.[78] Homebuilding began in the 1830s on lots facing Union Square and in the blocks extending eastward from its Union Place perimeter. During the city's recovery from the Panic of 1837, the area became the most fashionable place to live. Irving Place linked the enclaves of Union Square, Gramercy Park to the north, and Stuyvestant Square to the east.

The lots abutting Gramercy Park, perhaps the most famous of Samuel Ruggles' undertakings, stood largely vacant during George and Emma Cunningham's brief sojourn a few blocks from the south side of the Park. Though Ruggles deeded the land for the Park to its trustees in 1831, fourteen years later only two houses had been built on the surrounding parcels. The 1845 purchase of a house site by a distinguished civic figure, George Templeton Strong, led to the completion of what remains to this day the most elegant residential square in Manhattan. Strong's arrival virtually insured the neighborhood efflorescence that Emma had so ardently wished for when she and George moved to Manhattan. In a few short years, houses around the Park were built and occupied by merchants, industrialists and physicians. Peter Cooper, Cyrus Field, and Dr. Valentine Mott became neighbors in a beautiful quasi-private setting. [79]

Many of Emma Cunningham's Irving Place neighbors were members of New York's elite merchant families, boasting ties to the city's leading trading and shipping firms. Most residents became congregants at the local Episcopal, Presbyterian and Dutch Reform churches attended by New York's upper classes.[80] After moving into 26 Irving Place, Emma Cunningham followed suit, joining Rev. William Snodgrass's nearby Fifteenth Street Presbyterian Church.[81] The socially respectable Presbyterianism practiced by George Cunningham's father and sister was an attractive choice to Emma as a means of gaining the better social contacts and upper-middle class respectability that her parents' faith lacked.[82] This "trading up" in Protestant denominations in which Emma participated was commonplace among men and women throughout nineteenth century America who saw church affiliation as an indispensable tool in their ascent to status and wealth. The fundamentalist Baptist and Methodist congregations were filled with small-time merchants, tradesmen and manual laborers, many of them born overseas. More highly educated individuals and those with longer family histories in America frequently climbed the social and economic ladder through religious re-affiliation. Dutch Reformed, Presbyterian and Episcopalian churches were populated, in general, with wealthier and more sophisticated men and women than the fundamentalist groups, and wide-eyed Emma Hempstead Cunningham easily reckoned where to pray in order to do herself the most earthly good.

Emma's acquired Presbyterianism appears, however, to have been her personal predilection, and not a joint marital effort. Emma became a friend and individual admirer of Reverend Snodgrass, and remained involved with him and his young son, George Vail Snodgrass, for the next ten years, even after the Reverend removed to Goshen,

New York in upstate Orange County. George Cunningham, although born into a church-going Presbyterian family of Scotch descent, seems to have been otherwise occupied on Sundays while Emma sought spiritual counsel in the Fifteenth Street church. Emma's husband appears nowhere in Reverend Snodgrass' parish records. Publicly practiced faith came to George later in life, perhaps only after financial reverses had caused him to seek supernatural help in his speculative quests. Shortly before his 1849 departure for the hills of California, George joined the Brooklyn Presbyterian congregation that had accepted Emma as a member upon their return to Brooklyn three years before.[83]

The outcome of the Cunningham-Cornell partnership dispute was only one of several financial reverses suffered by George Cunningham, each of which shook young Emma's confidence further. The Cunningham-Cornell lawsuit was followed by several mortgage foreclosures brought against Cunningham and Harris as partners in 1846, and successful actions were also brought against Cunningham by various creditors in the late 1840s.[84] Emma was frightened over and over when process servers knocked at the door. The young housewife's bitterness grew even greater when she was named a party defendant in several of these suits. Not only had Emma failed to reach the plateau of wealth to which she had aspired at her betrothal to George Cunningham; even the meager assets she inherited from her late father were now at risk. Christopher Hempstead had neglected to protect his eldest daughter's paltry legacy from the contemporary law of marital property. Control over a wife's inherited assets vested in her spouse, absent testamentary provisions to the contrary, and George's creditors might make short work of Emma's small inheritance.

Emma's 1846 farewell to the Irving Place house was bitter. Trusting as she must in her husband's business acumen and truthfulness had proven ill-advised, and the hard truth set in as Emma turned the key in the entry-door one final time, and gazed north to Gramercy Park's gracious iron-gated lawn. Unlike her neighbors' husbands, George was no merchant prince. The prospect of parasol-shaded summer mornings on the paths beckoning nearby suddenly evaporated. Life would get grimmer and grimmer; there was little doubt of that. Sitting in modest parlors in a succession of increasingly modest homes, reading in *Godey's Lady's*

Book of the glamorous minglings of her former acquaintances dug deep into Emma's flesh. She had been so close, so very much a contender.[85]

Even as Emma's disenchantment with her mate grew, and despite repeated setbacks through the 1840s, George Cunningham remained optimistic. Though burdened with the education and care of three daughters, his desire for a male heir could not be restrained. Disregarding the clamor of creditors all around, George insisted that Emma do his bidding, and two sons were born, George D., Jr. in 1847, and William S.D. in 1848. The distilling business would have had to continue to prosper mightily after the family's exit from Irving Place in order to underwrite the considerable expenses of raising and educating the children, even by middle-class Brooklyn standards. Such was not to be the case, though.

Despite special treatment in the disposition of his father's estate, George and Emma soon fell economically far behind George's sister Margaret Cunningham, and her husband, William Harris. Although the proceeds of the William Cunningham Sr.'s estate had provided a foundation for George and Emma's relocation to Manhattan, within two years after their good fortune, salt was rubbed into Emma's wounded pride. Her sister-in-law Margaret's fortunes advanced apace, while George suffered one setback after another.

Margaret Cunningham, an observant Presbyterian and dutiful daughter, had married a Virginia gentleman, who relocated to Brooklyn to seek his fortune. William Harris had considerable social skills: the smooth talking southerner was elected as a Brooklyn City Alderman in 1842, and served two consecutive terms in the same Second Ward seat that George Cunningham had occupied seven years earlier. [86] Although Margaret's husband likely also suffered losses in the distillery partnership with his brother-in-law, the damage was not fatal. Harris succeeded in other business ventures. He turned to acting as agent for the Brooklyn Gas Light Company in 1849, and in 1852 co-founded and became President of the Brooklyn-based Nassau Fire Insurance Company.[87]

George and Emma's relationship with George's sister, Margaret, and her successful husband only added to their own woes. Parlor evenings became bitter when talk turned to the rising social success of the Harris family, while George and Emma languished in what would be their final home together in South Brooklyn's Red Hook. Beyond the growing disparity in social position, Margaret had other reasons to disassociate herself from her brother George. It seems that George Cunningham's lease of their late father's Front Street distillery did not last until 1856 as originally scheduled. The income from that lease was intended as a legacy to Margaret and her sisters. George's failure in the distilling business, and his lack of success in other ventures resulted in the early termination of an arrangement that had been intended by his father to support Margaret's and her sisters' lifestyles for many years to come. The disappointment among Emma and her sisters-in-law and their husbands that resulted from George's mismanagement of the family business came back to haunt Emma a few years later when her and George's finances drooped. No one with a Cunningham surname came to her aid. [88]

As their eldest child approached adolescence, one last opportunity presented itself to Emma and George Cunningham to recoup their good fortune. The national conflagration of greed brought on by the discovery of gold in California in January 1848 inspired George and Emma with a dream shared by tens of thousands of middle-class Eastern urban dwellers. Biting her lip, and knowing that certain deprivation faced her if George failed, Emma watched her husband head down to Brooklyn's East River docks with his valises. The couple's only hope lay in the California hills. With no financial support available from the Hempstead or Cunningham clans, Emma waited in ever more straitened circumstances for George to return. Weeks stretched on interminably as Emma pinched pennies. Many days she found herself staring into almost bare cupboards, desperately hoping for the shower of wealth George had promised. Emma's husband departed for California full of hope, taking the precaution of executing his last will and testament at the end of the summer of 1849. Unfortunately, George's stay was neither long nor profitable.[89]

Broken in spirit by yet another failure, George Cunningham lived out his last few years in quiet poverty when he returned to South Brooklyn. Rumor had it that he was suffering from a tropical disease contracted during his passage home to New York through the Panamanian isthmus. With the distillery business lost forever and no trade to fall back on, his family's standard of living steadily sank.[90] Emma struggled to hold her head high among her Fourth Place neighbors, but the truth was impossible to hide. Early each morning, workingmen hurried out of the rows of compact houses built in the 1840s and 50s to accommodate the exploding population of the borough. Stevedores and draymen hurried to nearby docks and storehouses as their children were hustled off to school, their ears still burning from the morning's lye soap. Wall Street counting house clerks with stiff paper collars and hair parted in the middle rushed by on their way to the Manhattan ferries, while wives scrubbed the remains of night-soil pickups from the sidewalks. Everywhere, signs of others' prosperity filled Emma's watchful eye.

First communions and lavish birthday parties for local children, usually the cause for neighborhood celebration, became unbearable for the still youthful mother as envy and bitterness swept over her. A soon-to-be poverty-stricken Emma found herself trapped once again. Life as the eldest daughter in a devout Wesleyan household had been horrible, but youth and beauty had promised a way out. Trapped in a marriage to a man more than twenty years her senior who was in failing health, her existence had become a dungeon. She could hardly get out of bed on some mornings. Interminable chores and an empty purse grated her mind mercilessly as she faced the dismal prospect of doing it all alone.

Despite his former prominence, George Cunningham's death attracted little notice. Readers of the obituaries in the inside pages of the June 3, 1854 issue of the *Brooklyn Daily Eagle* were informed of the passing of the one-time well-known distiller and Alderman. Only the simplest and starkest details were provided:

> DIED, in this city, on the 1st inst. Geo. D. Cunningham in the 57th year of his age, after a lingering and painful illness; The relatives and friends of the family are respectfully invited to attend his funeral from his late residence in 4th place, 5th house from Clinton St., South Brooklyn, tomorrow afternoon at 3 o'clock without further notice.

Although no notice of George's departure was taken in the press other than in the *Daily Eagle,* and no mention of foul play was suggested, Emma's behavior in the weeks prior to her husband's demise underwent intense public scrutiny three years later. At the time of Harvey Burdell's murder, rumors abounded of Emma having arranged George Cunningham's death in order to gain control of their modest

I, *Emma A. Cunningham the* Execut*rix*
named in the last will and testament of *George D. Cunningham*
late of *Brooklyn* in Kings County
deceased, being duly sworn, do swear and declare that I reside in the
City of Brooklyn and that I will faithfully
and honestly discharge the duties of Execut*rix* of said last will and testament.

Sworn this *Second* day of
October A. D., 185*4* before me, } *E A Cunningham*
L. C. Smith

Surrogate.

Emma Cunningham affidavit of domicile given in estate administration of George D. Cunningham

DIED.

In this city, on the 1st inst., GEO. D. CUNNINGHAM in the 57th year of his age, after a lingering and painful illness. The relatives and friends of the family are respectfully invited to attend his funeral from his late residence in 4th place, 5th house from Clinton street, South Brooklyn, to-morrow afternoon, at 3 o'clock, without further notice.

In this city, on the 3d inst., Mrs. HANNAH MOORE, widow of the late Mr. James Moore, in the 56th year of her age.

Obituary of George D. Cunningham in **The Brooklyn Daily Eagle**

assets. In the hysteria of February, 1857, many suspected Emma of harboring a nasty habit: having failed to enrich herself with George's departure, the well-heeled Dr. Burdell was said to have made a natural target for the monster's second try.

Though Emma's father was well known in Brooklyn's religious community, and notwithstanding the political and commercial successes of her first husband and her brother-in-law, scant personal details were reported to the public at the time of Emma's murder trial, nor during the months before. Periodicals and pamphlets published at the time of Emma's notoriety in 1857 offered mostly curt generalities and speculations about Emma and George Cunningham's marital career, the decline in their finances, and his demise. The initial article published in *Frank Leslie's Illustrated News* after Harvey Burdell's murder merely describes Emma as living in Manhattan after her marriage to George, and the birth of her first child "in splendid style, until her husband failed in business, when she again moved to Brooklyn." [91]

After Emma stood accused of causing Burdell's death, the *Daily Eagle's* editorial columns provided a different, although unsubstantiated, version of Emma's initial acquaintance with George Cunningham, as well as her family background and marriage. The newspaper first likened the circumstances of George Cunningham's sudden death in an armchair to the wealthy Dr. Burdell's unexpected demise and Emma's subsequent claim to being the dentist's wife and heir to his sizeable fortune. After informing readers that Emma had received $10,000 in life insurance proceeds when she became a widow for the first time, the *Eagle* then gave its pejorative opinion of Emma's character and the circumstances of her first marriage:

> *Mrs. Cunningham's father was a foreman of a ropewalk at Wallabout, and was a respectable member of the Methodist Church. He had a number of daughters besides Mrs. Cunningham, and they were all noted for being "high" girls, and for what is vulgarly called "carrying on" and as such attracted a large number of visitors of that class of young men who seek the society of such high-blooded females. They were exactly of that disposition, which, if balanced with good moral principle, might make sprightly and attractable [sic] members of society, but who are much more likely to graduate in the school of immorality and crime.*
>
> *Mr. Cunningham, it is said, paid $100 to some female diplomatist for an introduction to Miss Hempstead, and the result was as stated. When children had grown up as a consequence of their intimacy, a marriage ceremony was performed to legitimate the offspring.[92]*

Emma's moral fiber was similarly impugned on the witness stand during proceedings conducted by Coroner Connery after Harvey Burdell's murder. In addition to describing Emma as a prostitute, witness John Hildreth implicated her in Burdell's demise in the same manner as the *Eagle* had in its suggestion of her mercenary motive in George Cunningham's death. [93]

Whether or not Emma Cunningham was actually so upset with George Cunningham as a failed provider to plot his murder, her first husband had no inkling of such feelings when he executed his will on August 15, 1849. George left everything to his beloved wife. The instrument was presumably completed before his departure for the gold fields of California, and only three months after George finally joined Emma in membership in a Brooklyn Presbyterian Church.[94] George Cunningham's estate ended up totaling some $10,000 in assets, including life insurance and real property. Horace Laddin, who acted as a business agent for Cunningham prior to his death, continued to administer the estate assets for Emma's benefit when she became a widow. Laddin was a resident of Elizabethport, New Jersey in the early 1850s, and may have also been acquainted with Harvey Burdell as a result of Burdell's frequent trips to collect rents from the waterfront investment properties which the dentist owned in the rapidly developing New Jersey village on Arthur Kill. Although the gross size of George Cunningham's estate was not insignificant, potential creditors' claims may have overhung its administration and diminished the amounts actually distributed to Emma. The 33-year-old widow was left far from self-sufficient, even if her late husband's debts were small at his death.[95]

Two-and-a-half years after his client George Cunningham's death, Horace Laddin was called as a witness at the Coroner's inquest into the murder of Dr. Burdell. Laddin testified to his business relationship with George Cunningham prior to his decease and with Emma thereafter. [96] While telling the jurors of the preparations for George's California sojourn, Laddin also described the meager means available to Emma when she lost her first husband.

Laddin purchased passage to California for his friend George Cunningham during the summer of 1849. A year's hiatus in their dealings followed while George traveled to the West Coast, returning empty-handed. A brief venture by the unsuccessful '49er in Brooklyn home-building then failed, and Laddin loaned George funds to support Emma and her five children. The insurance policies that George had earlier purchased to provide security to his family were significantly compromised: a $5,000 policy was pledged to Laddin to repay a loan in that amount so that the family could eat. Laddin also paid out several thousand dollars to Emma's dressmaker friend, Hester Van Ness, around the time of George's death. $5,000 in proceeds from a second insurance policy went into real estate selected and managed by Laddin for Emma's benefit.

Widowed at a young age, and estranged from her brother and sisters and their families, Emma quaked with fear some days. The rents that Horace Laddin collected from her real estate investments could scarcely pay the upkeep on her Brooklyn home. Money for food, education, clothing, and the myriad other expenses of even a modest lifestyle for herself and her five children were far beyond her means. Fretting over a life that seemed destined not to be was a waste of precious energy. Gainful employment at a level that would keep her sons and daughters off the streets was, however, impossible in mid-nineteenth century America.

The text and engravings of William Burns' 1851 pamphlet *"Life in New York Indoors and Out of Doors"* tell the woeful stories of forty typical "female" professions and the paltry stipends then available to women in need of a steady independent income. Artificial flower-making, millinery and clothing manufacture, church choir singing, type-rubbing, book-folding, umbrella manufacture, gimp weaving and retail clerkship, gold-leaf packing and straw braiding are all depicted in Burns' heart-rending account of the lives of women of various ages and degrees of want. Certainly, no smiling faces greet the reader from the many engravings in the grim work. Although some of the youngest and healthiest workers (with or without dependent children) claim in Burns' fictional accounts to be able to at least avoid starvation on the pitiful wages paid them by the honest few among their employers, Emma Cunningham's predicament was clear: either find a well-to-do husband who would support her and her children, or face a rapid depletion of her modest inheritance, and a spiral downwards.

The 33-year-old mother knew, though, that she still possessed the one asset truly critical to her family's future well being. Though facing middle age, in 1854 Emma was still a comely, dark-haired beauty. Her handsome form and vibrant personality might aid her well in finding a second husband. The search for a man who would support her in the manner she deserved, as well as help raise her sons and daughters became a matter of life and death, and she went about it with fierce determination.[97]

CHAPTER 4

◆━━◆✕◆━━◆

Searching Saratoga:
A Widowed Mother's Quest

ELIGIBLE MARRIAGE PROSPECTS for Emma Cunningham were few and far between in her part of Brooklyn. Only a few years before her family moved in, the blocks surrounding her Red Hook home had been mosquito-infested wetlands. The infrequent local middle-aged bachelors and widowers were mostly coarse and uneducated, either prone to drink or sad reminders of her father's severe piety. Emma knew instinctively that a Manhattan base was vital if her manhunt was to succeed. Even though recently bereaved, Emma packed her family's meager belongings and boarded the ferry to New York. Economizing as best she could, a series of temporary living arrangements ensued during the summer and fall of 1854, first on Twelfth Street in the home of a Dr. Longfellow, then in a home on West 24th Street, where a handsome physician soon became a frequent visitor.[98]

The circumstances of Emma's initial acquaintance with Dr. Harvey Burdell are unclear, but the dark-haired, beautiful Emma Cunningham had no shortage of romantic possibilities among the many men who were attracted to her at first sight. Securing a marital commitment from one of the interested parties was a much more difficult enterprise, though, for a widow who brought, along with her physical and intellectual charms, enormous responsibilities.

Emma Cunningham romanced several suitors while Harvey Burdell pursued her during the latter months of 1854. Among others, Emma exchanged intimate letters for a year and a half with former Owego, NY resident, Whitehall C. Hyde, while he tried his luck in

– 62 –

California. Despite her energetic prospecting, no engagement result-ed, however, and as the fall and winter months crept by, Emma realized that she would rapidly sink into the poverty she so dreaded unless another opportunity was swiftly brought to fruition. [99] Under these urgent circumstances Emma may well have ignored any unsavory infor-mation that she had, or could have, gathered about the handsome, well-known Dr. Burdell. Her failure to fully vet his character before becoming deeply involved with the socially peripatetic gentleman was a decision Emma came to regret.

Emma's dressmaker and longtime friend, Hester Van Ness, gave emphatic testimony in the packed courtroom at Emma's murder trial about the dentist's ardent entreaties to Hester's employer. According to Miss Van Ness, Harvey Burdell enlisted her aid in his bidding to the widow to "throw off her black clothes."[100] In time his pleas were heeded: Emma joined Dr. Burdell in Saratoga Springs in August, 1855, prome-nading on his arm through the ornate lobby and across the columned veranda of the Congress Hall Hotel. Whether Emma was conscious of any reason that Dr. Burdell might be attracted to her beyond her physi-cal and social charms is unclear, but her escort certainly made his busi-ness friends aware that his desire for Emma as a potential investor in real estate speculations was as keen as his sexual interest.[101]

Saratoga Springs was the premier East Coast hunting ground for widows like Emma Cunningham through much of the nineteenth cen-tury. Few resorts, though, rivaled Saratoga in its density of male seduc-ers and swindlers, stalking their victims through the crowded summer-time streets. Caricatures of these men and their prey served as grist for many a contemporary sketch in *Frank Leslie's Illustrated News*, as well as in far less dignified journals. Sharp-nosed predators lost no time when a train arrived. Porters unloading trunks packed with finery at the rail-road station were shadowed right to the lobbies of their clients' hostel-ries. Women with wealth to trade for sexual companionship were much sought after by visiting Lotharios, whether or not youth and beauty formed part of the commerce. Emma had little time to lose before her modest resources would be exhausted, and although discretion and careful investigation were clearly called for, the desperately hopeful mother trod quickly along a treacherous path.

Guests came to mid-century Saratoga in droves from both sides of the Mason-Dixon Line, Canada and Cuba, as well as from many parts of Europe. Incoming visitors from far and wide were listed side by side with the dozens of New York City residents among the printed arrival notices for the major hotels. The village's *Daily Saratogian* commenced publication on June 25, 1855, during Emma and Harvey's first stay there, announcing in a masthead column its intention to satisfy its readers' thirst for a summer-time daily paper. Editor G.W. Demers' experiment in resort journalism was geared to the taste and convenience of an audience that the *Saratogian* estimated at the end of the season to include 20,000 guests at the major hotels alone. Thousands of others stayed in town in innumerable boardinghouses and second-rate hotels, as well as in the private homes of some of the 6,300 permanent local residents.

Saratoga had become an immensely popular watering hole by the time of Harvey and Emma's first visit. Visitors could now travel to the area for a short stay on recently consolidated single-carrier railroad service from New York City. 1855's rail trip of eight-and-a-half hours represented a vast improvement over the journey required in bygone years when only the leisure class could afford to enjoy Saratoga. In earlier times, access from New York was only possible via lengthy steamboat and stagecoach routes, connecting with patchwork lengths of independent rail service in the New York to Saratoga corridor. Consolidation of ten rail lines under the New York Central's umbrella in 1853 changed the economics of visits to the spa, manageable in earlier times only for members of the upper classes who could afford extended stays. Relatively fast and modestly priced mass transportation at mid-century to what, in the 1830s and 1840s, had been a fabled watering hole of the upper crust, caused a tremendous influx of visitors from all stations and walks of life.

The layout and content of the *Daily Saratogian* were heavily geared to the leisure tourist trade. A smattering of local, New York State and national news was mixed with the mid-nineteenth century serialized *romans* published in all but the most staid commercial dailies. The majority of column space, however, was devoted to jocular and sometimes snide editorial comment on the local social scene, and to paid notices, sold to advertisers on a season-long basis.

The *Saratogian's* August 6 "Hotels" column noting Dr. Burdell's arrival sat next to a display listing for *"Stile's and Brigham's Union Daguerrian Gallery"*. A slice of the 1855 *zeitgeist* in Saratoga and its mosaic of visitors was encapsulated in the poetic bid of the gallery proprietors to their customers, whose elegant carriages filled the dusty expanse of the Village's main thoroughfare. The public was invited to stop by the gallery, located on Saratoga's own Broadway just north of the Congress Hall Hotel, to sample the inexpensive photographic products only recently made available to a mass consumer audience.[102]

The obsession of individuals for permanent images of loved ones in the mid-nineteenth century, in which sudden death, particularly from contagious diseases such as cholera and yellow-fever was still an ever-present worry, created an enormous demand for these products when their retail cost came within the reach of middle class individuals. The Union Gallery's advertising copy offered salve for the psychological needs of Saratoga visitors and residents alike who lived in a culture of urgent striving for upward mobility, but were haunted at each step in the gay season with the transient, sorrowful state of human ambitions and emotions. Macabre though it may seem today, mid-century customers were solicited with these verses:

> *Secure the shadow ere the substance fade*
> *For when the lady's in the cold earth laid*
> *How oft their friends (who still on earth remain)*
> *Regret that they did not their Type obtain*
> *Arouse to action ere it be too late-*
> *We speak to all, the rich, the poor, the great-*
> *Now is the time, pass not the "Union" by.*
> *For* Stiles and Brougham *can your wants supply.*

Many visitors to Saratoga sought reconnection through supernatural means with loved ones who had departed before photographs could be taken of them. George Wheeler, "one of the most celebrated Mediums in the world," would admit visitors to his rented rooms at the Empire House on Front Street. Fifty cents admission entitled the curious to bridge the realms of reality and other worlds to participate in "Circles from 3 to 5 and 8 to 10 P.M." wherein "a full explanation of the principles on which these Phenomena are based will be given."

Visitors from across the western world also enjoyed the many diversions Saratoga offered. A typical morning included indulgence in the town's famous spring waters. Graceful pavilions at the many spring fonts in central Village locations provided a genteel atmosphere for the sexes to mingle and preen as they sipped the putrid-tasting but supposedly medicinal waters. Customers sampled the effluent of pipes branded with names such as "Empire" and "White Sulphur," comparing the local waters to the offerings of Germany's famed Baden Baden and other European spas popular with the wealthiest classes. After a morning's dalliance at one of the pavilions, the ladies decamped to elegant shopping along the Village's Broadway retail thoroughfare while the gentlemen departed for the famed Saratoga race track. Evenings were frequently consumed with enjoying the offerings at Leland's Opera Hall or making the rounds of endless parties and dances held in private homes and the larger hotels.

Harvey Burdell could choose from many activities with which to entertain the object of his desires when she arrived that August with her 14-year-old daughter Helen. In addition to the numerous indoor amusements, fresh-air recreation was advertised in the *Saratogian* with the offer of entrepreneur Lucius Howe. 1855 marked the twelfth year of tours of the famous Howe's Cave in the foothills of the Catskill Mountains, puffed by its proprietor as a "mammoth CAVE, second only to the giant Kentuckian." [103] An hour's train ride south from Saratoga to Schenectady connected tourists with private coaches. Customers then traveled 22 miles on a macadam road to the mouth of the cavern. Ladies were allegedly at no disadvantage to their male companions in navigating the wonders of the underground passages: In the Barnum-speak of the day, Howe bid adventurous females not to demur:

> *Every year . . . vast sums of money have been expended in clearing and widening the more difficult passages, so that now, ladies "clad in the voluminous skirts of the day, commonly hooped with gutta-percha cord," can pass through the entire length of the cave with as much facility as gentlemen, and in nearly every instance they seem to take greater delight in performing the journey than their companions of the opposite sex.*

All manner of entrepreneurs catered to the carriage trade circus of would-be politesse that dominated Saratoga's Broadway. The main hotels fronted on the tree-lined thoroughfare, and street-hawkers accosted customers day and night. During the month of Harvey and Emma's first visit together, itinerants such as Mr. Sackett, a "card writer," ensconced themselves on the piazzas of the Union and United States Hotels at regular hours each day, inscribing *cartes des visites* and penning letters for their predominantly female clientele. At modest cost, and with longhand and diction in many cases far superior to the buyer's natural abilities, the ghost-written correspondence would present a refined image to the recipients of these *billets-doux*.

Every taste and need could be catered to in Saratoga. Some of the more unfortunate results had to be attended to via a side-trip out of town or by mail order. If Harvey Burdell suffered that summer from any of the contagions with which his peers in the City's playboy demimonde were afflicted, he could easily locate discreet, local, professional treatment. The resort environs were not lacking in palliatives: "OLD ESTABLISHED HOSPITAL OF THE FRENCH SYSTEM" trumpeted an August, 1855, display ad placed in the *Saratogian* by Dr. C.W. Lispenard. The physician's clinic in nearby but conveniently anonymous Albany, New York, made a specialty of dealing with sexually transmitted diseases and sexual dysfunction. For men needing treatment for syphilis, gonorrhea and similar ailments, the valiant doctor boasted that he "continues to be consulted on all forms of PRIVATE DISEASES . . . By the aid of his matchless remedies, he cures hundreds weekly, no mercury used, and cures warranted . . . Young men who by indulging in secret habits, have contracted that soulsubduing [sic], mind prostrating, body destroying vice, one which fills our Lunatic Asylums, and crowds to repletion the wards of our Hospitals, should apply to Dr. Lispenard without delay."

At the opposite end of the spectrum, and of particular interest to Emma Cunningham, were the advertisements of local schoolmasters. Emma's adolescent daughters were in need of proper schooling, and if adequate financial arrangements could be made, Saratoga would be ideal for their education and social advancement. Side by side with the columns touting Dr. Lispenard's syphilis clinic stood display ads pur-

Saratoga Springs Female Seminary

< First Baptist Church – Saratoga Springs, NY

Saratoga Springs – Congress Spring

chased by local educators, Emerson F. and Pauline Carter. The Carters were proprietors of the Saratoga Female Seminary, situated on the southeast corner of Circular and Congress Streets, immediately across from the northeastern entrance to Congress Park. The *Saratogian's* August issues announced the start of the Seminary's second year of

Congress Hall,

SARATOGA SPRINGS.

SEASON 1855.

Dancing every evening, (Sundays except-
ed,) commencing at 8½ o'clock.

PROGRAMME.

1. Introduction.....................
2. Quadrille.......................
3. Polka...........................
4. Schottische.....................
5. Quadrille.......................
6. Polka Redowa....................
7. Quadrille.......................
8. Redowa Waltz....................
9. Polka & Schottische.............
10. Quadrille......................

Congress Hall Hotel dance card

Piazza of Congress Hall Hotel – Saratoga Springs

operation the coming fall, offering "a thorough course of useful and ornamental education." Despite her need, Emma Cunningham had to wait one year, though, before joining the institution's parent roster. Funds were scarce, and Harvey Burdell would have to be put in the proper frame of mind before favors could be asked of him.[104]

Although a smorgasbord of diversions were offered to Saratoga's summer visitors by legions of regional and local entrepreneurs, the major gathering places in the Village were the mineral springs. Fonts were ensconced in elaborate pavilions and surrounded by spacious gardens. Among the best known was the colonnaded Congress Spring pavilion, located a few steps inside the northern entrance to Congress Park. In contrast to the modest plantings and walkways that today adorn its bubbling mouth, in the 1850s, an esplanade paved with marble mosaic surrounded an ornate colonnade. Rustic seats, statuary and shrubbery also enhanced the site. Visitors entered an open-air hall, whose interior was columned and pilastered in classic style, mimicking for the multitudes of American anglophiles, the spring-water salons of England's celebrated Bath.[105]

Walking across Spring Street from their rooms at the Congress Hall Hotel, Harvey and Emma entered the northern edge of the Park arm in arm. A few steps east of the Spring Street entrance brought the elegant couple to the Congress Spring Pavilion. Under the ornate roof, a balustrade-encircled enclosure contained a spring-fed pool. A young male attendant dipped a tin cup hung on a pole into the pool, filling the glasses proffered by the crowd. Derbies, bowlers, top hats and straw boaters topped the thirsty gentlemen's faces, many elegantly adorned with the latest fashions in moustaches and whiskers. Even more so than for the men, the time of day dictated women's dress at the pavilion and elsewhere in town. Frocks, chemises, hooped skirts, fans, straw bonnets, veils and kerchiefs were carefully selected for the hour and weather. Every bow and ribbon had best be arranged flawlessly if a lady was to draw maximum attention from those whose eyes she wished to please.

The prominent engraver and publisher Frank Leslie, Jr. spent many summers in Saratoga chronicling and illustrating the fashions of the day and the goings and comings of the glitterati and lesser lights of the warm-weather season. Leslie did not hold his tongue when it came to pillorying local society. His widely read journal skewered the *hoi polloi* and social climbers as well as the era's elite as they tried to show themselves off to best advantage. The scene in the late 1850s among Emma Cunningham's and Harvey Burdell's contemporaries in the crowds of poseurs and desperate souls was painted by Leslie in his *Illustrated News* with acerbic vigor:

*Here, in this temple, from six in the morning until nine, there is one con-
tinued throng of people of all ages and nations, from the feeble old dotard,
whose trembling steps lead him here to take this last year's Congress water,
to the infant in arms, who sips it down with dislike. What a crowd is here.
Fashion and folly, age and youth beauty and ugliness, virtue and vice,
honesty and hypocrisy . . .*

Men were the first subjected to Leslie's merciless brush :

*Some old decrepit topers, with the shadow of the graveyard resting upon
them, and almost the sound of their tolling funeral-bell in their ears still
cling to this place, their grey heads, furrowed cheeks, stooping forms and
tottering walk tell of the frost of age and the gradual decay of vitality. . . .
They remember a thousand scenes of joy where they hoped to gather roses,
which are now but ashes, and the perfume of violets which is soon to be the
corruption of the grave. There is one we have now in our memory, he has
a wig, false teeth, a cane and eyeglasses, and the most fashionable of
clothes; his age is really sixty-five, and yet he talks of marrying still, speaks
of young ladies as 'devilish pretty creatures' and a young widow the other
morning as a "jolly woman." Poor wretch. Time has a scythe that cuts
sharper and truer than a razor, and all your memories of early flirtation
will grow dim as the stars in the morning, and die out colder than winter.*

Few were left standing as Leslie's scornful scythe swept through the
fairer sex:

*[T]here are old women, too fashionable old women, who would steal the
rose hue and plant it on their cheek, and rob the pearl of its whiteness in
their manufactured teeth. They move like vampires, they do not live, they
simply exist. They patronise young men, insist upon taking your arm,
promenading you up and down the piazza, sneer at beauty, direct your
attention to that little 'pert thing, that impudent minx, that upstart there,
whose father was a shoemaker,' and so on through a long catalogue. Old
women drink Congress Water, they like it amazingly - the iron strengthens
them and also makes them ironical. The crowd moves aside in fear when
they approach.* [106]

No longer youthful when they met in Saratoga, Dr. Harvey Burdell
and Emma Cunningham were in good company as they dodged the
grim shadows cast by Frank Leslie's depiction. The legions of aging
widows and decrepit "sporting men" who frequented the Springs were
a warning of things to come if the pair did not cement their friendship
into a permanent relationship. Congress Park was a field of dreams for

those bent on sexual adventure in Saratoga, but many would depart bruised and broken. There among the *faux* rustic trellises, lonely souls available to intrigue paraded daily, eyeing each other with whatever focus they could muster, straining to discern whether the dress and manners of a promenader, spied from a safe distance, showed some scintilla of promise. Family groups flaunting their wealth mingled among the widows and widowers crowding the park, trying to restore some semblance of health to their fractured lives. Slave-owning southern cotton barons, department store kings, factory owners and titled estate heirs mixed with men and women from far more modest circumstances, eyeing and commenting to their friends on the circus all around.

Saratoga Springs in mid-nineteenth century American operated much like modern day Long Island's East End. As a watering hole for the wealthy and the aspiring middle class, the Village was invaded every summer by thousands of wannabes, hangers-on, celebrities *du jour* and politicians. The hustlers and petty criminals who thrived in the environment of summertime adornment and physical and mental recreation plagued the spa's visitors. During the summer of Emma and Harvey's first visit together, the *Saratogian's* editor bemoaned a pestilence of "steerers" employed by third-rate hostels to snare the lesser classes of arriving rail travelers:

> [S]pecimens of this genus shark are just now very plentiful in this village. Wherever they come from or whither they go no one knows. They are animals. They make their appearance here every summer, hang about us and infest us with their presence as long as the rush of business continues, and when the season closes, presto! they are off, probably to besiege some other community with their detestable operations. _They are villainous, contemptible fellows, to the traveler what Banquo's ghost was to Macbeth.

Newcomers to the Village were duly warned:

> The chief theater of the runner shark's operations here is the railroad depot. He is there upon the arrival of every train. He watches for an unsuspecting traveler as the cat does for the mouse, and considers him quite as legitimate prey. He pounces upon him the moment he is fairly off the cars. He seizes him by the coat-tail, jerks him roughly by the arm, thrusts a card under his nose, or flourishes a driving whip threateningly about his head. He is not to be repulsed or driven off. He clings to the

stranger like grim Death to a defunct African. He eulogizes the merit of his hotel, perhaps, most probably, some sixth-rate, rat-trap of a boarding house, in an ineligible portion of the village. He follows the victim even through the street, and is only content when he has him safely booked for codfish chowder and saw-dust pudding at the 'Revere,' the 'Mansion,' the 'Caliope,' or the 'Jupiter' house. [107]

No runners were needed to obtain customers for Hathorn and McMichael's Congress Hall Hotel, though, where Dr. Harvey Burdell and Emma Cunningham registered in August, 1855. The original hotel structure was erected in 1804 by Saratoga Springs patriarch Gideon Putnam, and occupied a prime site on the easterly side of Broadway at the corner of Bath Street. Having been continuously improved since its founding, Congress Hall shared its premier status with the Union Hall and United States Hotels as centers of operations for those of Saratoga's summer season visitors intent on conspicuous and optimal public exposure. America's predilection for false fronts and *caveat emptor* knew no bounds in the 1850s, and Congress Hall's appeal to its clientele was a prime example.

The resort's double-height veranda spanned the entire Broadway frontage of the structure. Spanning its 251-foot length and 20-foot breadth stood a row of magnificent pillars wreathed with ivy. Shuttered windows opened onto the front deck from the formal ground-floor rooms. Eight deep, high steps led from the Hotel's gardens and Broadway's bustle up to the elegant colonnade. Wide-planked floors and generous dimensions comfortably accommodated the continuous daytime and evening promenades of hotel guests and other town visitors. Another amenity of the major Saratoga hostelries was a gargantuan dining room. Six hundred running feet of elegantly festooned tables filled Congress Hall's salons. Guests who had retired to their rooms for their personal toilette after afternoon activities were summoned to dinner by a giant gong. Immense repasts were served each evening to the patrons who entered in evening dress at the appointed time.

The grand entryway and luxuriant public rooms of Congress Hall masked the impoverished dimensions of its guest quarters and the crass commerciality of its proprietors. Cell-like rooms with fixtures likened by one contemporary commentator to "those articles as seen in penitentiaries" met only the barest of needs. Customers were packed herring-like floor above floor, and a prompt response to the meal-time gong was vital if one was to avoid being trampled at the sideboards in the dining hall. African-American servants were in attendance everywhere: Saratoga served a national clientele, and though abolitionist sentiments made the unabashedly racist Southern planters and merchants unwelcome in parts of Newport, Rhode Island and other northern getaways, Saratoga hoteliers did quite the opposite. Submissive white-gloved attendants joined with dark-skinned musicians who would "vex their instruments and keep time with their hands and heels, as if all their extremities had been hired." A visiting Alabama banker felt as comfortable in Saratoga as he did in a Mobile private club.[108]

Emma Cunningham and her daughter Helen had many opportunities to display their feminine charms and light-footed grace during their August,1855 visit: ballroom dancing at Congress Hall during the summer season took place every evening except Sunday. Several hundred revelers assembled each evening in the gaudily bedecked ballroom, where bachelors and *bon-vivants* mingled under the tasseled and globed chandeliers with family groups. Sculpted gowns, multi-layered crinolines, lace-shawled bodices and garlanded coiffures were the order of the day for ladies.

Mutton-chop-whiskered gentlemen paraded back and forth in their black frock-coats and silken cravats. Pre-printed dance cards dangled from the ladies' beribboned wrists, ready for inscription of their partners' names. Fluttering hopefully about on hoop-covered layers of petticoats, the confections surrounding Emma and her daughter posed and preened, smiling demurely, hoping that handsome beaus would quickly fill the lines reserved for an introductory tune and the assortment of polkas, quadrilles, schottisches and waltzes.

Summer's end in mid-century Saratoga featured grand balls at the Union and Congress Hall Hotels. Many socially prominent *habitués* showed up in town just in time to participate in these end of the season wonders. Contemporary guidebooks described the surreal vista which greeted nighttime travelers emerging from the piney woods skirting the Village. Gazing through the isinglass curtains of railroad cars, stagecoaches, or their private carriages, passengers were suddenly treated to a dazzling view of the brilliantly illuminated ballrooms and splendid, lantern-bedecked private mansions that filled the center of town. The fairy-tale atmosphere provided a suitable aperitif for the middle-class visitor. Fantasy served an indispensable role in most wayfarers' experience of the physical as well as the emotional parts of their Saratoga visit.

Their tiring journey at an end, Emma and her daughter Helen quickly turned to the business at hand after the bell-boys carted their heavy trunks upstairs to their Congress Hall room. The heavy footlockers that accompanied mother and daughter from the Saratoga depot in August, 1855 spilled over with weapons for their mission. Earnest competition in the regatta of ladies' fashion overwhelmed the opera houses, hotel salons and private homes of summertime Saratoga and the Cunningham women came as well-equipped as their modest budget would allow. Emma and Helen were painfully aware, though, of the potential shortcomings in their arsenal. Scant solace was likewise offered by the *Saratogian* to a husband or lover of limited resources. A man with any self-respect was expected to subsidize his wife or mistress's eagerness for keeping up with the latest trends. The funds floated for such enterprises could not be advanced with the expectation of the return on investment to which their sponsors were accustomed in the exchanges and counting-houses where they customarily dealt. Adherence to the dictates of the latest couture guaranteed nothing other than momentary notice.[109]

Social ranking according to wealth, and restriction of admission to the politest circles and conclaves ruled Saratoga's summers since the early part of the nineteenth century. A burgeoning American economy during the 1840s and 50s, created platoons of *nouveaux riches* who played an important role in expanding the boundaries of acceptability in the village. The top of the pecking order was sighted by aspirants to Saratoga status who spent the entire summer season in town. Newcomers such as Madame Eliza Jumel who could not obtain admission into the salons of the long-time summer "cottages" could, upon tendering the ever-upwardly ratcheting price of local real estate, buy and build their own expressions of *hauteur*.[110]

Members of both sexes battled for recognition and social advancement in Saratoga on many fronts. As night fell, the competition for mates and fortunes took on a particularly ardent tone after long, hot days of leisure. Emma Cunningham's fixation upon the sexual and economic sinecure that Harvey Burdell represented was but one of thousands of such dramas put upon public display. Editor Demers at *The Saratogian* published many portraits of characters who shared with Emma Cunningham the unfortunate potential to serve as prey for the Village's summertime social predators. Whispered confidences and averted glances followed both Emma and Harvey as they moved about town. The Village provided a second home to scores of their lower Manhattan acquaintances, many of whom were unaware of the months-long courtship. The chances of a union being consummated between the notorious playboy and his eager companion must have crossed more than one wag's tongue that August as they laid their bets down in a local casino and waited for the chips to fall.

Emma's aborted climb up the social ladder with her first husband George Cunningham both hardened her determination towards, and at the same time, blinded her judgment of the wealthy suitor who accompanied her in Saratoga's streets. Even if Emma actually read the *Saratogian's* warnings to widows to avoid the rakes and frauds among the gentlemen strolling through the Village, her discretion was too clouded by the dance of courtship and anxious desires for her to recognize her suitor's mindset as she perused the paper's editorials. The newspaper's columns from the summers of 1855-6 permit one to spy on the field available to Dr. Harvey Burdell, out and about in Saratoga Village in the days before Emma arrived to join him at Congress Hall. Though Dr. Burdell exceeded in wealth and social position many of the other single men prowling Saratoga's Congress Park during the late summer months, his deviant personality placed him squarely on par with the characters whose external physical characteristics and behavior were vigorously ridiculed by the *Saratogian:*

> *Every morning there passes through Broadway from Congress Spring to the Columbian Grove, one of those non-descripts, those butts of society, those animals of no genus – a lady's lover. – The specimen to which we refer is a rather singular being in his way. He stands no more than five-feet-four inches in his stockings, but within his composition there is*

embodied as much of impudence, arrogance and self-conceit, as would be possible to cram into such a limited space. He has an idea that what he lacks in stature is made up in beauty of person and mind, and confidently believes that he cannot pass through the street without attracting the attention and captivating the heart of every maiden who may chance to come anywhere within the radius of his magnetic circle. He is a firm believer in the theory of fascination, and has been known to assert with the utmost degree of confidence, that if he can only have the opportunity of fastening his eyes for the space of six consecutive seconds upon any lady made of mortal flesh, he can so completely charm her into the meshes of love that the only chance of escape is an immediate and final removal from his vicinity, and consequently from his influence. In carrying out his theory, he has a prevalent fancy for standing about on hotel stoops, and under pretense of cleaning his teeth with a gold pick, staring steadfastly and impudently upon every unfortunate lady who may chance to pass.— He excuses himself for his impudence by contending that it is his bounden duty to exert to the utmost the transcendant [sic] powers with which Nature has endowed him.[111]

Men and women alike were warned by the *Saratogian's* columns and many other purveyors of common-sense advice to investigate the claimed backgrounds of would-be lovers and potential spouses. Emma Cunningham was an experienced and sophisticated woman by the time she enjoyed the attentions that Dr. Harvey Burdell lavished upon her during the later months of 1854 and through the summer of 1855. She may have consciously disregarded these warnings. Inflated confidence in her own shrewdness may have coupled unfortunately, with Emma's urgent needs. Somehow she was mesmerized into believing that she could avoid the surprises that befell so many young widows who were courted and seduced during a visit to Saratoga and then abandoned.

Sealing her relationship with Harvey Burdell in a manner calculated to lead to marriage could have been Emma's considered plan during her most private moments with the wealthy dentist that summer. Nature took a predictable course. The borderlines between love and strategy began to shift violently back and forth between the couple when they returned to New York as waves of nausea coursed through Emma's body many mornings. The true nature of the man to whom she had pressed her lips one summer's eve soon became clear to Emma Cunningham, as did the changes once again overtaking her body.

CHAPTER 5

◆━━◆✕◆━━◆

The Ripening of a Sociopath

IMAGINERY WEDDING BELLS pealed to the rhythm of the New York Central's wheels, lulling Emma Cunningham to sleep as she and her daughter Helen headed back to New York at summer's end. Their visit to Saratoga had been a successful one, by all accounts, and if her luck held, a beautiful golden circle would soon grace the fourth finger of Emma's left hand. The ringing in Harvey Burdell's head was entirely different, though; a devilish pain of suspicion and greed had begun to creep around in his skull. The dentist's intentions and Emma's wishes were far, far apart. According to the testimony of his closest male friends at the inquest into Burdell's death conducted some eighteen months later, while publicly suing for Emma's affection, Burdell was privately telling the same men of his deep aversion to the female sex and utter distaste for matrimony. Emma had high hopes of consummating her second marriage and securing a stable financial future for herself and her large brood. Unfortunately, Harvey Burdell had other things in mind.

After having amassed tens of thousands of dollars in assets and risen to the top of the dentistry profession over a twenty-year career in New York, Burdell had also grown wealthy through his directorship of the Artizan's Bank, the Webster Fire Insurance Company, and from various real estate investments on Bond Street, along the thriving Arthur Kill waterfront in Elizabethport, New Jersey, and in his native upstate Jefferson County.[112] The elegantly dressed dentist was undoubtedly eager to see and be seen in Saratoga with his colleagues from the Bank's board of directors, and the more successful of his many patients and Bond Street acquaintances who frequented the Village in summertime. Having a beautiful, mature and respectable woman on his arm was an essential part of the act.

By 1855, Dr. Harvey Burdell was a well-known figure among the upper middle class set that shuttled between Manhattan and Saratoga Springs during the warmer months of the year. A brilliant and shrewdly calculating medical man, Dr. Burdell had come to New York to join his older brother John Burdell in dental practice in 1834. Harvey Burdell first located his clinic near City Hall, at 21 Chambers Street, only a few dozen yards from John's home and office at 69 Chambers Street. After two years, Harvey moved even closer to John, setting up shop next door at 67 Chambers Street (The address given for Harvey Burdell in the contemporary directory may in fact reflect the two brothers practicing from the same clinic space). They remained together in partnership for five years, until John's personal and professional life were destroyed by a series of hideous perfidies. An English apprentice, Thomas Gunning, who came to live and work with the brothers in 1839, created havoc in the clinic as well as in John's boudoir.

Though somewhat inconsistent with several contemporary accounts and extant genealogy records, an article published in the *New York Dental Recorder* at the end of 1857 furnishes plentiful detail about the family dynamics of the Burdell brothers' childhood. The account paints a sorry picture of young Harvey's personality that presaged both the future torrent of fratricidal warfare among the several Burdell siblings and their respective offspring, as well as Harvey's untimely and violent death. Though other published synopses of Harvey's early life insisted that he lost his father while still a toddler, the *Dental Recorder* implied that Harvey's parents were separated when the lad was nine or ten years old. About 1820, Harvey was said to have moved with his father to the Jefferson County village of Sackett's Harbor, New York where after being schooled for a couple years, the boy was apprenticed to a printer in neighboring Oswego. His formal education, ended, and Harvey became financially independent of his father. Parental supervision of the young man's moral and ethical development ceased forthwith.

Left to his own devices, the energetic youth worked as a compositor for a couple of years and then was said to have accepted an invitation from his older brother John to move to New York and learn the dentistry trade in the late 1820s. A term supposedly followed at a Philadelphia medical school, and thereafter Harvey returned to New

York and joined as a full-fledged member of John's dental clinic. Though undistinguished in the eyes of this professional journal as a practitioner, and reportedly only able to maintain a modest income from his dentistry skills, Harvey played upon his older brother's respectable reputation to enhance his own practice. The size of the murder victim's estate at the time of the publication of the *Dental Recorder* item was well known, and the author attributed Harvey's success in amassing wealth not to his skill as a dentist, but rather to the extreme parsimony with which he lived. Harvey Burdell learned to function alone in the world, fearful of all those around him, and became fixated with the accretion of wealth in lieu of acquiring intimate personal relationships. "[H]e was literally 'alone,'" the magazine reported sadly, "no one being dependent upon him, no really intimate associates; usually sleeping in a room adjoining his office, and procuring his meals at restaurants. A naturally frank-hearted disposition had been smothered or sacrificed by a morbid desire to grasp the almighty dollar. Friendship, the ties of kindred and affection, professional ambitions, were thrown aside or crushed the instant they came into collision with any prospect of gain. All the true happiness of life he seems to have sacrificed, and to what end? Simply to amass a bribe sufficient to nerve his murderers to the execution of one of the most diabolical murders on record." [113]

The several stories of Harvey and John's parentage published at his death are somewhat inconsistent as to the exact date of Harvey's birth and his father's given name, as well as where the family made its home when Harvey was a small boy. A sorry critical thread runs through all versions, though: young Harvey Burdell was forsaken by his mother in his formative pre-teenage years. It appears most likely that Harvey was born January 8, 1811 in the hamlet of Hounsfield, in Jefferson County, New York. Harvey, John, and their brothers James, William and Lewis, were the offspring of Polly Cunningham Burdell and her first husband, also John Burdell. During Harvey's early years, various combinations of the parents and their children lived in the villages of Herkimer and German Flats in upstate Herkimer County as well as in Sackett's Harbor, on the shores of Lake Ontario. [114]

Harvey Burdell's narcissistic personality was forged in adversity:

contact with his mother evaporated at a young age, whether via his parents' divorce, or through being thrown out of his childhood home after his mother was widowed. Some accounts insisted that John Burdell died leaving Polly with the five children to raise. One thing is certain, though: by the time Harvey Burdell reached the age of thirteen, Polly had remarried farmer James Lamon. Five new sons and daughters followed in short order.[115] A jealous husband and demanding little children surrounded Polly Burdell Lamon, spelling trouble for young Harvey and the other Burdell boys. The children from her first marriage became unwelcome in their mother's new home, and by 1824, Harvey was forced out of the house. His feelings towards women in general and his aversion to any emotional commitment to another human being, much less marriage, were a natural result of harsh preadolescent experiences.

Thirteen-year-old Harvey finished a few years of schooling at the Sackett's Harbor Academy and then struck out on his own, working as a compositor. In 1828 or 1829, the boy, still in his teens, became owner of a several-year-old weekly newspaper in the upstate area, the *Oswego* [New York] *Advertiser*. Renamed by Harvey *The Freeman's Herald,* the paper was founded to support the Republican administration of the newly inaugurated John Quincy Adams in 1825 and to compete with the opposite views of the long-established *Oswego Palladium*. Harvey gave up the unprofitable operation after one year and accepted employment in Oswego with Major James Cochrane, who published the anti-Jacksonian *Oswego Democratic Gazette.*[116]

According to one report published after his death, when Harvey's journalism career ended, he followed his older brother John to Philadelphia in the late 1820s or early 1830s, and attended lectures at Jefferson Medical College. [117] The College's lists of graduates for the years in question make no mention of either Burdell brother having been granted a medical degree, but it was a common practice at the time for young men without sufficient finances or educational backgrounds to merely attend a number of medical school lectures without matriculating, and then hold themselves out as physicians.[118] Thoroughgoing prevarication by men holding themselves out as experienced and educated in many other businesses and professions was just as commonplace. In later years, and regardless of how many hours, if any, Harvey spent in Jefferson's dank lecture halls, it was easy for the creative Dr. Burdell to concoct and pass off as truth various versions of his medical training credentials for consumption by patients and professional societies.

John Burdell arrived in New York in 1829, five years earlier than Harvey, and practiced dentistry at various locations on lower Broadway near City Hall. Harvey's arrival initially spelled even greater success for John, and the pair co-authored a book on dentistry in 1838.[119] The Burdell brothers became well known among the small group of dentists in Manhattan with some scientific medical training, and clients flocked to their doors. Their professional and personal lives took strikingly different paths, though, even while they maintained complementary practices in adjacent premises.

The respectability of dentistry as a profession in the United States during the entire first half of the nineteenth century was highly suspect. The absence of medicinal anesthesia until the mid-1840s, the use of crude extraction implements such as the notorious "turnkey", and the prevalence of impostors possessing only the crudest handicraft skills who implanted virtually any semi-solid substance in the cavities of the suffering public made dentistry more of a trade (and a dubious one at that) than a profession.[120] Dentists' parlors were set up by charlatans and quacks of every description. Quick money was often fleeced from ignorant customers in exchange for temporary relief from excruciating tooth pain. Flamboyant advertising was commonplace; anyone with board, brush and paint-bucket could hang out a shingle and begin accepting patients the same day. Whatever their former employment or education, predictable consequences followed at the hands of many of these novice practitioners.

Harvey and John Burdell's practice stood out as a reputable one, though, at least from a clinical perspective. The publication of their handbook, *Observations on The Structure, Physiology, Anatomy and Diseases of the Teeth, In Two Parts*, strengthened their already well-established professional standing. Part One of this slim volume is Harvey's work alone. The introduction laments the lack of licensing, and warns of the presence of many unsavory practitioners:

The profession of dentistry has obtained a degree of importance and respectability within the last twenty years, more particularly in our large cities, which enables its qualified and accomplished professors to rank with the educated physician or surgeon. Quacks and ignorant pretenders in this, as well as the other branches of the healing art, are numerous. It is a fact, universally admitted, that a majority of those who assume to themselves the title of 'surgeon dentists' and who palm themselves off by means of recommendations, advertisements etc., are persons who have devoted the earlier part of their life [sic] to pursuits widely different. Barbers, butchers, tailors, blacksmiths, carpenters, and in fact those engaged in almost every other capacity, (not that these occupations are less respectable) without the least preparatory education, quit their shops, issue their placards, and commence sans ceremonie, to gain an experimental knowledge at the expense of those who may be so unfortunate as to fall into their hands.

It cannot be supposed that the former pursuits of such individuals could have contributed much to their surgical knowledge; yet in almost every newspaper we see them pushing themselves into notice, with an impudence and boldness equaled only by the brazen-faced medical charlatan.

The text goes on to recommend the adoption of training, apprenticeship and licensing requirements in the United States for the practice of dentistry under a system that would protect an ignorant and vulnerable populace: "In many parts of the United States, particularly in small towns and villages, where the inhabitants have been so often duped and swindled by 'surgeon dentists', all those who practice dentistry are looked upon with ridicule and contempt, and are considered to be accomplished knaves or genteel impostors."[121]

Harvey Burdell departed from strictly professional concerns in the second half of his contribution to the brothers' opus, presaging his disastrous involvement with Emma Cunningham. An intertwining of Harvey's sexuality with his daily professional life informed the twenty-seven-year-old author's description of the unusual importance of well-formed and well-maintained teeth to an attractive female physiognomy. In a chapter entitled *"Effect of the Teeth on Personal Appearance"* Harvey described some of the benefits and detriments of his practice among his many female clients:

The expression and general appearance of the face depend much upon the condition of the teeth. If they are perfect, regular, pure, and clean, they contribute more to beauty than any of the other features; but if neglected,

– 83 –

diseased, or encrusted with an offensive accumulation, they excite in the beholder both pity and disgust . . .

Harvey found sympathy with a contemporary Parisian medical writer, whose words he quoted:

The influence which the teeth exercise over beauty justifies the pre-eminence which I attribute to them over all the other attractions of the countenance. This ornament is equally attractive in both sexes: it distinguishes the elegant from the slovenly gentleman, and diffuses amiability over the countenance by softening the features. But it is more especially to woman that fine teeth are necessary, since it is her destiny first to gratify the eyes before she touches the soul, and captivates and enslaves the heart.

I assent most cordially to the preceding remarks. The dark black eye may be ever so piercing, the soft blue eye may melt with tenderness, the rose may blossom upon a downy cheek, and the graceful form, even of the Venus de Medicis, may be found among the softer sex, yet all charms lose their power if the teeth are defective.

> *Let all fair readers remember Moore's - :*
> *'What pity, blooming girl,*
> *That lips so ready for a lover*
> *Should not beneath a ruby casket cover*
>   *One tooth of pearl !*
> *But like a rose besides the church-yard stone,*
> *Be doomed to blush o'er many a mouldering bone !* [122]

Far removed from his unmarried brother's froth of sexuality, the sections of the book authored by John Burdell concentrated on the anatomical and physiological aspects of dentistry. John, too, mixed a personal agenda with his professional opinions: Part 2 of the brothers' book is laced with religious and spiritual references to God's intentions, and exhortations concerning family values. A separate chapter was devoted to the salubrious effects of natural foods and their relationship to dental health, all contemplated in John's mind by the Creator in the divine order of the universe.

The publication of *Observations* marked the apex of John Burdell's professional career in New York. Well respected throughout the city, by 1838 John had built a solid practice of middle- and upper-class patients. The work was plentiful enough to require an assistant or two.

His ample income had also allowed marriage to a girl of solid social standing. By the time the brothers' book was published, John Burdell had been married for two years to Margaret Alburtis, daughter of the successful Manhattan harness and coach-maker, William Alburtis. Although the circumstances of Margaret's initial acquaintance with John are unclear, it may have been occasioned by John's tenancy in a house adjacent to one of his future father-in-law's properties. Unfortunately, his wife's moral compass was of a different cast, though, and brought disaster to John's health and wealth.[123] John's practice flourished while his brother Harvey took care of the spill-over of clients, and the older brother's Chambers Street house was filled with Brussels carpets, mahogany chairs, astral lamps and many other typical accoutrements of a comfortable middle-class life. Unlike his brother Harvey, who spent a great deal of time engaged in the extensive "sporting gentleman's" subculture of gambling and brothel-going of the times, John Burdell pursued intellectual and philosophical interests that complemented his dentistry practice. [124] His bookshelves at 69 Chambers Street were filled with religious texts such as *Finney's Sermons*, forty volumes of *The Moral Reformer*, twenty-six volumes of *Campbell's Illustrations of Prophecy*, and many numbers of the *Biblical Repository*, but also with tomes on natural foods and nutrition.[125]

John Burdell was a vigorous enemy of the use of tobacco, not only because of its deleterious effects on human teeth, but also for religious reasons. He contributed an impassioned essay entitled *Tobacco: Its Use and Abuse* to Dr. Joel Shew's 1849 collection of historical articles and essays condemning the habit. John was prominent enough to have his moral and medical viewpoint considered worthy of accompanying the collections' essays by Reverend Henry Ward Beecher, Horace Greeley and Dr. William Alcott. Harvey's older brother also had an abiding interest in healthy dietetic practices. John supported the then novel nutritional theories of Sylvester Graham, acting as a New York agent for the distribution of Mary S. Gove's Grahamite *Health Journal and Advocate of Physiological Reform*.[126]

Despite his material success and professional achievements, John Burdell's domestic life deteriorated severely when an English immigrant, Thomas Gunning, came in 1839 to learn the dentistry trade in

John's office. While apprenticed to John, Gunning also slept and boarded at 69 Chambers Street. Gunning proved adept at acquiring medical and business skills, as well as forging relationships with his master's patients and wife. He soon formed more than a passing acquaintance with the mistress of the house. By 1841, the apprentice had interposed himself thoroughly between the two brothers, and Harvey Burdell moved to a private office at nearby 310 Broadway. Gunning promptly had himself listed in contemporary business directories as John Burdell's partner.

Late in August 1843, the New York *Aurora* reported the inevitable: John Burdell had hauled Gunning into court, charging him with seducing Margaret Burdell. Bail was set at $5,000 in a civil action claiming $10,000 dollars in damages. Both sums were extraordinarily high for the times and the given nature of the alleged infraction. John was reported in the paper to have already left 69 Chambers Street and moved in with his brother Harvey a few blocks uptown. [127] By siding with Margaret in her pursuit of a divorce, her brother-in-law William Burdell, then also resident in New York, fired the first salvo in the skirmish with his brothers. The battle lasted for over a decade, well beyond Harvey's and John's untimely deaths.

Years elapsed between John's challenge to Gunning and his wife Margaret's response. Not until November 30, 1846, did Margaret Burdell file for divorce in New York County Chancery Court. Margaret's counsel, Edwards Pierrepont, was retained by her brother in-law William, and Margaret's father William Alburtis acted as her "next friend" in the litigation.[128] Margaret Burdell's divorce complaint recited various acts of economic abandonment and adultery committed by John. According to the transcribed sworn statement that forms part of the complaint, executed in her own hand, the couple was married July 8, 1836. Margaret gave birth to four children, among them Sarah, who was born June 6, 1837 and died at age four on March 28, 1842. Margaret's complaint recites that John Burdell abandoned her without means of support in December, 1836, when she was already pregnant with Sarah, and then ran off after an unsuccessful reconciliation.[129]

Apparently the couple's first separation during John's year-end 1836 trip to the West Indies did not end the marriage, for Margaret bore John three more children, Ann Margaret in 1839, Emily in 1840, and John C. Burdell in 1842. The divorce complaint also recites that John's Caribbean trip was preceded by an unspecified illness through which he was nursed by Margaret, and that John's dental practice and other business interests were left in the care of his brother Harvey, rather than with Margaret, while John was away. Numerous other acts of cruelty on John's part are alleged, including denying his wife food during a second pregnancy that ended in a miscarriage, elimination of any animal protein from Margaret's diet, an attempt to poison Margaret, and the removal of the family at one point to Utica, New York, where John walked out once more, leaving his wife and children penniless.

In his answer to his wife's allegations, John Burdell denied knowing of his wife's pregnancy when he left for the West Indies in 1836. No reference occurs in John's answer to his interest in Sylvester Graham's dietary programs and the possibility of his having attempted to impose the salubrious Grahamite regimen on his pregnant wife. His main defense to Margaret's complaints involved Thomas Gunning's evil presence in the marital abode and his wife's disingenuous scheming with her none too secretive lover.

Gunning's scheme in his master's home was complex. While John was ill, Gunning loaned his master money to pay rent and for other expenses in the spring of 1842. The debt was secured by a lien on the extensive personal property in both the residential and professional rooms of 69 Chambers Street.[130] With John distracted by ill health, Gunning committed a ruse to obtain title to the encumbered property. A letter appeared at the Chambers Street house addressed to John Burdell from a Mrs. Crane of Elizabethtown, New Jersey. Mrs. Crane stated that she was a person of means, in need of dental surgery and requested that John come to her home across the Hudson River. After John recovered enough to make the trip, Gunning secretly foreclosed on the lien and wrongfully bid on the encumbered property at auction. According to John's affidavit, only after this fraud was accomplished, did he detect an improper intimacy between Gunning and Margaret Burdell, whereupon he demanded that Gunning dissolve their partnership and leave 69 Chambers Street. Gunning refused, so John moved out instead, relocating first to his brother Harvey's premises at 362

Broadway, and then, in February 1847, to his own office on the east side of Union Square, at 2 Union Place. [131] John Burdell also alleged that his peripatetic wife Margaret was, as of the date of the legal answer, seeing yet another lover in her new separate abode in Franklin Street. Although her attorney was successful in obtaining a support award and temporary custody for Margaret of the couple's minor children, the case dragged on for years. No record of a final judgment survives. Meanwhile, William Burdell did not honor his promise to pay Edwards Pierrepont's legal fees, and Margaret's counsel obtained a judgment against William Burdell. The judgment sat uncollected for years, until it played a central evidentiary role in the inquest into Harvey Burdell's demise. [132]

John Burdell's relationship with his disloyal apprentice created a plethora of litigation, before and after the divorce proceedings. Suits and counter-suits intertwined the three Burdell brothers as well as Margaret Burdell and her lover Gunning. In a separate business contract action heard before Justice Jesse Oakley during the October 1843 term of the Superior Court in New York County, Thomas Gunning successfully recovered $93.23 plus costs from John Burdell. The case revolved around Gunning somehow renting out John Burdell's own home to the apprentice's master on a furnished basis, including use and enjoyment of "all and singular the household furniture, silver and plated ware, tools & implements used in the art trade and mystery of dentistry . . . for the sum of $1,100 per annum." Gunning must have been as skilled with the pen and a notary's seal as he was with the turnkey and Cupid's bow. How he gained legal title to 69 Chambers Street is anyone's guess. [133] Although Gunning also told the court (after taking title to the personalty at 69 Chambers Street in the episode involving the fictitious Mrs. Crane, *supra*) that John Burdell had incurred various other debts to him, the jury and Justice Oakley seem to have accepted at least a portion of Burdell's various defenses, among them that the chattel finance instrument in question and Gunning's possession of the property conveyed were obtained by fraud, and resulted from foreclosure of a fraudulent mortgage. The cuckolded John Burdell threw himself on the mercy of the court on account of Gunning having evicted him from the premises "by the criminal connexion [sic] or improper familiarities of the said plaintiff with the wife of the said defendant dwelling in the said premises," and on account of the trespasser having failed to apply a $300 distribution of dentistry partnership profits to the rent in question. The total judgment rendered against John Burdell was a small fraction of the various amounts claimed by Gunning.[134]

Gunning initiated yet another monetary action of an indeterminate nature against John Burdell in the Marine Court in September, 1843, in which Harvey Burdell also became embroiled. Harvey became incensed when he was accused by Gunning in open court during that case of being a thief and perjurer. Harvey then commenced a separate slander action against Gunning in Supreme Court in New York County on or about September 21, 1843, and had Gunning arrested and held on $1,000 bail. Unknown today, contemporary civil practice permitted the vengeful Harvey to have Gunning thrown in prison until he could offer a satisfactory bond against a potential civil judgment. Matters soon calmed down between the two rivals, at least temporarily: the action between Gunning and Harvey was discontinued by mutual consent filed April 21, 1844. For at least a brief period, though, Gunning had to limit his visits with his ex-partner's wife to brief, hushed interactions in a Tombs jail cell. [135]

Included in the surviving pleadings of Harvey's slander action against Thomas Gunning are four affidavits, all dated within the month of August, 1843. Servant girls in John and Margaret's home subscribed their names at the bottom of the quill-penned, curlicue-filled law clerk transcriptions of the goings on in the Chambers Street house. Although these affidavits antedate Margaret's initiation of her Chancery Court divorce proceeding, they either form part of the actual record of Harvey Burdell's slander action against Thomas Gunning or of the official docket in one of the other lawsuits between the Burdell brothers and Gunning. In a separate pleading in her subsequent divorce action, Margaret Burdell maintained that three of the affidavits were coerced from the affiants by John Burdell on peril of loss of their jobs and imprisonment "*in the tombs* [sic]".

John Burdell's affidavit in the bundle recounts his marriage to Margaret in New York City on July 18, 1836, and the birth of each of their four children. John pleaded to the court "that until within a short

Thomas Gunning   Dr. John Burdell

period past, he lived happily with his said wife, and had no cause to suspect her purity and virtue." The mortally embarrassed dentist went on
to recite the existence of his dentistry partnership with Thomas
Gunning, which included Gunning boarding and lodging in Burdell's
house for approximately sixteen months. A thorough and lengthy
"criminal connexion" ensued between Margaret and the rascal neophyte
dentist, with Burdell claiming to have been forced out of his own home
while Margaret remained *in situ* with her Adonis.

John Burdell's averrals are supported by the affidavits of the three
former servants in the 69 Chambers Street household. Mary Burchill,
placed "her mark" at the end of an affidavit stating that there existed
an "unusual improper familiarity between Mr. Thomas B. Gunning and
Mr. Burdell's wife. I have known them frequently to be alone together
after the rest of the family were all in bed; and have known her to take
up suppers to the room with him alone, frequently after ten at night."
28-year-old illiterate Margaret Cullough also inscribed her " X " to the
following account:

> [O]*n one Sabbath evening last winter (the precise day I have forgotten)
> about 9 o'clock, while Mr. Burdell was out, I, in company with two other
> persons, as we were about to enter the house, in passing the front basement*

window, saw Mr. T.B. Gunning and Mr. Burdell's wife standing very near together in the front basement in what I thought a very improper position, as Mr. Gunning had hold of her hand; and feeling ashamed at the sight (as one of my companions was a Gentleman) I turned away and walked some distance up Broadway, before entering the house. I have often known Mrs. Burdell & Mr. Gunning to set up alone till a late hour at night, some times as late as eleven and twelve even later.

The third servant's affidavit was made by a seemingly literate Ellen O'Brien, who signed her full name to a document repeating the allegations of her co-workers about the late night "sittings" of Margaret Burdell and Thomas Gunning. Margaret "ceased to lodge" with John Burdell in May of 1842, according to the affiant, when the nocturnal activities commenced. O'Brien accompanied Mary Burchill on an evening stroll with Burchill's gentleman friend, and was witness to the scene described above by her co-worker. It precipitated the same shamed response in Ellen. O'Brien recounted Margaret's weeks-long trip to Brooklyn during mid-summer, 1842. Ellen accompanied her mistress on the Brooklyn visit, having first fixed up Margaret's bedroom at 69 Chambers for Gunning to occupy in Margaret's absence. Gunning was a frequent visitor to the house in Brooklyn where his lover stayed that summer, particularly when John Burdell was away in the country. One thing had led to another, and as the summer ended, Ellen O'Brien noticed violent changes in her mistress' behavior as well as that of her distraught husband.

Housekeeping at 69 Chambers Street and the staffing of daily tasks in the building underwent wrenching changes during the autumn of 1843. John Burdell moved from a truly hellish situation to another, sharing his brother Harvey's home and office. Having won the contest with Thomas Gunning for John's allegiance, Harvey Burdell provided some assistance to brother John, but it lasted only briefly after John moved out of 69 Chambers Street. Though he shared an office with Harvey at 362 Broadway during many months in 1845-6, John's relationship with his brother was hardly one of mutual trust: John took pains to try and prevent Harvey from poaching John's remaining client base, which had already slipped as a result of Thomas Gunning staying in John's former abode and offices on Chambers Street. It was common knowledge that Harvey had capitalized in the past on his brother's reputation, using the public's confusion over the identities of the two brothers for his own advantage. John's entry in an 1845-6 business directory cautions visitors to the Broadway office shared by the two brothers: "[A]s I shall out of my office a portion of each day, it will be well for those who make appointments, to be particular in mentioning John___, in order to prevent mistakes."

Even though he had sided with John's wife Margaret in the couple's pending divorce, brother William Burdell turned to aid John in his attempts to physically separate from their scheming sibling. A loan from William helped John Burdell move into his own office at 2 Union Place, but the terms were hardly what one would expect between brothers. While his brother William ostensibly came to John's aid, Harvey continued to pursue John like a dog. In February 1848, only fourteen months after the filing of Margaret Burdell's divorce complaint, Harvey filed suit in New York County Supreme Court against John for $187.50 supposedly due on a promissory note. [136]

The 1844 settlement of the civil action that Harvey brought against Thomas Gunning did not end matters between those two rivals: Harvey Burdell had Gunning imprisoned for criminal forgery some years later. In the early reporting surrounding Burdell's murder, the *New York Tribune* recounted Gunning's complicity in breaking up John Burdell's marriage as well as the story of his incarceration.[137] The *Tribune* then pointed the finger at Gunning as a likely murder suspect: "This man, it is said, was a most vindictive rascal, and swore that if he lived to get out of prison he would be revenged on his prosecutor. Has this man finished his term at Sing Sing, and if so, has he returned to this city? And if he has, who is he and where is he and has he visited Dr. Burdell with this terrible vengeance?" The reporter was apparently unaware that Gunning had resided on Bond Street outside prison walls for several years prior to the 1857 murder.

Whether or not the *Tribune*'s speculation had merit, in 1857 it would have been easy for Gunning to find Harvey Burdell and exact his revenge. Thomas Gunning moved his office and residence into a house at 53 Bond Street in 1848, four years prior to Harvey's purchase of 31 Bond Street.[138] Hand-written ledgers from the New York State census of

1855 show Gunning as being 42 years of age, born in England and having resided in the United States for 16 years.[139] His affair with Margaret Burdell may have been torrid but it apparently did not mature into a longer commitment. The records show Gunning residing in the census index's dwelling 231 in the Fifteenth Ward, 2nd Election District, together with a 36-year old wife, a 9-year-old daughter named Mary, and two year old son William. [140] The children's names do not correspond with those of John and Margaret Burdell's children mentioned in the parents' respective estate proceedings. Gunning's household also included "Sarah Johnston, Boarder, 22, Mary Gallagher, Servant, 21, Ellen Dillon, Servant and Catherine Mulligan, Servant, 20." Dwelling 231 was valued at $10,000 in the census records.[141]

If the *Tribune*'s surmise as to Gunning's complicity in Burdell's death was correct, then the Englishman was indeed not only cold-blooded but supremely self-confident of evading detection: Gunning remained on the block for ninety days after Harvey Burdell was dispatched. When his lease expired on April 30, 1857, the survivor moved uptown. New York City directories of the times show a hiatus in Gunning's residence on Bond Street for the 1851-2 directory year, which may correspond with the prison stay recounted by the *Tribune*. No other mention of Gunning's role in the Burdell murder appeared in the *Tribune* after the initial article, and he was rarely mentioned by name, much less inculpated, in other contemporary journalism.

John Burdell never recovered form the blows dealt him by Margaret, Thomas Gunning, and his two brothers. On March 12, 1850, Harvey Burdell made application to Alexander W. Bradford, Surrogate of New York County for probate of John's last will and testament.[142] Little did the jurist know how deeply he would later become involved in adjudicating matters concerning the two brothers and their extended families. Bradford admitted probate on May 7, 1850, after the customary hearing and appointment of a guardian *ad litem* for John and Margaret's minor children, Ann, Emily, and John, Jr.

Those familiar with John and Harvey's relationship must have been stunned by the terms of the instrument. In his will, which was dated February 26, 1850, and signed in New York City in the presence of his brother James Burdell of Herkimer Village, New York, John appointed

Harvey "my administrator and guardian of my children." John's high-minded voice echoed through the transcription of his final wishes: "I also enjoin upon said H Burdell that he rear direct and educate them in the principles of virtue and religion and above all things protect them from vice and degradation and bestow upon them the same care he would were they his own children. The custody of the children being invested in me by order of the Supreme Court of the State of New York, I therefore transfer said custody and control to Said H Burdell, and would request that the Mother do deliver Said children of her own free will and accord without any further legal proceedings."[143]

Given their fractious history, and John's familiarity with Harvey's personal life-style and beliefs, one might question the authenticity of the entire will, but no contest was brought. The irony of John's charge to Harvey to take care of John's children as if they were Harvey's own is striking. Harvey's wanton behavior was well known in the Astor Place demi-monde, and caused his high-minded older brother no end of embarrassment. Strangers he met on social occasions and new dental patients constantly confused John with his profligate brother.

Public records do not disclose how the custody of John's three children was resolved. No mention is made of any of them ever having resided with Harvey at 31 Bond Street in the news articles about Harvey's murder seven years later, even though all three were still minors. The *New York Herald* reported what many suspected at the time of John's death: Harvey Burdell wrote out the suspect will and forced it upon his almost senseless brother to sign while he lay on his deathbed. Margaret Burdell also let the *Herald* know that the beloved Uncle Harvey had neither taken custody of the children, nor provided his nieces and nephews with funds from their father's estate.[144] Equally notable in John Burdell's will is the absence of any property bequests, but again Harvey Burdell had probably made such provisions irrelevant by stealing from John.

John never recovered from the deceit practiced upon him by Thomas Gunning and Margaret, and the ill will among Harvey, William and John Burdell literally drove the latter to his death. Like vultures circling fresh carrion, Harvey and William fixed upon independent schemes to take advantage of their sibling's emotional and financial troubles when Thomas Gunning drove John from his own home. Liens against John's miserable few possessions were recorded in favor of both William and Harvey, and John arrived at death's door a bankrupt. Even in sunnier days, John had owned no real estate in New York City. Other than his good name, his dentistry practice was his only significant asset. Whatever wealth John controlled when he left 69 Chambers Street must have vaporized in the ensuing combat. It is inconceivable that John owned anything of value by the time he signed the papers Harvey thrust in front of his glassy eyes. John left not a single bequest to any of his children, either directly or in trust.

John Burdell's sorrowful death and his brothers' complicity in his destruction foreshadowed the later, even more public scenes in the Burdell family tragedy. In its early coverage of Harvey's murder, the *Herald* provided a somewhat confusing account of the relations of the three brothers during the years of John Burdell's breakdown, informing its readers that all three young men had been ejected from their childhood home by their mother Polly upon her remarriage to James Lamon.[145] Not surprisingly, no love was lost among the three men during their adult lives, and this sorry order was embossed, in Harvey's case, with a tendency towards heterosexual predation. According to the *Herald's* reporting, Harvey rivaled Gunning in his adulterous admiration of Margaret Burdell, and William stepped in to try and prevent Harvey's felonious grab of the modest proceeds of John's estate. *"A Sketch of the Life and Character of Dr. Harvey Burdell"* published in the *Herald* on February 4, 1857 told readers of how the penurious Harvey cadged off his older brother for years while living with him at 69 Chambers Street. Dentistry clients of John's were lured away by his licentious younger brother, and after Harvey made more than one pass at John's wife, Margaret, he was ordered out of the house.[146]

Upstanding older brother John was a gullible fellow by nature, and Harvey led him like a sheep to slaughter. Not content with alienating his sister-in-law's affections, when divorce proceedings were imminent, Harvey approached John with a seemingly brotherly proposal: if John would grant a mortgage to Harvey on his meager assets, the lien would be binding in any divorce proceeding, and prevent Margaret from being awarded a share of the marital property. Without advancing any funds, he took control of his brother's property as he acted the part of concerned sibling and then gave John shelter after Thomas Gunning forced the cuckold from his home.

At the time, Harvey maintained his office and residence at 362 Broadway, on the corner of Franklin Street, and the almost penniless John Burdell, crushed in spirit, moved in and tried to re-establish his previously thriving dental practice. Harvey was not about to offer graceful charity. Blood relation or not, when John attempted to hang his own sign on the building's street-side facade, Harvey forbad it. A shingle hanging from a nearby shed was all John was permitted, with the expected results. After being rebuffed in his demand that Harvey tear up the mortgage granted at the outset of his divorce, John managed to take possession of a few items he had salvaged from his 69 Chambers Street abode, and moved to new quarters on Union Place. Harvey and William Burdell took turns playing ping pong with their brother's loyalties as well as his wallet, and in a gesture of feigned magnanimity, William Burdell (though recently the financier of John's adversary in their marital dispute), advanced funds to assist in the relocation. Needless to say, the transaction was purely commercial: William took care to obtain a mortgage from John on his new office and home furnishings.

The descriptions of Harvey Burdell as a quarrelsome and litigious miscreant, offered by his dentistry profession colleagues at the inquest seven years later, though hardly complimentary, gave little clue of the ghoulish gavotte Harvey and William Burdell danced as their older bother lay dying. [147] Harvey apparently got wind of the lien given to his brother William, and took prompt action. The early bird would get the worm, and as John Burdell lay on his deathbed, Harvey showed up at 2 Union Place with the New York County sheriff. *Rigor mortis* was next, and the two went about seizing everything they could "even the furniture of his death chamber, to the very feather bed from under his brother, leaving him to die on a sofa."

The *Herald's* account of John's last years is borne out by extant legal pleadings. A complaint signed by Edwards S. Pierrepont, Esq. and sworn to by his client, William Burdell on April 8, 1850, a short time after John's death, alleged Harvey Burdell's wrongful conversion of

John's personal property.[148] William Burdell sought recovery against his brother Harvey in the New York County Court of Common Pleas, alleging that Harvey had wrongfully taken possession of John's office furniture and miscellaneous household effects. Despite having secured his act of brotherly love with a mortgage, William fell prey to his then still healthy sibling with a keener command of the legal process. The complaint recites that Harvey

> ...unlawfully detains from the said plaintiff the following goods and chattels of the plaintiff, that is to say, Three Carpets, two large mirrors or pier glasses, one large mahogany wardrobe, one large mahogany bureau. Four small bureau's, one sofa bed-stead, one mahogany bed-stead Three hair mattresses, one large valuable centre table one mahogany leaf table Three breakfast tables, Twelve mahogany chairs, six cottage chairs one valuable mantle clock one instrument case, one Dentists operating Chair, all of which said goods and chattel belong to the plaintiff who is entitled to the possession of the same . . .

Harvey Burdell defended the action through his attorney Skeffington Sanxay, and swore to a general denial of brother William's claims. On April 26, 1853, after a jury trial, Judge Woodruff issued a judgment to William for $1,150.54 including court costs.[149] The size of this judgment did not pose a serious financial threat to Harvey Burdell; his battles with William continued over the next decade, while Harvey continued his ascent among the bourgeoisie of New York's commercial center. There is no record of the disposition of this judgment when Harvey Burdell's estate was liquidated.

As if there was not enough family strife to consume their fratricidal impulses, John, Harvey and William's lives were further complicated in the mid-1840s by the arrival in town of their brother James' son, Galen Burdell. Ambitious Galen, like his uncles John and Harvey, moved to New York to try and make his livelihood as a dentist, and first apprenticed himself to a Brooklyn practitioner, Abram Vosburgh. Cut from the same cloth as his uncle Harvey, Galen swindled his employer, and Vosburgh sued the youth at the end of his contractual term, alleging nonpayment of agreed upon rent and board. In a maneuver that his role model would surely have applauded, Galen defended the action in Brooklyn Marine Court on the grounds of legal incapacity, claiming that his status as a minor avoided any legal responsibility for his debts.

The case was reported on April 1, 1848 in William Cullen Bryant's *New York Evening Post*. Galen took great umbrage at the *Post's* ridicule of his defense of infancy, and he sued Bryant in New York County Supreme Court for libel. The *Post's* "news" article had poked fun at Galen's morals, recounting to its amused readers how the sitting judge in the case had raised his spectacles in disbelief when Galen, still a minor, threw himself on the mercy of the court. With his apprenticeship over and some money squirreled away as a result of having stiffed Abram Vosburgh for rent and board, Galen was able to move into Manhattan and open his own practice. Not just anywhere would do for the site of his new office, though.

Uncle Harvey had set a good example when he arrived in New York and set up shop next door to his successful brother John. Luring away the patients of blood relatives with the same surname had served Harvey well, and what greater respect than imitation could be paid? Galen rented an office across the street from Harvey Burdell's 362 Broadway clinic and promptly hung out a shingle. The sign totally confused the already clouded heads of sufferers who arrived on the block with bandaged jaws and desperate expressions. The judge sitting in Supreme Court when Abram Vosburgh's suit was finally heard was not amused as he tipped his spectacles to examine the defendant's youthful countenance. According to the *Post's* reporter, "Some one remarked at this juncture, if Dr. Burdell was an 'infant' he was the oldest infant he ever saw. The secret was soon out, and it reveals a novel way of getting into practice on another man's reputation." Young Galen had painted and hung outside his door a plank reading "Dr. Burdell, Dentist;" it was an exact copy of his uncle's sign hanging on the opposite corner. Infant or not, under the eyes of the law, the sly nephew was deemed unentitled to the usual protections. Galen suffered judgment for the full $75 claimed by his former master. Wounded where it hurt most, the defendant then sought revenge against the *Post*. The outcome of Galen's libel claim is unclear, though. The surviving legal files in the case are incomplete. [150]

Vosburgh's successful suit was only a minor annoyance to a young

Galen Burdell

man with the entrepreneurial drive possessed by Galen Burdell. America presented boundless opportunities for a smart, fast-talking swindler. As a confident young single man in a booming economy, Galen had the personal freedom and emotional wherewithal to strike out on his own at the end of the 1840s. Having destroyed any family bonds that might have benefited him in New York, Galen followed the path trod by so many of his generation, and joined the Gold Rush. Galen's rapid rise to wealth and fame in California forms a striking contrast to the sorry fate of his would-be aunt, Emma Cunningham.[151]

Far apart from her nephew Galen's nimble and amoral opportunism, Margaret Burdell's ability to physically separate herself from the Burdell family pathologies was substantial restricted by the burden of supporting three young children, limited financial resources, and an incomplete marital separation. After filing for divorce against John Burdell in 1846, Margaret Burdell did not join Thomas Gunning on Bond Street when he moved there in 1847. Margaret moved at least three times over the course of the next nine years among various lower Manhattan residences. No one took John's place, and Margaret spent her middle-aged years as a widow, constantly in straitened circumstances. After her father's death, Margaret Burdell inherited a modest sum. The old coach-maker died intestate in October, 1850, leaving Margaret a one-fifth interest as tenant in common in three properties on Duane and Chambers Streets. Within two weeks of her father's death, Margaret sued for partition of the properties, presumably out of financial duress, and then accepted an offer before the case reached trial for $2,500 from her relative, Edward Alburtis, in exchange for her share. Edward made a tidy profit on his relative's misery: the three pieces of real estate were sold for a total of $30,400 some 21 months later. Margaret would have more than doubled her inheritance if she had waited for her 20 per cent share of the money.[152] Years later, when her ex-brother-in-law Harvey was murdered, the newspapers virtually ignored the story of Margaret's unhappy involvement with the Burdell family. Like Thomas Gunning, Margaret had moved far away from the scourge of Bond Street after Harvey Burdell's wound-ridden body was buried.

CHAPTER 6

———◆━◆◆◆◆━◆———

Harvey Burdell's Funeral and The End of the Inquest

NOON BELLS rang out from Grace Church's tower on Wednesday, February 4, as thousands of spectators jammed the muddied corner of Broadway and Tenth Street by the churchyard gates. The sober sanctuary of Manhattan's most fashionable Episcopalian congregation was unusually busy for a mid-winter weekday. The crowd pressed forward against the rows of iron spikes that wrapped around the corner close, impatient to gain access to the limited pew-space. Although the Coroner's jury continued to sit and hear witnesses, hordes of curiosity-seekers had left the inquest site and walked the short distance north from 31 Bond Street behind the hearse bearing Harvey Burdell's coffin. The majority of the high-society parishioners avoided the public spotlight, and it was particularly strange that the funeral of a non-member, the suddenly notorious Dr. Burdell, was being conducted from the premises. No Burdell relative had bought one of the expensive pews whose ownership was required for registration on the congregation's membership rolls. How it came to pass that Burdell was buried from Grace Church with the head minister Reverend Dr. T.H. Taylor officiating remains a mystery.[153]

A heartrending scene unfolded on the second floor of 31 Bond Street earlier that day. Until the morning of the funeral, Emma Cunningham was barred from the room where her one-time lover had lain in a satin-lined rosewood coffin since the completion of an autopsy earlier in the week. As the undertaker's wagon drew up to the front door, Emma begged Coroner Connery once more for a chance to pay her last respects. Attendance at the funeral was out of the question:

Emma realized that Connery's legal strategy would be compromised if she were permitted to make a public display of grief over Burdell's passing. Though reluctant to show any mercy in his studied façade of avenging inquisitor, Connery finally relented, and Captain Dilks escorted Emma and her children downstairs into the hushed viewing room. The *Herald* reported the good-bye scene, which unfolded in a manner that could only lend credence to Emma's claim of being Harvey Burdell's widow and the rightful beneficiary of his estate. Clad in bulky mourning dress, Emma hesitated as she headed downstairs for a look at the sorry remains of her last chance:

> *Having descended the staircase half way, she burst into a fit of tears . . . sobbing heavily, she at length entered the dread apartment. The Captain could not support the scene which he knew must ensue, and therefore remained outside, but the lady and her family were accompanied by officers Smits, Davis and Williams, and from one of those gentlemen we have obtained the following particulars: Mrs. Cunningham entered the room first, and walked straight to the coffin. Standing motionless by it for a few seconds, she remarked "That's not his shirt, he never wore one like it." Then the full tide of agony and despair seemed to roll over her – the two daughters and little boys were sobbing bitterly – the mother sank upon her knees, and throwing herself upon the open coffin, she exclaimed: — "Oh I wish to God you could speak, and tell who done it.".*...
>
> *On one side was the younger daughter, Helen, supporting her mother and beseeching her, "Dear mother, don't cry so." Augusta, the oldest of the family, held her on the other side, whilst the two boys nestled together near the group, sending up a doleful cry of sorrow, the mother mingling her sighs with "O dear doctor," and such like exclamations.*
>
> *Finally the time came for the corpse to be removed and the tearful group ascended to their own apartments. Mrs. Cunningham was so affected by the appalling adieu that medical assistance had to be called in. She was put to bed, and Dr. Uhr [Uhl] waited upon her. We are happy to hear that her symptoms are not likely to prove serious.*[154]

Shortly after noon, the hearse pulled away from 31 Bond Street, and made its way slowly uptown. Crowds quickly overtook the slow-moving team as it drew into Broadway. Grace Church was still locked when the hearse and other carriages arrived, and the iron gates in front were shut tight. Bedlam reigned outside, as if a popular sporting event was happening nearby or the circus had come to town. The cortege halted and the iron bolts of the massive gates were thrown back. Their ponderous hinges creaked open. The crowds swelled to fill the gap, but brass-starred policemen promptly produced their billy clubs and used them to good advantage on those who ignored the order to halt. No one was allowed inside the sanctuary, and after a path was cleared through the protesting masses, Burdell's coffin was carried inside and placed on the waiting altar. The church doors were then barred and the gates swung back into place and bolted shut as angry cries arose from the disgruntled spectators. [155]

Despite access to the church being blocked, throngs continued to pour into Broadway and the adjoining side streets. Bodies were packed tightly on both sides of Broadway and into Tenth Street east and west of the churchyard, covering the sidewalks and stoops. According to the press, women far outnumbered men among the spectators: "Nearly the entire crowd immediately before the church were females – if their dresses had ever been extended and voluminous, they were then packed about as close and tight as dry goods on live forms ever were before." Public knowledge of the heinous nature of Dr. Burdell's treatment of his ex-lover had spread throughout the city, and high-pitched cries for justice rose in a raucous counterpoint. The tables had been turned in this instance, but many women nonetheless condemned Emma Cunningham as murderess of the precious order of genteel femininity. At times, the calls for her doom reached the typhoon level attending public executions of men convicted of misogynist violence. Despite the crowd's agreement about the victim's vile character, and the consensus that Dr. Burdell had received his just desserts, the multitude agreed that Emma should hang.

Over eight thousand people pressed for admission to the shuttered church as the hour for the service arrived. Confusion among the police was so great that even a cousin of the deceased, standing outside the gates with her feet wet and cold, could not gain entrance. After a long delay, the pallbearers, family and members of the press were admitted to the sanctuary, which remained half-empty even as the disappointed public milled outside. Before the elegant coffin lid was screwed shut, the mourners, passing by the bier, took a final glimpse at the solemn face of Dr. Burdell. An undertaker had dressed Burdell in a new black suit; and although a black cravat and a high shirt collar disguised the gruesome wounds in his neck near the carotid arteries, the extraordinary lacerations on the Doctor's face were unmistakable.

Just after 2:00 P.M., the decision was made to open the church doors to the public, and those nearest the gates were able to rush in. Disorderly lower-class women pouring into the pews drew amused looks from the church ushers. The shabbily-dressed visitors were used to sitting in segregated upstairs galleries in fundamentalist congregations, and the sight of the uncomfortable mob made a distinct impression on the *Herald*'s reporter: "Grace Church was probably never filled with such a congregation before; it was a different audience from the one that usually assembles there. The ladies were not the elegantly dressed ones . . . nor were the gentleman the merchant princes of our city . . . Some of the ladies, on entering, asked the sexton if they could go up to the gallery, and were much surprised to find that there was no gallery in the church."

Reverend Taylor promptly entered and commenced the customary Episcopal funeral service, intoning the familiar "I am the resurrection and the life" from John 9:25 and 26 with the well-worn verses from Job and Timothy. Rapt attention was paid as the choir chanted a hymn arranged upon Psalms 39 and 40, and Dr. Taylor then read the lesson from Paul's First Epistle to the Corinthians. A final prayer was uttered. With the Reverend's words ringing in the audience's ears and tears dampening onlooker's handkerchiefs, eight pallbearers moved into position. Harvey Burdell's mortal remains were marched outside to the beat of Reverend Taylor's stentorian tones: "we humbly beseech thee, O Father, to raise us from the death of sin unto the life of righteousness; that when we shall depart this life we may rest in him . . ."

Outside on Broadway, a procession of fifty carriages lined up to accompany the hearse down to the Battery. All along the two-mile trip to the wharf, spectators crowded the sidewalks and hung from windows, straining to get a glimpse of the much-celebrated victim's final carriage ride. A barge was waiting at South Ferry, and after the slow trip across the Upper New York Harbor to South Brooklyn's Hamilton Avenue dock, the cortege disembarked and made its way uphill through Green-Wood's ornate gates to the height of the Gowanus Hills. There, Harvey Burdell's coffin was lowered into snow-rimmed lot 3799. Few, if any, relatives made it to the graveside, despite the ample travel time afforded since his death. The murder victim's final resting place at the corner of Oak and Landscape Avenues was never marked with a permanent gravestone, a fact easily understood given the events of the next several months.[156]

* * *

By the day after the funeral, many of the important protagonists, possible motives, and physical evidence had already been presented to the Coroner's jury. Still to come, however, was a clutch of witnesses who would shed further light on the violent clashes between Emma and her would-be husband. Only days before his death, the Doctor had made one last attempt, armed with legal documents, to put an end to their months-long battle.

The confrontation between Harvey Burdell and Emma Cunningham that proved final had broken out in full force on the weekend of January 24. The flashpoint involved the presence, once again, of Harvey's 24-year-old female cousin, Dimis Hubbard, at 31 Bond. At the beginning of 1857, Dimis was once again single. Her marriage at sixteen to a neighbor in upstate Jefferson County, William Charles Vorce, ended eight years later in divorce. Following in the footsteps of her much older cousins Harvey and William Burdell, Dimis had come to New York with her husband within a few years after her marriage.[157] Harvey had moved away from Jefferson County when his cousin was a small child; the two would not become intimately acquainted until Dimis and William Vorce moved to the city and initially boarded at Harvey Burdell's home.[158] Dimis's marriage did not endure the transition from slow-paced Jefferson County to New York City's teeming streets. The end came when William Vorce's taste for brothel life became known to his spouse in the fall of 1855. In her divorce complaint filed in November, the young country-born wife recited the details of her March, 1849 marriage in Henderson township, and then asserted that during October 1855, as well as for months before, Vorce "at a house of ill fame in Mercer Street near Canal Street in the City of

New York, [the] number of which is unknown to the Plaintiff, did commit adultery and have carnal connexion with a female inmate of said house whose name is unknown to the Plaintiff . . ." Adding injury to insult, Vorce had placed his wife at risk for a potentially life-threatening illness: "The Plaintiff further shows that by means of the aforesaid acts of adultery or some or one of them the defendant has contracted a venereal disease."[159] The pleading stated that the couple was childless, and was signed by Dimis with a child-like scrawl.[160]

In addition to the marital deceit, yet another layer of malice and intrigue is embedded in the first few lines of the divorce papers. The caption of the lawsuit contained a smoldering fuse. Abandoned by her whore-mongering husband, and in all likelihood destitute, Dimis called upon Harvey for help in early November, 1855. The desperate young woman requested that Burdell provide her with shelter at 31 Bond Street, and assist her in the legal proceedings by acting as the then mandatory surrogate plaintiff. Not long back from their first visit to Saratoga together, and even with Emma's pregnancy looming over him, Burdell could not resist a damsel in distress. Who knew in what ways the favor might be re-paid? His passion for anonymity drove Burdell to act desperately, though. Using whatever combination of threats and promises he could muster, Harvey Burdell prevailed upon the indisposed Emma to subscribe her name as Dimis's legal representative in his cousin's divorce action.

In 1855, New York, among many states, denied a married woman the right to act for herself in initiating divorce proceedings. The law's chauvinist assumption of puerile female nature included the notion that a woman was incompetent to handle her own legal affairs. When instituting suit, she was required to find a suitable representative to act as nominal plaintiff. Although in many cases the father or brother of an unhappy wife acted in the requisite capacity, single widows also qualified for service. Hoping against hope that Burdell would change his mind and agree to marry her if she cooperated with his strange request, Emma consented to act as Dimis's "next friend" in the action. The divorce was granted, but little thanks came Emma's way. Less than two weeks later, Burdell caused Emma to abort the fetus she was carrying.[161] According to several witnesses at the Coroner's inquest, Dimis remained in the house at 31 Bond Street against Emma's wishes for many months after moving back there in the fall of 1855. Several individuals giving testimony at the inquest vouched for Emma's insistence that while Harvey Burdell was fending off her marriage campaign, he was also conducting a sexual affair with his helpless young cousin.

When Emma Cunningham took over as landlady of 31 Bond Street on May 1, 1856, one goal, above all, had to be accomplished: Dimis was to be ridded from the house once and for all. The young lady's whereabouts in New York during the winter and spring of 1856 are unclear, but Emma was certainly successful in ejecting Dimis from the house by the start of the summer. Six months later, Dimis was residing at 910 Broadway, near 21st Street, with Harvey's brother, William Burdell, and the three relatives were in the habit of socializing together.[162] In the months intervening between Dimis' departure and Burdell's death, Emma Cunningham could perhaps claim at least one non-violent victory: she was, for the most part, successful in keeping the young woman out of her home and her lover's bed. None of the testimony in front of the Coroner indicated that Dimis was a frequent visitor to 31 Bond Street after moving out of the house. Burdell had not been easily discouraged, though. When Burdell and Emma returned from their second summer in Saratoga together at the end of August, 1856, the doctor unsuccessfully implored Emma to permit Dimis to return and live at 31 Bond.[163]

Harvey Burdell's interest in his young cousin remained a poisoned thorn in Emma Cunningham's side throughout their relationship. Despite having rid her household of Dimis' daily presence, Emma had ample opportunity to hear of her lover's meetings with the competition outside of 31 Bond Street. Toward the end of January, 1857, Burdell even dared to bring Dimis back to the house. After visiting in Brooklyn on January 24 with his married cousin Catherine Dennison, Harvey Burdell returned to New York to pay a call on Dimis and his brother William. The next day, Mrs. Dennison called at 31 Bond Street, and when she arrived, Dimis was again sitting in the parlor with Harvey. With bitterness boiling inside, Emma lurked on the stairs of the house, spying on her rival, whose music and French lessons continued to be subsidized by the doctor. Despite having gotten wind of Dimis's having an appropriate beau, and Harvey's promise to will $6,000 to Dimis if she remarried as he wished, Emma remained obsessively jealous of the young woman.

Mrs. Dennison was not alone in noticing Emma's intense displeasure over Dr. Burdell's parlor get-together with Dimis that Monday. Two witnesses took the stand on February 6 in front of the coroner and provided further details of the late-January confrontation between Harvey and Emma that followed Dimis's parlor visit. Grand Street resident Alvah Blaisdell had been Burdell's dentistry partner in their Franklin Street office until May of 1853. Although he remained a close friend of Dr. Burdell's and visited with him frequently, Blaisdell had given up dentistry by 1857 and commenced running a wholesale liquor business.[164] By the time Blaisdell mounted the witness chair, Harvey Burdell had been painted as a sociopath by a number of witnesses, and in his testimony Blaisdell seemed anxious to preserve some dignity for his deceased partner.

During the mid-week prior to Dimis's January 24 visit to 31 Bond, Blaisdell came to the house and listened to his frightened friend's tale of being threatened with violence by Emma, George Snodgrass, John Eckel and Emma's older daughter, Augusta. Dr. Burdell pleaded with Blaisdell to stay overnight at 31 Bond the coming Friday, January 30, to protect Burdell against an expected assault, but Blaisdell declined. In an effort to divert the jurors' attention from decedent's deviant sexual agendas, Blaisdell informed the group that a late January screaming match at the house resulted from Emma Cunningham's rage at being left out of a will that Dr. Burdell had recently drafted.[165]

Soon after Alvah Blaisdell stepped down, Dimis Hubbard seated herself in the witness chair. With her answers to the interrogators' questions, the jury first learned of the bomb that Burdell was planning to drop on Emma during what turned out to be the final week of his life. Despite promising Emma continued tenure in 31 Bond Street in the October 1856 settlement papers that the couple exchanged, by the following January, Harvey Burdell could no longer bear to live with Emma under the same roof. Burdell persuaded his long-time acquaintance Catherine Stansbury to rent the home effective May 1, 1857. The doctor even showed Dimis the lease that he planned to have Mrs.

Stansbury sign, and made it clear to her that he would evict Emma as soon as possible. Ever the cautious one, at least when it came to documentation, Burdell had convinced Emma to execute a new settlement agreement on January 24 at the end of their quarrel, granting the doctor a general release and promising to leave the premises as scheduled on May 1, 1857. [166]

Dimis's brief account of the events of the final two weeks of January at 31 Bond Street was fleshed out by the next witness. Among Harvey Burdell's dentistry patients during the fortnight preceding his death was the rector of Zion Episcopal Church, the Reverend Richard H. Cox. Cox had been coming to Dr. Burdell for dentistry work for over a decade, and had formed a close friendship with the doctor. According to Cox's testimony, when he arrived at the house on January 15, the doctor was particularly out of sorts. Burdell apologized for the disorderly parlor, which also served as a reception room for patients. Emma Cunningham had thrown a noisy party in the house the previous evening and the place had been left a shambles.

Getting his teeth fixed was not the only reason Cox visited on the 15th; the Reverend had his own domestic problems, and came to solicit Burdell's assistance in the clergyman's own divorce. [167] While discussing Cox's personal affairs, Harvey Burdell also told his visitor of the plan to rent the house out from under Emma Cunningham. A follow-up clinical session was then arranged for Friday, January 30th, one that turned out to be the last in Reverend Cox's course of treatment.

The door knocker of 31 Bond clattered throughout that fateful day. After being admitted to the busy parlor floor, Rev. Cox overheard and then spied Catherine Stansbury, who had shown up for one last inspection of the premises before the following day's planned lease-signing. Burdell seemed agitated when Mrs. Stansbury arrived, and he refused to take her for a tour while Rev. Cox remained in the operatory chair. [168] Reverend Cox sat speechless, his mouth agape, while Burdell's friend and ex-partner Alvah Blaisdell also appeared, followed shortly by Dimis Hubbard. Having been shown a will drafted by Burdell during the doctor's visit to his Broad Street office a few days prior, and then hearing that Burdell had purchased a revolver, Blaisdell had come to check up on his apoplectic friend. Blaisdell was well aware of the variegated and occasionally tawdry nature of Burdell's clientele, and was concerned for his friend's safety. Though told by Dr. Burdell of his fears that Emma and her new boyfriend would do him in, Blaisdell knew his friend well enough to realize that among the prostitutes and other denizens of the area's demi-monde who formed the bulk of Burdell's patients, there were many who might wish to do the dentist harm, and would gladly partner with Emma in a homicidal plan.

All four of the parlor guests had been aware for months of Burdell's wish to rid himself of his ex-lover's pestilential presence. Emma's blood boiled when she found Burdell's allies gathering in her home that Friday, sharing plans for her enemy's victory. Ever one to rely on paper and legal procedures, Burdell had moved furtively around the house all day, avoiding Emma's glare. With her signed release in his pocket, the desperate dentist was close to fulfillment of his most intense desire: Emma would soon be out of his house, and out of his life. After a mid-day tooth-repair session, Reverend Cox left 31 Bond Street, having endured Dr. Burdell's rant about evil women and been made privy to his plans to rent the house to Mrs. Stansbury. Blaisdell departed about 4:30 that afternoon, promising Dr. Burdell that he would return at 7:00 in the evening, but the appointment was not kept. When Cox returned at 5:00 P.M. to explain to Harvey how he could assist Cox in divorcing his wife, the Reverend found that his friend had just gone out. Dr. Burdell had told cook Hannah Conlan that he would return between 9:00 and 10:00 that evening, and directed that if a tall gentleman called, to ask him to come back the following day.[169]

The door knocker sounded again after Burdell's departure, and a gentleman standing almost six feet tall entered the parlor-floor vestibule, asking for Emma Cunningham. When Emma was told that a Mr. Todd was calling, she seemed not to recognize his name, but came downstairs anyway. As the sandy-haired, bewhiskered guest identified himself, Reverend Cox noticed from his listening post in the adjacent parlor that Emma's greeting to the caller was an oddly warm one. What transpired between the caller and Emma does not appear in the record of Cox's testimony. Inexplicably, Mr. Todd was not called to testify in any of the subsequent legal proceedings.

The last several days of the fifteen-day ordeal orchestrated by

Coroner Connery and District Attorney Hall involved extensive appearances by all four of Emma's children. Several neighborhood merchants also spoke of weapons purchased in neighborhood shops by Snodgrass and Eckel in the days before the murder occurred. Testimony was given by a variety of witnesses who traveled to the inquest from upstate New York as to Harvey Burdell's whereabouts on October 28, 1856, the date Reverend Uriah Marvine executed a marriage certificate bearing Burdell's name as groom.

The *Herald* reported the eldest of Emma's children as being first to take the stand: "Miss [Margaret] Augusta Cunningham is perhaps a little above the ordinary stature of her sex, and is of a slender figure," the paper informed readers in its Sunday morning edition on February 8. Margaret showed no sign of sharing in her mother's grief. The paper's reporter did a careful study of the girl:

> She appears to be about twenty-three years of age and is the elder of the two [sic] sisters. Her complexion is blonde, her features regular, her face oval, her hair a very light brown, and her expression, instead of indicating hauteur or firmness of mind, is that of a quiet and rather amiable looking girl. Her countenance is rather prepossessing than otherwise, and she seemed to impress those present favorably towards her. While giving her testimony, this impression was removed, to a great extent, by the somewhat flippant manner in which she answered several of the questions, and by her laughing when speaking of Dr. Burdell's penuriousness. She was dressed in a plaid stuff, a large fur cape, and was without a bonnet.[170]

Margaret's emotional distance from the events at hand proved understandable. During most of her mother's affair with Dr. Burdell, the eldest Miss Cunningham had been living away from New York City, first in Cleveland, and then at Luther Beecher's Female Seminary. Contact with her mother's suitor had been limited to her initial acquaintance with Burdell as his dental patient, encountering him during her occasional stays at her mother's homes on West 24th Street and at 31 Bond Street, and during a visit to Cleveland that Harvey and Emma made in 1855. The interrogators left un-addressed, though, whether Harvey Burdell eschewed pedophilia, at least when it came to the offspring of his own lover. Perhaps the doctor kept his thoughts to himself as he hovered over the witness's beautiful form while she sat helpless in his dentistry chair.

The young woman's most cohesive testimony concerned the events of the last weekend of Burdell's life. The final row between Emma and Harvey began, according to Margaret, when Emma threatened to publish the "fact" of their marriage ceremony before Reverend Marvine in October, 1856. Emma had met with Burdell privately on Saturday, January 24 in an upstairs room in the house. When Margaret appeared in the doorway, Burdell suspected her of overhearing their conversation; he then pushed Margaret out the door into the hallway, and up against the stair banister. On the witness stand, Margaret recalled Burdell's having previously threatened to kill her if she joined with her mother in disclosing the October marriage. After being shoved out of the room, the frightened girl backed away from Burdell's angry glare and ran off, frightened for her life.

The complexity of Emma Cunningham's relationships was further revealed when Margaret informed the jury that during the month after the marriage ceremony, her mother shared her husband's bed every night. Ranks were closed as Margaret, not quite eighteen years old by her own account, corroborated her mother's posture of decency and marital propriety. According to Margaret, boarder and murder suspect John Eckel had a platonic relationship with her mother; only in a group with George Snodgrass did Emma and the boarders attend performances at neighborhood theaters. Margaret's final testimony estab-

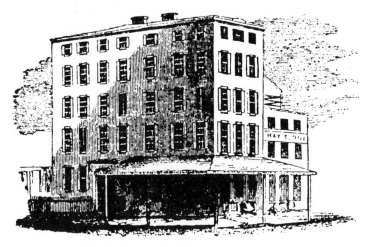

Oliver Wellington's Twelfth Street Water Cure Clinic

lished her own alibi for the night of the murder. She had sat up late with her sister Helen, who was scheduled to travel the next morning to boarding school in Saratoga with Reverend Luther Beecher. They heard nothing unusual until the two girls retired.

A timid, frightened Helen Cunningham took the stand next. One can only imagine the shame felt by the round-featured girl, who would be sixteen years old in less than a week. The city was blanketed with newspaper accounts of Helen's amorous adventures with George Snodgrass, and the discovery of her underclothes tossed among the bedding in his room at 31 Bond Street. As she waited in the witness chair for the interrogation to proceed, Helen's plain, neat black dress and modest demeanor contrasted sharply with her older sister's *hauteur*. Heaven only knew what Coroner Connery would ask when the questioning began. Helen's testimony proved inconclusive, though, and disappointing to the thrill-thirsty public.

Contrary to rumors in the streets and jury room that the murder victim had been a friend of Emma and George Cunningham during that couple's marriage, Helen asserted that her mother's acquaintance with Burdell was only of some two years duration. The younger daughter claimed to know little, if anything, about Emma's supposed nuptials with Harvey Burdell. In contrast to her older sister's account, Helen told the jurors that Emma and Harvey never slept together at 31 Bond, simply sharing adjoining bedrooms from time to time. Helen was at home during all of January, 1857, prior to her planned enrollment at Temple Grove Seminary, and a witness to all the goings-on in the house.[171]

At least the two sisters' stories agreed in one respect, though; alone among all the witnesses, they were able to shed some light on the identity of the mysterious Mr. Todd, who was one of the last callers at 31 Bond on the evening of Burdell's death. According to both girls, Todd was from out of town, and came calling upon Emma with a Mr. Coe. Apparently Todd was seeking introductions to suitable female companions in the City. Dr. Oliver Wellington, who maintained a water cure clinic on University Place and Twelfth Street, had been questioned by the jurors on February 5, telling the group that Emma had sought medical treatment for one of her daughters in the spring of 1855.[172] Wellington had failed to inform the Coroner that Coe boarded at the

Twelfth Street clinic late in January, and that Coe was an acquaintance of Emma's. Though both Margaret and Helen testified about these facts, inexplicably, the Coroner did not explore the matter further by subpoenaing Dr. Wellington's repeat attendance at the inquest.

Little nine-year-old William Cunningham, Jr. followed his sister Helen onto the stand, bravely climbing up into the makeshift witness chair and telling the jury all he remembered of the confusion of ten days prior. William recalled spending the evening of Friday, January 30 as his mother's helper, sitting with Emma and Helen, and assisting in whatever way he could in the preparations for Helen's departure for Saratoga the next morning. George Snodgrass had sat at William's side that evening, marking Helen's clothing for packing in the trunks, and when it came time for bed, William headed upstairs to share George's room for the night. Emma and her two daughters all slept together that evening, according to William, and the little boy's sleep went undisturbed until morning.

In contrast to his younger brother's brave deportment, George Cunningham, Jr. simply could not contain his emotions when called to testify: "This witness was a small boy," the *Herald*'s correspondent reported; he "advanced toward the witness stand in accompany [sic] of an officer. He sobbed, and cried very much, and was conducted into the chair used for the witnesses, opposite the Coroner's table." Recorder Smith immediately challenged the youngster, questioning not only his literacy, but his church going habits and dutifulness in Sunday school attendance. Pains were taken to warn the ten-year-old scion of the Cunningham clan that his eternal soul was at risk. The youth repeated an account of the night before the crime, in essence the same as that offered by his brother William, but Recorder Smith's bullying made George Jr. feel unwell. Sashes were thrown open to admit fresh air into the stuffy parlor hearing room, reported the *Herald*, "and [the] witness was held at the window, and water being brought in, he was abluted while he screamed and cried out." One of the physicians in the audience approached the youth to assist him off the stand. In danger of fainting dead away, the chalk-white boy was led back upstairs where he had been sequestered with his mother since the murder was discovered.[173]

Neighborhood merchants also played a prominent role during the final days of testimony at 31 Bond Street in the search for a murder weapon and incriminating evidence of Emma's designs. Storekeeper Sally Sallenbach, proprietress of a corset shop at 573 Broadway, remembered a visit during late October 1856 that Emma and her older daughter had paid early one evening. Stating that she was waiting for a gentleman to meet her there, Emma and Margaret Augusta, (whom Sallenbach identified in the jury room) declined the shop-owner's offer to show them goods. As Margaret sat in the front room of the premises trying out Sallenbach's piano, a man whom the witness identified as John Eckel entered. He was shown some papers by Emma, and the storekeeper overheard her whisper to Eckel that "all things are right now."

Shop girl Isabella Banford clerked at Clyde & Black's parasol and cane store at 401 Broadway, near the corner of Canal Street, and when questioned by the officials, remembered a couple coming into her establishment on Friday morning, January 30 in search of a sword cane. A request from a woman for such a weapon was rare, according to Banford, and she claimed that the incident thus stood out clearly in her memory. The female customer, said to be some thirty-six years old, carefully handled the first cane proffered by the salesgirl, and after bending it on a table, pronounced it too long and flexible. The couple hurried out after telling the witness they needed something much shorter and sturdier, and could not wait for the next morning's delivery of fresh merchandise.

At this point in her testimony, Banford was escorted upstairs to look at Emma Cunningham face to face. When she returned to the jury room, she stated with certainty that Emma was one of the two shoppers present that January morning. Banford was then sent in a carriage down to the Tombs to have a look at John Eckel. Upon her return, though, she told the group that she could not identify the prisoner. Just as Banford finished her statement, Dr. J.B. Morton entered the room and commanded the attention of the officials. With the support of Henry Clinton, Dr. Morton attempted to have the jury presented with the testimony of an acquaintance who had information about a similar couple who had shopped at Clyde & Black's store on the same morning, for similar merchandise. Neither Judge Capron nor the coroner was willing to allow hearsay testimony, and over Clinton's hissed objections, Dr. Morton was dismissed.

Clyde & Black had a number of competitors in the immediate area dealing in canes, umbrellas, and similar devices that could be put to lethal use. Henry Rohde kept a shop a few blocks north at 516 Broadway, but his testimony about a couple coming by during the last week of December, 1856, was inconclusive. Far more interesting to the jury was a pair of young girls, Margaret Alviset and Agnes Smith, who stood behind the counters at Margaret's father's Broadway storefront in the Metropolitan Hotel, just a few blocks south of Bond Street. The girls recalled waiting on George Vail Snodgrass a day or two before Burdell was stabbed to death, and having sold the youth a sturdy dagger. Snodgrass had sat in the witness stand immediately before Alviset's and Smith's testimony on February 14 and denied having bought a dagger from anyone, whether or not in the company of Emma Cunningham. Tension filled the air as the shop girls ended their answers to the coroner's inquiries: despite Snodgrass's protestations, when he took his seat in the audience, Margaret Alviset fingered him as the buyer of a wooden-handled, four-sided dirk. The coroner's physicians reported that just such a weapon was used to despatch Harvey Burdell.

The roles of downtown storekeepers in providing weapons and disguises to the suspects in Burdell's murder as well as the participants in the October 28, 1856 nuptials at Reverend Marvine's rectory formed a significant part of the mass of testimony presented to the jury by Coroner Connery. Identifying John Eckel as a participant in these scenes took on critical importance in the coroner's undertaking as he sought to bolster his conspiracy case against Emma Cunningham and her rent-paying paramour. Many witnesses called upon to physically identify John Eckel and Dr. Burdell were confused by Eckel's physiognomy as he sat in the Tombs, as well as that of Burdell's corpse lying in its coffin. Some recalled their encounters with gentlemen whose whiskers, haircut, or hair color were different than those visible after the jury convened its sessions.

Reading the *Herald*'s classified ads, Emma and her friend John Eckel could have selected several items from the menu of a hair parlor conveniently distant from Bond Street, if they were in the market for cosmetic changes to the tanner's appearance. The agate type advertisement from a shop patronized by John made clear where the tanner would have gone to conceal his identity. The simple display notice read: "Cristadoro's Hair Dye, Scalps and Wigs – don't be beat – wholesale and retail, and the dye privately applied at No. 6 Astor House. – Use none but Cristadoro's Dye – Wear none but Cristadoro's wigs. Your interests will be subserved by following this advice."

Joseph Cristadoro operated an establishment, in what remained, despite its City Hall area location south of the city's contemporary commercial hub, one of the most fashionable hotels in New York. Cristadoro's assistant, Joseph Wilson, was called to the witness stand on February 6. The witness promptly identified Eckel and Emma Cunningham as the couple that sat in the parlor rooms of his employer's barbering establishment on January 12 or 13, 1857. The pair ordered a toupée for Eckel, and insisted that it be ready the next evening. It remained unclear whether the hurry was to provide Eckel with a youthful look for the festivities in Emma's rooms planned for the evening of January 14, or for a more sinister motive, but Wilson's identification of his customers was nonetheless positive. Joseph Cristadoro, who testified the day before Wilson's appearance, had told of first greeting Eckel and a female companion when they entered his shop, and then turning the customers over to his foreman for service. Eckel was identified from a daguerreotype as being the same fellow who came down to the City Hall neighborhood that January day. No mention of the bald-headed Eckel availing himself of services other than toupée-fitting was mentioned.[174]

Notable among the retailers whom the coroner failed to summon to the inquest were any operators of the innumerable gambling parlors and private gaming rooms that flourished in Broadway saloons, and were interspersed among the brothels and taverns in the side streets along that great thoroughfare and the nearby Bowery. Devotees of virtually any game of chance could find ample company among the gregarious groups of visiting out-of-town businessmen as well as professional bunko operators who made their living in the neighborhood near Burdell's home. The Doctor was well known at local card games where he could participate as a banker with little risk. After days of insinuations, a link between Burdell's avocation and his untimely death was established on the witness stand.

For reasons that remain speculative, the authorities did not require testimony from individuals with personal knowledge of Harvey Burdell's gambling career. [175] The sole evidence creating a connection between Burdell's gaming and his untimely death came as John Farrell sat in front of the twelve jury members on the morning of February 10, and told what he saw as he walked down Bond Street late in the evening on January 30. Farrell had been located and called to testify as a result of an anonymous letter received the day before by Coroner Connery. The witness was identified as having observed Burdell returning home on the night he was murdered. Judge Capron began his interrogation of Farrell by repeating a rumor that Burdell had been seen at the corner of Bond Street and the Bowery that evening, arguing with a known gambler. Supposedly the two had gone upstairs at 31 Bond to settle the matter. Farrell responded that he knew nothing of such a dispute, but that he had in fact been in Bond Street at about 10:30 P.M. that evening. The witness related how he had seen two men walking together down the street when one of the pair stopped to enter 31 Bond. The companion continued on a few steps, then abruptly wheeled around and returned to enter the house. Farrell then heard a row break out and went over to knock on the door of 31 Bond. A bearded man of middling height, perhaps five-feet-eight inches tall, came to the door, and when he asked what Farrell wanted, the witness became afraid and quickly descended the stoop. Shortly afterwards, as Farrell waited a few yards down the block, he heard the cry of "murder" resound from the house. Strangely, no explanation was requested by Judge Capron nor was one offered as to why Farrell had not summoned the police immediately in such suspicious circumstances.

When pressed further by the authorities, Farrell, who worked as a shoemaker and at an appraiser's office, admitted that he had been tippling on the evening in question, but stoutly maintained that his beverage intake had amounted to only half an ounce of "reduced spirits." Farrell added gratuitously that he was not easily affected by liquor. A commotion broke out as the witness finished describing his drinking habits, and John Eckel was hustled into the jury room, looking a mess. After the quivering prisoner refused to doff his coat for a more thorough inspection by Farrell, he was hauled out, the crowd cursing him execrably. Despite Eckel's refusal to cooperate, the witness expressed no doubt as he assured the jury that the disheveled prisoner was the man who had answered the door that evening.

* * *

The final days of the inquest, which ended Saturday night, February 14, were marked by renewed appearances on the stand by each of the three suspects. Eckel was the first to again be brought uptown from the Tombs, but he refused to talk. After a lengthy colloquy among the Coroner, District Attorney Hall, and Henry Clinton, the suspect was remanded to the custody of the City Prison until the Coroner's jury could reach a decision. Emma Cunningham appeared again on February 9 and 11, her emotional state and mental acuity seeming to deteriorate over time as the damning testimony of so many witnesses established a violent antipathy between her and her murdered ex-lover. By the end of her final appearance, Emma could not even remember the name of the minister who had allegedly wed her with the deceased.[176]

During a visit to the Tombs on Friday, February 13, the Herald's reporter found Emma Cunningham weeping disconsolately, with one of her daughters at her side. Coroner Connery had found reason several days before to end her house arrest and incarcerate Emma in a prison cell. Henry Clinton's petition of *habeas corpus* for her daughters had freed them from the coroner's custody, but the plea failed for their mother. In the fetid and damp Tombs, few comforts were available, but Emma at least managed to arrange to have their meals brought in from outside the prison walls. A few pieces of furniture were also procured for Emma's cell. In contrast to Eckel's voluble confidence that he would be exculpated once a suitable tribunal heard the case, Emma seemed to the reporter to be overwhelmed with grief and in mortal fear of the jury's conclusions.

Testimony on February 14th finally brought an end to the inquest, with Harvey Burdell's sister-in-law Adeline Louisa Burdell called as the last witness. With Adeline's help, the Coroner had hoped to determine

Harvey Burdell's whereabouts from 5:00 P.M. to 11:00 P.M. on the night of his death, but the gap in information was left unfilled. The sum and substance of her testimony concerned only her late brother-in-law's plans to join the witness, her husband William Burdell, and their niece Dimis on Saturday January 31 for a night on the town. The outing never took place.

At 4:45 Saturday afternoon, after two full weeks of hearings, Coroner Connery addressed his final charge to the jurymen. It lasted forty-five minutes, and the group then retired to deliberate upstairs. Almost six hours later, the panel descended, and Connery's son John, who had acted as his father's deputy throughout the proceeding, called the roll. Juror John Hall stepped forward and delivered the inquest verdict to the anxious crowd. It came as no surprise: the verdict not only stated homicide as the cause of Burdell's death; the panel also declared Emma Cunningham and John Eckel responsible for the carnage, with George Snodgrass judged an accessory to murder. The group charged two of Emma's daughters, Margaret Augusta and Helen, with withholding information about the crime. Emma, Eckel and Snodgrass were taken back to the Tombs that evening, and the coroner once again took custody of the Misses Cunningham, pending action by a grand jury. Legal control of 31 Bond Street was turned over to the public administrator, who had been appointed by Surrogate Bradford during the past week to temporarily control the decedent's estate because Harvey Burdell died without leaving a will. Officials deemed the testimony of the cook, Hannah Conlan, housemaid Mary Donahoe, and crime scene passerby John Farrell vital to further criminal proceedings, so all three were held in police custody over the weekend. As midnight struck, Captain Dilks ordered his officers to guard the house over the weekend, insuring that Emma's children were kept indoors until Oakey Hall assumed control of the situation on Monday.

While the inquest jury was deliberating upstairs, journalists in the makeshift hearing room rushed to transcribe their shorthand notes of the coroner's closing address for publication in the next editions. Competition among the New York dailies had been fierce throughout the past two weeks. The *Tribune*'s Horace Greeley, James Gordon Bennett of the *Herald*, and their counterparts at the *Sun*, the *Times*, and many competitors fought to boost circulation by "scooping" each other in reporting each day's ever more incredible events. The jury's verdict had been rendered early enough for printing overnight in the papers that published on Sundays, and a gaggle of reporters raced downtown soon after the late evening decision. Word of the formal charges lodged against Emma Cunningham and John Eckel spread through the Bond Street neighborhood like wildfire, and crowds from all over lower Manhattan gathered in the cluster of blocks at Park Row, Ann and Nassau Streets known as "Newspaper Row." Thousands of the curious, whether mere thrill-seekers or those blood-thirsty, waited for the *Herald* to post its early edition of Sunday's paper on the pressrooms' outdoor walls.[177]

In a trend-setting example of the news media's behavior itself being deemed newsworthy, Monday's *Herald* described the raucous scene at its offices in the freezing cold, pre-dawn hours: "As soon as the jury in the Burdell case had finished their labors at 31 Bond Street, and the result of their deliberations was partly made known, the scene of the excitement attending this extraordinary case was at once removed to the HERALD establishment, and before one o'clock yesterday morning, an immense concourse of people thronged the entire lower part of the building . . . Men, women and children, to the number of five thousand souls, found their way into the salesroom of the HERALD office yesterday morning and departed with bundles of Sunday's edition amounting in the aggregate to 85,680 copies." [178]

A near riot had ensued outside the *Herald's* offices that night as the eager public and aggressive newsboys shouted and shoved to get their hands on the earliest press run: "At 1½ o'clock," the paper boasted, "all approach to the establishment was cut off. Fulton, Nassau and Ann streets, in the vicinity of the building was one mass of human beings. In fact, there was a grand mass meeting of the news dealing fraternity, which astonished even the newsboys themselves . . . never did each vendor of newspapers imagine he had so many rivals in the business."

As the clock struck two, the superintendent tried to open the Ann Street door that led to the paper's sales room. Only by liberal use of a hickory cane and great deal of exertion could the burly foreman force the crowd back into the black night. His efforts were ultimately of no avail, though: "Two efficient policemen were stationed at this door for the purpose of maintaining order, but when the lock was turned and the barrier flew open, all their exertions to stop the human tide from pouring into every nook and corner of the basement were for several moments unavailing, and at one time it was feared that a serious loss of life might ensue, so great was the crushing weight that was directed against those who had found their way into the room below."

The tidal wave of eager newsboys and hungry Park Row hangers-on, eager to seize a small profit from their middle of the night efforts, turned the usually raucous nightly setting into one of complete bed-lam. "For seven or eight hours the scene in the salesroom was one of wildest excitement. Persons who were usually in the habit of buying twenty-five or thirty copies eagerly pressed forward and demanded hundreds instead . . ."

Though salty language was *de rigeur* at any time of day around the flophouses and saloons that lined Park Row, this Sunday morning was unusually defiled: "The conduct of the newsboys was anything but pleasant for a religious person to look upon. They had no regard what-ever for the sanctity of the Sabbath, and poured forth oaths and curs-es that would make even a Jack tar blush to the very ears." The *Herald's* pressroom porters were besieged by their raffish acquaintances outside the loading docks. Boys as young as five or six years old, clad in rags and covered in dirt from head to toe, begged for extra bundles to sell, offering whatever pittances they could muster to secure a favor from the mustachioed eminences who ruled over their daily lives with con-tempt. "Various were the means used to attract the attention of the salesmen in the delivery of the papers . . . 'Don't take his money, it's bad.' 'Here, take mine, all in specie.' 'Don't you do it, his is fiddler's change.' 'Hurry up your cakes, Hope.' . . . coming from the lips of a thousand persons, made the entire neighborhood resound with clam-or and excitement."

In a burst of self-congratulation, the *Herald* published several statis-tics to impress its readership. The cash value received for its precious bundles, as compared to the always-dubious banknotes in common cir-culation at the time, was flaunted before the public, much as ratings from A.C. Nielsen rank the success or failure of today's mainstream television programming. James Gordon Bennett boasted tartly to all who would listen, "It my be well to remark here that there is no scarcity of change in this city at present, for out of the $1275 received yesterday for Sunday's HERALD, over $500 of the sum consisted of specie, all in American currency. We have consumed, during the past week, one ton of ink, and thirty-one tons, or one thousand and two hundred reams, of paper in the production of the HERALD." [179]

In the custom of the day, the paper had from the outset included in its front-page news stories much opinion about the protagonists' conduct both in and out of the jury room, and various forensic theories. Twenty-one years earlier, editor Bennett had forged a new path in the reporting of violent crime. When prostitute Helen Jewett was found hacked to death and burned in her bed in a bordello on Thomas Street in 1836, Bennett pushed his way past police sentries to give his readers an eyewitness account of the gruesome crime scene. Though virtually unknown at the time, this technique had been thoroughly adopted by the time of Harvey Burdell's death, and the *Herald's* staff reporters at 31 Bond Street were forced to bid against their peers for access to information as well as cordoned off areas. Captain Dilks' men obeyed the strict instructions given them, at least until the gleam of silver appeared.

Though the news articles in the *Herald* seem to the modern eye to be a peculiar mix of fact and opinion, the left-hand column of page four of the paper was reserved for what the publisher deemed to be pure editorials. As the inquest wore on, a generous helping of sociology, linked with ethical encomiums, was heaped upon the public's plate. Editor Bennett warned of the descent of the revered democratic American republic into a godless state of barbarism, epitomized by the Burdell crime. The *Herald's* dissection of the benighted state of New York society was not limited, however, to merely explaining the murder in social terms. Portraits of typical members of the criminal class painted by the paper preached morality. Skewed by gender, a misogynist undertone was also evident. Although Emma Cunningham was not mentioned by name, the nefarious courtesan's behavior described in the lesson of the February 16 editorial bore a striking resemblance to the woman reported in many witnesses' testimony a few days before.

The contrasted male gambler and pimp seemed far too hardened a career criminal, though, to be likened to Harvey Burdell.

The *Herald*'s sermonizing revolved around a comparison of the ninth and nineteenth centuries, implicating money and the very social democracy the paper held dear as complicit in Burdell's murder. So high-minded was its tone, Bennett's text might as well have been adopted by Grace Church's Reverend Taylor for a sermon one Sunday morning late that winter: "The present position and past history of the parties accused afford a sad record, the moral of which should not be lost upon the community. It is the cant of the day to talk wisely about the progress, the learning, the refinement, the education of our people, the enlightenment and the superior civilization of the nineteenth century. Scholars philosophize about it – editors turn pretty periods with it – politicians make its praises share with the American eagle and the star spangled banner in their fustian harangues."

First reminding its readers of the abysmal violence of the Dark Ages, the paper then described the absence of justice and social disorder that permitted unfettered criminal behavior on the part of the well-connected during the earlier millennium, in an epoch "when there were no steam engines, telegraphs, newspapers, Brussels carpets, daguerrotypes, glass windows, brown stone front modern improvement houses, patent leather boots, Bible societies, republican institutions, primary elections, revolving pistols, missionary meetings, and many other humanitarian luxuries of the nineteenth [century] . . ." Tales of random violence perpetrated by strangers in the ninth century, according to the *Herald,* could easily have been taken from contemporary reports of the garrotings and worse, published in recent issues of the paper. Brigands and highwaymen towards the end of the first millennium operated in a society much like that of mid-nineteenth century New York, if the paper's view of history was believed.

Remarking upon the tremendous opportunities afforded urban Americans for rapid personal enrichment during the latest financial bubble, the *Herald* shook a disapproving finger at the disorderly egalitarianism brought on by the burgeoning New York economy. According to editor Bennett, "Money, or the appearance of money, is the only passport to what is called good society. No questions are asked as to how he obtained his money – if he has it he may enter the sacred circle . . ." Any crime could be committed with impunity, in this analysis, and the supposed progress embodied in the enumerated educational and technological developments and economic growth were severely questioned. "People are just so far educated that they can commit crime scientifically . . . They guard against all chances of detection; but if some accidental circumstances should bring the matter home to their doors, they rely upon the spoils of the crime to shield them from the legal consequences . . ."

A thousand years of human progress was tartly summed up by Bennett, who cautioned that well-to-do murderers could stalk their victims in urban New York much as their privileged but savage forbears did centuries earlier, in reliance on the fact that "Civilization only makes acquittal a little more expensive." A walk up Broadway on the arm of the columnist threw a harsh light on the organza-frocked and topcoat-clad pedestrians whose elegance was understood by the correspondent in many instances as an expression of something quite different than urban refinement. Characters embodying a distillation of the personal histories and worst traits of Emma, and then Harvey, were encountered on the stroll, as the author continued preaching on the sins of New York's demi-monde:

> . . . [W]e will show you the brigands and the assassins of this cultivated epoch – this golden age—this enlightened nineteenth century. You shall see that woman, born in poverty, defectively educated, allowed to riot in secret lust, stepping by virtue of a few thousand dollars, into the domestic circle where virtue, chastity, and modesty should alone be permitted to enter. You shall see her at her devotions loudest in responses, most fervent in the amen. You shall see her, as the money begins to vanish, quartering herself upon some wealthy victim, securing him by her woman's wiles – you shall see how she makes his house a hell – you shall hear their quarrels as he resists her growing demands upon his purse – you shall see how she gives grand parties without the remotest possibility of paying honestly for them – you shall see her finally disposing of her victim by steel, poison, the cord, or the pistol bullet. You shall see her escape punishment, and again at liberty to prey upon society. You shall see in the fashionable hotels and boarding houses hundreds of men and women who have no occupation, no fortune, no means of support, and yet who luxuriate on the fat of the land . . .

The lesson continued, as ignorant, newly-admitted members of "polite society," eager to aggrandize themselves through new acquaintances in the explosive growth of ante-bellum New York, were blamed for admitting swindlers and robbers into their midst through a sloppy vetting of credentials. The resemblance of Emma and her daughters Helen and Margaret Augusta to the characters described in the *Herald's* unflattering representation is unmistakable:

> *Mrs. Plash met Madame Dagger and the Demoiselles Dagger at Saratoga last year. They seemed to be quite nice, quiet, ladylike people, and cards are sent to them. Now Dagger mere is an accomplished brigand, and the Demoiselles Dagger having no money, and being above sewing machines, are in training for the same line of business. Once their feet cross the threshold of Mrs. Plash's first class house, their position is safe. They have the Archimedian lever with which they can move the cheque books of the heaviest men in Wall street. And they do it.*

With Emma Cunningham well along on her way to the gallows, the editor's choice of a male counterpart to the female temptresses underscored the *Herald's* conservative outlook on the sexes. Rather than describe a well-to-do and older member of New York's vast "sporting gentlemen's society" of sexual predators, the male image chosen was that of a con artist with no social aspirations: "The male brigand is generally a man of pleasing address, who pimps for gambling houses and other disreputable places, and who takes in young men to ruin on the most reasonable terms. He always comes late to the party, but he is a great man to lead the German, very assiduous in attending upon the ladies, and altogether a very handy thing to have in the house. He makes it pay."

The outing on Broadway ended with the sermon's conclusion, as the columnist inveighed his audience to cease its supercilious social posturing and learn the true lesson of Burdell's savage death:

> *We are really worse than the barbarians we affect to despise. Your Feejee cannibal tells you that he is going to kill you and eat you. Your New York savage tortures you stealthily, year by year, profanes your domestic hearth – robs you of your substance – deprives you of your self-respect; and, when you are no longer valuable, ruins your character or murders you in your bed.*
>
> *Mark: The cannibal of the Feejee islands is a barbarian. He has never heard of the dispensation of our Saviour; he cannot read the Bible; he is*

a naked, dirty savage. You send to him your theologians, with raiment for the mind and the body. The savage of Manhattan Island is civilized, clean, well clothed and enlightened. Let us return to first principles, and have some missionaries for the barbarians of New York.[180]

The peals of the *Herald's* editorial thunder resonated with the sensibilities of many upper crust New Yorkers, among them New York attorney and diarist, George Templeton Strong. The prominent Gramercy Park householder commanded the respect of several thousand wealthy and influential citizens, and the private musings expressed in his diary often expressed sentiments shared with many of his peers. Strong recorded a vivid account of the temper of the times in his diary entry dated February 1, 1857, two weeks before the *Herald's* column:

An epidemic of crime this winter. 'Garroting' stories abound, some true, some no doubt fictitious, devised to explain the absence of one's watch and pocketbook after a secret visit to some disreputable place, or to put a good face on some tipsy street fracas . . . Most of my friends are investing in revolvers and carry them about at night, and if I expected to have to do a great deal of late street-walking off Broadway, I think I should make the like provision; though it's a very bad practice carrying concealed weapons. Moreover, there was an uncommonly shocking murder in Bond Street. (No. 31) Friday night; one Burdell, a dentist, strangled and riddled with stabs in his own room by some person unknown who must have been concealed in the room. Motive unknown, evidently not plunder.[181]

This orgy of outrage had not occurred in a vacuum. The hysteria, exposed in the press and pulpit, and underscored by the influential diarist's personal observations, reflected a deeper social concern. The Burdell murder had taken place during a pivotal period in New York's history. The civic consciousness, laden with tides of immigrations, street crime, political corruption, religious intolerance and racial unrest, had been suddenly set ablaze by news of the ghastly murder of a well-heeled citizen. All over the city, cries were heard for swift and firm execution of criminal justice, and a game of political football threatened to overwhelm any concern for the proper administration of criminal justice. Emma Cunningham and boarder John Eckel might well be hung by the neck for the sins of an entire nation.[182]

* * *

The verdict of the coroner's inquest, on its surface, established a clear path for the vindication of public morals while upholding the efficacy of the city's police and prosecutorial teams. Battles erupted, though, at every step of the way as local Democratic and Republican factions locked horns in a struggle for municipal hegemony. That fight would play out many months after the mid-February inquest verdict, with the criminal justice process frequently subordinated to partisan goals. It would be almost fifteen years before victory could be fully claimed by the good government supporters, several of whom rose to fame on the stepping-stones of their successes in the Burdell litigation. Accounts between Oakey Hall and Henry Clinton, as well as Samuel Tilden, would only be truly settled with the downfall of William Marcy Tweed and his henchmen a decade and a half later.

Edward Downes Connery knew the deeper implications of Harvey Burdell's death as soon as he was summoned to the crime scene. Not only was civic decorum at stake; front and center in the coroner's mind was allegiance to New York's Tammany Hall machine, and his critical role in fending off the onslaught of local patrician do-gooders and their upstate Republican allies in this dangerous situation. Loyalty to the almighty Democratic clubhouse might well have to supersede the fair and efficient administration of justice. On the other side of the fence, opposing forces quickly closed ranks. Sensing a prime opportunity to do their enemies great harm, local Republicans relished the occasion to involve one of their party's local leaders in the fray.

Even though his party was generally out of power in municipal politics, the antagonistic district attorney, A. "Elegant" Oakey Hall, took personal control of the high profile prosecution as was his right. No flunkie could be trusted with such a delicate matter. Hall would do his level best to use this case to lop the tail off the Tammany tiger. If the reigning Democrats were to continue local rule, they would have to demonstrate an ability to keep rein on the wave of violence that had run rampant in New York. Through newspaper editorials and clergy's sermons, the tenor of the times reflected a deep disgust with the abuse of power in which Democrat Mayor Wood and his cronies had recently engaged. Oakey Hall aimed to make the best of it.

CHAPTER 7

───◆◈◆───

The Lions Roar

WHISKEY-SWILLING revelers from New York City's main Democratic Party clubhouses, Tammany and Mozart Halls, were cautioned to tone down their traditional revelries on New Year's Day, 1857, as they gathered at mid-day with Mayor Wood in his City Hall chambers to exchange best wishes. Unusually circumspect in tone, the mayor's invitation had warned his guests not to expect the customary beverages. The classified newspaper advertisement for the reception placed by First Marshal W.H. Stephens reflected the sober political climate that had descended over some of the city's political societies: "The Mayor will be pleased to see his friends at his office on New Year's Day, between the hours of 11½ and 12½ o'clock. In consequence of doubts as to the propriety of the practice in a public office, he has determined to offer no refreshments at the Mayor's office as heretofore on that day."[183]

New Year's Day 1857 had dawned chilly and damp that Thursday. After paying their traditional calls, New Yorkers with a taste for legitimate entertainment could choose among a host of daytime diversions as well as the evenings' theatrical and music hall offerings in the venues clustered below Fourteenth Street on the Bowery and Broadway. With Harvey Burdell recovering from a long night of debauchery, Emma Cunningham could take her children and confidante John Eckel to the wholesome atmosphere of Barnum's Museum at Fulton Street and Broadway at minimal expense. The great showman's no-alcohol policy insured that drunkards would not disturb patrons of the current stage production in the building's vast auditorium, and the entry tariff was also family-friendly. Barnum's ticket price was all-inclusive: customers could wander for hours in the arcades filled with such humbug wonders as the "Russian Giant" and the "Living Skeleton," interspersed with dioramas of "The Happy Family" and other maudlin scenes.

Once sobered up, men of Harvey Burdell's means could stop by the show windows of Lord & Taylor's Grand Street emporium on that quiet holiday, perhaps planning a gift for a female companion from the Russian sable sets and royal ermine capes being offered in the season. Gentlemen at leisure might take a Broadway omnibus uptown to Forty-Second Street to watch the target-shooting competition being presented at the Crystal Palace in Reservoir Square. Niblo's Garden offered an operatic version of *Cinderella,* while Laura Keene starred on her own stage in *The Marble Hart* and a new one-act tearjerker *I Dine with My Mother.* Early-evening shows were the rule of the day, with 7:00 P.M. curtains in most houses. Theatergoers could dine after the final act in the plush salons of Delmonico's or one of the many elegant dining rooms in the clutch of new hotels recently built on Broadway near Bond Street. Late night dining was commonplace after enjoying theatrical fare that ran the gamut from Burton's Theater's current production of *Twelfth Night,* to the vulgar black-face minstrelsy presented at Christy and Woods's hall on Broadway near Grand Street.

With the courts and government offices closed for the New Year's holiday, Mayor Wood took a break from his tiresome duties once the City Hall revelers left him in peace. A short respite would be a good idea before the beleaguered politician faced the storm of political warfare brewing in Albany. At stake in the coming months were control over the city's police force, the enactment of stringent temperance legislation, and wholesale changes in the municipal charter that would radically reduce local control of immense pork-barrel opportunities. The rampant corruption and woeful ethics that had plagued civic and commercial life in New York for decades dictated that Albany legislators manufacture statutory changes in the complex state-city relationship. These efforts, although part of other political agendas, were all supposedly geared to the realization of "good government" and efficient, economical accomplishment of public works.

The city's economy, strengthened over several decades as the center of the nation's capital markets, had shown significant resilience after the nationwide financial depression of 1853-4. Hard times had not halted a twenty-year-long juggernaut of railroad construction and attendant financial speculation. The four years that preceded Harvey Burdell's demise had seen more miles of track laid in America than were put down over the previous two-and-a-half decades.[184] Though the vast majority of this construction occurred many hundreds of miles outside the city, the burgeoning railroad industry generated immense wealth within New York's borders. Securities were floated with ease to finance operations that would never emerge from red ink. The techniques of financial legerdemain developed during the mid-century rail boom were copied by legions of promoters in other industries. Credit was frequently extended to newly formed companies by banks and insurance companies located many hundreds of miles from the debtors' places of business, and with no regulatory oversight. Wall Street profits flowed into New York's economy in much the same manner as they would through the later half of the nineteenth and the entire twentieth centuries. Consumer excess reached new heights in a city where new millionaires were minted almost every day.

The culture of wealth and ostentation that dominated New York was decried in many of 1857's public New Year greetings from the pulpits of ever-conservative clergy, and in the columns of the daily newspapers. James Gordon Bennett's *Herald* tartly criticized the excesses of contemporary life and wholesale departure from the lofty republican ideals of the nation's history in its January 11 editorial. Unbeknownst to Bennett, his address foreshadowed the grim civic moralizing he would give vent to after Burdell was found butchered to death:

The wonderful prosperity of our country has in a measure turned the heads of the people. The influx of gold has led to an outlet of expense. Economy no longer exists pure and simple; extravagance of habits is the rule, not the exception . . . A fashionable lady . . . cannot now venture abroad without a silk dress worth perhaps fifty dollars; laces, fifty more; sables, fifty more, a French hat, almost fifty more. With bracelets, watch, and charms to match, she moves along with a capitalization of the floating funds of her husband, and this is but an item if compared with the costly contents of her boxes and bureaus at home. A dinner party is a heavy investment; course succeeds course, servants in white Berlin gloves help the guest to delicacies which would astonish a Heliogabalus, and wines of the finest flavor, such indeed as intelligent travelers assure us can no where else in the world be found in combination, moisten the throats of the appetizers . . .

Such ostentation could not occur in a vacuum. The destruction of the social order of the earliest decades of the nineteenth century, when New York commercial society was dominated by descendants of the original Dutch settlers and Revolutionary War patriots, was much despaired of by the paper's editor. Bennett's criticism of popular mores and cultural standards wove together his keen observations of the moral bankruptcy of contemporary religious observance with the plague of personal aggrandizement, in prose strikingly similar to much *fin de siecle* rhetoric in twentieth century America, and just as grimly prophetic:

> *To accomplish such luxuries, every effort is made by the aspiring, and honest industry does not so easily find the means. Business is pushed to its furthest limits, speculations are entered into of the greatest magnitude; the more ardent cannot wait, but boldly seek by fraudulent transactions to reach the summit of display at a single leap. The mania for sudden success pervades every class of operators, from the man who trims your beard to the adventurer who sends his half paid for steamers over the ocean. The steadier and brighter virtues of humanity fall into disrepute . . .And what are the consequences already? A general demoralization of feeling, a reducing of the standards of public opinion; an indifference to crime; audacity in official plunderers; the court room turned into a debating society for the amusement of spectators, instead of being a forum for dignified justice; the money marts changed into vast gambling places, where fortunes are made and lost at a blow, in transactions which the laws of the land actually prohibit and denounce as illegal.*
>
> *Our very religion has become infected with the temper of the times. Christians vie with each other in the gaudy construction of their churches; hundreds of thousands of dollars are expended to erect architectural caverns, where the preacher is scarcely visible, in which morceaus from the opera are poured forth in harmony with the "dim religious light," and sinners, buried in soft cushions, hear doubtingly and with regret there is "another and better world." . . . To be distinguished at all hazards, to appear, if not to be, rich, to float in the sea of fashion, to be even a drop of the "cream of cream" is just now the folly of the hour, and the attainment of distinction is often at the price of honor. . .*

Once again, the paper's sermonizing might well have been adopted for use in the pulpit on the immediately succeeding Sabbath morn, as editor Bennett's prose foretold an apocalypse:

> *When men and women of fashionable position constantly meet each other at celebrated refreshment saloons; when double veils are worn even by*

respectable ladies; when clerks give expensive dinners to fellow clerks, and their families are starving at home; when debts are now chiefly collected by criminal process, and any man's liberty may be taken from him by an affidavit drawn up by a Tombs lawyer; when companies with vast nominal capital are torn to pieces by greedy managers; when the peace and war of neighboring countries hang on the decisions of speculating monopolists; when the municipal, state and general governments are becoming one vast theatre of corruption; we may well deprecate the accursed love of gold for which the world is madly bartering its virtue, which is infusing itself into all business and monopolizing every thought – we deplore the prevalence of the sensuous over the mental tastes and tendencies of the day – we lament over the weakness of human virtue, which cannot endure prosperity. [185]

* * *

Fernando Wood was re-elected as mayor in the fall of 1856, having been chosen by Democratic supporters once again despite his conflicts with the Tammany stalwarts who would control New York politics during the following decade. Wood's ascent to power during the 1840s was itself part of a sea change in the social landscape of Democratic politics in the city. Elected to Congress in 1840 at age 28, Wood enjoyed tremendous support among Irish immigrants, having developed the art of vote gathering to what historian Gustavus Myers called the rank of an exact science.[186]

Myers, in his history of Tammany Hall, aptly described Wood's rise to power as a qualitative change in the social classes controlling of New York politics: Fernando Wood had been a Quaker, clerk, grocer, cigar-roller and the "keeper of a low groggery." With his plebian manners and modest upbringing, he represented a decisive break with the gentlemen merchants who had previously held power in New York.[187] A supporter of states rights, Wood frequently sided with pro-slavery Democrats in Washington, and was a staunch supporter of Jacksonian policies, opposing efforts to maintain a national bank and protective tariffs. Fernando Wood's ascent in municipal politics exemplified a crucial change in the city's governance, as wealthy businessmen and lawyers were forced by the sheer number of new voters to relinquish control of the electorate in the decades before the Civil War. [188]

Municipal politics and patronage in New York City had long been the scene of tremendous battles between the traditionally Republican-controlled state legislature and the frequently in-power Democratic municipal administrations. While the city's mayoralty and board of aldermen nominally controlled local affairs, all of their power derived from state legislation. The balance of power was continually readjusted over the early decades of the nineteenth century. Amendments to so-called "home-rule" laws and the creation of independent state-empowered commissions having capital project and regulatory authority governed the course of local affairs and the physical landscape of the city.

The year 1853 saw a massive change in New York City government as a result of a particular spasm in the continual upstate-downstate struggles. Elections in the fall of that year, required by Albany pursuant to amendments to the city charter, replaced the existing forty-member board of aldermen and assistant aldermen with new legislative structures. William Marcy Tweed, who had served for less than two years as alderman from a lower Manhattan ward, was forced from his seat with the demise of the infamous "Forty Thieves." The gang was swept out of office, though in some cases only temporarily. [189]

Elected with a plurality of only one-third of the votes cast, Fernando Wood was propelled into the mayoralty in 1854 with the backing of a significant number of disreputables, among them a group of liquor dealers. Much to their chagrin, upon assuming his post, the new mayor surprised his followers by announcing a purge of corrupt bureaus, the Sunday closure of saloons, suppression of brothels and casinos, and a campaign to reduce rowdyism. Displeasure with Wood's initial campaign for civic morality as well as the ongoing strife between the "hardshell" and "softshell" factions in Tammany Hall led Wood to make many compromises over the next two years, and his reputation for civic virtue eroded severely. Bloody street battles between Tammany factions broke out during the election contest in the fall of 1856 in many wards, but at the end of the day, Wood emerged victorious.

Perhaps the greatest struggle that faced Fernando Wood in the days after his 1857 New Year's Day party involved control of the municipal police force. Harvey Burdell's gruesome end added fuel to this already bright-burning blaze, coming on the heels of the previous year's horrific wave of street crime. The new year also saw tremendous conflict over the creation of Central Park. A replacement for lower

Manhattan's City Hall was proposed by the mayor, to be situated in Madison Square, several miles north of the existing seat of municipal rule. Wood justified the attempt by an alleged concern for situating the halls of government closer to the current center of Manhattan's population.[190] The struggles over pork barrel patronage and potentially lucrative capital project contracts paled, however, in comparison to the disputes among Wood's supporters, the Albany legislature and Republican Governor John King's office over the imposition of temperance laws in the city and wresting control from the mayor of the notoriously laggard police force.

New Yorkers cried for police protection and the rapid apprehension of robbers and murderers who were suddenly preying on the public at whim during the latter months of 1856. The citizens' pleas were mostly to no avail, though. The streets around the house shared by Emma Cunningham and Harvey Burdell were particularly dangerous, being only a few steps off the center of the transient-filled Broadway Entertainment District, and the long-notorious Bowery saloons and pleasure palaces. New York City's municipal police force at mid-century was controlled by a three-man commission headed by Mayor Wood and two members of the local judiciary, the Recorder and a city judge. Public accountability was virtually nil. Although, in the opinion of the *Herald*, the force was well prepared for any repeat of the wholesale civil disturbances experienced in years past (among them the infamous 1849 Astor Place riot, fomented by nativist gangs), the number of officers available for patrol was said to be woefully inadequate.[191]

Compounding the problem, according to the *Herald*, was District Attorney A. Oakey Hall's dereliction of duty. Upon winning election to head the office in 1854, the Republican prosecutor inherited hundreds of pending indictments from his deceased predecessor, Nathaniel Blount. Rather than devoting his attention to the disposal of pending cases and vigorous procurement and prosecution of new indictments, Hall instead focused on sponsoring legislation in Albany that would transfer New York's municipal police department away from the control of local voters and their political leaders, and into the hands of a five-man commission appointed by Governor King and ratified by the Republican-controlled State Senate.

Hall's bill was but one of several such Republican sponsored proposals, some of them linked to wholesale changes in New York City's charter itself. The Republicans sought to remove control of many administrative functions of city government (and the allied patronage positions) from the local electorate, and thus from the machine politics of Tammany and Mozart Hall Democrats. Although the corruption of New York's Democratic officials had been decried for years by all of the established newspapers, "good government" principles honored by some of the city's upper-class establishment dictated that Albany maintain only loose control over local government. *Herald* editor James Gordon Bennett and other influential civic voices stoutly opposed the Republican Hall's proposals. Oakey Hall worked vigorously to secure passage of his police bill, one that would give him a seat on a new police commission, as the *Herald* ridiculed him in its January 28 edition:

> *For some time past the journals have been filled with accounts of street robberies, burglaries, and other crimes of the most heinous character. In a few instances, the police have made arrests, and the guilty persons have promptly brought before the bar of the Sessions, where summary justice has been dealt out to them by the City Judge, Mr. Russell, who has properly recognized the true theory of criminal law, which is to protect society by imposing severe exemplary punishments.*
>
> *But the administration of criminal justice in New York does not rest altogether with the bench. . . Under some circumstances, the duties of the prosecuting officer for the people are far more important than those of the magistrate, the former having the power to arrest the course of justice by neglecting his duty, which is to initiate proceedings, to draw indictments, to make motions for the trial of cases, to compel the attendance of witnesses – and finally to move for sentence upon the convicted criminal . . .*
>
> *It is competent for us to inquire how far the person now holding the office of District Attorney has performed his important duties.*
>
> *The District Attorney who preceded the present incumbent died suddenly, leaving a large amount of business unfinished. His successor had been his assistant, and, although young, was supposed to have sufficient experience for the post to which he aspired. He found that during the last few years, a great number of indictments had accumulated in the office, and he at first displayed considerable zeal in the public service.*

Editor Bennett went on to report a sad decline in Hall's efficiency in office, describing an aborted attempt to bring to justice the keepers of literally hundreds of houses of prostitution and gambling dens in Manhattan:

A few of the offenders were tried, judgment was suspended, the prosecuting officer not pressing for sentence, the gamblers walked coolly out into Broadway, their diamonds flashing and their broadcloth glistening in the summer sun; the old indictments were allowed to accumulate more dust in the Attorney's office, and a fresh batch was placed in the same dignified retirement to keep the veterans in countenance.

Hall's diligence in pressing his Albany proposal was then attacked head-on:

This bill has been cooked up in an obscure private parlor of a hotel by the District Attorney, while criminals whom he should have prosecuted were walking about free as air, clothed in purple and fine linen, and faring sumptuously every day . . .

As we have said before, the bills hashed up by the lobby, which has been driven from Washington to New York, conceal a grand spoils scheme under the pretence of city reform. The proposed police bill would make matters worse than they are now. Before the District Attorney attempts so sweeping a change, the public have a right to demand that he shall reform the abuses said to exist in his own office. He was elected to perform certain specific duties. Let him pluck out the beam from his own eye before attempting to remove the mote from that of his neighbor.

Early on the morning of Saturday, January 31, only three days after the *Herald*'s attack on the district attorney, the newspaper's Nassau Street print room disgorged its usual bundles of freshly inked broadsheets. Harvey Burdell's office boy, John Burchell, had not yet begun his morning chores at his employer's Bond Street house as the presses started to roll. The day's issue made no mention of the murder alarm on Bond Street that would be raised just as the ragamuffins of Park Row filtered out through the city streets with the morning edition. Unaware at deadline of the soon to be discovered horror, the *Herald* laid into Hall again:

Our Albany correspondence [sic] informs us that Mr. Oakey Hall, the District Attorney of this city, has taken up his quarters at the State capital, to lobby for his police bill through the Legislature. We have no announcement of Mr. Hall's resignation of the office he now holds, but does not fill. We presume, however, that he intends to resign – first, because it is inconsistent with his official position that he should be a member of the Albany lobby, and second because his bill gives new powers to the District Attorney; and Mr. Hall has several times acknowledged that he labors of his office were too onerous for any one man to perform.

Editor Bennett excoriated Hall, first for trying to increase his own power and compensation while arranging to sit on the new police commission, second, for his dereliction of duty in the courthouse, and last, for his participation in a *"grand spoils scheme"* seeking to *"remove the government of the city from the hands of the people of the city."* A forceful challenge to Hall's professional capability and ethics, one equal to that which would face him the next morning, was then flung down: "With reference to the District Attorney, it appears to us that he will find it more to his future interest to discharge the duties of his office with all diligence, and with as much ability as he has been gifted. His business is in New York, not at Albany. Let him act in accordance with this fact, or resign his office."

The battle over control of New York's police force and the prosecutor's integrity was joined, both in the halls of the State legislature and the columns of the *Herald* and its competitors. This all-important struggle would continue to distract Hall and the other protagonists in the Burdell case for many months to come, but the next morning's paper put the matter aside as it blared news of the horrible discovery at 31 Bond.

CHAPTER 8

———◆•✕•◆———

Rugged Individualism and Sexual Predation: The Cultural Context of the Burdell-Cunningham Affair

ESPITE THE EARLY YEARS of plenty Emma enjoyed during her marriage to George Cunningham, and by Harvey Burdell during much of his adult life in New York, misery had accompanied them throughout their childhoods. Their personalities developed in remarkably similar ways as both struggled to adulthood in the midst of privation. Harvey and Emma shared two traits with many of their peers: desperate grasping for wealth and amoral interpersonal manipulation were widespread in mid-century America. Emerging feminist credos provided a novel context for Emma and Harvey's interaction, though, and on that springboard, violence virtually unknown in their middle class world was launched.

Emma Cunningham and Harvey Burdell shared with countless Americans of their generation an obsession with the creation of personal wealth, regardless of means or methods. The art of the swindle had become the American *raison d'etre* in the second quarter of the nineteenth century as legions of young men and women, equipped with little more than their optimism and vigor, arrived in urban centers from rural and exurban areas of the United States, as well as from abroad. Many newcomers were eager to amass material and social fortunes in the free-wheeling climates of major American cities.[192]

Simultaneously with this explosion of materiality, significant changes occurred in the nature of how and why many Americans sought sexual relationships and marriage opportunities. Always important to the formation of marital bonds, wealth took on new meaning and complex characteristics as prospective partners dealt in mid-century with a novel problem. Social mobility and rapid demographic change frequently rendered useless the traditional markers of land ownership and established connections that had long guided such decision-making. Marriageable individuals now frequently met as total strangers in urban environments, courting without the benefits of long-standing mutual acquaintances. In the 1830s and beyond, men and women of very modest backgrounds could, as never before, realistically strive to join the rapidly growing upper middle class in Eastern seaboard cities, both via personal industry and fortuitous commercial events (and, in the case, primarily, of women, via well-planned sexual adventure). Marriageable individuals in unprecedented numbers came to see each other as opportunities for instant riches, much like promising mining claims.

Early nineteenth century America witnessed the migration of legions of young people of modest means to its larger cities.[193] Men took positions in all kinds of business and industry, while women were employed principally as domestics, seamstresses and factory workers. During the first two decades of the century, single urban male immigrants, many serving in quasi-apprenticeship status, were usually housed with their employers. One building would house both the proprietor's family and the store or workshop in which the young man was employed. Female domestics also lived-in, optimizing their masters' labor bargain.

Residing in the employer's household also subjected the employee to ethical supervision and provided some basis other than the morals and behavior patterns of the employees' now-distant childhood homes for regulating sexual activity. This structure was not to last, though. With the growth of many mercantile and manufacturing establishments in the early part of the century, the scarcity of land in central business districts led to the development of exclusively residential neighborhoods where prosperous businessmen could afford to live in relative cleanliness and quiet, away from their factories and warehouses. Living arrangements for young workers became separated from those of their employers and thus devoid of the supervision that had to some extent insured moral behavior. The liberation of young men (and some young women) to live where they might, on very modest sources of income in relatively anonymous urban hostelries, created explosive growth in what came to be known as the "male sporting culture" of American cities of the 1830s. Unwatched by parents, pastors or employers, young male clerks fraternized with women in theaters, restaurants and ice-cream parlors, as well as in venues less open to public inspection, with a degree of openness and sexual expression that would have been unthinkable in previous decades.

A psyche of personal freedom for the young entrepreneurial class, be they shop-clerks, aspiring dentists, or petty criminals, prevailed among a large segment of these youthful urbanites. The advent of the California Gold Rush in 1848 added an immense quantity of libertarian fuel to this fire. Sexual adventure for men and women, independent of regulation, and geared to the rapid aggrandizement of personal wealth and social status, replaced many of the more stable psychic foundations of marriage that so recently prevailed in what had been a largely agrarian society. But men and women brought different tools to the field in which social mobility was sown, as well as being subjected to different restrictions. Marriage to a well-off man or one with bright prospects provided the only hope of economic betterment to vast numbers of women who lacked substantial family backgrounds. By comparison, men from lower classes could rely on their own entrepreneurial skills to better themselves, free from the bonds of traditional domesticity if they so chose. Laws that put at risk any property owned in a woman's own name at or after her marriage existed side by side with paternalistically administered, common law rights to damages for seduction and breach of promise. Single women who were swindled in the sexual marketplace in these decades could resort to the law, but usually only with the assistance of male family members as their legal representatives.[194] Unsuccessful marriages were difficult to sunder: in New York through the mid-1850s, women such as Margaret Burdell and Dimis Hubbard Vorce who sought divorce could not pursue relief in chancery court in their own names, regardless of the grounds.

A woman seeking divorce had first to secure the assistance of a legally competent individual to act as her "next friend." Margaret's father, William Alburtis, satisfied the requirement as an adult male, but widows also qualified under New York statutes to act in such capacity. Somehow the law considered the mere bereavement of a married woman to instantly invest her with sagacity equal to that of a man. The day before her loss, however, the same woman was deemed incompetent to handle her own affairs, much less represent another woman in court. The law was surely an ass in Emma Cunningham's case. It seems that a more determined surrogate could have been found when Dimis Hubbard needed help. Unfortunately the circumstances of her engagement by the plaintiff were not destined to provide maximum advocacy when Dimis's wily older cousin, Harvey Burdell, made the introduction. Emma was desperate to please Burdell. Agreeing to lend her name to Dimis's divorce petition in November, 1855 might convince the recalcitrant dentist to finally offer Emma his hand.

Prevailing mid-century attitudes towards women's rights among well-respected editors were frequently laced with ridicule of the suffragist cause. James Gordon Bennett's *New York Herald* was not alone in the snide calumny it directed towards efforts in the New York legislature at the start of 1857 aimed at liberalizing New York's climate of gender discrimination in all legal affairs. Sitting in her bedroom in early January, tossing over in her mind again and again the insults and injuries that Harvey Burdell had inflicted upon her, Emma Cunningham's blood would have boiled when she read the paper's report of current goings-on in the Albany state house:

The blue stocking Amazons are again petitioning for "women's rights." Mr. Scott, a member of the House from Saratoga, a very modest gentleman, too, presented a petition this morning. The Speaker immediately referred the subject to the Judiciary Committee. . . The petitioners ask that there may be established by law an equality of rights between the two sexes. The Judiciary Committee is composed of married and single gentlemen. The bachelors on the committee, with becoming diffidence, have left the subject pretty much to the married gentlemen. They have considered it with the aid of the light they have before them, and the experience married life has given them. Thus aided, they are enabled to state that ladies have the best piece and the choicest bit at the table, the warmest place in winter, and the coolest place in summer. They have their choice of which side of the bed they will lie, front or back. A lady's dress costs three times as much as that of a gentleman, and at the present time with the prevailing fashion, one lady occupies three times as much space in the world as a gentleman. It has thus appeared to the married gentlemen of your committee, being a majority, (the bachelors being silent for the reason mentioned, and also probably for the further reason that they are still suitors for the favors of the gentler sex) that if there is any inequality or oppression in the case, the gentlemen are the sufferers. They, however, have presented no petition for redress, having doubtless made up their minds to yield to an inevitable destiny. On the whole the committee have concluded to recommend no measure, except that as they have observed several instances in which the husband and wife have both signed the same petition – in such case they would recommend the parties to apply for a law authorizing them to change dresses, so that the husband may wear the petticoats and the wife the breeches, and thus indicate to their neighbors and the public the true relation in which they stand to each other.'

As it is not very probable that the [chairman] has changed his mind since the last session, there is good reason that he will refer the Bloomer petitioners to his opinions enunciated then which stand recorded in the Assembly journals, as above quoted.[195]

Horace Greeley's *Tribune* took a far more liberal approach to many women's rights issues than the *Herald*, albeit also sometimes couched in paternalistic prose. A column published in the *Tribune* five months after the *Herald* article stoutly endorsed equal pay for equal work. Though omitting any reference to suffrage, the author dealt with other controversial interpersonal issues, enunciating positions hardly shared by the likes of Harvey Burdell. Greeley boldly offered that "[t]hen, again, woman has rights as a wife. She has a right to know her husband's business; she has a right to know his friends and habits; she has a right to his company and respect . . ." Women's education was also supported by the *Tribune*, albeit only in the disingenuous form echoed by the U.S. Supreme Court decades later when its decision in *Plessy vs. Ferguson* articulated the separate but equal doctrine for the rights of African Americans to public education: "Woman has rights as a daughter," wrote the Tribune; "She has a right to as good an education as her brothers receive. She should not be put off with 'reading, writing and cyphering.' We do not say that she should have the <u>same</u> education, but we say as <u>good</u> an education." Reform of discriminatory laws of intestate distribution was also advocated: ". . . and if her father leaves any money when he dies we moreover say that his daughters have a right to an equal share with the sons. It is a great mistake to suppose that because women don't smoke, nor chew, nor keep fast horses, nor drink, &c., that daughters need only half shares."

The *Tribune*'s liberal views extended to altering even the most basic principles underlying heterosexual interaction, particularly among marriageable single individuals. One can only imagine the guffaws exchanged over Harvey Burdell's faro table when Greeley's sentiments were repeated:

> We would beg to suggest another right which we think a woman is entitled to, and that is, to have something else beside _flattery and nonsense talked to her_. We would venture to remark to our young men, that a sensible young lady is at least as sensible as [sic] a fool as a young man; perhaps in some cases, even more so. Don't think yourself disagreeable, if your face is not always spoiled with a smirk, a moustache, or a simper. The laughing hyena is not the beau-ideal of every young lady. Take our advice, and venture to talk good sense, in good grammar, and with a natural voice and countenance, to the first young lady you meet; it is _her right_ to be addressed in this way, and it is your right and duty to do it.[196]

* * *

Evaluating the long-term economic potential of a prospective husband was a particularly difficult task for Emma Cunningham, or any young woman determined to escape the strictures of her parents' narrow-minded home. The volatility of urban economies such as New York's put even the best-informed decisions at risk. Even a suitor with steady employment in a dependable trade did not necessarily represent a source of security to his intended bride. Enormous pressures were brought to bear on the living standards of the lower-middle class and middle class "native" Americans residing in the population centers, as tremendous numbers of immigrants with artisans' skills made their way to American cities, principally from Germany and Ireland. Periodic depressions in wage rates and living standards caused by an ongoing torrent of cheap labor from abroad, coupled with the lack of a federally-backed national currency and a dearth of control over the already long-tentacled banking and securities industries accompanied a series of major and minor financial panics that swept across the country during the first half of the nineteenth century. Many a young man whose prospects seemed sanguine at a marriage engagement turned out to be a pauper by the time he lifted his bride's veil. [197]

Ante-bellum America's widespread legitimization of marginally honest business behavior was reinforced by the licentious conduct of urban politicians. Suffrage for virtually all white males of voting age had become commonplace in the largest American cities by 1830. Proof of naturalization was virtually irrelevant as a condition of being permitted to vote. Local ward officers recruited immigrants from the dockside droves to show up at polling places and cast their votes for the machine candidates. Fraudulent election practices, rowdy-ism, and the outright purchase of the franchise created corrupt control of vast municipal patronage systems manipulated for personal financial gain.[198]

The corruption of electoral politics was exacerbated in 1848 as news from California of the discovery of gold at Sutter's Mill spread. Tens of thousands of lower and middle-class Easterners headed west over the next two years. Public morality was seriously eroded by the sight of men returning east after brief sojourns by placer streams, having risen from rags to riches in a matter of a few months.[199] Travel to California offered legions of the hopeful, both young and old, the opportunity to put behind them their past failures and leap frog over limited opportunities in competitive urban environments. The Gold Rush may also have been responsible for a contemporaneous decline in the public morals of East Coast population centers, as droves of hard-working, generally law-abiding citizens headed west in greater proportion to the general population of their home communities than their more stationary criminal-class neighbors. Considerable public debate, though, occurred in the East as to the morality of pursuing instantaneous riches. Boston's Reverend Edward Beecher, (cousin of Emma Cunningham's favorite New York Presbyterian minister, Luther Beecher) preached a sermon in January, 1849 condemning the westward exodus. Rising to the occasion with the same declamatory vigor often attributed to his storied Brooklyn relative, Henry Ward, the pastor inveighed against *"the inordinate desire to obtain any kind of earthly wealth,"* and admonished his listeners to renounce such excitements *"that destroy the balance of the mind, the power of sober forethought, sagacious calculation and enlarged views."* Beecher advocated that his audience of members of the New England and California Trading and Mining Association *"take at least as great pains to secure the eternal treasures of heaven"* unsullied by any *"base alloy of avarice, selfishness, luxury and vice."* [200]

The vast majority making their way to the gold fields were working- and middle-class men, significant numbers of whom were married fathers. The typical prospector was unaccustomed to the rigors of outdoor life. When he booked passage through the Panamanian isthmus, George Cunningham was hardly the footloose adventurer romanticized by contemporary ballads. Men in the diminished circumstances of George Cunningham and Harvey Burdell's nephew, Galen, were too distracted by the pains in their stomachs and the clouds on their personal horizons to dwell at length on the lofty principles espoused by Reverend Beecher. These men were archetypical participants in the Gold Rush: along with tens of thousands of their peers, they seized upon a trip to San Francisco as a panacea. [201]

The combination of rapid human communication made possible by the invention of the telegraph in 1844, and the psychic possibility of instant wealth for masses of individuals otherwise incapable of achieving economic advancement exerted massive pressure on personal ethics and American social institutions in the 1850s. Even before the start of the decade, Charles Dickens, on his first trip to the United States, noticed flaws in the national character that were developing into the nationwide slough of fraud that dominated pre-Civil War America. Dickens described the ethical vacuum in which the self-made Dr. Harvey Burdell and many of his contemporaries operated:

> *Another prominent feature is the love of "smart dealing" which gilds over many a swindle and gross breach of trust; many a defalcation, public and private; and enables many a knave to hold his head up with the best, who well deserves a halter; though it has not been without its retributive operations, for this smartness has done more in a few years to impair the public credit, and to cripple the public resources, than dull honesty, however rash, could have effected in a century. The merits of a broken speculation, or a bankruptcy, or a successful scoundrel, are not gauged by its or his observance of the golden rule . . . but are considered with reference to their smartness.* [202]

The floodgates of personal avarice and lust, both economic and sexual, were already straining at their hinges when the Gold Rush began. The deluge threw them wide open as wealth literally washed into the hands of many 49ers. At mid-century, it became possible to a far greater degree than in earlier decades for Americans, regardless of their participation in religious institutions, social connections, or national or racial heritage, to accumulate riches, independent from ownership of land, inventories, or other tangible physical assets. The mindset of unfettered individualism in the rapid accumulation of wealth of all kinds, quite outside the traditional Protestant ethos of the deserving elect, overwhelmed a significant proportion of post-1848 America. The milieu of greed was held responsible by leaders of public opinion for New Yorkers' ever-increasing indifference to crime, the debasement of the legal system, and the transformation of fondly remembered houses of worship from centers of pious pursuits into temples of commerce.

Preaching from a widely visible pulpit, the *Herald* waxed apocalyptic as New Year's 1857 dawned: "What an excited city is ours under all these influences! Society is a crust on the side of sleeping volcanoes, which every now and then startle us with their explosions and horrify us with their desolations."

In the opinion of the columnist, New York at the beginning of 1857 existed as the urban epicenter of an international ethical morass:

> *To the uninitiated, the city of New York is a curious spectacle. If it were unroofed, Asmodeus himself would be astonished. In this capital might be found most of the singularities of other cities – the gaiety and the freedom of Paris, and its unembarrassing social arrangements, the animal pleasures and sturdy deep drinking of London, the intrigue and stilettos of Madrid, the solemn and bigoted devotion of Rome, the licentiousness of Vienna, the falsehoods and furtivity of St. Petersburg, the harems and the beastliness of Constantinople, the usury and extortions of Jerusalem in its palmiest days. And every day it grows larger, and wealthier, and gayer and more audacious. Such are our social tendencies at present.* [203]

The *Herald* was not alone in the late ante-bellum years in depicting New York as a fantastic canvas of shadow and light. Aghast observers of the scene noted that the city's streets were overwhelmed with amorality, both commercial and sexual. Even more disturbing to some was the adulation that this new race of urban entrepreneurs earned from the masses. Popular journalist George Foster's 1853 collection of essays,

Fifteen Minutes Around New York, harpooned the heroic figures and *modus operandi* of the American entrepreneurs so idolized by Harvey Burdell and Emma Cunningham. The author seemed in the middle of a bad dream as he wrote about Wall Street's denizens:

> *Who then are these favored and powerful individuals who exert this immense control over society and the world ? What they were, we will say nothing about: as to who and what they are, go to Jullien's or Ole Bull's or Sontag's and you will see.*[204] *They are the patrons of the Opera – the hope of Art in this country and this age: and the beauty of it is that they know as much of painting, of statuary, or architecture, and the belles letters, as of music . . . They have that which is so much better than knowledge, or study, or experience, or brains, or in fact, than anything but money – they have position; and that position they have obtained and can only keep because of their money. No one cares to dispute with them their claims to fashion and exclusiveness. No one dares to exhibit the ludicrous mockery of their pretensions to elegance and social eminence. No one dares to lay bare the lie upon which they live, nor to hold them up for what they are. No one dares to question them, as they stride insolently through the temple of fashion and good society, or march disdainfully and with their flying colors to their velvet-cushioned pew in Grace Church . . .*
>
> *Let us return from our long and interesting detour to Wall street and the purlieus of the Exchange. Let us watch the process by which the fortunes are accumulated that enable their possessors thus to lord it over the world, and to climb to these places of eminence and distinction which should be reserved alone to the wise, the brilliant, and the good. We will not descend to the particulars of the various transactions which go to make up the sum of that profession known as trade. Suffice it to say, that the foundation of it all, the secret of success, the key to wealth and power, is the cautious overreaching of the neighbor. So long as the merchant or the speculator maintains untarnished that conventional honor which thieves find it absolutely necessary to enforce in the division of their plunder; so long as his bank account is good and his credit untainted in the "street," no matter how savagely he may oppress the poor man within his power – no matter how many hearts he may have wrung with anguish, how many lips may turn white with hunger, how many desperate souls driven to crime, how many milk-white virgin bosoms be given to the polluting touch of lust, for money to buy bread – how many fellow human beings may be wholly crushed and made forever desperate by the iron grasp of this man – he is still respectable, 'one of the most respectable of our citizens . . .'*
>
> *Such is a fair and not overdrawn picture of a type of money, shop-keep-*

ing aristocracy of the New World – a race of beings who, as a natural historian, we undertake to say, have never been equaled on the face of the earth, in all that is pompous without dignity, gaudy without magnificence, lavish without taste, and aristocratic without good manners.[205]

* * *

Despite years of financial success, Dr. Harvey Burdell was still climbing the social ladder of George Foster's New York when he met Emma Cunningham in 1854. Emma's suitor embodied what Alexis de Tocqueville described as the archetypical anxious American of his class in *Democracy in America,* published sixteen years earlier: "With all the parts of his universe, himself included, in erratic motion, with no fixed terminus and no secure resting place, the democrat develops an acute awareness of loss and failure." [206]

Thrown out of his childhood home by his widowed mother upon her remarriage, Harvey Burdell developed into a fratricidal sociopath early in life, engrossed in what has been described as an autophobic sexuality. As a physician trained in the 1830s, Burdell was exposed to the new field of obstetrics and gynecology, whose solely male practitioners drove many midwives out of business. Modern medicine did not approach women's health benignly, however, when it came to issues of sexual politics. Linked with Burdell's fear of his own sexuality and perhaps in reaction to it, the desperate young medical student fashioned a convenient psychic defense strategy by adopting the prevalent misogyny: "Nineteenth-century medicine did not merely sexualize woman's nature;" according to historian Karen Haltunnen, "it pathologized it . . .; male practitioners argued the urgency of their medical takeover of female sexuality; in their view, women were too dangerous to be left in the unprofessional hands of their own sex . . ." At the same time, though, male doctors evinced a distinct revulsion at their new work. It is easy to picture Harvey Burdell recoiling with his lecture class-mates at the subject, for his personality fit four-square with the prevailing attitudes articulated by Haltunnen:

What lay behind such pronounced repugnance on the part of the new obstetricians was a whole complex of male attitudes towards female sexuality, which mingled fear with hatred and disgust. Expectations placed

*upon masculine identity in the nineteenth century when individual eco-
nomic success and social order were believed to depend on rigorous self-
control, helped shape these attitudes. "The ideal of self-sovereign middle-
class manhood produced an autophobic sexuality, such that erotic arousal was chronically attended by dread and was experienced as disgust and
guilt when it was felt to stray beyond the boundaries of self-control," and
that dread and disgust were projected onto women as the source of sexual
arousal. Beneath the passionless ideal lay the fear that women were always
in danger of succumbing to sexual appetite, and thus undermining male
self-command; men insisted on women's innate purity in an effort to overcome their dread of female sexual pollution.*[207]

Genteel treatment of one's mate was an essential facet of the reigning middle-class cult of domesticity in which Emma Cunningham so
desperately wished to participate. In stark contrast, Harvey Burdell led
a heterosexual life infused with the same avaricious amorality that he
applied in his various professional enterprises.[208] Though daring to
publicly violate the behavioral standards endorsed for gentlemen by
respected clergy and opinion makers of the day, Harvey Burdell's personal life nonetheless embodied the most basic and revered of
American ideals, a fierce independence of will.

Professor Christine Stansell's articulation of the philosophical
foundation of "respectable" male society's view of womanhood shows
the common ground that Harvey Burdell shared with the Beechers,
Horace Greeley, and James Gordon Bennett, though it seems likely
that neither the clergy nor the editors would have deigned to dine with
the notorious dentist. Women presented a threat to male independence, and justification for male domination of the culture and control
of its governance took on many forms, not the least of which was the
genetic argument: "In a republican culture which placed the independence of the male citizen at its zenith, the dependent status of all
women put them in the same lowly category as servants, children,
apprentices, slaves, and the poor - all inferiors whose lack of reason
and virtue necessitated for the common good that they live under the
care and supervision of wise citizens." [209]

Harvey Burdell made little pretense of gentlemanly intentions
with his male acquaintances as his relationship with Emma
Cunningham ripened into intimacy. Ever the calculating conniver,

Burdell believed that Emma had inherited significant property from her late husband George Cunningham. The dentist's predatory instincts fixed on Emma as a realistic opportunity for yet another economic and sexual conquest. Emma made an ideal vulnerable target for Harvey Burdell. The well-to-do dentist represented to the widowed mother a scarce opportunity for economic security. Ever able to play the polite and gallant suitor, Burdell's ardent attentions caused Emma to jump in with both feet during the first few months of courtship.

With the exception of the temporary Manhattan lodgings that she and her children occupied after her husband's sudden death, it had been almost ten years since Emma Cunningham had lived in lower Manhattan when she first moved into Harvey Burdell's home. Bond Street and the adjacent blocks had changed markedly since Emma's removal to south Brooklyn with George Cunningham after his liquor business declined in the mid-1840s. The Bond Street block that greeted Emma in 1855 was hardly the sort of genteel residential street to which Emma had aspired as a young woman. Just returned from Saratoga, Emma chose not to protest when her lover insisted that she takes rooms in his home as a boarder with Mrs. Jones, the current landlady of 31 Bond. Each step with Harvey Burdell had been difficult, and rushing him into matrimony might well scare away a good prospect. But Emma quickly noticed that some of the dentistry patients calling during the business day were flamboyantly dressed and vulgar in speech. Why Dr. Burdell pushed his operatory door firmly shut as Emma passed by, particularly when the patient was a young woman, made her sick with worry. The new boarder knew in her heart that some of the cries escaping from under the door during those long office visits were hardly due to lack of medical anesthetic, but it seemed best to bide her time. Where else were she and her children to lodge, after all, especially upon such favorable terms? The alternatives would be far worse, and Emma would just have to hope for the best.

26 Bond Street

CHAPTER 9

———◆◆×◆◆———

Burdell on Bond Street

HE BOND STREET environs in which Harvey Burdell chose to live and practice his profession at the peak of his career mirrored the tortured doctor's personal conflicts as well as the city's cultural schizophrenia. By 1855, the street's two short blocks linked the wealth and social pretensions of the decade's nouveaux riches with the tawdry nature of New York's sizeable lower-class underbelly. Bond Street was bounded on the east by the Bowery, with its infamous mix of proletarian gambling dives, beer halls and whorehouses; and on the west, by the glittering Broadway Entertainment District whose trade in vice was also ubiquitous, albeit better-dressed.

At one time Bond Street had been entirely residential, part of an affluent district of private homes built for and traded among well-to-do families during the 1820s, '30s and '40s. The irrepressible drive of real estate development and New York City's burgeoning population caused the relocation of the most fashionable residential districts to the blocks north of East Fourteenth Street by the time of Burdell's and other dentists' arrival in the area. Harvey Burdell acquired 31 Bond Street in 1852, but he was not the first dentist on the block. His nemesis, Thomas Gunning, had moved there in 1847, and many physicians followed suit over the coming decade. The concentration of commercial activity and easy transportation provided optimal commercial conditions for growing a medical practice. [210]

By the early 1850s, the Broadway blocks near Bond Street had filled up with new hostelries, fancy department stores and glittering restaurants, in a wholesale re-centering of New York's hospitality and retail industries. The sumptuous lobbies and dining salons of the hotels were filled with businessmen and politicians from the area and across the nation, who gathered to wheel and deal in financial and political influence, while wining and dining without restraint.[211]

One of Broadway's principal attractions in the 1850s was its profusion of live entertainment venues in the blocks north of Canal Street. In mid-century America, theatrical performances were still considered by many respectable elements as being immoral. Commercial travelers from all over the nation came to New York to enjoy its dramatic offerings, many of which were unavailable in more prudish population centers. The city's largest and best-known theaters were situated in the Bond Street area, among them Laura Keene's Varieties, Wallack's Theater, and the Mechanics Hall, home of the popular black-faced Bryant's Minstrels. Prostitutes of every description used the balconies and private boxes of these theaters as well as the crowded tables of the dining salons and beer gardens to solicit and entertain clients. Niblo's Garden, renowned among the many restaurant-cum-performance spaces during its several decades of existence, stood at the nearby intersection of Prince and Crosby Streets. The landmark structure was ultimately incorporated in the Metropolitan Hotel where Harvey Burdell took many of his meals during his last days.[212] Adjacent to the large Broadway hotels and theaters were a multitude of daguerreotype and fine art galleries, "fancy goods" stores and gaudy saloons. Brooks Brothers' clothing emporium, the Tiffany glass shop, Lord and Taylor's department store, and the studio of photographer Matthew Brady occupied premises in the neighborhood. Cheek by jowl with these uses, though, stood somewhat less respectable establishments, whose economic magnitude in pre-Civil War New York was considerable.

Prostitution was one of the largest industries in Harvey Burdell's hometown. and a plethora of courtesans greeted male visitors at every step along muck-filled Broadway. Members of Mayor Fernando Wood's personally controlled police force turned an official blind eye, both to the flesh trade and the innumerable gambling parlors. Overnight, in casinos and private clubs, unsuspecting and thoroughly inebriated country rubes and small-town swells were deftly relieved of the proceeds of their daytime visits to the city's marketplaces and exchanges.

The size of the vice industry in mid-century New York was well-doc-umented by the New York State census conducted in 1855. Of the twen-ty-one separate industries whose annual "cash value" was measured, prostitution in New York City ranked second only to clothesmakers' shops. Whoredom's yearly take was said to exceed $6.35 million, as compared to the tailoring industry's 20 per cent larger gross annual revenue (leveraged by the splendiferous sartorial needs of Broadway district professionals and their managers). The fabrication of silver wire, steam engines, and boilers, as well as shipbuilding, distilleries and breweries, paled in comparison to the annualized value of the trade in illicit sex.[213]

Prostitution, though technically illegal in New York in the late 1850s, was rarely the subject of prosecution. Timothy Gilfoyle's metic-ulous modern study confirms that in comparison with the previous two decades, (themselves hardly models of Puritanism in terms of police suppression of such vice) "[b]y the 1850s, leniency toward prostitution was even more pronounced. Of the 143 different addresses advertised in the city's leading guidebooks, only 7 were charged with any type of disorderly conduct during the decade." [214] The patronage of many public officials and law enforcement officers in these establishments minimized official scrutiny. Rumor had it that the immediate, intense focus on Emma Cunningham and her boarders as suspects in the Burdell case resulted from the police department and district attor-ney's intentional misdirection of the murder investigation so as to avoid disclosure by the true perpetrator of politically embarrassing facts about vice and graft in the neighborhood. Captain Dilks and his men of the Fifteenth Ward seemed to ignore multiple tips passed to them about men and women who had been involved in recent fracas-es with the obstreperous decedent.

The interplay of politics and the sex industry that surrounded Dr. Harvey Burdell's residence and day-to-day activities was also the subject of many popular contemporary novels, among them George Thompson's story of depredation and sexual pathology, "The Gay Girls of New York." In Thompson's tale, star courtesan Hannah Sherwood dresses in high fashion, reads novels, drinks champagne, and engages in numerous "amorous delights." Her moral side, though, serves as the linchpin of the story. One evening she prevents Arthur Wallingford, a wealthy alderman, from seducing a young sewing girl in the brothel. Even when Wallingford offers Hannah $300 to disappear so he can have his way with the novice, she refuses. Justice is done when the avenging Hannah humiliates the alderman, forcing him to kneel and apologize. [215] Author Thompson's story, though published several years before Harvey Burdell's demise, could well have taken place at any number of houses and hotel rooms in the Bond Street environs. Thompson promptly seized upon the Burdell case as grist for another *noir* novella.

The hostelries dominating the Broadway blocks near Harvey Burdell's home provided a veneer of respectability for many transient visitors to New York's teeming commercial center. The Metropolitan Hotel, Lafarge House, St. Nicholas and St. Denis Hotels, and the neighboring Prescott House and Union Place Hotel set new standards of luxury for the Southern cotton brokers and other merchants visiting the city during the decade before the outbreak of the Civil War. Each of the ornate establishments offered luxuries well above the level of the long-reigning Astor House on lower Broadway.[216] Before or after attending performances at nearby theaters, guests dined in the vast hotel dining rooms or in the male-dominated eating salons of Delmonico's, Frederick's, or Sweeney's. Several course meals were topped off with ornamental confectionery that flattered the swaggering pretensions of the diners. Would-be tycoons who joined director Harvey Burdell for a meal while they discussed the possibility of a loan from his Artizan's Bank could tuck into dessert concoctions with appellations such as "St.George and the Dragon," "Roman Helmet," the "Temple of Liberty" and "Apollo's Lyre" while they sipped fine champagnes.[217]

The tenor of the times and the scene of Broadway ostentation traversed by Dr. Burdell daily was floridly described by statesman and public policy advocate Carl Schurz.[218] In his memoirs, Schurz recalled a dinner he attended as a young man, not long after his arrival in this country from his native Heidelberg. The affair was held at the Union Place Hotel on the southeast corner of Fourteenth Street and Broadway. In a diary entry for September 17, 1852, Schurz recalled his amazement at the rough-edged goings-on in what was then a fashion-able and respectable urban hotel dining room, at least according to American standards:

It was a table d'hote if I remember rightly at five o'clock in the afternoon. Dinner was announced by the fierce beating of a gong, an instrument which I heard for the first time on that occasion. The guests then piled into a large bare dining room with one long row of tables. Some fifteen or twen-ty negroes, clad in white jackets, white aprons, and white cotton gloves, stood ready to conduct the guests to their seats, which they did with broad smiles and curiously elaborate bows and foot scrapings. A portly, colored head-waiter in a dress coat and white necktie, whose manner was strik-ingly grand and patronizing, directed their movements. When the guests were seated, the head-waiter struck a loud bell; then the negroes rapidly filed out and soon reappeared carrying large soup tureens, covered with bright silver covers. They placed themselves along the table at certain intervals, standing for a second motionless. At another clang of the com-mander's bell they lifted the tureens high up and then deposited them upon the table with a bump that made the chandelier tremble, and came near terrifying the ladies. But that was not the end of the ceremony. The negroes held fast with their right hands to the handles of the silver covers until another stroke of the bell resounded. Then they jerked off the covers, swung them high over their heads and thus marched off, as if carrying away their booty in triumph. So the dinner went on with several repetitions of such proceedings, the negroes getting all the while more and more enthu-siastic and bizarre in their performances."

With his banking industry responsibilities and prominence in med-ical practice, Harvey Burdell was a commonplace table guest at scenes such as those recalled by Schurz. As a bachelor without need for fami-ly accommodations or sizeable entertaining rooms in his home, Burdell also adopted other practices of his male peers. Soon after his 1852 purchase of 31 Bond Street, Burdell began leasing his home out to a succession of landladies. Of the many rooms in the four-story struc-ture, Burdell reserved for his private use only a bedroom and his sec-ond floor dental operatory. The dentist joined the other inhabitants of 31 Bond at the boarding table, when not out on the town. Once his clashes with Emma Cunningham broke out in October, 1856, though, Harvey Burdell began taking most of his meals in the dining room at the nearby Lafarge House. Facing Emma's wrath across a dining table

Metropolitan Hotel, Broadway, New York, Chromolighotraph by Sarony & Major

Lafayette Place and Great Jones Street, c. 1866

Broadway between Amity (now Third) and Bond Streets, c. 1860

was unbearable, and right after New Year's Day 1857, Burdell switched to dining in the splendor of the nearby Metropolitan Hotel.[219]

The Metropolitan was built in 1852 on the site of Contoit's Garden by the sons of Stephen Van Renssalaer, and initially operated by the Leland family as lessee. Despite the 250 servants provided for the 1,000 guest rooms, its 300 feet of brown free-stone clad Broadway frontage, 12 miles of gas and water pipes, and incorporation of the famed Niblo's Garden entertainment venue within its courtyard, the Metropolitan was not an immediate success. Though the hostelry was a pioneer in the commercial development of the Bond Street area in the early 1850s, it was still considered too far uptown in 1852 to attract a large clientele. With the explosion of mid-decade commerce in New York and the agglomeration of a critical mass of complementary public accommodations, the Metropolitan soon prospered, and acquired a reputation for hosting the "power breakfasts" of the mid-century.

La Farge House, menu for December 12, 1856

Ever sociable when it suited his purposes, Harvey Burdell fit right in with the swells and social climbers who crowded the Metropolitan's early morning tables. The hotel's reputation for vainglorious consumption by its patrons was characterized decades later by one journalist as one "which drew custom from all parts of the country . . . Cotton was king and for a long time the cotton princes of the South gathered at the Metropolitan until the Civil War. There was also a large California patronage. At one time the profits of the Metropolitan were said to have reached $1,000 a day. The hotel gave a series of hops each Winter at which it seemed as if all the diamonds of

Golconda were worn by the ladies. The gratuitous suppers given on these occasions were superb . . ." The Metropolitan's popularity among the nouveaux riches of Harvey Burdell's day presaged its fame a decade and a half later; Boss Tweed's son operated the hostelry in the years immediately before his father was jailed by Special Prosecutor Henry Lauren Clinton upon conviction of municipal corruption.[220]

*   *   *

Harvey Burdell's ascent by the mid-1850s to the fashionable tables of the Metropolitan Hotel and the Lafarge House did not occurr overnight. The previous two decades were consumed with building his professional practice, social connections, and personal wealth. The dentist-cum-speculator's prominence brought diverse investment opportunities, including places at high-stakes gambling tables, and made Burdell a prized object for female acquaintances. As a newcomer to the tumultuous society of upwardly mobile, single young professional men who flocked to New York in the mid 1830s, Harvey Burdell immersed himself in the aggressive behavior of his male peers. Ejected from home by his mother Polly during early adolescence and forced to seek his emotional and financial fortune alone, Burdell's camaraderie among men and women of rakish independence was foreordained. Excited by the pleasures of a lengthy, peripatetic bachelorhood, and emboldened by his success as a popular dentist and financial risk-taker, Harvey Burdell became well known as a cunning competitor on many a playing field.

The shape of Burdell's young adult years in New York during the 1830s were part and parcel of the changing ethos and expectations of the many young Americans who divorced themselves from the religious and ethical institutions of their parents to pursue wealth and upward social mobility in anonymous city environments. The consequences of these disruptions were sometimes ghastly. The murder in 1836 of a well-known Manhattan courtesan, Helen Jewett, of which her customer, Richard Robinson, was accused, brought into sharp focus the trends in the sexual and economic forces of the day that predicated the Burdell-Cunningham fiasco.

Harvey Burdell was only one of thousands of young Manhattan

men who both cringed and thrilled when they read the news: twenty-three-year-old Jewett was found murdered in her bed on the morning of April 10, 1836 by Rosina Townsend, madam of the brothel where Jewett lived and worked at 41 Thomas Street.[221] A nineteen-year-old shop clerk, Richard Robinson, an émigré from Durham, Connecticut known by Jewett and her colleagues as Frank Rivers, was arrested and charged with sinking a hatchet into Jewett's skull during an overnight visit. Robinson was indicted but ultimately acquitted of the grisly murder, after a trial that was the focus of civic life for many weeks.

Jewett's murder and Robinson's inculpation created a variety of public confrontations among citizen groups buffeted by the rapidly changing economic and sexual forces present in America in the 1830s.[222] Historian Timothy Gilfoyle explained the social context of this horrible crime in his 1992 work *City of Eros – New York City, Prostitution, and the Commercialization of Sex, 1790-1920*:

> *To the American public in 1836, Richard Robinson was on trial for more than just the murder of Helen Jewett. As the boardinghouse, peer group, and market economy replaced the craft economy, family and "moral economy," young men frequented brothels and visited assignation houses in growing numbers. ...Robinson's promiscuous adventures aptly illustrated the restructuring of male sexual behavior in New York City after 1820. Numerous young men courted prostitutes, "kept" women, paid their rent, and assumed aliases to hide such activities. Sexual desires were now expressed through institutions of public leisure and commercial exchange – the theater, the boardinghouse, and the brothel. More significantly, Robinson's behavior was defensible in the minds of his supporters. Jewett was a social leech out to ruin a rising but poor clerk, a female threat to "Young America." Indeed "no man ought to forfeit his life for the murder of a whore," concluded some apologists. As the cry for justice in the murder of a prostitute rang out, Robinson's contemporaries saw themselves on trial. Many ran to his defense. Diarist and one time Mayor of New York Philip Hone noted during the proceedings; "I was surrounded by young men about his own age, apparently clerks like him, who appeared to be thoroughly initiated into the arcana of such houses."* [223]

The notion of a "war" between the sexes took on its modern meaning during these times, and one can easily imagine Harvey Burdell's reaction as he learned of Jewett's and Robinson's involvement. Young, single, and recently arrived in the chaotic city, Burdell was part and parcel of a widespread phenomenon of sexuality and economics. Prolonged bachelorhood had become a highly desired state, in no way impairing the earning prospects of its adherents. The earning power of women, although they were freer than ever before to enter the job market in many employments, still condemned most single females to lives of destitute misery. The economic disadvantage of women of modest means and marriageable age in comparison to the prospects of their male peers, coupled with an explosion of the "double standard" of sexual morality, created significant new tensions between young men and women. Sexual violence, including assault and murder connected with breach of promise situations, was a natural result of this disequilibrium. Gilfoyle distilled the environment down to its essence:

> *Organized around various forms of gaming – horse racing, gambling, cockfighting, pugilism, and other "blood" sports – sporting-male culture defended and promoted male sexual aggressiveness and promiscuity. For young men like Robinson, bachelorhood was the ideal. Prostitution, sexual display, and erotic entertainment brought excitement to a prosaic world. Respectable, reproductive heterosexuality, in contrast, was associated with femininity and female control. Self-indulgence, not self-sacrifice, meant freedom; unregulated sex was the categorical imperative for the sporting male.*[224]

Although many downtown blocks, including Thomas Street, those of the notorious Five Points, and other locations in the City Hall vicinity, continued to be centers of streetwalking, brothels, houses of assignation, and other variants of "residential" prostitution well into the 1850s, by the start of the decade the area in the immediate vicinity of Bond Street and present-day Lafayette Street had also become a notorious tenderloin, with many blocks of Mercer, Greene, Crosby and neighboring streets filled with bawdy houses and complementary establishments.[225] As with the Plaza district of modern-day New York, the sex trade in Burdell's day flourished on the side streets adjacent to Broadway and Astor Place in a neighborhood occupied by the finest hotels, restaurants and retail establishments.

The microeconomics of whoredom were as important to Harvey Burdell as was the larger scale of the industry to greater New York. By the account of several witnesses in the proceedings following his death, Burdell made a significant portion of his living servicing the dental needs of the participants in the neighborhood sex trade. Burdell's reputation as a liberal-minded *bon vivant* also extended to many a high stakes faro game in the neighborhood.[226] By day, though, his dental clients included respectable members of society, among them a long-standing professional relationship with a Justice of the Brooklyn Marine Court.

Novelist George Thompson, one of the most popular pulp-fiction authors of mid-nineteenth century America, quickly fastened upon the widespread fascination with Harvey Burdell's untimely death and tawdry notoriety. Thompson's works were frequently first published in serial form in second-class newspapers, followed quickly by cheap pamphlet editions. Titillating titles such as *Venus in Boston* and *Confessions of a Sofa* thrilled readers with tales of fallen women and profligate men encountering woeful fates in urban environments. With the public's attention riveted to the Burdell case, Thompson put pen to paper forthwith. Weeks before Emma Cunningham's murder trial began, the author had churned out a ninety-page novella based on the events that had electrified the city. Although some portions of the work remain subject to conjecture or are simply imagined, the accuracy of many characters and scenes in *The Mysteries of Bond Street; or the Seraglios of Upper Tendom* can be corroborated through contemporary journalism and primary archival sources.

Among the events fleshed out in Thompson's depiction of the days before Burdell's demise were those testified to by shoemaker John Littell during the coroner's inquest. Littell had seen the murder victim enter his home late on the evening of January 30 in the company of a man who walked towards 31 Bond with the doomed dentist from the Bowery end of the block. *The Mysteries of Bond Street* first portrays Burdell (named "Hurdell" in Thompson's work) in 1839 as a young doctor out on the town. The protagonist is an accomplished and light-fingered faro banker, well known as a patron in many underworld entertainment venues. In an early gambling den scene, the doctor's dexterity with items other than dental instruments is described by two players as they enter a back room in a saloon:

> *The scene, presented to an uninitiated person, would have been as mysterious as the rites of Egyptian priests of Iris [sic], but to the young men,*

who evidently belonged to that class of society of New York, known as the sporting fraternity, it was familiar.

Around a large deal-table, covered with baise, and on which was past-ed a suit of hearts, were seated some twenty individuals, who were court-ing industriously the goddess of Fortune, at the fascinating game of pharo. Piles of red and white checks were placed in unequal numbers on various cards, and each of the players expressed their opinions, as the Doctor drew the documents that decided their fortunes from a silver deal-ing box.

The fictional murder victim's arousal at the gambling table matched several accounts of the real Dr. Burdell's makeup: "The banker [Hurdell] was a young man of about eight-and-twenty years of age, decidedly good looking, with a dark, heavy beard, and an eye black as jet, that seemed to sparkle with excitement and to take in every thing that occurred about the table at a single glance." Given the deal-er's finesse, the novella's game proceeded to a predictable result, with one of the losing players remarking to the other afterwards: "I am inclined to think that the Doctor don't pull the cards on the dead level, though what game he is playing on the boys I am unable to decide. Even Wright and Hinson, who are, most assuredly, the sharpest dealers of which the Bowery can boast, are out of the Doctor's secret, for he always wins." [227]

*   *   *

Gambling profits, dentistry fees, real estate speculation and a variety of other business ventures made Harvey Burdell a solidly ensconced member of the upper-middle class by the mid-1850s and an especially promising marital catch. As his means increased, Burdell began to summer in Saratoga with other *nouveaux riches* of his day, joining his banking and professional acquaintances in flight from Manhattan's oppressive summer heat and noxious streets.[228] 1855's female embodi-ments of "arm candy" were also important to Burdell as he made the rounds of balls and fashionable dinners both in New York and Saratoga. Marriage, though, was by all accounts the last thing on his mind when he developed an acquaintance with Emma Cunningham during the later part of 1854 and the spring of 1855.

In testimony given after his death by several of his acquaintances, Burdell was said to have been under the impression that Emma Cunningham was self-sufficient, and had inherited considerable property from her late husband. Believing Emma to be no threat to his independence, Dr. Burdell could enjoy her genteel manner and handsome demeanor as an ideal consort for the1855 summer season. How and why Harvey Burdell came by these impressions of Emma Cunningham's finances and intentions remains a mystery. The truth about her background and state of mind that either eluded him, or was simply single-mindedly ignored during the early months of their courtship, became apparent only after the summer's passion produced all-too-frequently unwanted results.

The abortion that Harvey Burdell forced upon Emma at Thanksgiving in 1855 set into motion a chain of events with disastrous consequences. The true depth of evil of which Harvey Burdell was capable came to the fore when he learned of Emma's pregnancy. To the devious dentist, Emma's medical condition was of little concern, and the fact that she could easily die during the risky procedure was of no consequence. What her pregnancy did represent was a golden opportunity, one that he could use to good advantage. With Emma literally quaking with fear, Burdell easily coaxed his lover into assisting Dimis Hubbard with her divorce.

Having yielded to Dr. Burdell's sexual desires, and submitted to an abortion, Emma felt justified in trying to force a marital commitment from her lover. With his desires satisfied, though, the would-be groom was more unwilling than ever to consent, and a fatal spiral downward commenced. Burdell's anger at Emma's forceful importunings overwhelmed a man not accustomed to submitting to demands from a member of the opposite sex. Prolonged personal carelessness and violent fits of temper followed, ending late one night in a bloody struggle in Burdell's dental operatory. Who and how many persons were present as Harvey Burdell coughed out his last breaths would remain a mystery, though, perhaps forever.

CHAPTER 10

❖◄►◄❖

Emma On Trial

ONCE the coroner's inquest ended in mid-February, the Burdell matter remained relatively quiet in the press while the public awaited a formal indictment. The commencement of the grand jury's consideration of the charges leveled against Emma Cunningham and John Eckel was by far the most prominent item on the calendar in the Court of General Sessions Monday morning February 16. Only those both blind and deaf could have remained ignorant of the case, but Recorder Smith nonetheless provided the group with a lengthy account of the coroner's findings and the police investigation. The grand jurors then retired to begin their deliberations. Because such proceedings were conducted in secret, the *Herald's* reporter was forced to turn to other sources for the day's reporting of the case, and he joined the hundreds of citizens who had been trouping through the corridors of the Tombs for the past several days, gaping into Emma's and Eckel's cells at will. To the newspaperman's surprise, Emma was seated at a writing desk, penning an inventory of the furniture at 31 Bond Street which she claimed as her property. The public administrator of New York County had taken possession of the house the previous Saturday night, and the frightened prisoner busied herself with trying to insure that her meager household possessions were not auctioned off with the rest of the contents of 31 Bond.

Over the next several days, stories about the case, although not as voluminous as in the first two weeks, continued to occupy a prominent place in the New York papers. The public read about clairvoyant Elizabeth Jane Seymour's suit against Coroner Connery for false imprisonment, and witnessed the first salvo fired in the battle over control of Harvey Burdell's estate. On Wednesday, February 18, Surrogate

Bradford heard applications of the competing parties for legal authority to administer the estate. One of the initial items agreed upon between Henry Lauren Clinton and his client was that Emma would move as swiftly as possible to take control of Burdell's assets. It was no accident that in her first tear-stained appearance in front of Coroner Connery Emma displayed her best evidence that she was Burdell's lawful wife, and thus entitled to preference under the law. She repeated her act for Surrogate Bradford, but given the complexity of the situation, he decided to play it safe, and disposition of Emma's plea as well as the competing claims of Harvey Burdell's blood relatives was put off until March 3.

News of the grand jury's action appeared in the *Herald*'s issue of February 21. A. Oakey Hall subscribed his florid signature to the indictment issued by the grand jurors finding probable cause that Emma Cunningham and John Eckel had murdered Burdell. With the group's findings a foregone conclusion, and the defendants already incarcerated, press coverage of the indictments was scant in comparison to that of the previous two weeks' events. Much attention was given in the day's paper to a newly discovered witness in the case, Dr. Ervin Spicer of Sackett's Harbor, New York.

Spicer's affidavit, transcribed in the *Herald*, told a story never heard by the coroner's jurors. Why the physician came forward at such a late date would remain a mystery. News of the case had reached his village at the outset of the two week long sitting of the coroner's jury. An acquaintance of the murder victim for over thirty years, Dr. Spicer had practiced dentistry in Burdell's adolescent hometown in Jefferson County on the shores of Lake Ontario.[229] Spicer swore that during an upstate visit by Burdell in August 1856, he and the decedent made plans to go into partnership in New York City. Spicer arrived in New York City on the following September 10 and promptly commenced practice in Dr. Burdell's clinic. Approximately ten days later, the affiant was surprised to find two policemen in the first-floor parlor of the house in the company of Emma Cunningham and her sometime lover. Spicer resisted Emma's entreaties to leave, and Burdell then told his partner of having his pockets picked and the key to his desk safe removed. A promissory note made by Emma to Burdell had promptly gone missing. After the police departed, Spicer recalled Burdell leaving the premises to go to the bank. Emma gave Spicer her keys, imploring him to search her rooms for the lost document. Burdell returned after his partner had complied with Emma's request, and was told of the fruitless search. With Emma Cunningham and John Eckel now officially charged with Burdell's murder, the rest of Spicer's tale became even more interesting: later on the afternoon of the incident described, Burdell confided in Spicer that his entire story about a stolen note was a fabrication, retold in Spicer's presence merely to inflame Emma's anger and encourage her to vacate the house so that Dimis Hubbard could move back in. Burdell also admitted to Spicer that Emma and he had in fact been married by Reverend Marvine.

Regardless of its shocking contents, it would be weeks before Dr. Spicer's affidavit could be considered by a court of law. The grand jury's action was final, and the affidavit could only be admitted at trial if one of the sides saw fit. Prosecutor Hall seemed in no hurry, though, to set a trial date once the grand jury acted. As with every other decision, the schedule would be set by Hall so as to maximize the chances of a conviction.[230] With no criminal hearing in sight, Emma Cunningham could concentrate during the remainder of February on plotting revenge against Harvey Burdell for the havoc he had caused. Litigation over control of his estate was scheduled to resume early the following month, and her counsel was well aware that the health and welfare of Emma's children hung in the balance. With Harvey Burdell lying cold in his grave, and no courtroom scenes to portray, the newspapers' sermonizing was stilled for the time being.

Despite the many curiosity seekers who trooped through the corridors of the Tombs and stopped at the barred door of her cell to gawk, Emma Cunningham had ample time during the last weeks of winter to quietly contemplate where life had taken her. How the widow had come to suffer another catastrophic misfortune after such promising beginnings with the once wealthy George Cunningham, and where fate would lead her and her children, drove Emma almost insane with grief and rage. Her scheme to gain her freedom and access to the wealth that Harvey Burdell had denied her was stropped sharp as a razor's edge while she awaited trial. Contingency plans had to be made, and Emma's keen intellect and burning desire for revenge produced a fantastic strategy.

Though criticism of his misconduct was heaped upon Coroner Connery by New York's major newspapers and its more enlightened citizenry during the inquest into Harvey Burdell's death, the outcome was endorsed by all: Emma Cunningham was convicted of homicide in the court of public opinion even before a grand jury was convened. The initial outrage of the *Times, Herald* and *Tribune* over the murder of a supposedly respectable upper-middle-class professional changed considerably, though, after some of the less than honorable details of Harvey Burdell's personal life became widely known. The overall conclusion, however, reached by both the public and press was almost unanimous: though initially abused by Dr. Burdell, the consensus was that Emma was ultimately done justice by the dentist via their solemnized marriage. Common belief held that Emma Cunningham had conspired with John Eckel to assassinate her unwilling groom and take control of his sizable estate in recompense for years of maltreatment.

Emma had been represented by attorneys B.C. Thayer and Levi Chatfield in her October 1856 suits against Burdell, but she did not involve the pair in settlement negotiations, nor in guiding her through the second agreement that she and her ex-paramour entered into late in January, 1857.[231] Apparently her confidence in Thayer and Chatfield was modest, at best. On the same afternoon that Burdell's corpse was discovered, Emma turned elsewhere for legal help, summoning the young but seasoned New York trial lawyer, 36-year-old Henry Lauren Clinton. Clinton's involvement in the case would catapult him to fame and fortune in New York legal circles, lasting throughout the balance of the century.[232]

Henry Clinton rushed over to Emma's house that wintry Saturday afternoon and managed to make his way past police sentries to the third floor. Captain Dilk's men were under instructions to admit no one, but somehow Clinton finagled an opportunity to speak briefly with his client. Coroner Connery discovered the ruse, though, and had Clinton ejected. For the next seven days, both before and after Emma Cunningham was put on the witness stand, Clinton was barred from any contact with his client, even though she had become a prime suspect in the case. Facing a concerted effort by Connery to inculpate her, Clinton filed a *habeas corpus* petition with Judge John P. Brady of the

Court of Common Pleas. On Saturday, February 7, Connery was forced to produce Emma, John Eckel, George Snodgrass, and Emma's daughters in court. Clinton insisted that Connery was wrongfully holding the detainees and illegally denying Emma access to counsel.

After hearing arguments and taking into consideration the content of the testimony heard to date at the inquest, Judge Brady ordered Eckel remanded to the City Prison as a suspect, but freed Snodgrass and Emma's daughter Margaret Augusta entirely. Emma was returned to the coroner's custody at 31 Bond Street, but Clinton was granted appropriate future access to her. Emma's daughter Helen was also remanded to Connery, but only for so long as would be necessary for her to complete her current testimony. Clinton had accomplished only one of his two goals with Brady's decision. His client's daughters were freed, but the decision left Emma in limbo: had his client been formally incarcerated as a suspect with Eckel, Clinton could have prevented Emma from being forced to incriminate herself in further appearances at the inquest, while retaining access to her to plan her legal strategy. As matters stood, though, she would be compelled to take the stand again upon Connery's demand.

Letters poured in to Clinton and Connery during and after the inquest, offering assistance and theories supporting the positions of each side. Many were from cranks, and most were judiciously ignored. In a demonstration of the keen legal and political intellect that would be a hallmark of his illustrious career, Clinton concentrated his attention on crafting an optimal defense strategy for Emma's upcoming murder trial. The chosen tactics placed a risky bet on the defense's ability to reverse the tide of public opinion. Clinton and his co-counsel, Gilbert Dean, Esq., decided that the single greatest damage done to their client by the coroner's malevolent buffoonery lay in the popular belief that Emma and John Eckel had faked her marriage to Harvey Burdell in Reverend Marvine's rectory parlor on October 28, 1856. Although cognizant that proof of the marriage and her entitlement to a share in Burdell's estate might well solidify a trial jury's belief that Emma had a strong motive to bring about Burdell's death, Clinton concluded that removing the enormous stain on her credibility would be more important to his client's vindication.

Clinton painstakingly reviewed the evidence proffered by various inquest witnesses placing Burdell in New York City on the day of the marriage ceremony, as well as contradictory testimony suggesting that the groom was out of town on business in upstate Herkimer and Saratoga Springs, New York on the day in question. Coroner Connery had done everything in his power to impugn Emma's veracity and to question testimony indicating that Dr. Burdell was at least physically present in New York City on the day of his alleged trip to the altar with Emma. With a trial date conceivably months away, if Henry Clinton was to have any chance of effecting a turnabout of the juggernaut rolled along by Oakey Hall and Coroner Connery, Emma's lawyer would have to find a forum in which to successfully establish the validity of her second marriage before the murder trial commenced.

Fortunately for the defense, a tailor-made opportunity was ready at hand in the form of the wrangling which erupted over the administration of Harvey Burdell's estate. Although mention of a will having been drawn up by the decedent made its way into the inquest record at several points, none of the many attic-to-cellar searches of 31 Bond Street uncovered such a document, and no claimant filed a probate petition claiming existence of a will. By February 9, many of the potential heirs to Harvey Burdell's estate were already maneuvering to gain control of his assets. The three minor children of the deceased's late brother, John, joined in their uncle William Burdell's application for authority to control the estate. Another young attorney whose fame and fortune would be elevated via his role in the case was selected to represent the group. Samuel Tilden began attending the inquest sittings even before he made his first appearance before Surrogate Bradford on behalf of the Burdell blood relatives.[233]

When hearings on the competing applications commenced on March 3, Henry Clinton appeared for his client, "Emma Cunningham Burdell," seeking a judicial determination of the validity of her marriage to the late dentist. Clinton fully expected that a fresh opportunity would be afforded his client to prove the *bona fides* of her second nuptials in a court of law rather than in the center ring of Connery's circus. Even if Surrogate Bradford delayed his decision on the matter beyond the start of the murder trial, at least Emma's story might be freely told beforehand. This time, Clinton, instead of his adversaries, would manage the scenery changes and curtain falls before the public's eager eyes.

The case presented by Henry Clinton to the Surrogate was predicated on convincing the jurist of the pristine innocence and untarnished credibility of Emma's daughter Augusta, who was admitted by both sides to have been present at the ceremony conducted in Reverend Marvine's rectory. Augusta positively identified the decedent as being the man she stood beside in the rectory parlor. Clinton also emphasized that the first version of the "settlement" documents between Burdell and Emma in October, 1856, were not actually executed by her, and thus posited that Emma had refused any remedy to her breach of promise and slander lawsuits against the doctor other than through solemnization of their nuptials. The January, 1857 version of these documents introduced at the inquest, one seemingly fully executed by Emma, was rejected by Clinton as a forgery. Clinton then reminded the Surrogate of the testimony given by one of the doctor's friends at the inquest: the witness told of being asked by Harvey Burdell to examine Emma's signature on the January papers and to give his opinion as to its genuineness. Clinton pointed out to Bradford that this was a strange request unless uttered by a forger.

Potentially damning testimony in support of the argument that Emma faked Dr. Burdell's participation in the marriage ceremony came from a variety of sources. A string of witnesses swore to the Surrogate of Burdell's presence in Herkimer and Saratoga Springs, New York during the days immediately prior to the October 28 wedding. Clinton scrupulously analyzed the witnesses' offerings, and presented his rebuttal to Bradford: not only was each member of the group mistaken by a month in their recollections of Burdell's upstate visit; the witnesses were also alleged to be conspiring with the Burdell family to defeat Emma Cunningham's suit and line their collective pockets with the estate assets.

The balance of Clinton's case rested on impugning Connery's conduct of the entire inquest, and an attack on the morals of Dimis Hubbard and her role in luring Burdell away from Emma Cunningham. Any flaws in Emma's case, including supposed discrepancies in

Augusta's testimony at the inquest as compared to that rendered before the Surrogate, were explained away by Clinton. His impassioned plea presented the judge with a stark philosophical choice between upholding Emma's marriage to Dr. Burdell, and declaring the marriage a nullity. Surrogate Bradford would either render chivalric treatment to Mrs. Cunningham and her daughter in their roles as prototypes of the contemporary ideal of "true womanhood," or support the rapacious greed of Burdell's blood relations and endorse the decedent's immoral conduct. Henry Clinton waxed poetic as he beseeched the court to forgive any inconsistencies in Augusta's accounts:

> *With a view to account for any discrepancies that may appear between her [Augusta Cunningham's] testimony before the Coroner and this court, I will invoke your attention to the extraordinary and unparalleled circumstances under which she first testified. Her home for one long week had been converted into a prison. It was filled with the police and besieged by a mob. Her mother, her sister, and herself were confined there as prisoners, and treated as outlaws; for even the right to see and advise with counsel was denied them – a right guaranteed by the Constitution, and which, in practice, has always been accorded to even the most abandoned and desperate criminals. Every one who spoke to them in words of kindness was branded as with the mark of Cain. The fearful and appalling murder of her step-father was quite sufficient to overthrow and exhaust one of weak constitution, and who had suffered for years with broken health. Surrounded by scenes of tumult and brutality – worried, jaded, worn out with sufferings, indignities, and calamities; her strength gone, her nervous system, for the time, broken down, she went upon the stand to testify; the atmosphere of the room contaminated and fetid; her eyes compelled to meet the concentrated gaze of a gaping crowd – can you not excuse the trepidation, nervousness, or confusion, under such circumstances? She might well be excused for any statements then made by her. But she has been remarkably accurate and consistent upon material points, thus showing the power of innocence and truth . . .[234]*

With all of Clinton's persuasive logic and heart-rending rhetoric, one point, though, remained unexplained by his client: every individual testifying in support of the marriage being valid agreed that Harvey Burdell had expressed multiple demands that the union be kept secret until June of 1857. No plausible reason was presented by Emma's side for this insistence.

As arguments droned on in front of Surrogate Bradford, the murder defendants languished in prison. Meanwhile, collateral events in the Burdell-Cunningham conflict were featured almost daily in the New York press. Coroner Connery was facing consequences from his recent behavior far more serious than mere ridicule in the City's daily papers. Republican Governor John King led the Albany enemies allied against Tammany Hall, and loyal clubhouse member Connery made an ideal political target. The coroner's previous employment history as a theater and music critic for the *Herald* added a note of mirth to the criticism heaped upon him for the spectacle he had conducted at 31 Bond. On complaint of Henry Clinton, Governor King served impeachment papers upon Connery at the end of February, 1857, seeking his removal for unbecoming official conduct.[235]

Emma's counsel protested bitterly over his client's treatment throughout the inquest. The most serious charge involved her having been strip-searched in front of the Coroner's son, "Deputy John" and other male officials. Prior to the March 24 commencement date of Connery's trial in the Court of Common Pleas, the Coroner produced a written statement, purportedly signed by Emma Cunningham, wherein she admitted having consented to the search. Though at first it acknowledged having believed the Coroner's side of the story, the *Tribune* sent its reporter to the Tombs on Monday evening, March 16, to interview Emma, whereupon the paper's representative was informed that her signature had been forged to the document. Emma protested: "I can assure you, Sir, that I was ordered to strip myself; that I was stripped down to my toes, and stood in a perfectly nude state before Deputy John, an officer, Dr. Woodward, and a lady, who was permitted to remain in the room at my special request."

Despite an opportunity to gain political advantage, Emma halted further malicious speculation in which some of the press had also recently engaged. Although Coroner Connery had required her to defrock completely, she was emphatic that no sexual abuse had taken place: "No, certainly, Dr. Woodward took no improper liberties with me; . . . the examination was, I presume, conducted in as delicate a manner as it were possible to do it ... I believed that it was legal to strip me, and so I submitted."[236]

Accompanied by his sometime deputy and dutiful son John, Edward Connery stood trial before Judge Charles P. Daly, dressed in the same genteel blue coat with brass buttons familiar to those who had attended the lengthy homicide inquest. Connery was accused by Clinton of multiple instances of "gross impertinence and bestiality" towards Emma Cunningham and many other witnesses during the course of the hearing.[237] With proceedings still ongoing in Surrogate's Court, Henry Clinton was forced to juggle both lawsuits as well as continue planning for Emma's criminal trial. Connery's impeachment trial proceeded slowly, though, and testimony concerning the most egregious of Connery's alleged outrages was not presented until the end of April. The case proffered by Clinton and other complainants was apparently not compelling. Governor King informed Clinton in mid-May that the evidence was insufficient for a conviction.[238]

The climate of public opinion for Henry Clinton during the initial weeks of his Surrogate's Court attempt to cleanse Emma Cunningham's reputation was far from optimal. The gruesome nature of Dr. Burdell's death and his ex-lover's vilification in the popular press were never far from the public eye, even while the criminal case was temporarily dormant. Readers of the *Tribune* gaped with open mouths through the late winter as they read of the wave of violent crime sweeping over the city during those weeks. Among others, the murder of pitiful young Emma Green especially shocked the paper's audience when this gruesome story was published on February 26.

Only three days prior, the *Tribune*'s editors had once again bemoaned the wave of random violence engulfing New York. Late February's issues enumerated multiple stabbings and garrottings in many wards of the City, none more woeful than the horrid story Miss Green gasped out during her deathbed deposition. The unfortunate youngster had been lured with a five-dollar bill into a house of assignation on Elizabeth Street by a passing stranger who claimed to recognize his prey from an earlier encounter in the Crystal Palace uptown. Their commerce resulted in a violent outburst, and a pistol shot pierced Green's abdomen, producing the fatal wound.

Editorial sentiment as to Emma Cunningham's guilt or innocence published during the weeks before her trial for murder began was thinly disguised in many instances, while frightful murders continued to occur in the streets of many of the nation's large cities throughout the spring. When an unfaithful young male daguerreotype shop-owner was stabbed in New Orleans in broad daylight by his jilted patron and lover, the local paper eagerly compared the assailant and the circumstances to Emma Cunningham's case. The *New York Tribune* endorsed its own slant on the story in its headline prefacing a story quoted from the New Orleans *True Delta* issue of April 24:

"A WOMAN'S REVENGE – ALMOST A SECOND BURDELL AFFAIR" read the *Tribune's* reprinting of the sordid Louisiana events: A "charming widow . . . flush with sordid lucre," named Mrs. Mary Jane Charles, was persuaded by a young artist of "lofty aspirations and Byronic exterior" to provide monies that were quickly misdirected. Two photo parlors were built instead of the Italian country retreat authorized by the swain's lover. Insult was added to injury when the youth abandoned his 30-year old paramour. Driven to distraction by jealousy, Mrs. Charles purchased a pearl-handled dagger, intending to strike her victim "while in the act of transferring the features of some fair one to the metallic plate." The victim encountered his assailant on the sidewalk instead, and was gashed severely in the neck and thigh. Mrs. Charles made her way through the crowd of astonished bystanders to a waiting carriage and rushed homeward. Her indictment on murder charges followed shortly, with the *Tribune's* headline giving voice to many New Yorkers' conclusions about Emma Cunningham's culpability and motives.[239]

* * *

With the Surrogate's Court disposition of Emma's marriage claim expected to take months to complete, a temporary administrator was appointed for Harvey Burdell's estate, opening yet another avenue for dispute. Although Clinton managed to delay the personal property auction at 31 Bond Street as a result of Emma's claim that the parlor furniture was hers alone (or failing that, at least being part of a valid leasehold estate that was to last until May 1), the administrator succeeded in scheduling an auction of the contents of Burdell's dental operatory and office, as well as the parlor-floor furnishings, books and bric-a-brac, for March 30.

The impending dispersal of the contents of the Bond Street home presented another opportunity for New York women to fantasize revenge against their own errant lovers and husbands. The March 31 issue of the *Tribune* reported crowds outside 31 Bond Street on the day of the auction not seen since the end of the coroner's inquest. Hours before the start of bidding, Bond Street was once again thronged with curiosity seekers. *"Some of the women quite lost their temper at being crowded, yet, they pushed on with might and main, and strange smile[s] of satisfaction lit their features as they gained the hallway,"* the paper reported. Once inside, some visitors tried to go upstairs to Emma's rooms, which she had vacated when taken away to her prison cell, but police officers kept the crowd confined to the first two floors of the home. Several hundred persons crowded into the house, mostly women, and among them many elegantly-dressed courtesans. Fights broke out repeatedly among the prospective bidders, as jockeying ensued for prime positions in front of the auctioneer's stand. Many men left the premises in disgust after witnessing the shrill scene inside.

The auctioneer moved from room to room on the two floors, selling off the furniture and furnishings. Among other items, a copy of *"Snodgrass on Apostles"* was put to the hammer, though why the Administrator believed the work authored by Emma Cunningham's preacher friend to be part of Burdell's estate is unclear. Most pieces brought bids of but a few dollars, with one of the top prices paid by Burdell's neighbor, Dr. Roberts, for the late dentist's rosewood secretary. Harvey Burdell's death had evoked a broad spectrum of sentiments among New Yorkers, both male and female, as the pieces of his ghastly relationship with Emma Cunningham and her children became common knowledge. Souvenir hunters of every sort paid visits to the crime scene and fixated on the physical details of 31 Bond and its environs that most strongly evoked their own emotions about the case and its resonance in their personal lives. Broken promises, wasted friendships, and manipulative personal excess all came forth in the responses of supposed friends of the deceased as well as complete strangers.

Among the oddest of the auction audience was a Mr. Ebling, a gentleman who had played no public role in the case before. Strange looks followed Ebling throughout the home as the process was completed; his ghoulish demeanor was of a different cast from that of the average curiosity-seeker. Besides being the successful bidder for lots of Burdell's books, Ebling won a macabre souvenir of Harvey Burdell's and Emma Cunningham's lives together: a bid of two dollars brought him the "Specimen of 'Foetus,' preserved in spirits, in a large glass jar," as an astonished crowd whispered their comments. Details of Ebling's personal life and his acquaintance with the deceased and the accused murderess would remain a mystery, and his name was not mentioned in subsequent press. All told, a few hundred dollars were collected in cash, and the bidders left the house by 5:00 P.M., save those persons lingering for a last few moments among the haunting shadows inside what the *Herald* described as "a dwelling-place and yet no habitation . . ."

Within two weeks after the auction, Henry Clinton completed his presentation to the Surrogate, establishing what he felt was an unimpeachable case for Emma's marriage claim. Unfortunately, the very quality of the proof might well have been the reason for an unfortunate interruption in the proceedings: District Attorney Hall, ever mindful of the potential impact of a decision by the Surrogate in Emma's favor, suddenly decided to schedule the opening of her murder trial for May 5, and with that deadline suddenly imminent, Clinton was forced to move the Surrogate for an adjournment so that the criminal defense team could ready themselves for battle in the Court of Oyer and Terminer.

Jury selection in Emma's murder trial began with the impaneling of five hundred prospective jurors on Saturday April 18. In an effort to find men who had not formed an opinion as to the guilt or innocence of the defendant, a pool was assembled numbering over twelve times the normal size. No request for a change of venue by either side was reported, however.[240] The political climate surrounding the opening of Emma's murder trial was packed with controversy, much of it calling into question the credibility of the city's entire system of law enforcement and criminal justice. The Mayor's defeat in Albany in early April in the battle for control of the municipal police force provided a dramatic background to the events unfolding in the Burdell saga. The State legislature's dissolution of Wood's personally-controlled constab-

Surrogate A.J. Bradford   *Justice Henry Davies*

ulary was not accepted by the Mayor as a *fait accompli*: even as the jury panel was being selected for Emma Cunningham's murder trial, the Mayor busied himself in obtaining a temporary injunction against implementation of the new police act. The injunction was quickly vacated, though, and chaos resulted in many wards as street fights broke out between the Mayor's "Municipals" and the newly appointed "Metropolitans" over rights to display police force badges and assert authority.[241]

The May 4 report of the commencement of the murder trial in the *Tribune* was tucked among the *"CITY ITEMS"* describing dirty streets, and the appearance of America's pre-eminent Shakespearean actor, Edwin Booth, as Richard III at Burton's Theater that evening. Blaring headlines were deemed unnecessary to announce what was already known throughout town: the Burdell trial would commence at 11:00 A.M.. in the Supreme Court Circuit Room, over the Court of Sessions. Rumor had it that the hall of the Marine Court adjoining the Supreme Court would be thrown open for spectators, but the officers of that tribunal objected to the invasion of those premises, which had just been newly fitted up. With a tornado of publicity swirling in the courthouse corridors, maintaining pristine décor in the newly-renovated Marine Court was shoved to the wayside. The trial opened with a full complement of spectators looking on through the broad doorways separating the two courtrooms that were thrown open for maximum visibility.[242]

Oakey Hall led off for the prosecution when court commenced Tuesday morning May 5. With characteristic flourish, his address depicted Emma Cunningham as one of the most violent and despicable murderesses in human memory. After painting Emma as a modern-day Lady Macbeth lying in wait to assassinate her innocent quarry, Hall began his evidentiary presentation by placing Dr. J.W. Francis on the stand. The physician had examined Burdell's mutilated corpse on the morning of Saturday, January 31; his grisly testimony told of finding Burdell's corpse encased in what the *Tribune* took pains to describe in detail as "a mass of soaked linen . . . supersaturated with blood," surmounted by "a plethoric full distended face, with the eyes obtrusive, with the mouth firmly drawn together, and with the tongue protruded between the teeth."[243] Hall's plan of proof became clear as soon as he placed his next witness on the stand.

Cook Hannah Conlan stepped up and took the oath in her thick Irish brogue. The witness, who had been widowed four years earlier, joined the Burdell house staff out of financial necessity in 1855. The courtroom atmosphere was a frightful one for Hannah, according to the paper's reporter: "She is a genuine looking Irish girl, of the most intense kind," reported the *Tribune.* The descriptive power of the paper's account could scarcely have been improved upon, even by modern-day courtroom television: the witness *"manifested great trepidation on going on the stand, and some minutes elapsed before she could compose herself sufficiently to give her testimony. By the gallantry of the Judge, a glass of water was offered to her, and her equanimity was restored."* [244]

Oakey Hall's twofold reason for putting Conlan on the stand became evident immediately: Conlan was employed by the prosecutor to establish an impassioned motive for Emma Cunningham having murdered Burdell, while at the same time impugning the defendant's morals. Through a series of questions, and over the objections of defense counsel, Hall brought out many details of an abortion that Emma underwent at Burdell's hands at Thanksgiving 1855. Emma had taken to bed ill at holiday-time, and after being attended to personally by Burdell, she handed over a full "chamber" to Hannah. In that vessel the cook discovered a fetus. Violent illness followed for the poor mother: it was a full month until Emma first came downstairs to dine with her children.

Clinton and his co-counsel Gilbert Dean's protestations to Justice Davies over permitting the testimony of the cook Conlan and her co-worker Margaret Donahoe were listened to but overruled. What defense counsel characterized as the "unreliable memories of domestics" were deemed perfectly admissible by the Court. Dean's objection to prosecutor Hall's strategy may have been eloquent, but it failed to block her damaging testimony.[245] The district attorney showed that emotions between Burdell and Emma grew even more complicated, not only by the aborted pregnancy, but also by Emma's relationship with boarder John Eckel. Hall inquired as to Conlan's knowledge of the relations among the three housemates, and over Clinton's objections, the triangle was outlined distinctly by the witness: Emma had told Conlan that Burdell was violently jealous, having found Emma and Eckel together and alone in her rooms. All hell had broken loose when Burdell "looked through the keyhole and saw that [which] he did not like." [246]

Yet another reason impelling Emma to murder her ex-lover was elicited from Conlan, although perhaps unintentionally on the part of Henry Clinton. Upon cross-examination by Clinton, Conlan described her conversations with the mistress of the house about Burdell's dalliance with his young cousin Dimis Hubbard, as well as other female visitors to 31 Bond Street. The picture of Harvey Burdell's immorality could not have been more clearly presented to the jurors. Control meant everything to Harvey Burdell, and Emma and Dimis were mere pawns in a sexual war game that the wealthy householder played out for his own amusement. Clinton then used his cross-examination opportunity to present another basic pillar of the defense strategy. Conlan had been incarcerated by Coroner Connery's order since the end of January, and the illegitimacy of this conduct as well as the hardship brought upon Conlan as a result were presented to the jury in conjunction with the defense team's portrayal of Emma as the victim of prosecutorial misconduct both on the part of the coroner as well as the district attorney.

Having exhausted all other objections, Clinton accused Conlan of being a drunkard, and by implication an unreliable witness. The voluble Irishwoman fended off his attempts with deft humor as she left the stand:

Q. Have you been in the habit of getting drunk a good deal?

A. I could always take my share, but never so much as not to be able to work; I never saw any one who would throw it over their shoulders, whether they were rich or poor. [247]

*   *   *

The prosecution's witnesses during the first days of the trial presented a story already familiar to the public; Burdell's neighbor, Dr. Stephen Main, housemaid Margaret (a/k/a Mary) Donahoe, Catherine Stansbury (would-be replacement for Emma as boarding house operator), and Police Officers Davis and Moore all testified to much the same facts as they had presented to Coroner Connery and prosecutor Hall during the inquest nine weeks before. Donahoe repeated for the jury's ears the story of Emma's disclosure to her that Burdell had pulled a gun on Emma during a quarrel, as well as telling her of Dr. Burdell's general wickedness. Margaret Donahoe was particularly forthcoming in her defense of Emma Cunningham's morals. Countering the innuendo that Emma had started sleeping with her indicted co-conspirator, John Eckel, before Burdell's death, Donahoe maintained that her mistress always spent the night alone in her own bed while Eckel lived in the house. The witness was in as good a position as anyone to testify on these matters: her daily duties included making up the beds each of the many sleeping chambers on the occupied floors of 31 Bond. Margaret had become expert in reading wrinkle patterns in the bedclothes she straightened. Surely the serving girl would have noticed any article of Eckel's clothing left behind on a morning after.

In contrast to Emma's upstanding character, Donahoe also repeated the stories of Harvey Burdell's infidelities with Dimis Hubbard that she had heard from Emma, and the violence threatened against her by the frequently angry dentist. The police officers then confirmed their testimony of the altercation between the unhappy couple that they had witnessed when called to the house in the fall of 1856 during the fracas over the supposedly purloined promissory note.

Wednesday, May 6, was the second day of testimony, and the Supreme Court opened to a scene of pandemonium: "At an early hour yesterday morning," reported the *Tribune* the next day, "before the opening of the court or the court-room, a great crowd of people gathered around the door, and lined the stairways up and down, from the third story to the street; and when the doors were finally thrown open, there was a grand rush for seats . . . At 10 o'clock the order of 'Hats off!" was passed like an order through a phalanx of filibusters. Then came the order of "Hear ye, hear ye !" when everybody held his breath, and listened for what he could hear. The Judge took his seat, the jury took theirs, and the wheels began to move."

Readers were treated to the first description of the defendants crowded around the defense table:

> *Mr. Eckel sat at a table reading in THE TRIBUNE the report of Tuesday's proceedings. He has somewhat of the look and air of a legal gentleman; and a person might suppose him to be one of the counsel in the case, rather than a prisoner at the bar. There is general surprise manifested by strangers on first seeing Eckel. He is a quiet-looking man, somewhat undersize in hight[sic], though rather stout in frame. He is exceedingly self-composed, puts on a frequent smile, and is not by any means the tiger he is supposed to be by "people from the interior." Mrs. Cunningham, one of her daughters, and her two boys, occupied seats near her counsel; while their mutual friend, Mr. Snodgrass, who was also present, sat at a little distance and beguiled the tedium to some of the reporters occasionally dropping a remark in the way of friendly conversation.* [248]

Dr. Stephen Main continued his testimony from the previous evening, when the proceedings had gone quite late. Dr. Main described the crime scene he encountered when summoned to 31 Bond on the morning of January 31, and analyzed for the court the wounds to Burdell's lifeless body. Dr. Samuel Parmly followed, and swore to having encountered two strange, shabbily dressed men on Burdell's block after 10:00 P.M. on his nightly perambulation outside his Bond Street house.

Prosecutor Hall then called Coroner Connery's son, John, to establish the young deputy's discovery of a pistol and two daggers as Emma's rooms were searched during the February inquest. This move might have given Clinton another opportunity to present the coroner's conduct in a light sympathetic to his client, but Justice Davies blocked Clinton's attempts to elicit testimony from John as to the controversial strip search of Emma's person while in the custody of the witnesses' father. Clinton's patience with the judge's uncooperative ruling quickly paid off, though: Dr. David Uhl then briefly took the stand. In describing the condition of Burdell's corpse, Uhl negated the possibility that the weapons found in Emma's rooms could have created the lethal wounds.

Coroner Connery himself was sworn in by Oakey Hall as the next step unfolded between the two rivals over the political fallout of the Burdell case. Connery produced for admission in evidence Emma Cunningham's signed deposition at the inquest, and then subjected himself to questioning by both sides, cautioning that because of the pending charges of misconduct against him, certain questions would perhaps not be answered. The deposition contents spoke strongly in favor of at least one of the prosecution's arguments: Emma admitted to being jealous of Burdell and his having refused to marry her for reasons she preferred not to disclose. Though she made it clear that Burdell had acquiesced to matrimony in the fall of October, 1856, Emma informed the coroner's jury that virtually all of the furniture in the first and second floors of 31 Bond belonged to her alone, in case the matter became relevant in future proceedings. Now that Harvey Burdell was cold in his grave, Emma could try and play both sides of the fence. Though she claimed to have married the decedent, Emma could not rely on the good graces of the courts. Laying claim to the parlor and bedroom fittings as hers alone might be inconsistent with a husband's rights to his wife's property, but Burdell's estate administrator would certainly not compromise his position that Emma had never married the murder victim just to try and lay claim to a few cheap sticks of furniture.

Once Connery was on the stand, Clinton and Dean could tell the jury the story of the Coroner's mistreatment of their client. In addition to the by-now infamous strip search, the defense team impugned the validity of the entire inquest on the grounds of nepotism. In addition to hiring his son John to assist in the investigation, Connery had taken the opportunity to put his son-in-law, Dr. William Knight, on the public payroll. Knight was retained as part of the post-mortem examination team. Why four physicians were retained to assist the coroner in a single case remained unquestioned throughout the proceedings.

Ethnic stereotypes were also employed by the defense team in a manner calculated to appeal to the jury's prejudices as Emma's lawyers energetically attempted to protect their client. As with Irish cook Hannah Conlan, Clinton and Dean attempted to show that Connery had been drunk from the outset of the inquest:

Q. When you got there [31 Bond Street], what was your first official act?

A. To commence the inquisition.

Q. Well, how did you commence it – that is what I want to know?

A. By subpoenaing [sic] a jury and going through the regular process; of course I saw the body and examined it a little before the jury came in.

Q. Was your first official act to apply to Mr. Eckel for a bottle of brandy and to tell him that you would have it?

A. No, sir.

Q. Didn't he furnish a bottle of brandy to you at your request.

A. No.

Q. Pitcher?

As Clinton pressed onward, Connery laid the responsibility for the fetching of the brandy onto a friend of Emma Cunningham's. The witness then refused to testify further about his tippling on the morning of January 31, claiming the right to remain silent because of the pending impeachment proceedings. [249]

The balance of the district attorney's case consisted of various neighbors offering inconclusive accounts of what they saw and heard on the night of Burdell's demise. Although many heard cries of "murder" at the late evening time alleged as that of Burdell's death, none of the residents could offer eyewitness testimony to the commission of the crime, nor was any dispositive evidentiary link established between Emma and the physical circumstances of Burdell's death. Hall's final offerings to the judge and jury were again motive-related: the prosecutor put in evidence the unexecuted October, 1856 litigation settlement documents that ended Emma's breach of promise suit against Burdell, and then called upon another acquaintance of the decedent, Dr. Benjamin Maguire.

Maguire's testimony was delayed, though, as Emma's lawyers rose and demanded attention from the bench. After Oakey Hall declared to Judge Davies that Dr. Maguire would be the final prosecution witness, Clinton and Dean insisted that the court first entertain their motion to dismiss the case. Claiming that the State's failure to call to the stand the Misses Cunningham, John Eckel, and George Snodgrass was a fatally prejudicial defect, Emma's defenders argued that Judge Davies had an obligation to end the proceedings. The defense team alleged that the knowledge of persons within the house at the time of the murder was an essential part of the prosecution's theory that the murder was committed by a resident, and that the district attorney had an obligation to present all available evidence on the matter. Judge Davies was unreceptive to the arguments, though, and after he denied the defense motion, Dr. Maguire took the stand.

Prosecutor Hall focused his questioning of Maguire on a pistol that the witness' friend Harvey Burdell had purchased four years ago. Gilbert Dean's cross-examination was aimed at far different matters, though, swiftly turning a prosecution witness into a defense resource. Seeking to solidify the defense's assertions that several individuals had more than adequate reasons to wish Burdell dead, Dean questioned Dr. Maguire intensely about Dimis Hubbard's relationship with Burdell. The witness told little, but the mere line of questioning gave the jury ample reason to doubt Emma's having been the only one who hated Harvey Burdell enough to do him in. Dean managed, via his interrogation of Maguire, to recap the story of Harvey Burdell having permitted Dimis Vorce and her whore-mongering husband William to reside at 31 Bond Street in the fall of 1855. The audience heard of Burdell having taken more than a fraternal liking to Dimis, and helping her procure a divorce. William Vorce was said to have hated Harvey Burdell, fiercely swearing vengeance against his wife's libertine cousin. Over the strenuous objections of the prosecution, Messrs. Dean and Clinton then elicited a brief account of Harvey Burdell's strife with his brothers John and William, seeking to cast the decedent in a further unsympathetic light.

District Attorney Hall cut this line of questioning off as soon as Judge Davies would permit, and then rested the prosecution's case.

* * *

Despite exhaustion from the day's proceedings, Clinton gathered his strength, and late on the afternoon of May 7, Emma's lead counsel rose from the defense table and turned to face the jury. Adopting the posture he had practiced in Surrogate's Court as the noble protector of ideal womanhood, Clinton declared the vile accusations against his client to be without precedent. While claiming to be part of a generally shared sentiment that the State had failed miserably in presenting a plausible case, Emma's defender turned the tables on the prosecution, accusing the District Attorney of having "dogged and hunted" his client "as though she were a wild beast." Prosecutor Hall was also denounced for trying to prevent the jury from "giving utterance to the feeling of manly sympathy" for the defendant.

Expressing amazement at the performance he had just witnessed, Clinton explained at length the strange circumstances in which the jury was being asked to render a guilty verdict. In a clever attempt to turn the tables of justice, Henry Clinton substituted Oakey Hall as the defendant: "I have often listened with pleasure to my learned friend as he addressed juries in capital and other criminal cases; but what was my surprise when I saw that he, usually so fair, so candid, so cautious, and so just, had overstepped all bounds of moderations, not contenting himself with stating the facts of the case which he expected to prove, but as my associate has said, ransacked the classics, had traveled over history, sacred, profane and modern, with the view of selecting demons, female fiends, in order that he might typify by means of them the character of my unfortunate client . . ."

Though at first stoutly maintaining that he would not review Emma's painful personal history, nor attempt to countervail District Attorney Hall's depiction of his client as a scheming liar, Clinton nonetheless proceeded to do his best to evoke sympathy for the twice-widowed Emma as a victim of immense prosecutorial misconduct. Oakey Hall might as well have been charged with the rape of an entire home full of widowed mothers:

– 187 –

He told you that she came before you a vailed [sic] picture of sorrow – a miserable hypocrite – that all the suffering which she seemed to have experienced was entirely feigned. She does come before you a picture of sorrow, and unfortunately as she comes before you with the weeds of widowhood, it is not the first time that her heart has been pierced with anguish; it is not the first time that she has been called upon to deplore the loss of a husband. I will not attempt to depict to your minds the anguish of her soul, when scarce three years ago the husband of her youth was entombed beneath the sod; but gentlemen, when she lay stretched upon the bed of sickness herself, as she supposed, about to be drifted into the oceans of eternity, she was told that the husband of her youth had departed this life; that his spirit had found its way, we trust, to a better world. Yet, gentlemen, she put her trust in the widow's God; she had faced affliction before, and she had come through it unscathed; since that time had rapidly, but smoothly been borne down the stream of time, until, unfortunately for her, she was dashed upon an epoch in her history, the fearful moment when suddenly there shown [sic] out from the horizon of the future, not that star of Bethlehem whose serene, hallowed light burst the darkness of her affliction as the grave which she supposed closed over the lifeless form of her husband, and in which her earthly hopes were all entombed; but alas the star of destiny shed its baleful light upon the ill-fated union of herself with Harvey Burdell. [250]

With the Surrogate's Court case regarding Emma's claim to her lover's estate suspended for the time being, Henry Clinton could assert the bona fides of Emma's marriage to Harvey Burdell without restraint, arguing that the marriage itself disproved the prosecution's alleged motive for Emma's alleged homicidal attack. Why would a woman married to a man with a steady and sizable income do him in, queried the defense? Many others had substantial reason to kill Harvey Burdell. [251]

While dissecting the inconsistencies in the prosecution's totally circumstantial case, and impugning District Attorney Hall's forthrightness, Clinton also excoriated the coroner for having denied his client her basic civil rights. Once again the jury was reminded of the naked indignities suffered by Emma at Connery's hands. Even Clinton's worthy opponent in the Surrogate's Court, Samuel Tilden, was not spared the defense's barbs. Tilden, who represented the blood-relative claimants to Burdell's estate, had been present many days at Emma's murder trial, supporting the State's case. Assuming victory in the pending estate litigation, Clinton reminded the jury that his client's conviction and trip to the gallows would be of immense benefit to Tilden's clients.

Ever a powerful orator, Clinton attacked the character of the decedent with full force, contrasting the murder victim's dalliance with Dimis, the "kept mistress of her own blood cousin" with his client Emma's moral purity and her children's spotless innocence. Emma's protector then completed his address by throwing his widowed client and her soon-to-be-impoverished children upon the jury's mercy:

> *I venture to say that when you have listened to this testimony, the pleasantest duty you ever performed will be to acquit this woman. To remove the dark cloud of disgrace . . . you will rejoice that you are not called to throw over her and her children and her whole family, one and all, the black mantle of infamy, whose folds may attack and encumber them through life . . . And you will send them forth into the community, relieved of this infamy, this baseless, diabolical charge. When you have done that, you will have discharged your duty to your conscience; you will have satisfied the prosecution; and the whole community will have reason to award to you the thanks due to twelve honest and upright men.*

With Clinton's opening speech complete, the defense case then consumed the court's attention over the next two days. Reverends Luther and William Beecher and William Snodgrass were put on the stand, as well as medical expert Dr. John F. Carnochan. Emma's children, her dressmaker, Hester Van Ness, Burdell's cousin, Catherine Dennison, and many of Burdell's social acquaintances then followed. No shocking disclosures came forth in the defense case, and Judge Davies frequently prohibited witnesses from answering questions aimed at establishing the moral character or psychological profile of the defendant or the decedent. Fully aware of the burden of proof beyond a reasonable doubt that the prosecution faced, defense counsel took every opportunity to poke holes in the mound of circumstantial evidence upon which the State's case was based.

Despite the admitted strife between the defendant and her ex-lover over many months, and despite Judge Davies' strict management of admissible testimony that resulted in the exclusion of conjectural psychological portraits of the opposing parties, Clinton and Dean were successful in establishing a picture of domesticity in Emma

Cunningham's abode during late January hardly consistent with that of a scheming murderess. Dr. Carnochan's opinion about the massive physical strength necessary to inflict the fatal wounds on Burdell's body also did much to counter the prosecution's focus on Emma Cunningham's supposed left-handedness and the common belief that the actual murderer was similarly inclined.

Images of sanctity and grace were skillfully introduced to the jury as the defense team guided Emma's daughters through their paces on the stand. Burdell's death had interrupted young Helen's plans to leave for Saratoga the next morning with Reverend Beecher to resume her studies at the Temple Grove Female Seminary. The teenager's innocence and a hint of the just ways of the Almighty in countenancing the death of Helen's evil stepfather were somehow allowed by the Court to be paraded before the jury as Gilbert Dean inquired of the young witness whether there was any singing at 31 Bond Street on a Sunday so soon after Burdell's death:

Q. I wish you would state what you sang?

A. It is the first verse of the twelfth hymn in the Book of Common Prayer *(indicating the place in the book, which was handed up for inspection).*

Mr. Dean then read as follows:

> *"God moves in a mysterious way*
> *His wonders to perform,*
> *He plants His footsteps on the sea,*
> *And rides upon the storm.*

Dean's intoning of the hymn was juxtaposed with the predictable: the young woman then denied any knowledge of how, when or by whom Harvey Burdell was despatched.[252]

* * *

The defense's case lasted less than two days, and with the public expecting an exciting climax, the courtroom was once again packed on Saturday morning May 9th. By 9:00 A.M., over three hundred women were counted among the spectators crammed into every available space, waiting to hear the closing speeches of opposing counsel. The *Tribune* reported a dramatic finale in the hall, in which "the most intense interest pervaded the immense audience, and perfect stillness prevailed." Clinton and Dean had rested their case the night before, and the court and jury had recessed for a visit to the scene of the crime. Several jurors supplemented the testimony proffered in the court room by noticing the ease with which 31 Bond Street could be entered from both rear and side doors as well as the main entrance from the stoop, and the group was soon escorted back downtown.

Judge Davies allotted four hours for each side to sum up before he began his jury charge. Prosecutor Hall's assistant, Charles Edwards, first presented the state's summation of technical points of law. [253] Gilbert Dean then rose in front of the jury box, and for two-and-a-half hours, laid out his client's defense. Once again, the state was put on trial, as Dean excoriated the District Attorney and Coroner Connery: "A crime has been committed – Dr. Burdell has been killed, But a greater crime has been committed since his death – a crime not by the midnight assassin – not by the man who steals stealthily in the darkness of night and plunges his dagger into the heart of his victim – but a greater crime has been committed in the name of the law and by its sworn officers. I stand here today to rebuke officially their corruption or incompetency . . ."

Oakey Hall rose to face the court after Dean's lengthy speech came to an end; his closing argument would take even longer than Gilbert Dean's address on Emma's behalf. The chief prosecutor's opening words confronted head-on the weakness of a circumstantial case, shaping, nonetheless, a powerful incrimination of the defendant in an emotional oration. Hall sought to overcome the his adversaries by focusing on the sheer evil of the crime itself: "Murder – old common law murder – moved and instigated by the devil, and with malice aforethought, has always about it such an element of secrecy, that unless we bring to bear all the reasoning powers of our nature to put together circumstances and trivial facts, we can never arrive at that conclusion which we think we have arrived at when we act on positive testimony."

Avoiding any further fictional comparisons of the defendant to the furies of ancient legend or murderesses of renown, Hall systematically led the jury through the prosecution's case, establishing motive, means, opportunity and likelihood. In what might seem to today's listener to be a quite modern statement of sexual equality, the district attorney cautioned the jurors to ignore Clinton's touching pleas about matters irrelevant to the proof at hand:

If mawkish sympathy enters the jury box – as it may have hitherto to some extent have entered the box of the prosecuting officer of this county – If ever mawkish sympathy takes control of the jury box, if men surrender their feelings as men, then there is but one other step to take. Mawkish sympathy has then but to extend to the judiciary, which, thank God, it has not yet reached. Then strike the scales of justice, pull the bandage away from one eye and place it on both, and let the community know that while it is true that juries

> *"When human life is in debate,*
> *Can ne'er too long deliberate-"*

yet, if they deliberate to such an extent as to give immunity to crime, by acquittal, when circumstances are damning, there will come into the world and be inaugurated that millennial triumph of the powers of darkness of which we have all read in the holy writ, and which my learned friend in his speech so strongly placed before you.

Following the district attorney's speech, Judge Davies recessed the trial until 3:00 P.M. Meanwhile, as the *Herald* reported, "[t]he court-room was cleared, except of ladies, and the passages, staircases, and landings became so choked up with masses of people that it was next to an impossibility to make one's way through . . ." [254] When the Court of Oyer and Terminer reconvened in mid-afternoon, chaos again prevailed as masses of eager spectators clamored for admission to hear Henry Clinton's final speech. Court officers had been obliged for days to fashion elaborate ruses to smuggle Emma Cunningham in and out of the building without detection. As soon as word leaked out of her movement, gangs of street urchins would announce a sighting to the throngs on Chambers Street who had waited for hours for a glimpse of the notorious defendant. Those at the head of the crowd had a terrific fight on their hands if they came close to getting a seat inside from what the paper described as a cattle-yard: "The pressure to get into the courtroom was tremendous. Up the flights of iron staircases squeezed, and pressed, and struggled the thousands of human beings who were so anxious to be present at the closing scenes of this celebrated case. Two-thirds of the spectators in the inner court room were women –

well dressed ladies, who had managed to obtain admission – a much coveted privilege. Behind was a complete jam of men, who had pushed and elbowed their way up."[255] Judge Davies gaveled the afternoon session to order, and Henry Lauren Clinton embarked upon his final ninety-minute discourse in the perfectly still chamber. Castigating prosecutor Hall for the illegality of his presentation, Clinton now limited his pleas for sympathy for his client, for the most part staying the course of evidentiary rebuttal. Once again Clinton emphasized the existence of other individuals with ample motives to murder Burdell and the prosecution's twisting of the many threads of circumstantial evidence into a weak strand of proof. Ultimately, though, Clinton returned to playing on the jurors' pity for his client. The *Herald* reported the touching scene, focusing on the distraught defendant:

> *During portions of the counsel's speech in which he referred to 'the brutalities of the brute Connery' – (according to his own words) his rudeness to her, and his refusal to let her see the dead body of her husband, the prisoner for the first time during the trial manifested deep grief and emotion. For some time she kept her handkerchief to her eyes, and afterwards the traces of weeping were on her face. Her daughters were present all the time, but as they kept their faces veiled no emotion was discernible in them. Snodgrass sat near them, and beside him one of the little boys. As counsel wound up his peroration the accused wept and sobbed violently.*

Attorney General Cushing joined District Attorney Hall on the final day of the trial, and his remarks were the last to be heard before the jury was charged. Cushing made one last attempt to parry Clinton's previous attack on the State's most important witness, cook Hannah Conlan. While declaring Emma Cunningham's marriage to Burdell to be a sham, and smearing her character as that of a selfish mother who had willingly submitted to seduction by the murder victim, Cushing implored the jury not to be swayed by the defense's attempt to question servant Hannah Conlan's sobriety and veracity: "The girl who earns her livelihood by the sweat of her brow is as much entitled to respect as the one dressed in gaudy colors, who lives in the Fifth avenue, and perhaps entraps others to ruin."

If anyone deserved pity during the jury's deliberations, maintained Cushing, it was the poor murder victim, and the twelve men were urged to steel their consciences and harden their hearts in their deliberations:

Gentlemen, if this woman was the assassin, if she was the one who did it, when Harvey Burdell stood there trembling between life and death, asking permission to say his last prayer, did she say "I will extend this mercy to you?" No: with that hardness of heart which you have not got, the dagger was driven there. The consequences of conviction are awful. This whole family may be ruined. These young daughters are lost forever. They must suffer beyond redemption. And these boys, too. But with that you have nothing to do except so far as that it should lead you the more carefully to scan the evidence and see that your verdict is warranted by the evidence. Standing in the position which I do, charge you on your oaths to look to it that you do not convict her but on evidence which is irresistible in your own mind, and which carries deep conviction to your bosom. On the other hand, if you do convict her, gentlemen, it is a duty, though a painful one. When you entered that box, you took the responsibility of standing between her and justice. God and the community so deal with you as you deal with yourselves, your own conscience and your God.

With the case closed, Justice Davies' charge laid out in sophisticated, technical rhetoric the law of circumstantial evidence, while at the same time instructing the jury in plain English to cast aside the emotional and tawdry historical comparisons invoked by counsel on both sides. The twelve men were clearly told: if Emma Cunningham was to be convicted on circumstantial evidence, their inference from the facts presented must not only be reasonable and natural; it must also be "to a moral certainty."

After reviewing the evidentiary record with excruciating care, Justice Davies sent the group out to deliberate with these solemn words ringing in their ears:

To your decision I now commit the fate of this unfortunate woman, and the future of herself and her family. While you deal justly by her, it is your privilege also to deal mercifully; for as I have before remarked, if you have any reasonable doubt of her guilt, that doubt is to be cast into the scale in her favor, and entitles her to your verdict of acquittal. If, on the contrary, on a review of the whole case, you deem the charge contained in the indictment proven, it is your duty to your country and your God to say so, though it be with anguish of heart and may cause deep shame and sorrow to others. But if, in this final reviewing, you are not satisfied of her guilt, pronounce a verdict of acquittal, and let the accused go free.[256]

The jury charge had been lengthy, and it was 7:00 P.M. before the group retired. Emma Cunningham sank down in her chair at the defense table, totally exhausted from the tension of the day's lengthy proceedings. Beside her, the *Tribune* reported, sat her daughters "fanning themselves beneath their thick brown veils to partially escape the heated and unhealthy atmosphere which pervaded the room." [257] Despite the late hour, no one left the courtroom except the jury panel.

As it turned out, though, the two sides and the myriad onlookers had not long to wait. Only thirty minutes after the jurors filed out of the room, Justice Davies ordered the doors closed between the official courtroom and the adjoining chamber that accommodated the mass of spectators, so as to prevent unseemly outbursts as the verdict was announced. The jury panel filed back in, and after the roll was called, Emma was ordered to rise and face the twelve men, as Clerk Vandervoort quietly intoned: "Jurors, look upon the prisoner; prisoner, look upon the Jurors. How say you, gentlemen, do you find Emma Augusta Cunningham, otherwise called Burdell, guilty or not guilty."

The few spectators seated in the closed-off courtroom were quickly restrained from applause as the foreman pronounced Emma not guilty in a subdued voice. Gilbert Dean and Henry Clinton reached out to support their client as she sank into her seat in a swoon. Only a few minutes passed, though, before Emma regained her composure and strode next door to receive hearty congratulations from her friends and the jury. John Eckel was released on his own recognizance, and Emma was free to go. The *Tribune's* reporter completed the tale of the day's events: "An hour later she and her daughters . . . were rolling in a carriage toward the house No. 31 Bond Street, where they will remain for the present." [258]

Despite her exhaustion at the end of the final trial day, Emma had started out early that Saturday highly confident of the trial's outcome. During her last night in the Tombs, the accused arranged for her wardrobe to be carted back to 31 Bond Street before being escorted in custody down Centre Street for what turned out to be the last day of the hearing. By the following morning, both the *Times* and the *Herald* had pronounced the jury's verdict warranted, while the *Herald* continued to criticize Oakey Hall for not having pressed a thorough investigation into Burdell's whereabouts on the night of his death. District Attorney Hall and Coroner Connery were soundly ridiculed by the more aggressive *Tribune*.

Editor Horace Greeley minced no words in recapitulating the officials' misconduct, as well as the shameful pretrial inculpation of the defendant during the previous February by some of the popular media. The *Tribune*'s widely respected editor voiced what had become popular sentiment concerning the ludicrous behavior of the state's servants and certain organs of the press:

> The trial of Mrs. Cunningham-Burdell for the murder of Dr. Harvey Burdell, resulted, on Saturday evening, as everybody for days had known it must result, in a verdict of acquittal. In fact, since the close of the first day's testimony, there has been virtually nobody on trial but the District-Attorney, whom the public have adjudged guilty without leaving their seats. His opening harangue would have been utterly inexcusable in the public prosecutor of the Marchioness de Brinvilliers, the dramatic Lucretia Borgia, or any other wholesale murderer whom History has pilloried for the abhorrence of generations; but such an abusive opening with such a flimsy case behind it, we trust, for the honor of the legal profession, was never before made in any other than a political prosecution, where the king's instrument had orders to procure a conviction at all hazards . . .

> As to Mrs. Cunningham or Burdell, we do not hesitate to say that she has been treated with great harshness not only by the ministers of justice but by the Press – unintentional no doubt, but none the less real. By whose cunning and address the finger of suspicion was first pointed toward her, we do not know: when the point is ascertained, we may be able to give a guess at the name of the real culprit. From the moment that Dogberry took into his sage cranium the notion of her guilt, she has been dealt with as though no treatment could be bad enough for her. The proceedings before the Coroner, the indecent examination of her person, the opening of the District-Attorney, were all of a piece.[259]

With his client freed of criminal suspicion, Henry Clinton had accomplished the goal that his half-litigated suit in Surrogate's Court was designed to produce. Henry Clinton and co-counsel Gilbert Dean could now move ahead in their attempt to secure at least a significant share of Harvey Burdell's estate for Emma and her children. Months of litigation loomed, and the presence of crack attorney Samuel Tilden on behalf of the Burdell family heirs would make the task immensely more difficult. Little did Clinton and Dean know, however, that their lawyerly efforts would be supplemented in a most unexpected fashion.

CHAPTER 11

———◆◆✕◆◆———

The Surrogate's Conclusion

WITH Emma's reputation restored, the storm clouds lifted over Henry Clinton's efforts to pursue the Surrogate's Court case to a successful conclusion. On May 24, hearings over the disposition of Harvey Burdell's estate resumed in front of Surrogate Bradford, and by June 18, when testimony ceased, over one-hundred witnesses had been called. Clinton's summary of the evidence created a credible, consistent narrative of Burdell's presence in New York City on October 28, 1856, the date his name was entered in Reverend Marvine's marriage register, while at the same time suggesting to the judge that the several witnesses from upstate New York testifying to the contrary for the Burdell blood relatives were doing so out of mercenary self interest. The weakest links in the chain, however, were Emma and her daughters. Their affirmations that Burdell wanted the marriage kept secret and evidence of rowdy battles between the newlyweds in the Bond Street house ensuing only days after the marriage knot was supposedly tied did not present a convincing case to the Surrogate.

Samuel Tilden was joined by counselor Charles Edwards as special representative for the minor children of John Burdell in opposing Emma Cunningham's marriage claim. Although Tilden's arguments to the court provided little that Clinton could not rebut, co-counsel Edwards took a different tack, again appealing to the Surrogate's emotions by reviling Emma's character. Describing the allegedly twice-widowed litigant's claim as "a thread spun by a cunning spider," Edwards ended up admitting that Burdell was indeed in New York on the evening of October 28, as Reverend Marvine's marriage register indicated. However, the testimony of many others whom Burdell visited that day in Brooklyn and New York, and a careful calculation of feasible travel times and distances allowed Edwards to argue that Burdell's presence on Greenwich Street that evening was physically impossible. Tilden's co-counsel laughed at the idea of Burdell and Emma being secretly married, declaring the notion an idle one.[260]

Edwards' presentation ended with a review of Emma's and Burdell's behavior toward each other after the supposed marriage, showing a couple divided by the deepest enmity. Chambermaid Mary Donohue's averment that the couple never slept together after the alleged marriage, Burdell's plot to replace Emma with Catherine Stansbury as lessee of 31 Bond Street put into motion in a few days before his death, and the decedent's mid-January protestations to his colleague Dr. Cox *"that he had never been married, and meant never to be married,"* were all offered to Surrogate Bradford as hardly the sorts of circumstances from which one should conclude that a marriage had taken place. No rebuttal was offered, though, to Clinton's position that these words and behaviors were entirely understandable if the marriage was agreed to by Burdell as a means of settling valid and potentially damaging legal claims made by a woman whom he abhorred.

Counsel presented their concluding arguments to the Surrogate on June 30 and July 1, with Gilbert Dean having the final say. The hearing lasted through late Wednesday night as Dean pleaded with Surrogate Bradford to remove the stain of illegitimacy that continued to plague Emma and her children even after her acquittal on the murder charges. Woven into the final sentences of Dean's closing words, in strange juxtaposition to the florid legalese, was a hint of the bizarre turn of events about to take place. Clinton's co-counsel urged the court that if by some chance an unborn child sired by Harvey Burdell were delivered by his client, all concerned would have to admit to the bastard's rights. Dean insisted: if Emma were to give birth "all the dictates of humanity, and interests of society, as well as the presumptions of law,[would] unite in favor of the claims of that innocent child to a recognition by this court." [261] With a simple and perhaps unwitting pronouncement, Dean set the stage for a return engagement between Emma Cunningham and Oakey Hall. In this redux, Dean and his partner would play no part, though, and Hall would exact dramatic revenge for his ignominious defeat at the May murder trial.

* * *

Having expended every conceivable effort in his client's behalf, Henry Clinton took a much-needed rest in the countryside for the entire month of July, 1857, confident that his triumph in Emma's criminal defense would be repeated when Surrogate Bradford issued a decision in the estate case. Clinton's hopes were dashed to pieces, though, when he returned from upstate Sharon Springs on August 4. Bradford had not yet issued his opinion, but when Clinton opened his copy of the *New York Times* the following morning, he knew that all hope was lost. Emma Cunningham's defender stared with amazement at the front-page story. Once again, the top left-hand column banner shrieked his client's wickedness with a notice of her arrest for having tried to pass off a borrowed baby as the product of her final union with Harvey Burdell.

Never one to place all her eggs in one basket, Emma Cunningham quietly developed a strategy all her own during the months she was imprisoned in the Tombs. Henry Clinton and his co-counsel worked closely with the despondent widow in their efforts both to secure a criminal acquittal and to place her in the best possible position to inherit a sizable portion of Burdell's estate. Emma's confidence in the outcome had been less than total, though. In her desperation, the prisoner called for Dr. Samuel Catlin to visit her in the Tombs, letting him in on a secret that would have a tremendous impact on the distribution of her ex-lover's estate.

Dr. Catlin had served as Emma and George Cunningham's private physician during the later years of the couple's marriage and had attended George Cunningham at his deathbed. Catlin testified during the proceedings that led to Emma's murder acquittal without creating significant controversy, and though never suspected of wrongdoing during the previous months, the Brooklyn-based doctor was suddenly hauled into Jefferson Market Police Court when his patient was re-arrested on August 4. The public read with astonishment over the next several days of an elaborate sting operation that a gleeful Oakey Hall had conducted for the past four weeks. According to Dr. Catlin's affidavit filed with the fresh indictment, the physician had visited Emma in the Tombs about a dozen times before her acquittal on murder charges. Catlin gave a full accounting of being unwittingly drawn into

- **199** -

Emma's nefarious scheme: "Whilst in the prison she told me that she was with child. I have no recollection of any positive statement from her that she was with child by the late Harvey Burdell, but that was my inference from her conversations. . . Soon after her acquittal I noticed that her appearance corresponded to the fact of her statement. And thereafter I noticed she increased in size pretty regularly. Sometime in the month of June I was formally requested to become her medical accoucheur by herself, and I consented." Catlin's disingenuous patient informed him of the fortunate consequences of her condition in one of their last private interviews: "About this time, speaking of the child with which she was pregnant, she said that Judge Dean had told her if she had a child it would be heir to the property and she hoped it would live." [262]

While Gilbert Dean implored Surrogate Bradford to validate his client's wedlock with Harvey Burdell, Emma's imagined gestation took on a life of its own. In her desperate fight to reap the rewards she felt due her, Emma ended up playing directly into the hands of Oakey Hall as well as the Burdell heirs, even as Hall was being ridiculed throughout New York for his mishandling of the murder case. One doctor's opinion was not sufficient for Emma after she returned to 31 Bond Street a free woman on May 9. The delivery of such precious cargo might require more than one attending doctor. Emma's judgment was fatally flawed, though, in her selection of a consulting physician. Shortly after Gilbert Dean's July 2 courthouse disclosure of her "condition," she called for Dr. David Uhl to minister to her needs.

Under orders from Coroner Connery, and then Oakey Hall, Uhl had given medical care to Emma since Harvey Burdell's death, and had testified at his employers' request in all legal proceedings to date. David Uhl's bedside manners were undoubtedly genteel, for after three months' time, the usually suspicious Emma Cunningham let down her guard. After disclosing that she expected to deliver Dr. Burdell's child in August, Emma asked Dr. Uhl for help in supervising her pre-natal care. The results were disastrous. A simple gynecological examination confirmed Uhl's suspicions. Regardless of his personal feelings about his patient's morals, Uhl was not himself devoid of ethics, and the doctor sought legal advice from his personal attorney as to the proper course of action. Having been advised of his overriding responsibilities to the state, Dr. Uhl informed Oakey Hall in early July of his patient's strange somatic complaint. In his first interview with the prosecutor, Dr. Uhl was still reluctant to compromise Emma's confidences, but upon being cited the New York State penal code provisions concerning fraud, Uhl quickly relented, and promised his full cooperation in enforcement of the law.[263] With the chastened doctor's help, Oakey Hall designed a snare in which to trap the miscreant. Emma Cunningham escaped his grasp the first time, but revenge would now be his for the ridicule Hall suffered at Henry Clinton's hands during the murder trial. At the prosecutor's bidding, Uhl arranged a further interview with Emma during which she disclosed to him the true state of affairs as well as her motives. Emma offered Uhl $1,000 if he would undertake the job of producing a suitable infant upon the appointed day, and otherwise assist in its delivery.

Invention of a source for an infant that would not strain Emma's credulity was a simple task for Oakey Hall and his henchmen. Middle-class society in the eastern United States in the decade after the start of the gold rush was still filled with "California widows," women whose husbands had departed to make their fortunes on the West Coast in the aftermath of the Golconda. David Uhl was instructed by the district attorney to tell Emma about the impending availability of a newborn whose mother had been summoned west by her newly rich husband. Hall felt sure that Emma would buy the story: the donor would be said

Dr. David Uhl

Dr. Samuel Catlin

to be in a delicate predicament, as the *Times* put it: "ready to present her lord with a 'responsibility' for which, in law, he was not responsible." [264]

As for the baby, the indigent lying-in wards at Bellevue Hospital were a ready source of infants and needy mothers who could be pressed into service in the district attorney's masque. Several Hospital and City Almshouse officials as well as Oakey Hall's long-time personal physician, Dr. De La Montagnie, were enlisted to procure a suitable newborn.

Given the specification by her counsel in Surrogate's Court of the onset of Emma's condition, Dr. Uhl decided that August 3rd would be an optimal date for her pregnancy to come to fruition. Hall and his cohorts put themselves to the task of locating suitable lying-in rooms in which Emma could visit the indisposed California widow. Requisite furnishings for the staged deliveries, both real and fictional, were also needed. "Fitting apartments" were sought, according to Henry Clinton's personal recollections, "whereto might come the messenger of Mrs. Cunningham with a basket, and wherein (in the apartments, and not the basket) the mythical widow of California was to reside. Elm Street was found to be particularly full of 'apartments,' but there were none private enough except some in the house of Mr. *****, a lager beer gentleman of No. 190 Elm Street." [265]

No second-hand narrative could improve upon the tale of Emma's visit to Elm Street on the evening of August 3, as the story unfolded in the *Times'* reportage:

> . . .*Dr. De La Montagnie being unprovided with baggage, Mr. Hall lent him one of his wife's trunks, marked "K.L.H." which rendered necessary (lest suspicion being excited by the inmates, they might impart it to the bearer of the child when she should make her appearance, basket in hand) the taking of a name corresponding to the initials. The name selected was "Karl L. Herwig." It may here be remarked that the doctor from Dutchess County has a remarkably German appearance, and will do credit to the Saxon race anywhere. A card with that name upon it was given to the worthy host of No. 190 Elm Street, rooms were selected, and by twelve o'clock, noon, of Monday August 3rd, the first act of the drama of "My Little Adopted" was over.*
>
> *The denouement of this strange story now rapidly approaches.*
>
> *It was necessary to furnish the room in Elm Street, for it was probable that a messenger from Mrs. Cunningham might come to see it.*

Accordingly the District Attorney sent from his residence a cart of olla podrida furniture, the inventory of which is something like the following: One sofa-bedstead, one round table, one rocking chair, one roll of carpeting, five plain chairs, looking-glass, crockery, candle, matches, nursing-bottle, one trunk marked "K.L.H.," containing bedding and pillows, etc. It arrived, and was sent to the room a few minutes before Mrs. Cunningham, in person walked past to take a survey! She found it all satisfactory. Pending the despatch of the furniture, Dr. De La Montagnie proceeded to Bellevue in a coach, removed the child in its hospital clothes, accompanied by a nurse named Mary Regan for the occasion. The child – a female one – is the daughter of a poor woman in the hospital, named Mrs. Elizabeth Ann Anderson, and was born about ten or eleven o'clock last Saturday morning. Dr. De La Montagnie arrived at the house No. 190 Elm Street about half-past eight o'clock on Monday. In the meantime the furniture had been put in place, and a gentleman in the vicinity went to bed as the afflicted widow, in case Mrs. Cunningham's messenger insisted upon seeing the bona-fide lady. Thus all was arranged, including a basket belonging to Mr. Hall, with a neat pillow in it, ready for the conveyance of the petite enfant.[266]

Inspectors Speight, of the Twenty-first; Dilks, of the Fifteenth; and Hopkins, of the Third precincts, had been selected to take charge of the police arrangements; also patrolmen Walsh, S.J. Smith, and Wilson of the Fifteenth. Just after dusk on Monday evening the patrolmen were at the station-house. Inspector Hopkins was on the watch at the alley-way leading from the rear of 31 Bond Street into Bleecker Street. Inspector Speight stationed himself in Bond Street, to watch the outgoings and incomings. Insepctor Dilks selected the front of Burton's Theater [the east side of Mercer between Amity (now West Third) and Bleecker Streets] as his place of surveillance. Shortly afterwards Officer Walsh was sent to No. 190 Elm Street to watch, and Sergeant Smith brought to Burton's.

About nine o'clock Inspector Speight saw a female come out of the house No. 31 Bond Street, dressed in darkish clothes and a hood. She proceeded to the Bowery and got into a down-going car.[267] *Inspector Speight also got in. While there a friend came to him and said, "There is Mrs. Cunningham," pointing to the lady who had emerged from No. 31 Bond Street. The Inspector turned it off, and no more was said. At the corner of Broome and Marion streets, she got out. Mr. Speight tarried on the car half a block and then doubled and succeeded in seeing her enter No. 190 Elm Street.*

She soon came up-stairs and presented herself at the door. She contented herself with looking in the room merely. There were terrific moanings heard from the inside room, caused by the pain of the afflicted "paternal" mother, and the basket was delivered and taken out. So quick were her motions that Officer Walsh, in the obscurity, just missed her, but followed into the Bowery with Dr. Montagnie. The doctor came close to her, but could not see her face. He, however, distinctly recognized the basket as the one brought from Mr. Hall's house, and the one last seen in No. 190 Elm Street. She turned into Bond Street and re-entered 31 Bond Street, seen both by Dr. Montagnie and Inspector Speight and Patrolman Walsh, carrying the basket.

A messenger was observed to go to Dr. Uhl's house [listed in the indictment documents in the case as 41 East Twentieth Street] from No. 31 Bond Street about half-past nine o'clock on Monday evening in a great hurry. Patrolman Matthews, of the Twenty-First Precinct, had been sent to Brooklyn to watch Dr. Catlin (the physician, it will be remembered, who swore on the trial to Mrs. Cuningham's rheumatism). About half-past ten o'clock both physicians entered, and in due form Mrs. Cunningham was "brought to bed." A fictitious after-birth had been prepared and a large pailful of lamb's blood. The bloody sheets of Mrs. Cunningham's bed and the placenta, stowed away in the cupboard, completed this mock confinement, which had also been systematically accompanied by imaginary pains of labor.

Mrs. Cunningham, however, despite her illness, arose from her bed to partake of a delicate lunch, and then went back again. Dr. Uhl left first, and rejoining the police, informed them how the land lay. Soon after Dr. Catlin left, and was arrested by Patrolman Wilson as he was turning the corner of the Bowery, and taken to the station-house.

Inspector Dilks, accompanied by Dr. Montagnie as a physician, then went to No. 31, under and by virtue of that section of the Metropolitan Police Act which authorizes Inspectors at all hours of the day and night to enter any house wherein they have reason to believe a felony is being committed. They rang at the door, and were admitted. Objection being made to their going up,[268] Inspector Dilks courteously said he had been informed by a physician that there had been a birth of a child under curious circumstances, and it was his duty to inquire. They advanced upstairs, preceded by the "two ladies" – one being an aunt of Mrs. Cunningham and the other a nurse. The room in which Mrs. Cunningham was "confined" was the second-story front room – the same in which Dr. Burdell was laid out for his funeral, and which he occupied as a bedroom in his lifetime. The back room – where the murder was committed – had been newly papered and painted, and was set out for a lunch.

As Dr. Montagnie and Inspector Dilks were entering, one of the nurses said, "Here are some gentlemen who wish to come in." Instantly her *voice was heard saying, quickly, "Shut the door, don't let them come in here." But Dr. Montagnie and Mr. Dilks entered and made known their business. The child was found lying very sweetly asleep by her side, and was unmistakably the child taken from Bellevue and delivered to Mrs. Cunningham in Elm Street. It may here be stated that the child was marked with lunar caustic in the armpits, on each ear, and a new string, capable of being identified, tied about the navel.* [269] *On being examined, the string was also found, but of course, the lunar caustic marks will not be found visible for a day or two.*

The officers, with the District Attorney, now came up. Mr. Hall was apprehensive that, when discovered, Mrs. Cunningham might attempt to kill the child, and Inspector Dilks therefore immediately proceeded to take it away from her. She resisted, speaking of it as "her dear baby." "Don't touch my baby;" and, addressing Dr. Montagnie and others, said distinctly, "This is the child of Harvey Burdell."

Dr. Montagnie and Mr. Hall now leave No. 31 Bond Street, and taking the child with them, return it to its mother, Mrs. Elizabeth Ann Anderson, in Bellevue Hospital. The hospital clothes, which were found in Mrs. Cunningham's house, and which the child wore when removed form Elm Street, having been changed by Mrs. Cunningham for new and costly garments, its mother returns thanks for the exchange.

Yesterday [August 4] Mrs. Cunningham, Dr. Catlin, "accoucheur," and the midwife were arrested for the felony, under the statute of falsely pretending that Mrs. C. had given birth to a child who would be entitled to inherit the property of the late Harvey Burdell.

In a hearing before Police Justice William S. Davison of the Second District Police Court at Jefferson Market, Oakey Hall offered his affidavit of the circumstances, disingenuously portraying his enterprise with Dr. Uhl as a routine law-enforcement matter. Hall was well acquainted by now with Emma Cunningham and took precautions against any potential entrapment defense that his adversary might raise. Evidence was given by Drs. Uhl, De La Montagnie and Catlin, and by Inspectors Speight and Dilks. Sworn statements were submitted from Emma's sister, Ann Barnes, friends Catherine and George Wilt, Catherine's sister, Jane Bell, and Emma's daughters Helen and Margaret, who had all attended the new mother when she returned to 31 Bond Street, carrying her precious cargo in a fishmonger's basket. The testimony of a Fourth Avenue railroad car conductor, James

Carroll, was also heard by Justice Davison. Carroll had spied Emma riding downtown in his horse car on the evening in question. The evidence presented by these various witnesses in the indictment records was all substantially as reported in the *Times* article, minus certain colorful verbiage apparently not found fit to print.

Dr. Catlin had been summoned from his Brooklyn office by Emma's friend George Wilt between 7:00 and 8:00 P.M. on August 3, to attend to the indisposed mother. From Court Street it took Catlin not more than two hours to reach the Manhattan ferry, cross the East River, and make his way to 31 Bond Street. Upon examining the patient, Catlin determined that Emma had contracted *cholera morbus*, and gave her an emetic. After Emma vomited green bile, further inquiry led Catlin to conclude that she had not given birth, and that he had been tricked by his patient into participating in a fraudulent scheme.

At the end of preliminary hearings in his Sixth Avenue courtroom, Justice Davison traveled cross-town to 31 Bond Street to interrogate Emma Cunningham, who was held there under police guard once again. Emma refused to answer any except the most basic questions concerning her age, residence and occupation, stating that her main day-to-day business was "to attend to my family." Despite her reticence and general lack of cooperation, Justice Davison's statement in the indictment papers showed his charitable disposition: " [T]he unfortunate woman seemed greatly shattered, and excited to a considerable degree. The signature to the paper [Emma's sworn statement of her limited testimony] bears all the indications of having been penned by a person in a very debilitated condition . . ."

The gravity of Emma's alleged offense was soon made clear to the court. George D. Bulen, husband of Harvey Burdell's half-sister Alice Lamon, showed up at the Fifteenth Ward stationhouse in Mercer Street, and gave his affidavit as to the many lawful heirs of Harvey Burdell who would have suffered if Emma's trickery went undetected. Among them were Harvey's brothers Lewis, William, and James, the three surviving minor children of their late brother John; infant children of Allan McKee and Esther Lamon McKee (another half sister to Harvey); a half brother, Lester Lamon, and a half sister, Mary Ann Lamon Fields. Public Administrator Charles May presented himself to

Justice Davison on an earlier occasion, affirming that if the child in question was not Harvey Burdell's, then Harvey's siblings and their offspring would inherit his entire estate.

Once again, Emma Cunningham was transferred to the custody of warden John Gray at the Tombs, bail having been refused. Her removal from her rooms at 31 Bond Street occasioned great mirth, as neighbors and passersby once again witnessed the indecorous goings on at the house. When the police arrived, a crowd gathered quickly, and Emma's children were put to shame on their mother's account. This time around, there would be no hiding of the truth, according to the *Tribune's* account:

> *Her daughters Helen, Augusta and Georgiana were with her; and as soon as the subject of removing was broached, Augusta (the eldest) fainted, and was revived with some difficulty, only to suffer a relapse. A physician was sent for, but more than two hours passed before she was sufficiently recovered to bear her mother's removal. For some time past Miss Augusta has been afflicted with a nervous disorder, and is subject to fainting fits. Helen, the second daughter, bore the blow with great fortitude, and insisted on accompanying her mother, who still appears to be very ill and weak. Since the arrest of Mrs. Cunningham, her daughter Helen has been almost constantly with her, using every means in her power to alleviate her sufferings.*
>
> *Everything being arranged, a carriage drew up to the door, and a quantity of clothing and bedding was placed in it without unnecessary display. The door was thrown open and Mrs. Cunningham was brought out on a mattress by Inspector Dilks and Officer Smith and carefully placed on the back seat. She was dressed in black, and wore a thick veil over her face, and appeared to be entirely helpless. Her daughter Helen took a seat by her side. The officers next entered the carriage, drew the curtains, and the vehicle was driven down Broadway toward the Tombs.*

Due to the discretion that the police had exercised in arranging Emma's arrest, a mere forty people gathered outside to witness her departure, many of them servant girls employed by local residents. The predominantly Irish maids and cooks scarcely shied from expressing their dialect-laced opinions, according to the account of the paper's reporter: " 'There she goes, and may the divil go wid her' said a brawny Irish girl, with her sleeves rolled up, exposing her red arms. 'The divil will get his mate now, faith,' exclaimed another. 'She's a murtherin auld hag,' chimed in a third; and 'what a pity to make such a fuss over her,' said a fourth. The domestics of the vicinity . . . were in high glee, and some considerable time elapsed before they left the sidewalks and returned to their household duties." [270]

It took her counsel several motions and three weeks before Emma was finally freed from prison. Judge Charles Peabody of the New York Supreme Court permitted the defendant to be bailed on September 10, basing his decision upon the absence of a crucial element from the criminal case proffered by district attorney Hall. Emma had not attempted as of yet to claim the estate for her baby in any official proceeding, and thus, in the judge's opinion, she could not be charged with attempted fraud. Emma's successful bail application was, for all practical intents and purposes, the end of her prosecution. Notwithstanding Judge Peabody's decision, Oakey Hall obtained a grand jury indictment of Emma on the fraud charges on the very same day that she made bail, but the case was not brought to trial. After being removed to the Court of Oyer and Terminer and then to Supreme Court, the prosecution was abandoned.

Oakey Hall may have been defeated twice by Emma Cunningham, but what the angry and frustrated politician failed to accomplish, Surrogate Bradford achieved. While the legal wrangling proceeded in the bogus baby case, and Emma once again sat behind the Tombs' bars, the Surrogate issued his decision late in August. Once again the final result was much as expected. When oral arguments ended in Surrogate's Court on July 2, Henry Clinton had been convinced that his client's marriage would be declared enforceable, just as he had been confident of her acquittal on the murder charges some eight weeks prior. Surrogate Bradford seemed suitably impressed with the evidence supporting Emma's claim. The bogus baby ploy turned the tables completely, though, and when the Surrogate issued his ruling on August 24, no one was surprised. Although no explicit mention was made in the text of the opinion of the as yet unproven fraud charges, Bradford's subtext was clear: a woman who could concoct a scheme to produce a false heir could and probably did fake her marriage to the infant's supposed father. Standing on what had been the brink of victory, the desperate litigant fell in mortal defeat: Emma's marriage to Harvey Burdell was declared non-existent, and her rights to any share in his estate were totally foreclosed. Never popular among many New Yorkers, Emma Cunningham fell victim to mass ridicule. Four decades later, Henry Clinton recalled sadly a case that, in his view, attracted more public attention than any in the City's history: "The public career of Mrs. Cunningham-Burdell began with the most startling and thrilling tragedy; it ended in thoroughly disgusting low comedy." [271]

*   *   *

From the mid-winter discovery of Harvey Burdell's lacerated corpse until Emma's second arrest at the end of the summer, the attention paid by the popular media to the Burdell-Cunningham affair throughout the United States was enormous. In addition to extensive newspaper coverage in cities and towns across America, popular magazines such as *Harper's Weekly* and *Leslie's Illustrated* provided the hungry public with a steady diet of lurid details. Cheap pamphlets, mass-produced engravings, ministers' sermons and endless political rhetoric devolved from the case that had enthralled America throughout the year. Although public fascination with Emma Cunningham abated somewhat after her acquittal of the homicide charges, the press continued to cover her fight to control and inherit her ex-lover's estate. Though the outcome of the murder trial lessened the number of idlers peering through the windows of 31 Bond Street in the early summer months, the August 4 discovery of Emma's outlandish scheme to take control of her deceased lover's wealth rekindled immense popular interest in the matter as the media jumped to publicize the "Bogus Burdell Baby" scandal.

Emma Cunningham's smirking visage shone out from an engraving on the cover of a pamphlet rushed to publication as soon as the taking of evidence was completed in Police Court. Headlines billowed around the evildoer's image, adapted from a daguerreotype by the popular Wilton studio:

FICTITIOUS HEIRESS OF DR. BURDELL.
CONFESSIONS OF THE ACCOUCHER
BOLD GAME OF MRS. CUNNINGHAM

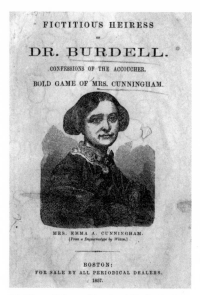

Fictitious Heiress of Dr. Burdell, Confessions of the Accoucher, Bold Game of Mrs. Cunningham; pamphlet, (published in Boston: 1857)

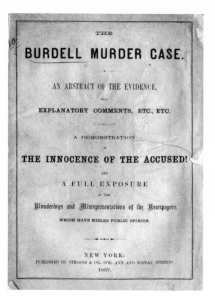

The Burdell Murder Case, an abstract of the evidence…; newsstand pamphlet (published by Stearns & Co., NY: 1857)

blared the cover page of the pamphlet, published in Boston and distributed "FOR SALE BY ALL PERIODICAL DEALERS". Its rough newsprint pages were crammed with finely printed narrative as well as a mass of affidavits and testimony offered when Oakey Hall obtained Emma's indictment on a second set of felony charges. The millstone of public opinion, so skillfully turned by Henry Clinton during the murder trial, reversed direction after news of her desperate maneuver in Elm Street became known. The popular press descended like jackals once again, and the belittling of Emma and her cause spread through the channels available to the mass of illiterate New Yorkers as well as their more educated neighbors.

Included among the many parodied embodiments of the bogus baby story was one of the most popular live-performance genres of mid-nineteenth century America: music hall presentations of blackface minstrelsy. Caucasian performers donned costumes and make-up to ridicule African-American stereotypes in what would be viewed today as virulently racist dialogue and song. A well-known and oft-performed favorite among the performers who smeared their faces with charred cork was "Villikins and His Dinah." The tune, borrowed from "Sweet Betsy From Pike", was also employed in numerous take-offs on Emma Cunningham's errant behavior, among them a song entitled "The Bellevue Baby – Mrs. Cunningham's Adopted," attributed to the pen-named "Saugerties Bard." [272] Dinah's tale of innocence seduced and wealth squandered at New York's famous Crystal Palace exhibition of 1854 was sung under the Villikins title, and three years later, the piece was converted from a minstrel stage hit to the purposes of Emma's detractors. Late-summer beer garden and music-hall offerings in 1857 also included adaptations of several folk songs such as "The Fine Old English Gentleman" altered by the pseudonymous songwriter "Brickbat" to be "Mrs. Cunningham's Darling Babby," Another waggish lyricist created "The Cunningham Baby. Or the Heir from Over Jordan." From the Battery to the Bowery, saloons and opera houses rang with mockery of this most immoral of mothers, one who violated

The Cunningham Baby. Or the Heir from Over Jordan

Mrs. Cunningham's Darling Babby [sic] Air— Fine Old English Gentleman or The Cork Leg, by Brickbat; song sheet, 1857

all notions of chastity and true womanhood in order to line her pockets and those of her children.

Classified advertisements in The New York *Herald* during the months of August and September, 1857 announced the blatant advantage taken of the situation by the greatest of the contemporary media-moguls. Readers of handbills plastered on P.T. Barnum's multi-canopied, flag-bedecked American Museum at Broadway and Ann Street told their friends of the amazing current offering: "BARNUM'S AMERICAN MUSEUM – THE VERY LAST chance to gaze on the Bogus . . . Admittance 25 cents; children under ten, 12 cents."

After a career in journalism in Bethel and Danbury, Connecticut, America's legendary showman had moved to New York and began his urban career. His commercial success with such hoaxes as "The Feegee Mermaid" and 161-year-old "Joice Heth – George Washington's nurse" was followed by even greater fame and fortune as the promoter of Jenny Lind's sold-out concert appearances in the United States, and the discovery of General Tom Thumb. Barnum operated his first incarnation of the American Museum at 222 Broadway for fifteen years before Burdell was murdered. The museum originated early in the nineteenth century in rooms in City Hall as a collection sponsored by the Tammany Society, and was later operated by a series of private individuals. In 1830 a permanent home for the museum was erected on Broadway at the Ann Street building, and its operations were sold to Barnum in 1842. [273]

Always interested in natural history, whether in living or mummified state, Barnum invested significant funds in the enlargement and physical upgrading of the Ann Street structure. Appalled by the drunkenness he witnessed in many entertainment venues, and wishing to increase attendance by families as well as temperate single individuals, the master promoter prohibited alcoholic beverages on the premises. Thousands of wonders of the ancient and contemporary worlds, be they animal, vegetable or mineral, were displayed in numerous salons to the curious public, along with concessionaires in indoor arcades offering a multitude of astrological services and astounding sleight-of-hand performances. By 1857, Barnum had installed the first large-scale aquarium viewable by the general public.

With the public imagination re-kindled by Emma Cunningham's desperate travails, Barnum smelled easy money. Always eager for new performance material that would attract large New York City area audiences, the inveterate showman contacted the bogus baby's impoverished natural mother and offered to solve her immediate money problems. Elizabeth Ann Anderson and her infant daughter appeared for many weeks in Barnum's gigantic lecture and concert hall in the Ann Street complex, alongside a wax figurine of the little girl's notorious would-be mother. The curious public trooped through the auditorium daily at no additional charge above the basic museum entrance fee, and gazed upon a *tableaux vivant* of impoverished debasement and immoral womanhood.[274] By early fall, though, interest in the many-months long spectacle had subsided. As the estate litigation dragged on among Burdell's blood relatives and his creditors, and more pressing events overwhelmed the public's attention, Emma Cunningham and her children dropped from the pages of the press, with only occasional sightings being mentioned over the next few years.

EPILOGUE

WITH THE BOGUS BABY excitement finally exhausted, Emma Cunningham's notoriety died down, and the popular press as well as law enforcement officials virtually abandoned their efforts to identify a convictable murder suspect in Burdell's death. Urgent personal concerns were distracting all New Yorkers: by October 1857, financial panic gripped the nation. The wave of gold-fever and speculative railroad construction sweeping over the country through the decade ended with the failure of hundreds of banks and insurance companies. Thousands of other large and small-scale enterprises followed suit. New York's Wall Street was the epicenter of the crisis, and massive unemployment spread rapidly throughout the city. On August 24, the New York branch of the Ohio Life Insurance and Trust Company closed its doors, setting off a chain reaction among financial institutions across America. Over the next thirty days, runs on New York banks reduced their specie reserves by almost 20 per cent, and some of the largest and most trusted houses of commerce failed in every American city. Autumn's economic devastation started on the very same day that Surrogate Bradford ruled against Emma Cunningham's claim to Harvey Burdell's fortune.

Chief among the causes of the Panic of 1857 was the collapse in value of hundreds of railroad companies established during the previous fifteen years. As with both earlier and later cycles of boom and bust, investors flocked to purchase securities issued by technological and communications innovators of the day. Many of these enterprises had never produced a dime of profits before they tapped public capital markets, nor would they ever. Speculation in railroad stocks and bonds and the paper floated by issuers in telegraphy and related industries, together with the sponsors' defalcation with offering proceeds for their personal use ran rampant. Institutions such as Ohio Life eagerly participated in the inflationary bubble by lending funds to stock market plungers, who were then wiped out quickly during the deflation that set in during the fall.[275]

The Panic of 1857 created havoc among all strata of society. Unemployment grew exponentially, and the concomitant lowering of working class wages led to a significant reduction in immigration during 1858. Less than forty days after the Ohio Life Company's failure, the *Tribune* predicted an avalanche of doom: "There is manifestly a hard Winter in prospect for our Laboring Class —for those who are usually workers for wages. Tens of thousands of them will not be able to find employment, while others will be forced to work in some vocation in which they will earn very little, and will probably receive even less . . . Of course, this involves a very large aggregate of individual privation and suffering."[276] Subsequent articles chronicled the woeful circumstances of laborers across the nation who flocked to New York seeking employment when local conditions became desperate. The paper pleaded with the itinerant unfortunates to stay away from the city so as not to exacerbate New York's plight, and bemoaned the disruption of staple prices caused by the failure of transportation systems.[277]

Poverty spread throughout the city that fall and winter, and even Mayor Fernando Wood joined the innumerable unfortunates. Despite commandeering a significant proportion of the votes in December's annual mayoral election, Wood was defeated by Daniel Tiemann. The new mayor's backers included many Republican stalwarts as well as the nativist Democrats led by Boss Tweed and middle-class Democratic merchants. Wood fell from power by year's end, just as Emma Cunningham slipped from public view.

Rotogravure impressions of Emma's face had become known across America earlier that year, and through the fall and winter, journalists gave the public sporadic notice of her whereabouts. Over the summer, Emma liquidated property she had held since her first husband's death. The burden of normal living expenses and the pressure of unpaid legal fees forced her to sustain a $2,000 loss when Emma sold a lot on West Forty-sixth Street in late August to a friend who had offered to bail her out of the Tombs while the bogus baby case was still pending. Even Emma's former cook, Hannah Conlan, suffered as a result of her employer's misfortune. Conlan had to bring suit for $35 against Emma Cunningham, representing five months of back wages. Judgment was rendered in Conlan's favor for 60% of the amount claimed.[278]

Emma and her children were evicted from 31 Bond Street as a result of Surrogate Bradford's ruling extinguishing her claims to Harvey Burdell's property. With her finances and reputation in ruins, Emma headed west. The relative anonymity still afforded many newcomers in many American communities and in post-Gold Rush California might allow the disgraced miscreant to assume a new identity. With luck, Emma might struggle out from under the notoriety that doomed her to poverty and worse if she stayed in New York. *Harper's Weekly* printed several reported sightings of the infamous mother and several of her children during the twenty months after her release from custody in the bogus baby case. The first found Emma residing in Ohio: "[June 19, 1858] The Cleveland (Ohio) Plaindealer says that Mrs. Cunningham Burdell has purchased a farm in Carroll County, about four miles from Carrollton, and about seventy miles from that city. She bought the farm from the heirs of the late Samuel Sears, paying $5000 down for it, and we understand that she will take immediate possession." [279]

By the Christmas season of the same year, though, *Harper's* reported Emma as having returned to New York City, residing in inexplicably comfortable circumstances: "[December 25, 1858] A correspondent of the Rochester Union writes from New York that "Mrs. Cunningham, of Burdell murder notoriety, and her two daughters are living in an elegant mansion in Twenty-third Street, and apparently in easy circumstances. They give parties occasionally, and the 'head of the family' it is said was visible at the Opera the other evening. Augusta was married recently, to a young Southern Planter, and Helen, it is understood, is in a fair way to follow the example." [280]

With her elder daughter safely married off, Emma Cunningham could devote her energy to finishing Helen's education and admission into polite society. *Harper's* item the following spring informed its readers of the resourceful widow's progress: "[April 9, 1859, in the column entitled "Domestic Intelligence"] : 'Mrs. Cunningham of Burdell notoriety' says the Greensburg Herald of the 16th ult. 'was in Blairsville, Pennsylvania a few days since. She was seeking to place her daughter in charge of the principal of the Female Seminary. Several gentlemen, who had seen her during the excitement in her case in New York, recognized her; she became aware of it and soon decamped. She dresses well, travels in a fine equipage, and has a gentleman who accompanies her as her agent.'"[281]

As with similar notorious events, journalists remained watchful for opportunities to cater to the public's durable fascination with the Burdell-Cunningham saga. From the outset of the murder inquest, and for months thereafter, letters published in the New York papers from eccentric publicity seekers contained fantastic accounts of newly discovered evidence and witnesses implicating new suspects in the crime. Emma's attorney, Henry Clinton, recalled in his memoirs several instances of questionable confessions to the murder made after Emma's acquittal, all from individuals seeking the dubious fame.

One such confession, though, had the ring of truth, and became the cover story of *The National Police Gazette* in one of its 1863 issues. Word reached the *Gazette*'s correspondent that a credible confessor to Harvey Burdell's murder had made a clean breast of his crime in a death-house scene in New Jersey's Mercer County Penitentiary early in April of that year. Local newspapers were filled in March, 1863 with coverage of the impending execution of violent career criminal George W. Symonds for the cold-blooded murder of a Princeton jeweler during the previous November. The swarthy, large-boned convict was said to have employed many aliases throughout his adult life. Two issues of the enormously popular *National Police Gazette* were devoted to Symonds' purported confession to the Burdell homicide.[282]

The first of the two *Gazette* articles, entitled "THE PRINCETON MURDER. THE BURDELL MYSTERY UNRAVELLED" chronicled the New Jersey murder trial up to the point of Symonds' execution. The second installment, reported under the by-line of "Peter Thomson, Official Reporter of Special Sessions" recounted Symonds' thirty-year career of rape, arson, larceny, robbery and murder in the northeast, and informed the public of the death-house confession of "The

Burdell Murderer." Thomson's biography of the convict portrayed a violent and thoroughly depraved sociopath who could well have done Burdell in. The Bond Street dentist had reportedly encountered dozens of similar men, both in his dental operatory as well as across baize-covered faro tabletops in downtown casinos, but other contemporary journalism corroborated the rumors of Symonds' complicity in Burdell's demise.[283]

George Symonds' intermittent residence in New York City spanned two decades in which Harvey Burdell reached the peak of his notoriety in both the dentistry profession and the demi-monde of the Broadway Entertainment District. Born in approximately 1818, either in Templeton, Massachusetts, or Portsmouth, New Hampshire, Symonds made his way to Roxbury, Massachusetts in the late 1830s where he found work as a baker.[284] The young man showed signs of grotesque maladjustment, even as a youth, according to the *Gazette*'s reporter, who traced the misfit's path from his Roxbury apprenticeship to Boston, and then on to New York City. Beginning with his misdeeds at a small-town Massachusetts bakery, it was evident to the reporter that no good would come by George Symonds' hands:

> [E]ven then the outlines of his future are traceable, as his master seemed to be under his control, for during the greater part of his apprenticeship he was engaged in driving the wagon and distributing the bread. The employer was fearful of the apprentice; the man quaked in the presence of the boy. If offended at a trifle he would as it were accidentally spoil a batch of bread, or mix some substance with the flour that would affect the customers seriously but not dangerously. It was an innate part of his devilish nature in the early part of his life, not to kill, but to sit, Iago like, aside in the shade, and witness the lingering tortures and writhings of his victims. . . .He was caught attempting to set fire to the bakery of his employer, the motive for which was a simple reprimand for having abused a child of tender years. For this offence – his first attempted case of arson – he was forced to flee for safety to Boston.
>
> Of his doings in that city at that time we know very little, but we can safely say that he had then for twin companions Poverty and Crime.
>
> Leaving Boston, which did not afford him a wide enough field for his criminal operation, he made his FIRST APPEARANCE IN NEW YORK in the spring of 1842.

Symonds' criminal enterprises in New York became more sophisticated when he met a Portsmouth, N.H. acquaintance in Union Square Park. The pair opened a bakery at 187 Canal Street, and promptly devoted it to heinous purposes. In a scheme repeated twice at the Canal Street shop and again at a new store on Broome Street, Symonds employed defenseless widows and impoverished young women as shop clerks, whom he would tempt with talk of shop management and marriage in order to gain sexual favors. Frustrated by their rebuffs, Symonds turned to force, and ended up arrested for attempted rape on more than

National Police Gazette cover "Burdell Mystery Unraveled"

one occasion. When he failed to win the attentions of a young widow living behind the Broome Street store, the vicious felon became enraged, and the object of his desire and her child barely escaped with their lives when Symonds put a torch to the building. The supposed baker opened his last store in New York at 30 Sixth Avenue, just north of Canal Street, but it was shuttered after only one month. The landlady threw Symonds out after unspecified misdeeds occurred.[285]

After being evicted from the Sixth Avenue bakeshop, Symonds turned to other handicrafts, developing skills at forgery and counterfeiting currency and lottery tickets. The itinerant hired a series of rooms into which he lured robbery victims on various pretexts; he also took advantage of the opportunities for larceny afforded by setting small fires in downtown hotels and creating chaos in the corridors and guest suites. After being arrested in 1844 for cracking open guests' trunks at Lovejoy's Hotel, Symonds faced felony charges and possible lengthy imprisonment. He had recently married a seventeen-year-old New York woman, and due to the respectability of her family, the proprietor of the Park Row establishment declined to press charges. When the prisoner was freed, he and his young wife, Eliza, fled back to Boston. Honest employment eluded the pair there also, though, and in February 1845, Symonds was sentenced to the Boston House of Correction on three counts of larceny committed with Eliza's assistance during the previous month. The prisoner escaped in April 1845, but was caught almost immediately. His sentence was then extended until May 1850, with much of it served at hard labor after he was remanded to Charlestown State Prison. [286]

Eliza Jane Symonds, though named as a co-conspirator in the Boston court's sentencing of her husband, was not incarcerated. According to the *Gazette*, the young bride, already mother of an infant, was the victim of a ruse that her husband attempted to perpetrate on the court, seeking mercy for himself. The *Gazette*'s reporter related how, in a scheme worthy of Dr. Harvey Burdell, Symonds disowned his wife in open court, claiming that she was only his mistress, and then pleaded to the judge that her elaborate life-style demands had forced him into a life of crime. Symonds also had Eliza arrested for seduction, but a kindly court officer doubted Symonds' word. The intervenor wrote to the pastor in New York City who had married the couple and obtained a copy of their marriage certificate, thus putting an end to the defendant's trickery. After her husband's conviction and incarceration, Eliza Jane Symonds fled Boston for the comparative safety of hometown New York.

The *Gazette* also enlightened its readers as to why George Symonds wanted Harvey Burdell dead: While her husband was at hard labor in a Boston prison, Eliza Symonds found her way to Harvey Burdell's dentistry office in 1846 or 1847 and became a steady client in his practice, also making the acquaintance of Harvey's nephew and competitor, Galen Burdell. A romance may have occurred between Eliza and Galen, and according to the *Police Gazette*, George Symonds got wind of the affair, confusing Harvey with his nephew as the presumed adulterer.

Symonds returned to New York City embittered after his 1850 discharge from the Charlestown jail, and after an encounter with a mutual acquaintance in a Park Row saloon, managed to locate his wife. At first resisting his attempts at reconciliation, Eliza finally agreed to rejoin her husband if he could complete a six-month trial period of honest employment. A supposedly penitent George Symonds left the city by steamboat alone, debarking from his Hudson River voyage at Kingston, New York, where he found work in a bakery. The newcomer took up attendance at Sunday prayer meetings with his employer, Mr. Gillet, and through him made the acquaintance of a single woman toward whom Symonds made marital advances. Only the suspicious baker Gillet's opening of a letter from Eliza to George interrupted this next spoliation; Symonds departed Kingston forthwith, but not without first ruining two batches of bread, breaking open several trunks in his master's premises and stealing enough money from Gillet and the household servants to carry him to Albany. After robbing an upstate hotel and staying away from New York City for three more months, Symonds returned to Eliza, convincing her that his stay with Gillet was a successful one. Displaying a bankroll of supposed savings from his wages, George convinced Eliza to cut short the probationary period, and she departed with him from New York via steamboat for what she thought was a trip back to Kingston and her spouse's continued employment there.

Symonds kept his wife on board the ship all the way to Troy, New York, though, and after docking at night and taking rooms at the Congress Hotel, she discovered the ruse. Her protests were to no avail; at gunpoint, Symonds insisted that Eliza stay with him as he took the next steps in his upstate career. With Eliza in tow, Symonds set out on a tour of Lansingburgh and Troy, where he seduced, fleeced and robbed employers, neighbors, and the general public. The couple arrived in nearby Hudson, New York in June, 1852, where Symonds found employment in a Warren Street bakery.[287] Once again, though, baking did not occupy Symonds for long; after getting the lay of the land, he began a spree of larceny and burglary that yielded copious results. The successful thief soon found himself with nowhere to store his loot pending its liquidation. The *Gazette* reported his solution to this problem: "Just about this time [late spring 1852] the lady who kept the Franklin House [a Hudson hostelry], becoming tired of keeping the hotel, advertised her lease of the house for sale. This was an opening for Symonds; he bought the lease and a portion of the fixtures of the house, such as bedsteads and chairs, and other articles that he could not very well steal; but everything else that he could possible obtain by robbery to furnish the house was refused by him."

The *Gazette* also took note of Symonds' ingenuity while relating the sordid tale: the parsimonious thief manufactured bed-sheets from a roll of stolen cloth, and carpeted the premises with a rug from a church that had been left outside to be cleaned.[288]

The story continued with Symonds, ensconced as operating lessee of the Franklin House, engaging in a rampage, robbing the henhouses, stores, dwellings and yards of the surrounding neighborhood. The thrifty hotelier then served up the edible spoils to his "guests" at the Franklin House. This rampage, including the robbery of a gentleman described by the *Gazette's* writer as a "Jew Peddler" at the hotel led to a concerted plea by the citizenry of Hudson to the Chief of Police in New York City for assistance in ferreting out what they believed to be an entire gang of marauders in their midst. Matters became desperate for Symonds with this outcry; his wife Eliza was so frightened that she slept every night with a bowie knife close by her side. After George attempted to rape one of the household domestics, the victim drove a carving fork through her master's right hand, thus assuring his future inclination toward left-handedness.[289] Eliza then left her husband for good, and in December, 1852, Symonds set fire to the Franklin House.

The hue and cry raised by Hudson's terrorized citizens caused their Mayor, George H. Power, to commence an investigation that led to Symonds' mid-January indictment on charges of arson, burglary and grand larceny. The state could not produce enough admissible evidence to support conviction, however, and after an unsuccessful change of venue to Troy (where the Hudson authorities had hoped additional charges based on occurrences in the neighboring city could be prosecuted successfully), Symonds was returned to Hudson and convicted on a charge of petit larceny. He was sentenced to a six-month term in the Albany Penitentiary.[290]

The second of the *Gazette's* articles reported Symonds' return to New York City after being released again from jail in the fall of 1854: "Symonds is not again seen in New York until some months before the murder of Dr. Burdell. He was then, as has been previously stated, a frequent visitor at the house of Dr. Burdell, as was also his wife, although he did not know it – she to get her teeth fixed, and he to see Mrs. Cunningham. After swindling the English lady at the hotel on Union Square he left her and that hotel, and removed to the Bancroft House in Broadway, kept by two ladies, sisters.[291] There he registered his name as "Paul, from Babylon." In the summer of 1857, after the Burdell murder, he left New York . . ."

The peripatetic felon's stay at the Bancroft House provided one more piece of circumstantial evidence of his supposed acquaintance with Emma Cunningham's would be husband: Harvey Burdell's brother William Burdell and his niece Dimis Hubbard resided in the Bancroft House during the later part of 1856 and January, 1857.[292] The *Gazette* article made no further mention, however, of another lodging on New York City's Wooster Street occupied by Symonds in January, 1857, that played a critical role in his avoiding indictment for Burdell's murder, and little further condemnatory evidence of Symonds' association with Harvey Burdell was furnished. The story focused instead on the miserable scene before the convict's execution in Trenton, when a woman claiming to be Symonds' wife Eliza appeared one evening at the Mercer County Penitentiary shortly before his trip the gallows, and implored the condemned man to make some provision for their young daughter. The prisoner refused to recognize his visitor, and Eliza was led away empty-handed.

Harvey Burdell's unsolved murder remained in the public consciousness for decades after Emma Cunningham's acquittal and Symonds' execution, but it was not until twenty-seven years after the *National Police Gazette*'s stories were published that another article was appeared in the *New York Herald* pinning the crime on George Symonds. Suddenly, and for no apparent reason, a lengthy, illustrated history of the Burdell murder and Symonds' gruesome biography was printed by the paper in late June 1890, above the byline of Miller Hageman. The reporter's familiarity with the case and Symonds' career were obtained first hand: during his youth, Hageman's father, John Freylinghausen Hageman, acted as chief prosecutor in sending Symonds to the gallows.[293] Through "facts verified by more than fifty witnesses," Hageman *fils* claimed to have solved the case, exposing the dereliction of the police and prosecutors in 1857 in an article captioned "The One Suspect Who Disappeared During the Long Examination" [294]

Much of the same information from the *National Police Gazette's* coverage decades earlier was interwoven with a recapitulation of Burdell's murder and what the reporter claimed was Emma Cunningham's entrapment in a chain of legal proceedings stretching from the Coroner's inquest through the bogus baby fiasco. Proclaiming the imperative of retributive justice, Hageman then lauded his own detective powers:

> *There is an old fabled Avenger that sits with sleepless eyes by the shore of the Dead Sea of Oblivion and rakes with its long, bony fingers the tangled seaweeds of mystery and the shells of echoing secrets, breathing in their sleep.*
>
> *Retributive truth has relentlessly dragged to light at last after long years a ghastly handful of such a swelter of horrors.*
>
> *The facts contained in this story of a fearful crime constitute from first to last an unbroken chain of evidence, which, although woven about a man after the lapse of thirty-two years, would be considered sufficiently strong to convict any criminal on a like charge.*

Once again, the alleged left-handedness of Burdell's assailant was connected to the accused, except that in this version of the story, Symonds' right hand was said to have been mangled in an accident in the Roxbury, Massachusetts bakery where he found employment as a young adult. The *Herald's* reporter left no room for doubt about Symonds' antisocial and even psychopathic disposition from birth onwards: "This child seemed to have been begotten with certain vicious tendencies. They developed early. He was fond of inflicting cruelty upon living beings. He had a country school education. He neglected his opportunities and shirked study. He grew up while yet a young man to be a monstrous size, being known to all about that section of the country as the 'boy giant.'"

A critical circumstantial connection between the confessor and the Burdell case was introduced by Hageman when he told why Symonds, although initially identified as a suspect by the police, was never arrested. George Symonds was said to have lodged in a brothel at 105 Wooster Street under the name of Lewis Lefferts in the days prior to Burdell's death, and the house was reported to have been *"frequented by persons of influence who would not allow a scandal to grow inside its walls."* [295]

The article claimed that the New York City police briefly sought Symonds/Lefferts for questioning immediately after Burdell's body was discovered, and that Symonds was reputed to have lost a large sum of money to Burdell in a gambling game on the night of the homicide, which he recovered from the decedent by resorting to lethal force. Hageman implied that Mayor Wood's police abandoned their search for Symonds because of the potential embarrassment he could cause through his familiarity with the patrons of his Wooster Street lodging house.

No notice was taken, though, by the reporter of another bizarre connection between Symonds and the Burdell matter. One of the twelve members of the coroner's jury was named Lewis T. Lefferts, residing at 105 Wooster Street. Symonds adopted the man's name as one of his aliases. [296]

Yet another newspaper article purporting to solve the Burdell crime appeared seven years after the *Herald*'s 1890 feature story. On August 1, 1897, the front page story in Sunday's edition of the usually stodgy *New York Times* blared: "Burdell Murder Cleared – Mrs. Cunningham Confessed the Crime-She and Eckel Were Guilty." An individual named William Woods provided the information to the *Times*, repeating a supposed confession made in 1860 by Emma to Woods' grandmother, Mrs. James D. Fowler, whose husband was a one-time dentistry partner of Burdell's. Dr. Fowler had disappeared after a single year of business with Burdell, deserting his family, and ultimately immigrating to France. Fowler's death in 1896 led to litigation over his sizeable estate and the resultant disclosure of his relations with Harvey Burdell, as well as his first wife having acted as confidante to Emma Cunningham. The *Times* offered few other details of the supposed confession despite its bold assertion that the crime had been solved once and for all. Emma and John Eckel were pronounced guilty as originally charged in lurid headlines: "The Woman Strangled Their Victim While the Man Stabbed Him to Death." [297]

Although John Eckel was released from police custody shortly after Emma's acquittal, the district attorney did not file a writ of *nole prosequi* abandoning prosecution of the case for many months. As a free man, Eckel returned to his tallow and hide business, operating a dealership on Stanton Street and Fourth Avenue in lower Manhattan, as well as a bone-boiling and fat-rendering shop in the abattoir district in First Avenue near Forty-fifth Street.[298] Eckel's troubles with the law did not end, however, after his involvement with Emma Cunningham came to a halt. The creation of the Metropolitan Sanitary Commission by the Republican-dominated Albany legislature in response to Tammany Hall's laxity in the promotion of municipal health measures spelled trouble for John Eckel. In 1867, the commission attempted to close down Eckel's East Forty-fifth Street facility due to its rampant violation of public health regulations. [299]

John Eckel was not alone among those of Harvey Burdell's friends who profited from their acquaintance with the well-known dentist, even after his death. In one of the stranger twists to the story, Burdell's colleague Alvah Blaisdell admitted John Eckel into Blaisdell's wholesale liquor business during 1860s. Though reportedly worth $300,000 at the inception of the partnership, Eckel was apparently not satisfied with trying to make an honest profit from the venture. In early 1869, Blaisdell and Eckel were convicted in Federal court of evading whiskey taxes in a scheme connected to officials in the corrupt Ulysses S. Grant presidential administration. The partners were sentenced to several years in prison. Eckel died in the Albany Penitentiary in late 1869, leaving a son in Brooklyn whose mother's identity could not be ascertained by the press.[300]

"Elegant" Oakey Hall's career in the Tammany machine was not harmed in the long run by his defeat in the Burdell murder trial, but his final run-in with Henry Lauren Clinton certainly proved disastrous for the sartorially splendid politician. William Marcy "Boss" Tweed had exercised significant control over municipal affairs in New York even during Fernando Wood's mid-century mayoralty, and by the end of the 1860s, Tweed, though holding no elective office, ruled New York City through his designated officials, including Mayor A. Oakey Hall. With the onset of the bribery indictments of the Tweed Ring, Mayor Hall faced Clinton once again late in February, 1872. This time, though, Hall was not seated in front of the judge's bench at the district attorney's table. Instead, a place was reserved for him in the prisoner's dock.

Henry Lauren Clinton capped a decades-long civic career as special prosecutor in the municipal bribery trials that Thomas Nast sketched for the world to enjoy. After three trials, Oakey Hall was finally acquitted of all charges on Christmas Eve, 1873, but his career had been destroyed. Twenty-five years of ignominy would pass before his death in 1898, one widely reported in the press. Today, a grandiose mausoleum silently greets visitors as they enter the gates of Trinity Church's uptown cemetery on 155th Street west of Broadway. Simple block letters memorialize the name of Clinton's arch-enemy on the copper-knobbed door of Hall's final resting place.[301]

Once Surrogate Bradford rejected Emma Hempstead Cunningham's claim to Harvey Burdell's estate, supervision of the estate passed to Harvey's brother, William Burdell. To secure the mandatory administrator's bond that he filed in Surrogate's Court, William mortgaged his pending inheritance of a one-eighth interest in the decedent's properties at 2 and 31 Bond Street. Although the murder victim's personal property was long disposed of by the fall of 1857, liquidation of Harvey Burdell's real estate consumed years, complicated by the foreclosure of a $20,000 mortgage he placed on 2 Bond Street in 1856, as well as the claims of many smaller lienors. More than twenty individual blood relatives of Harvey Burdell were named in the foreclosure maintained by The New York Life Insurance and Trust Company, which itself was named a defendant in a suit for partition of the estate's real property brought by Harvey's half-sister Alice Lamon Bulen and her husband George.

Charges and counter-charges were traded in the estate proceedings among the relatives as several sought reimbursement for legal fees incurred to defeat Emma Cunningham's marriage claim in Surrogate's Court. Creditors of the deceased (both family members and others) stepped forward to collect debts, some many years old. The Bulens' partition case lingered in court for years. As late as 1874, affidavits were still being filed in connection with the claims of a mechanic for work done on one of Burdell's properties located in Elizabethport, New Jersey.[302]

Miller Hageman's 1890 *Herald* feature story and the *Times'* 1897 disclosure of a supposed confession by Emma Cunningham represented only two of the cords that continued to tie the public's consciousness and imagination to the gruesome crime story, keeping it alive for years after Emma's eventual death. Sightings of Emma and her daughters were commonplace during the decades after her acquittal on murder charges.[303] Only days after the tenth anniversary of Harvey Burdell's demise, *Harper's Weekly* spotted her out west. The February 2, 1867 issue reported in a column entitled "Home and Foreign Gossip" on the latest employment of her already well-proven business acumen: "Mrs. Burdell-Cunningham, who obtained such an unenviable notoriety some ten years ago, resides in a small town in Lower California. She has been engaged there in superintending the operations of a silver mine purchased by herself, and has displayed remarkable energy and capacity for business."

A notice in the April 10, 1870 edition of The *San Francisco Morning Call* reported another step for Emma in her struggle to resume a respectable middle-class life: the preceding March 5, a Reverend Cox married "William Williams to Emma A. Hempstead (no cards)" in that city. Many individuals bearing the bridegroom's name appear in California's 1870 U.S. Census, but only one matches the information provided in a comprehensive history of one of California's active mining counties of the day and seems most likely to have been Emma's last spouse.[304] Welshman William Ellis Williams resided in New York during the years of Emma's first widowhood, returning to California to resume a mining career in 1856. His final stint as a prospector was conducted in Nevada County. Luck just would not hold for Emma Cunningham, however. Although twelve years her junior, William E. Williams unfortunately predeceased Emma; their 13-year-long marriage ended with his death on September 3, 1883. [305]

Destitute and alone, the once-again widowed Emma A. Williams returned to New York within the next 15 months. A *Times* reporter discovered her at Thanksgiving-time, "scantily clad and shivering with cold," standing alone in First District Civil Court seeking alms. "There was nothing noticeable about her appearance to distinguish her from the hundreds of others who apply for summonses to 'Thunderbolt Norton[,]'" reported the paper, "save her piercing black eyes, still undimmed by age and her swarthy complexion. Her hair was only streaked with gray, and had she been fashionably dressed she would have easily passed for a woman of 50." Hearing that Justice Norton was not sitting on the bench that day, Emma (actually 66 years old at the time) left without filing her petition for relief, *"poor and evidently friendless."*[306]

Whether or not she lived out her days in the New York City Almshouse is unclear, but at least one family member took pity on the luckless Emma at the very end of her life. Emma Augusta Hempstead Williams passed away in September, 1887, at the home of her niece, Phoebe Morrell, at 321 East 119th Street. Even so many years after the conclusion of the Burdell trial, and despite her pitiable circumstances, Emma remained a notorious, reviled person in New Yorkers' minds. The *Times* reported crowds gathered outside Phoebe Morrell's Harlem home jeering the deceased, even as Reverend Merritt Hulburn of Trinity Methodist intoned the funeral service in the upstairs parlor. [307] Emma's coffin was transported to Green-Wood Cemetery after the service, where she was laid to rest in the Morrell family plot. Only Mrs. Morrell's family was present at graveside, though it is possible that the group described by the *Times* included some of Mrs. Morrell's (and the decedent's) Hempstead relatives. Phoebe Morrell had survived her father (Emma's younger brother Christopher Hempstead, Jr.) by many years, but what contact, if any, she had maintained with the Hempstead clan is unknown.

Having made her way home after so many years out West, Emma was not allowed to lie in her grave among strangers for long. After consents were gathered from the surviving Cunningham family members, Emma was reburied in 1891 beside her first husband in his family's Green-Wood plot. The mercy of the Cunningham family had its limits, though. No tombstone tops Emma's pitiful spot, one hard by the polished granite epitaph of her sister-in-law Margaret Harris.

* * *

Visitors to Green-Wood today find a scene of peaceful repose as they walk the paths connecting the unmarked graves of Harvey Burdell and Emma Cunningham. Violent combat and widespread disgrace attended the lives of the unfortunate pair, but now only the sound of songbirds and the rustle of shade trees accompany a visitor's footsteps past the final resting places of the two lovers. Harvey and Emma lie quietly and anonymously, a few hundred yards apart, surely closer to each other in death than they ever were in life.

BIBLIOGRAPHY

GOVERNMENT RECORDS, ARCHIVES AND MANU-SCRIPT COLLECTIONS

COLUMBIA COUNTY, NY CLERK'S OFFICE: Real estate records and corporation/partnership filings

KINGS COUNTRY CLERK'S OFFICE: Pleadings records of various Kings County courts

MASSACHUSSETTS SUPREME JUDICIAL COURT ARCHIVES AND PRESERVATION OFFICE: Boston Municipal Court Records and Commitment Register for Charlestown, MA State Prison

NEW YORK CITY MUNICIPAL ARCHIVES AND RECORDS CENTER: New York County District Attorney indictment records

NEW YORK CITY REGISTER'S OFFICE: New York and Kings County real estate records

NEW YORK COUNTY CLERK'S OFFICE, OLD RECORDS DIVISION: Pleadings records of various New York County courts

NEW YORK AND KINGS COUNTY SURROGATES COURT: Estate administration records

NEW-YORK HISTORICAL SOCIETY: Quinn Collection of Hotel Files

NEW YORK PUBLIC LIBRARY: Samuel J. Tilden Papers [Special Collections]

NEW YORK STATE ARCHIVES: Handwritten ledger of admissions to Sing Sing Prison 1842-1852 ; Ledger of inmates discharged from Sing Sing, Clinton and Auburn State Penitentiaries for the years 1848-1852; List of Convicts Discharged by Expiration of Sentence or Pardon, Sing Sing Prison, 1848

UNION COUNTY NEW JERSEY CLERK'S OFFICE: Real estate records

CHURCH RECORDS

Encyclopaedia of World Methodism; Noel B. Harmon Gen. Editor, Nashville, United Methodist Publishing House: 1974, Volume I

A General Register of the Names of The Trustees Local Preachers and Leaders Etc. In the City of New York [c. 1816] in *Methodist Episcopal Church Records – New York City- Vol. 79* [NYPL Special Collections]

Inventory of the Church Archives in New York City - The Presbyterian Church, The Historical Records Survey, Works Projects Administration, New York: 1940

Presbyterian Historical Society, Philadelphia, PA: *Sessional Records of the First Presbyterian Church* [Brooklyn, NY]; *Brooklyn First Presbyterian Church Sunday School Directors' minutes 1824-31*; Marriage Register of the Second Presbyterian Church Brooklyn NY 1833-58; *Brooklyn NY Second Presbyterian Church Members 1839-1875;* Brooklyn N.Y First Presbyterian Church Sessions Records 1838-1859; *The Second Presbyterian Church of Brooklyn Session Minutes 1831-66*

Records of the Greenwich Reformed Dutch Church [Gardner Sage Library at Rutgers University, New Brunswick, NJ]

United Methodist Church Archives-GCAH, Drew University, Chatham, NJ: *A Record of the Methodist Episcopal Church Brooklyn Long Island New York March 2, 1831; Records of the First Methodist Episcopal Church of Brooklyn, N.Y. formerly known as The Sands Street Methodist Episcopal Church*, Brooklyn, 1938

Edwin Warriner, *Old Sands Street Methodist Episcopal Church, of Brooklyn, N.Y.: an illustrated centennial record, historical and biographical*, Phillips and Hunt, New York: 1885

Works Progress Administration Guide to Church Records in New York City for The Reformed Church in America, New York: 1939

PRINTED PRIMARY SOURCES

Act of incorporation: charter and by-laws of the Nassau Fire Insurance Company of Brooklyn, I. van Anden, Brooklyn: 1852 [NYPL] and *Special report of the insurance commissioners appointed by the Comptroller to examine into the conditions and affairs of the fire insurance companies in the cities of New York and Brooklyn, 1856*, C. Van Benthuysen, printer to the legislature; Albany: 1857 [NYPL].

Annual Report of the City Inspector of the City of New York for the Year Ending December 31, 1857, Chas. W. Baker, Printer, 29 Beekman Street, New York: 1858 [NYC Municipal Reference Library]

Catalogue of officers and graduates of the University of Nashville with an appendix, containing sundry historical notices, etc., A. Nelson & Co., printers, Nashville: 1850 [Tennessee State Library]

The Child at Home; or The Principles of Filial Duty Familiarly Illustrated, American Tract Society, New York: 1833. A digitized version of the work is viewable in *Hearth*, Cornell University's archive of domestic American publications at http://hearth.library.cornell.edu/

Fictitious Heiress Of Dr. Burdell. Confessions Of The Accoucher: Bold Game Of Mrs. Cunningham — For Sale by All Periodical Dealers, Boston: 1857. [NYHS]

Members of the New York County Medical Society From Its Organization 1806-1861: [ms. Collections of the New York Academy of Medicine]

The Mysteries of Bond Street; or the Seraglios of Upper Tendom [American Antiquarian Society, Worcester, MA]

"The Princeton murder : the Burdell mystery unravelled! : confessions of Charles Lewis, alias Symonds, and Life and adventures of George W. Symonds, the Burdell murderer / by Peter Thomson, official reporter of Special Sessions," in *The National Police Gazette*,1863 [NYHS]

Saratoga Female Seminary catalogs for 1856-7 and 1857-8 [Skidmore College Library Special Collections]

Villikins and His Dinah, Ross & Tousey, NO. 121 Nassau –st., N.Y. [NYHS]

CITY DIRECTORIES

Directory of the City of Hudson, [William B. Stoddard, Hudson, NY]

Doggett's New York Directory

Longworth's American Almanac, New-York Register and City Directory

Parmenter and Van Antwerp's Hudson City Directory [Hudson, NY]

Rode's New York Directory

Spooner's Brooklyn Directory

Trow's New York Directory

Webb and Hearne's Brooklyn Directory

NEWSPAPERS AND MAGAZINES

Alta California, [San Francisco]

Brooklyn Daily Eagle

Brooklyn Eagle & Kings County Democrat

The Coastal Post, [Marin County, CA]

The Daily Saratogian

Frank Leslie's Illustrated Newspaper

Harper's Weekly

The Kinderhook (N.Y.) Sentinel

New York Aurora

New York Courier

New York Daily Tribune

New York Dental Recorder.

New York Herald

New York Times

Putnam's Monthly

San Francisco Morning Call

The Trenton State Gazette and Republican

White Man's Newspaper [New York City]

BOOKS AND ACADEMIC JOURNAL ARTICLES

Harold J. Abrahams, *Extinct Medical Schools of Nineteenth Century Philadelphia*, Philadelphia: University of Pennsylvania Press: 1966

Louis Auchincloss, ed., *The Hone and Strong Diaries of Old Manhattan*, Abbeville Press, New York: 1989

Peter J. Blodgett, *Land of Golden Dreams: California in the Gold Rush Decade, 1848-1858*, Huntington Library, San Marino, CA: 1999

6 Bradford's Reports

Croswell Brown, *The Elegant Oakey*, Oxford University Press, New York: 1956

Sarah C. Bull, *Ole Bull, a memoir by Sara C. Bull; with Ole Bull's 'Violin notes,' and Dr. A. B. Crosby's 'Anatomy of the violinist,'* Houghton, Mifflin and Company, Boston: 1883.

Harvey Burdell and John Burdell, *Observations on The Structure, Physiology, Anatomy and Diseases of the Teeth, In Two Parts*, Gould and Newman, New York: 1838.

Edwin Burrows and Mike Wallace, *Gotham–A History of New York City to 1898*, Oxford University Press, London and New York: 1999

Henry Lauren Clinton, *Celebrated Trials*, Harper & Brothers Publishers, New York: 1897

Patricia Cline Cohen, *The Murder of Helen Jewett*, Alfred A. Knopf, Inc., New York: 1998

Russell Crouse, *Murder Won't Out,* Doubleday and Doran, Garden City, New York: 1932

Helen Deese, "'My Life . . . reads to me like a Romance' – The Journals of Caroline Healey Dall" *The Massachusetts Historical Review*, Vol. 3, 2001

Helen Deese, ed., *Daughter of Boston: The Extraordinary Diary of a Nineteenth-Century Woman*, Beacon Press, Boston: 2005

Harold J. Abrahams, *Extinct Medical Schools of Nineteenth Century Philadelphia*, Philadelphia: University of Pennsylvania Press: 1966

Alexis de Tocqueville, *Democracy in America* [trans. Henry Reeve], J. and H.G. Langley, New York: 1841

Charles Dickens, *American Notes and Pictures from Italy*, Oxford University Press, London: 1957

H.D. Eastman, *Fast Man's Directory and Lover's Guide to the Ladies of Fashion and Houses of Pleasure in New York and Other Large Cities*, New York: 1853 [NYPL microfilm]

Robert Ernst, *Immigrant Life in New York City 1825-1863*, Syracuse University Press: 1994

George Foster, *New York by Gas-Light*, ed. Stuart Blumin, University of California Press, Berkeley, CA: 1990

Timothy J. Gilfoyle, *City of Eros – New York City, Prostitution, and the Commercialization of Sex, 1790-1920*, W.W. Norton and Co.: New York, 1992

Edmund Grinrod, *A Compendium of The Laws and Regulations of Wesleyan Methodism With Notes and An Appendix; Printed for the Author and Sold By John Mason, 14 City-Road and 66 Paternoster-Row*, London: 1842. [included at:

http://www.isle-of-man.com/manxnotebook/methdism/gndrod/index.htm]

John Freylinghuysen Hageman, *History of Princeton and its Institutions*, J. B. Lippincott & Co., Philadelphia: 1879

L.M.A. Haughwout, *Genealogy of the Lefferts-Haughwout Family*, Wright Press, New York: 1903

Karen Halttunen, *Confidence Men and Painted Women – A Study of Middle Class Culture in America 1830-1870,* Yale University Press, New Haven: 1982

Karen Halttunen, *Murder Most Foul,* Harvard University Press, Cambridge, Mass.: 1998

T. Walker Herbert, *Dearest Beloved: the Hawthornes and the Making of the Middle-Class Family,* University of California Press, Berkeley: 1993

Eric Homberger, *Scenes from the Life of A City – Corruption and Conscience in Old New York,* Yale University Press, New Haven: 1994

Kenneth Jackson, ed., *The Encyclopedia of New York City,* Yale University Press, New Haven: 1995

Crisfield Johnson, *History of Oswego County,* L.H. Everts & Co., Philadelphia: 1877

Carole Klein, *Gramercy Park An American Bloomsbury,* Houghton Mifflin Company, Boston: 1987

Marc Linder and Lawrence S. Zacharias, *Of Cabbages and Kings County: Agriculture and the Formation of Modern Brooklyn,* University of Iowa Press, Iowa City: 1999

Charles Lockwood, *Bricks and Brownstones,* Abbeville Press, New York: 1972

Jack Mason, *Early Marin,* House of Printing, Petaluma, CA: 1971

Gustavus Myers, *The History of Tammany Hall,* Boni & Liveright, New York: 1917

New York City Landmarks Preservation Commission, *Historic Designation Report for The East 17th Street/Irving Place Historic District,* New York: 1998

George C.D. Odell, *Annals of the New York Stage,* Columbia University Press, New York: 1927-49

6 Parker's Criminal Reports

Edward Pessen, "A Social and Economic Portrait of Jacksonian Brooklyn," *New York Historical Society Quarterly,* Vol. 55, No. 4 (1971)

Jeffrey I. Richman, *Brooklyn's Green-Wood Cemetery: New York's Buried Treasure,* The Cemetery, Brooklyn: 1998

Brian Roberts, *American Alchemy: The California Gold Rush and Middle-Class Culture,* University of North Carolina Press, Chapel Hill, NC: 2000

Witold Rybczynski, *A Clearing in the Distance - Frederick Law Olmsted and America in the Nineteenth Century,* Scribner, New York: 1999

A.H. Saxon, *P.T. Barnum: The Legend and the Man,* Columbia University Press, New York: 1989.

Carl Schurz, *The reminiscences of Carl Schurz ... illustrated with portraits and original drawings,* The McClure Company, New York: 1907-8

Kenneth M. Stampp, *America In 1857: A Nation on the Brink,* Oxford University Press, New York: 1990

Christine Stansell, *City of Women – Sex and Class in New York 1789-1860,* Alfred A Knopf, Inc., New York: 1986

Henry R. Stiles, *A History of the City of Brooklyn, Including the Old Town and Village of Brooklyn, the Town of Bushwick, and the Village and City of Williamsburgh*, Brooklyn, N.Y., Published by Subscription: 1869

I.N. Phelps Stokes, *The Iconography of Manhattan Island, 1498-1909*, Robert H. Dodd, New York: 1928

William L. Stone; *Saratoga Springs: Being a Complete Guide to the Mineral Springs, Hotels, Drives and All Points of Interest Around and In the Immediate Vicinity of This Celebrated Watering Place. Views Taken on the Spot by William Gellatly*, T. Nelson & Sons, New York: 1866

George Thompson, *Venus in Boston and Other Tales of Nineteenth-Century City Life*, University of Massachusetts Press, Amherst and Boston: 2002, edited by David S. Reynolds and Kimberly Gladman

David Thomas Valentine, *Manual of the Corporation of the City of New York*, D.T. Valentine, New York: 1857 and 1862

Peter N. VandenBerge, *The Historical Directory of the Reformed Church in America 1628-1978 (The Historical Series of the Reformed Church in America No. 6)*, Wm B. Eerdmans Publishing Co, Grand Rapids: 1978

Harry Laurenz Wells, *History of Nevada County*, Thompson & West, Oakland, CA: 1880

Nathaniel Parker Willis, *American Scenery; or Land, lake and river illustrations of transatlantic nature*, G.Virtue, London: 1840

WEBSITES

http://politicalgraveyard.com/bio/davie-davila.html [Nineteenth century political biographies]

http://www.Ancestry.com [U.S. Census and Civil War military records, and various other genealogy sources]

http://www.cagenweb.com/marin/1854assessmt.html#B [Marin County, CA real estate tax records]

MAPS

G.H. Beers Survey Maps of Hudson, NY, 1871 [NYPL

Map of the City of Brooklyn and Village of Williamsburgh, Compiled, Lithographed and Published by Richard Butt, Surveyor, 1846; NYPL Ford Collection

William Perris block and lot maps for Brooklyn and Manhattan, 1855 et. seq. [NYPL]

ILLUSTRATION CREDITS

Jacket: Frank Leslie's Illustrated News , February 21, 1857

Frontispiece: Frank Leslie's Illustrated News August 22, 1857

Facing p. 1: Harvey Burdell from *Frank Leslie's Illustrated News,* February 21, 1857

p. 10: Rev. Uriah Marvine marriage register entry for Emma Cunningham and Harvey Burdell: Gardner Sage Library, Rutgers University; Marriage certificate: Samuel Tilden Papers, Manuscripts and Archives Division, The New York Public Library, Astor, Lenox and Tilden Foundations

p. 14: Portraits of Edward Downes Connery, John Eckel, Emma Cunningham, George Snodgrass, Augusta Cunningham, and Georgiana Cunningham from *Frank Leslie's Illustrated News,* February 21, 1857

p. 15: Portraits Of Abraham Oakey Hall, Esq. and Henry Clinton, Esq.: from Henry Clinton, *Celebrated Trials*

p. 38: 94 Classon Avenue: The Brooklyn Historical Society

p. 58: Emma Cunningham's affidavit of domicile given in estate administration of

George D. Cunningham: New York County Clerk's Office, Old Records Division

Obituary: George D. Cunningham: *Brooklyn Daily Eagle,* June 3, 1854

p. 68: First Baptist Church and Saratoga Springs Female Seminary – Saratoga Springs, NY: author photos

Saratoga Springs – Congress Spring: *Frank Leslie's Illustrated News,* August 27, 1859

p. 69: Piazza of Congress Hall Hotel: Collection of The Saratoga Springs Public Library

Congress Hall Hotel Dance Card: Skidmore College Library Collection and Saratoga Springs Historical Society

p. 90: Thomas Gunning: University of Chicago, Crerar Library

Dr. John Burdell: General Research Division, The New York Public Library, Astor, Lenox and Tilden Foundations

p.112: Oliver Wellington's Twelfth Street Water Cure Clinic *The Water-Cure Journal,* February, 1853

p. 152: 26 Bond Street: Author Photo

p. 158: Metropolitan Hotel, Broadway, New York, Chromolithograph by Sarony & Major, New York, Gift of Evert Augustus Duyckinck, 1864, PR 020, Geographic File, negative number 76889d: Collection of The New-York Historical Society

Lafayette Place and Great Jones Street, ca. 1866 stereograph by unidentified photographer, negative number 45867: Collection of The New-York Historical Society

Broadway between Amity (now Third) and Bond Streets, circa 1860: Robert N. Dennis Collection of Stereoscopic Views, Miriam & Ira Wallach Division of Art, Prints & Photographs, The New York Public Library, Astor, Lenox and Tilden Foundations

p. 159: La Farge House, Menu for December 12, 1856, N-YHS Library Menu Collection, negative number 46691: Collection of The New-York Historical Society

p. 179: Portraits of Surrogate A.J. Bradford and Justice Henry Davies: from Henry Clinton, *Celebrated Trials*

p. 201: Portraits of Dr. David Uhl and Dr. Samuel Catlin: *Frank Leslie's Illustrated News,* August 15, 1857

p. 210: Fictitious Heiress of Dr. Burdell, Confessions of the Accoucher, Bold Game of Mrs. Cunningham; pamphlet, published in Boston, 1857, call number KB153.B94 F44: Collection of The New-York Historical Society

The Burdell Murder Case, an abstract of the evidence . . . ; newsstand pamphlet, published by Stearns & Co., NY, 1857, call number HV6534.N5 B949, negatvie number 78847d: Collection of The New-York Historical Society

p. 211: Mrs. Cunningham's Darling Babby [sic] Air— Fine Old English Gentleman or

The Cork Leg, by Brickbat; song sheet 1857 lyrics only; call number SY-B1857

no.17, negative number 78848d: Collection of The New-York Historical Society

The Cunningham Baby Or The Heir from Over Jordan: Collection of The New York Historical Society

p. 219: National Police Gazette, April 1863 issue: The Burdell Mystery Unravelled. Collection of the New-York Historical Society

ACKNOWLEDGEMENTS

During the seven years that have passed as this project has been brought to fruition, countless individuals and institutions have provided me with generous assistance. Urban historian Deborah Gardner deserves first mention as the woman who introduced me to Green-Wood Cemetery, and who provided advice and encouragement throughout the process. One of the first suggestions Deborah made after I fixated on the Burdell story was to recommend a book entitled *The Murder of Helen Jewett*, written by University of California – Santa Barbara Professor of History, Patricia Cline Cohen. Pat befriended me forthwith and has given me incomparable, invaluable and magnanimous support. Jeffrey Richman, resident historian of The Green-Wood Cemetery History Fund and author of *Green-Wood Cemetery: New York's Buried Treasure*, deserves credit for my initial inspiration as well as ongoing assistance. I bought a copy of Jeff's wonderful book on my first visit to Green-Wood in May, 2000, and therein first encountered the Burdell-Cunningham story. Jeff and his colleagues at the Cemetery have been tremendously generous with their time and advice.

I owe thanks to Eric Homberger for his sage comments on an early draft of my manuscript, to A.H. Saxon for his assistance with matters pertaining to P.T. Barnum, to Joseph Van Nostrand and Bruce Abrams of the Old Records Division of the New York County Clerk's Office, Kenneth Cobb and his staff at the New York City Municipal Archives, Arlene Shaner of the New York Academy of Medicine library, Rev. Kenneth J. Ross at the reference library of the Presbyterian Historical Sociey, Russell Gasero of Gardener Sage Library, Rutgers University, Elizabeth Bouvier of the Massachusetts State Archives, Doris Lamont of the Saratoga Springs Historical Society, Ellen de Lalla, Local Historian at the Saratoga Springs Public Library's Saratoga Room, Wendy Anthony at the Skidmore College Library Special Collections, Lynn Hoke, archivist of New York City's Grace Church, Andrea Matlack, Archivist of the American Dental Association, and the staffs of the American Antiquarian Association library, Drew University's Methodist Church archives, the Old York Library of the City University of New York, the New-York Historical Society, the New York Public Library, the New York State Library at Albany, and the New Jersey State Library at Trenton. These institutions provided a treasure troves of information to me, over and over. Last but surely not least, my thanks go to Deanna Smith, a private genealogist of Palatine Bridge, New York, whose excitement and interest in my assignments to her produced a veritable goldmine of information.

For my brother Henry's enthusiastic support and to the many readers and friends who have offered uncountable suggestions and advice, I owe a debt of enormous gratitude.

NOTES

[1] In 1859, Davies was appointed to New York State's highest judicial body, the Court of Appeals, and served as its Chief Justice during 1866-67. See the compendium of individual political histories at http://politicalgraveyard.com/bio/davie-davila.html.

[2] *New York Daily Tribune*, May 6, 1857, p. 6 col. 4.

[3] Hall's penchant for elegant attire as well as the details of Emma's trial attire are noted in Croswell Brown, *The Elegant Oakey*, Oxford University Press, New York: 1956. See esp. p. 8. Bombazine is a fine-twilled fabric usually loomed with silk or artificial silk warp and worsted filling.

[4] Only a few years later Hall would switch parties to become New York's mayor under the reign of William Marcy "Boss" Tweed.

[5] The indictment is available on microfilm in the New York County District Attorney's records at New York's Municipal Archives, 31 Chambers Street.

[6] Hall's opening address is transcribed in Henry Lauren Clinton, *Celebrated Trials,* Harper & Brothers Publishers, New York: 1897, pp. 121-136.

[7] Although only 63 homicides are listed by the New York City Health Inspector out of a population of approximately 500,000 for the entire calendar year 1857, that year's total vastly exceeded the 30 persons "killed or murdered" in the official tabulation for the previous calendar year. New York City's homicide rate, on a per capita basis, far exceeded the 1856 measure during most of the last quarter of the twentieth century, although more recent years have seen a significant drop in reported murders. See *Annual Report of the City Inspector of the City of New York for the Year Ending December 31, 1857*, Chas. W. Baker, Printer, 29 Beekman Street, New York: 1858, p.10, and the Inspector's report for 1856 transcribed in the *New York Herald,* January 1, 1857, p. 6, col. 5.

[8] Luther Beecher's testimony in the litigation brought against Harvey Burdell's estate by Emma Cunningham contains an extensive account of his initial acquaintance with Emma and two of her daughters as well as the details of their enrollment at Temple Grove. Handwritten transcripts of this testimony are located in Samuel J. Tilden's papers in the manuscript archives at NYPL.

[9] *New York Herald,* February 2, 1857, p. 1, col 2.

[10] Ibid. p. 1 col. 1.

[11] *Ibid.* p.1, col. 2.

[12] Ibid.

[13] On Monday morning after the discovery of the crime, the *Tribune* led its readers through the house, including the professional quarters and Dr. Burdell's bedroom:

> The back room or operating room is neatly fitted up; on the walls are several small pictures, a large map entitled 'Historie de France' containing portraits of that country from 'Pharamond, year 420, to Louis Philippe, 1846.' An engraving of Harvey, demonstrating the circulation of blood to Charles First, is suspended over the mantelpiece. The furniture and upholstery consists of Brussels carpet, sofa, large looking glass, operating

chair, case containing dental instruments, book case, center table, rocking chair, and iron safe. A political map of the United States and a small case of preserved insects.

In the front room is a Brussels carpet, mahogany bedstead, 'French' marble basin, with hot and cold water, bureau, looking glass, with gas burners each side, two human jaws preserved in glass cases-pictures of Napoleon, and a map containing pictures of Presidents of the United States.

See *New York Tribune*, February 2, 1857, p. 5, col. 3.

[14] A copy of the document is included in the Burdell estate case files in Samuel J. Tilden's papers held in the manuscript division of NYPL. The copy also contains Emma Cunningham's endorsement in blank of the assigned judgment, taken by Harvey Burdell as a precaution. As with many legal documents from contemporary files, although the text is largely handwritten, this document appears to be only a copy. The signatures of some of the various parties do not match those on other primary source documents whose provenance indicates that the execution is in the subscriber's own handwriting.

[15] Inexplicably, the Tilden case files in the Burdell estate litigation also contain the original of this marvelous document. Marvine's signature and the rest of the handwritten entries match the entries in his marriage register (where the groom's surname is spelled correctly) located by the author in the records of the Greenwich Reformed Dutch Church held at Gardner Sage Library at Rutgers University in New Brunswick, New Jersey. The initials of Emma's chief counsel, Henry Lauren Clinton, adorn the upper left-hand corner of the certificate, and were perhaps inscribed to identify it as a plaintiff's exhibit in the estate litigation brought by Emma Cunningham to prove her marriage to Burdell and her entitlement to appointment as administratrix of the the deceased's intestate estate, as well as her rights to a significant share of its assets. Apparently to the victor belonged the spoils, and thus his adversary's evidentiary exhibit somehow ended up in Tilden's files.

The Greenwich Reformed Dutch Church was located on the south side of Amos Street (now Tenth Street) from 1826-1863 before moving to its final location in the vicinity of 43rd Street and Sixth Avenue. See *Works Progress Administration Guide to Church Records in New York City for The Reformed Church in America, New York: 1939*. The officiant at Emma's second marriage ceremony is listed in *Peter N. VandenBerge, The Historical Directory of the Reformed Church in America 1628-1978 (The Historical Series of the Reformed Church in America No. 6), Wm B. Eerdmans Publishing Co, Grand Rapids: 1978*, as "Marvin, Uriah, b. Albany, NY Jan 8, 1816. Williams College AB[Bachelor of Arts] Union College, 1835; Princeton Theological Seminary, 1847. Licensed. Presbytery Troy, 1846 ordained Classis Washington, 1848. Pastor Greenwich, NY 1848-55; Greenwich NYC 1855-58; First Nyack, NY 1860-70. D. Troy NY Nov. 18, 1898. (see *ibid.* p 113). Marvine's rectory in Greenwich Village was located at 732 Greenwich Street.

[16] *New York Herald*, February 1, 1857, p. 1, col. 3.

[17] *New York Herald*, February 1, 1857, p. 1, col. 3.

[18] *New York Herald*, February 2, 1857, p. 1, col. 5.

[19] The 1836 murder of courtesan Helen Jewett in a lower Manhattan brothel remained etched in the public consciousness over twenty years later as one of the most gruesome and brutal crimes of the century. The social context of that crime and its relation to Emma Cunningham's plight are discussed in Chapter 9, infra. John Colt was hung in the courtyard of the old Tombs prison on November 18, 1842, after a year-long struggle to avoid the hangman's noose. Colt had been convicted in the homicide of Samuel Adams in September of the previous year. The murderer had packed Adams' body in a box and arranged shipment to a southern port, but a delay in sailing led to the ghastly discovery of the moldering corpse and Colt's arrest. New Yorkers read with astonishment how on the morning of his execution the condemned man married Caroline Henshaw in his death-row cell, and then asked to be left alone to meet his doom. See *New York Times,* July 4, 1896, p. 9, col. 3. The article also recounts the history of the original 1838 Demotic-style Tombs jailhouse and several of its most famous residents.

[20] *New York Herald,* February 2, 1857, p. 4, col. 3, and February 3, 1857, p. 4, col. 4.

[21] *New York Herald,* February 3, 1857, p. 8, col. 2.

[22] Ibid.

[23] The spelling of the witness' surname is that adopted in the official transcript of Emma Cunningham's subsequent murder trial (See 6 Parker's Criminal Reports 432). Variant spellings of this surname appear in contemporary journalism and Henry Clinton's memoirs.

[24] Donahoe's testimony refers to an argument that occurred on "Saturday the 24th." At first glance, one would infer that the witness testified about the weekend before Burdell was murdered; January 24 was indeed a Saturday. However, a closer reading of her testimony, in conjunction with that of Snodgrass and others, makes it virtually certain that Donahoe was referring to a dispute that occurred over a weeken, late in October 1856, at a time when suits were pending between Emma and Harvey Burdell. One evening during that fall weekend, Burdell left the house, and returned late at night to find himself locked out of his own home. After the angry dentist pounded on the door repeatedly, George Snodgrass came downstairs and admitted him. Dr. Burdell then threatened to kill Snodgrass if the situation ever occurred again. The events of that weekend may well have crystallized Burdell's suspicions that many of the residents in his home were part and parcel of a fraudulent scheme aimed at him and master-minded by Emma Cunningham.

[25] *New York Herald,* February 3, 1857, p. 8, col. 2.

[26] Eckel and Snodgrass shared the same cell in the Tombs. See Ibid., p. 8, col. 4.

[27] *New York Herald,* February 4, 1857, p. 1, col. 1.

[28] Ibid. p. 1, col. 6. Mr. Stevens' veracity was called into question months later when two local police officers testified in the Burdell estate litigation that the witness was a well-know miscreant in the Fifteenth Ward. A copy of Stevens' 1832 indictment for second degree forgery was also read into the Surrogate's record by John Sparks, Deputy Clerk of the Court of Oyer and Terminer. Transcripts of this testimony are filed in the Samuel J. Tilden papers at NYPL.

[29] Ibid. John T. Hildreth was a stagecoach line operator in Brooklyn and was

active in Methodist affairs. Hildreth acted as steward of a new Methodist Church erected in 1856 on DeKalb Avenue between Franklin and Kent Avenues in the Wallabout area. See *Brooklyn Daily Eagle*, March 31, 1853, p.2, col. 5, and April 25, 1856, p. 2, col. 3.

[30] The 'Mains' testimony is transcribed in the *New York Herald*, February 4, 1857, p. 5, cols. 4-5.

[31] The last testimony transcribed on page 2 of the February 9, 1857 issue of the *Herald* is that of Louis Petelier, who owned a confectionery shop at 691 Broadway. Emma walked by the store virtually every day while she lived at 31 Bond Street, and had been a customer since October, 1855. Her order for the party of January 14th went unpaid, and by the 19th, Petelier took her promissory note for amount due, having been promised repayment in a few weeks. Petelier's shop sat on the west side of the tumultuous Broadway thoroughfare in a substantial mid-block building, a few steps north of Amity (now West 3rd) Street. One block south, Bond Street's western end faced Broadway. Petelier's neighbors included the magnificent Lafarge House, Burton's Theater, the Brandt glassware store, Scott & Co.'s lace shop and countless purveyors of luxury goods, fine restaurants, glistening hotels and prime entertainment venues that populated the "Broadway Entertainment District."

[32] *New York Herald*, February 4, 1857, p. 5, col. 6. The *Herald*'s description is substantially transcribed in an article accompanied by an engraving of Snodgrass with his banjo that appeared in *Frank Leslie's Illustrated Newspaper*, February 21, 1857, Vol. III, No. 63, p. 192.

The mention of Emma's third daughter in this news article is virtually the only reference made to another sister of Helen and Margaret Augusta in the *Herald*'s reporting. Helen Cunningham's testimony transcribed in the *Herald* on February 9, 1857, can also be read to establish the existence of a third sister, but scant corroboration appears in contemporary journalism. Henry Clinton's published memoirs of the case refer in one location to Emma having five children, but only two daughters and two sisters are described elsewhere in his book. The *New York Tribune*'s coverage of the subsequent murder trial again makes reference to the existence of three daughters. See Henry Lauren Clinton, op. cit. p.178, and *New York Tribune*, May 8, 1857, p. 4, col. 2. At Emma Cunningham's murder trial, the Rev. Luther Beecher testified at length about his relationship with the accused murderess's family, describing his meeting Emma at Saratoga in July of 1856 and enrolling her daughter "Georgiana" at his Temple Grove Female Seminary the following September. Rev. Beecher states that he was in New York at the end of January 1857 and had planned to escort his pupil back to Saratoga on Saturday January 31. The girl in question appears to be Emma's younger daughter, Helen. See 6 Parker's Criminal Reports 549, including George Vail Snodgrass's testimony about helping Helen pack her trunks for the trip at p. 579, and Helen Cunningham's testimony at p. 590. Dispositive, though, are the listing in the 1850 U.S. census of the family in the 16th Ward in Manhattan with three daughters, Augusta, Helen and Georgiana, as well as their parents and brother, and the fact that when George Cunningham died, a special guardian was appointed for all of his children. The order mentions five: Margaret A., Helen E., Georgiana A., George D. and William S.

[33] Ibid., p. 8, col. 3.

[34] Both lawsuits were filed by Emma Cunningham in New York County Superior Court. The Old Records Division of the New York County Clerk's office, located on the seventh floor of the ornate Surrogate's Court Building in lower Manhattan, provides access to site thousands of pleading files for the time period in question, covering civil cases in the Superior Court as well as many other courts of both law and equity jurisdiction in New York County. The pleadings are indexed not only by a massive set of card catalogs, alphabetically by plaintiff and defendant, but also by a searchable computerized database. Although entries in the indices as well as the actual pleadings in dozens of actions involving Emma Cunningham, Harvey Burdell, and other figures in this case are all present, no trace of the breach of promise and slander actions brought by Emma against Harvey in October, 1856, are to be found among the files.

[35] Benjamin Thayer, Esq. is mentioned as a subscribing witness on November 19, 1856 to Emma Cunningham's assignment in blank of the judgment obtained by Edwards Pierrepont against William Burdell.

[36] Chatfield's and Thayer's testimony in the matter is transcribed in the *Herald* on February 9, 1857 on p. 2. Although the transcript specifies the date in question as "June 18, 1856", this appears to be a typographical error, and 1855 is the intended year. This date matches other testimony concerning the first year of the Burdell-Cunningham romance in which Dr. Burdell was engaged in showing Emma Cunningham the extent of his wealth, and their romantic entanglement was at its height. The 1855 date is also mentioned as the accurate one in Henry Clinton's memoirs. See Henry Lauren Clinton, op. cit.,p. 366.

[37] Ibid.

[38] *New York Tribune*, February 6, 1857, p. 6, col. 2.

[39] *New York Herald*, February 5, 1857, p. 5, cols. 1-6.

[40] *New York Herald,* June, 22, 1890, p. 8, cols. 1-6. The inquest verdict is contained in the New York County District Attorney's indictment files for the Burdell murder case located in the New York City Municipal Archives.

[41] Completed in 1838, the original Tombs prison (the first of three to be constructed in the same general location) replaced the old Bridewell jail in City Hall Park and the Bellevue prison (whose distance to the courthouses in and near City Hall was a significant inconvenience for officers of the law). Executions had been conducted in public since colonial times in New York, attracting large crowds of jeering, hooting citizens who listened sometimes impatiently to the execution sermons customarily preached in the early nineteenth century before the trap door was sprung. Popular sensibilities changed later in the century, and by the time executions were moved to the Tombs courtyard, frequently only a prescribed group of twelve witnesses attended the carrying out of the sentence. See Edwin Burrows and Mike Wallace, *Gotham–A History of New York City to 1898*, Oxford University Press, London and New York: 1999, p. 506-7, and 636.

[42] Edmund Grinrod, *A Compendium of The Laws and Regulations of Wesleyan*

Methodism With Notes and An Appendix; Printed for the Author and Sold By John Mason, 14 City-Road and 66 Paternoster-Row, London: 1842. [See http://www.isle-of-man.com/manxnotebook/methdism/gndrod/index.htm]

[43] Few traces remain today in riverside Corlear's Hook Park and the adjoining streets of the shipping industry and maritime commerce that dominated the area's densely-packed, early nineteenth century streets and alleys. A cluster of wood frame buildings on the southwest corner of the intersection of Grand and Columbia Streets somehow survived the wholesale demolition and reconstruction of the neighborhood through the twentieth century, and gives the pedestrian visitor some sense of the scale and form of the structures standing on the streets during Emma's infancy.

[44] Hempstead is listed as in *Longworth's American Almanac, New-York Register and City Directory* beginning in the 1808-9 edition, plying his trade at addresses through the years on Third Avenue near Stanton Street, and on Orchard, Eldridge, Rivington and Broome Streets. It is likely that the family made its home in the immediate vicinity of the father's rope-making loft, perhaps in the same or an adjacent structure; the directory entries for Hempstead for the years in question do not distinguish between the family's residence and the father's business address. The addresses for Christopher Hempstead, Sr. listed for the year closest to Emma's birth date are 39 Rivington Street, and Eldridge Street near Stanton Street, a 15-minute walk from the waterfront.

[45] See Hempstead family genealogy tables from Ancestry.com

[46] The 1796 Brooklyn volume is located in the microfilm reels at the New York City Municipal Archives; it lacks a title page, but seems to have been published by John Bull of 115 Cherry Street. The last page of the microfilm record of this volume is an advertisement for *The New-York Weekly Magazine* also published from that address.

[47] Nathaniel Hempstead, Emma's paternal grandfather, acquired a 50 ft. by 100 ft. lot in an area near the local wharves on the south side of Brooklyn's Sands Street, west of Gold Street in October, 1803 from Joshua Sands for 150 pounds sterling. Longworth's American Directory for Brooklyn in 1811 also lists Nathaniel Hempstead as a rope-maker in Adams Street. Probate documents for various of Emma's ancestors verify their modest means, particularly in the details of Emma's grandfather Nathaniel's will, which was not offered for proof to the Surrogate's Court until six years after his death in 1834. [See: Kings County Surrogate's Court records, Liber 7 Page 256, probated on March 25, 1840] The instrument makes mention of the testator's "deceased son Nathaniel [B.] Hempstead" and leaves to each of that son's three children (Emma's first cousins) $100, to be paid four years after their grandmother Elizabeth's death. Emma's uncle, Nathaniel B. Hempstead, apparently predeceased his father: Spooner's 1822 Brooklyn Directory, while listing a Nathaniel Hempstead as a grocer at 47 Front Street, also lists Mary Hempstead, widow of Nathaniel Jr., at 129 Fulton Street, and Christopher Hempstead Sr., Emma's father, as a rope-maker at 6 High Street. Nathaniel Hempstead Sr.'s will leaves to Emma's father, Christopher Hempstead Sr., the entirety of the testator's modest-sized estate, subject only to (1) a lifetime annuity of $70 per year to the testator's sister (Emma's aunt) Ann[a] Van Winkle, and four years after her decease, a flat $200 distribution to each of her three children (Emma's first

cousins), (2) the payments to Nathaniel B.'s three children mentioned above, and (3) a payment of $600 to Christopher's sister, Hannah M. Powers (another aunt of Emma's). Christopher is listed as sole executor of his father's will, which was, for the times, a not insignificant, but hardly rich estate. It is unclear who carried out these executor's duties, as Christopher himself passed away on March 14, 1839, before probate of his father's will was accomplished.

[48] The yellow fever epidemic of 1822 that decimated Manhattan's poor neighborhoods may also have propelled the young Hempstead family across the East River to the less crowded and healthier climate of upland Brooklyn village.

[49] Marc Linder and Lawrence S. Zacharias, *Of Cabbages and Kings County: Agriculture and the Formation of Modern Brooklyn,* University of Iowa Press, Iowa City: 1999, Table 18, p. 316.

[50] The 5,222 acres devoted to farming in the Town of Brooklyn (whose land area was approximately 30% of Kings County) was exceeded only by the total cultivated acreage in the Town of Flatbush. Total lands devoted to farming in the Towns of Flatlands, Gravesend, New Utrecht and Bushwick were each approximately half of that employed in the Town of Brooklyn. [Ibid. Table 21, p. 318]. The tremendous demand for fresh vegetables of the much greater population of Manhattan, accessible to the Brooklyn farm wagons by dirt and plank roads and then by ferry across the East River, made the "truck" farms of Kings County competitive with the produce from more southerly locales for many decades during the nineteenth century, even after the mid-century development of railroad access to Southern agricultural areas with their far lower production costs and longer growing seasons. Farm labor, originally staffed by Dutch farming families in Kings County with family members and African slaves, soon absorbed significant numbers of the least-skilled and most poorly-educated Caucasian immigrants to America, including especially large numbers of Irish and German men.

[51] Cordelia was born in April, 1823. See *Records of the First Methodist Episcopal Church of Brooklyn, N.Y. formerly known as The Sands Street Methodist Episcopal Church,* Brooklyn, 1938; United Methodist Church Archives-GCAH, Drew University, Chatham. The Church was also known at The First Methodist Episcopal Church of Brooklyn.

[52] Christopher is listed in the New York City Methodist Episcopal Church Records volume entitled "A General Register of the Names of The Trustees Local Preachers and Leaders Etc. In the City of New York," dating from approximately 1816. It is unclear to which Manhattan congregation Christopher Hempstead belonged, although the downtown congregations at John, Allen, and Forsyth Streets, as well as that on the Bowery, are all possibilities located near the family's domicile. See *Methodist Episcopal Church Records – New York City- Vol. 79.* NYPL Special Collections]. Several items pertaining to the Hempstead family history are also noted in *Fictitious Heiress Of Dr. Burdell. Confessions Of The Accoucher: Bold Game Of Mrs. Cunningham — For Sale by All Periodical Dealers,* Boston: 1857. Anna does not appear in the baptismal records of the Sands Street church, but her parents may have baptized her in a ceremony conducted at one of the several other Methodist Wesleyan worship groups with which they affiliated after ending their membership at Sands Street.

[53] Methodist congregations, as well as many other Protestant denominations, granted formal "discharges" and "acceptances" when members moved between communities. See *Spooner's Brooklyn Directory of 1822*, Brooklyn, NY; published by Alden Spooner at the office of *The Long Island Star*, 60 Fulton St. Brooklyn, NY: 1822

[54] The Trustees of the Methodist Episcopal Church in Brooklyn paid $600 in May, 1829 to George Suckley for a 100-foot-square lot at the northwest corner of York and Gold Streets approximately seven months after Suckley also sold to Christopher Hempstead a 25 ft. by 100 ft. lot on the south side of Front Street just west of Gold Street. The conveyance of the 100-foot-square parcel to the Church trustees by Suckley was confirmed in 1835 when he also conveyed to the Trustees an interest in an irregular parcel containing the church parsonage, located on the north side of Concord Street, east of Jay Street, and a one-third interest in the portion of the Town of Brooklyn's burial ground located at Auburn Place and Portland Avenue allocated to Methodists. That burial ground was established in 1824, and legal title to the various congregations who shared the grounds was conveyed to them in 1828. See Brooklyn *Daily Eagle* January 23, 1844 p. 2, col. 3, and January 29, 1844, p.3, col. 3. The site of the Town burial ground is now occupied in part by Cumberland Hospital and other institutional structures on a plot in the central part of Fort Greene in northern Brooklyn. No trace of the cemetery appears above ground at the site today. The remains of the Methodist burial section were transported en masse to Cypress Hills Cemetery in the mid-nineteenth century. See deeds recorded in the Kings County Register's Office in Liber 24 Page 169, Liber 25 Page 431, and Liber 51, Page 492. Apparently the offshoots of the Sands Street Church shared a parsonage as well as a burial ground.

The original frame structure of the Sands Street church was not demolished when its successor was erected. The building was moved to a lot in Fulton Street, opposite High street, and remained devoted to church purposes. The African-American members of the Sands Street congregation also seceded and occupied a separate structure in the Village during the second decade of the century. In consideration of $325, Ebenezer and Lucretia Stevens conveyed a parcel of four-to-five thousand square feet on the west side of High Street, 160 feet south of Jay Street to The African Methodist Episcopal Church Trustees by deed dated July 1, 1819. See deed recorded in Kings County Register's Office in Liber 12 Page 505.

As a Class Leader in 1825 at the Sands Street church, Christopher Hempstead acted as a sub-pastor, holding weekly meetings and exercising the functions that Class Leaders typically fulfilled. These duties included visiting sick congregants, meeting with the pastor and the stewards of the church, collecting funds solicited from the class members, and procuring the attention of clergy for congregants desiring the services of pastors in their homes. [Class Leaders were first appointed by Methodism's patriarch, John Wesley, in 1742; their contribution collection responsibilities were among those first defined by Church hierarchy. See Volume I entry "Class Leaders" in *Encyclopaedia of World Methodism;* Noel B. Harmon Gen Editor, United Methodist Publishing House, Nashville: 1974). In addition to his other functions, Christopher Hempstead served as a trustee of the Sands Street church from 1826 through 1834. [See Spooner's Brooklyn Directories 1826-34].

Christopher Hempstead was made a trustee of the York Street church spin-off at the first meeting of its independent Board of Trustees held in June 1835. As the Sands Street congregation and its Sunday school grew, the need for separate structures in the neighborhood became apparent to the church trustees. The Sunday school was established in 1816 in Kirk's Printing Office on Adams Street. The formation of the York Street church occurred as early as 1824, when a frame building was erected at 162 York Street at the corner of Gold Street; it was enlarged in 1835. As leader of the Sands Street church Class organized in 1825, Christopher Hempstead formed, with his Class, the backbone of the congregation of the second church [See Edwin Warriner *Old Sands Street Methodist Episcopal Church, of Brooklyn, N.Y. : an illustrated centennial record, historical and biographical*, Phillips and Hunt, New York: 1885. Christopher was removed "by certificate" from the rolls of the Sands Street church in 1835, contemporaneously with his election as a trustee of the York Street church.

Until the formal independence of the York Street church, its congregants operated in tandem with the Sands Street congregation: ledgers of the two churches from May, 1831 indicate the presence of multiple shared pastors, exhorters, leaders, elders, stewards, and trustees. Emma's father and the other Leaders met on the first Monday evening of each month; quarterly collections were held on the second Sabbath of January, April, July and October. Holy Sacrament was administered in the Sands Street church on the first Sabbath of each month and in the York Street church on the third Sabbath of each month. Christopher's wife Sarah is also listed as a member of an 1831 Class, which met at 4 P.M. in the congregation's schoolroom. In accordance with Methodist custom, Class membership was segregated by gender.

[55] The reference to Adams Street as the location of the Class meeting led by Wells may refer to the Adams Street Sunday School facility operated by the various Methodist congregations.

[56] A third Methodist Episcopal church was erected in Washington Street near Tillary Street in approximately 1832. Each of the three affiliated congregations held an equal share in "burial grounds at Concord-st. and Wallabout". See Warriner, *op.cit.* pp. 24-5. Christopher Hempstead and his family apparently remained members of the York Street Church until May 1837, by which time the family had moved to Classon Avenue.

[57] No physical trace is visible today at the sites of the pre-1857 incarnations of the Methodist churches attended by the Hempsteads; indeed few structures of any kind have survived from the first half of the nineteenth century's Vinegar Hill and Fulton Ferry neighborhoods. The burgeoning prosperity of the maritime and industrial economies led to the replacement of the low-density religious, residential and industrial and other commercial structures of Emma Hempstead's childhood by a plethora of large masonry warehouses. Construction of the massive footings and lengthy approaches to the Brooklyn and Manhattan bridges in the late nineteenth and early twentieth centuries and subsequent "urban renewal" projects such as the creation of Cadman Plaza have left solely to the visitor's imagination the street scenes represented in William Perris' 1855 colored block and lot maps which detail the state of development of the Vinegar Hill and Fulton Ferry blocks from the days of Emma Hempstead's childhood through her marriage to George Cunningham.

[58] These businesses intermingled with the residences and churches in Vinegar Hill's street grid, and spread through Wallabout as Brooklyn's industrial economy burgeoned throughout the first half of the nineteenth century. Their proximity to Emma's homes during her teenage years is validated by various Brooklyn business directories for the period 1833-39.

[59] See *Brooklyn Eagle & Kings County Democrat,* January 10, 1843, p.2, col. 2.

[60] Such unions had become common by the advent of Emma's marriageable years, although the pairing of wealth with wealth remained of paramount importance. See Edward Pessen, "A Social and Economic Portrait of Jacksonian Brooklyn," *New York Historical Society Quarterly,* Vol. 55, No. 4 (1971), pp. 346-7.

[61] An interesting specimen of the child-rearing manuals in vogue during Emma's pre-adolescent years is represented in John S.C. Abbott, *The Child at Home; or The Principles of Filial Duty Familiarly Illustrated,* American Tract Society, New York: 1833. A digitized version of the work is viewable in *Hearth,* Cornell University's archive of domestic American publications at http://hearth.library.cornell.edu/.

[62] The neighborhood in which the first Cunningham establishment was located is colorfully depicted in a well-known painting of Brooklyn's village waterfront *Summer View of Brooklyn,* executed by Francis Guy, c. 1820. The oil on canvas work is in the collection of the Brooklyn Historical Society. A wintertime version of the same scene hangs in the Edna Barnes Salomon room on the third floor of the New York Public Library at 42nd Street and Fifth Avenue. See Henry R. Stiles, *A History of the City of Brooklyn, Including the Old Town and Village of Brooklyn, the Town of Bushwick, and the Village and City of Williamsburgh,* Brooklyn, N.Y. Published by Subscription: 1869, illustrations between pp. 88-89.

[63] Stiles, *op. cit.,* Vol. II, p. 93. Only one individual is listed as a distiller in Longworth's 1811 Brooklyn Directory; by 1841, there are 40 entries for "Manufacturer or distiller". See Pessen, pp. cit., pp. 327, 330. William Cunningham, Sr. was well off enough to acquire various parcels of prime Brooklyn waterfront area real estate during the spring and summer of 1810 for over $10,000: In May, 1810, Cunningham paid $4,250 to Robert Morris, Jr. and his wife Frances for a 200 ft. x 135 ft. lot at Washington and Water Streets; In May, 1810 Cunningham was the successful bidder at a court-ordered auction conducted on behalf of the Bank of New York in Manhattan's famed Tontine Coffee House. Cunningham's bid of $515 won a 25 ft. square lot near the Brooklyn Ferry that was part of a giant assemblage lost to the Bank by Brooklyn patroon Comfort Sands as a result of non-payment of various debts; In July, 1810, Cunningham also bought six lots, each 25 ft. x 100ft, for $4,750 from Robert Hodge, in a block bounded by Prospect, Adams, and Sands Streets. See deeds recorded in the Kings County Register's Office in Liber 9 Page 571, Liber 9 Page 579, and Liber 11 Page 44. William Cunningham Sr.'s early purchases also included $7,650 paid in 1813 for eight lots "East of the New Ferry" (near the foot of today's Old Fulton Street along the Brooklyn Heights waterfront) with significant frontage along Dock and Water Streets, that were also part of the Comfort Sands/Bank of New York foreclosure. Cunningham and a partner purchased and resold four lots on Willow and Middagh Streets in today's Brooklyn Heights neighborhood for considerable profits in the mid-

1830s, and Cunningham himself acquired and resold 33-35 Cranberry Street in the same area for a high four-figure sum.

[64] See Pessen, *op. cit.* pp. 331, 351-3.

[65] Between 1810 and 1814, George's father, William Cunningham Sr., owned a house, that he built on a lot at 38 Sands Street, on the north side of the block between Washington and Adams Streets. The house stood among a group of fashionable residences, across the street from the Sands Street Methodist Church's second edifice, erected in 1811, where Emma's parents were active members (although the date of inception of their membership is unclear). William Cunningham sold the property in 1814; his daughter Margaret and her husband William Harris also occupied the Sands Street house beginning in 1848, according to contemporary directories. Curiously, neither of them is listed in the Kings County Register's office as owning the property at any time. It is important to bear in mind in such cases of mismatch that individuals with title to valuable assets were frequently engaged in commercial disputes. Assets were often held in the names of friendly acquaintances to avoid exposure to suits.

William Cunningham Sr.'s first distillery in Brooklyn was located on the north side of Water Street near Dock Street; he resided at 38 Front Street and 35 Cranberry Street during some of the years in which his son and Emma Hempstead likely became acquainted. William and George Cunningham also occupied properties at 29 and 34 Front Street during Emma's childhood years, and later operated the distillery, ultimately inherited by George, at 57-61 Front Street. During many of the same years, Emma's grandfather, Nathaniel Hempstead, Sr. resided at 47 Front Street while her father, Christopher Sr. maintained addresses (whether for business and/or as a family residence) at numbers 3, 6, and 142 High Street, 143 and 163 Sands Street, and at the corner of Front and Gold Streets. All of these locations were within a small circumference in the waterfront Brooklyn Village of the times. Some of the addresses stood together on a single block. See Stiles, op. cit.,Vol. II, pp. 93,114; William Cunningham Sr.'s will is recorded in Liber 9, Pages 18 et. seq. in the Kings County Surrogate's Court Records, and the purchase and sale deeds to his Sands Street property are recorded in The Kings County Register's office is Liber 11, pages 44 and 50.

[66] The couple's relationship as man and wife, at least in the common-law sense, is validated, however, by references to the couple in probate documents of both families.

The *Tribune's* early coverage of the crime portrayed the Hempstead family in a generally favorable manner while at the same time disclosing alleged details of Emma's personal history and relationship to George Cunningham that were potentially controversial, such as the characterization of George as "*a distiller of 'liquid death' in Water street, Brooklyn, under the name of Cunningham & Harris.*" About the year 1839 they dissolved partnership, after which the senior partner was engaged in various pursuits. One article in the *Tribune* asserted that Cunningham had paid a third party to introduce him to Emma, and that after an intimacy developed, several children arrived outside of wedlock. Emma was said to have made her residence in Yonkers in Westchester County, New York during a portion of this time, while Cunningham lived with a woman in Brooklyn, whose maiden name was Pierce. Some time after Ms. Pierce's death Cunningham supposedly brought Emma back to Brooklyn, and lived with her in Jay Street; and about ten years after his introduction, he married her, on account of their daughters, who were then growing up to womanhood. See *New York Tribune*, February 5, 1857, p. 5, col. 5. Federal census records for Westchester County for 1840 and 1850 do not list a Emma Cunningham or Emma Hempstead. This is not dispositive, however, as to Emma's presence in Westchester County for the years in question, as the only single females listed by name in contemporary census records were widowed heads of households. The George D. Cunningham listed in the 1840 census in that county is not likely to have been Emma's husband, because that man is stated to be part of a large household in which six white males and three white females over the age of 15 resided. In addition, the entry in question is listed under the Town of Greenburgh rather than the City of Yonkers.

[67] See deeds and assignments of judgment recorded in Kings County Registers Office in L. 76, P. 184, L. 82, P. 203, L.229, P. 123, L.240, P. 428, L. 175, P. 197, L. 60, P. 240. Emma's father was dilatory in concluding his son's financial workout; the deed in L. 82, P. 203 recites his father's failure to carry out the terms of the trust, and a re-conveyance of the trust corpus to Christopher Jr.; one of the subsequent judgments against Emma's brother, initially obtained in 1842, was sold in 1850 at a discount to Horace Ladd of Elizabethtown, New Jersey, who then released the judgment as a lien against Christopher Jr.'s interest in property on Front Street. Ladd (also known as Horace Laddin) was George and Emma Cunningham's business agent during the 1840s and 1850s. Christopher Hempstead, Jr. is listed in Brooklyn directories after his father's death and will probate as being a milkman located at Kent and Myrtle Avenues and then at the Jamaica Road near the 2nd Toll Gate. See Webb and Hearne's Brooklyn Directories, 1841-2 and 1842-3. The size of their father's estate apparently was not sufficient to lift Christopher Jr. out of this modest profession.

[68] Kings County Surrogate's Court Records Will liber 7 p. 159. The paucity of the estate is indicated by the fact that the decendent's son sold his legacy for approximately $200 in an 1842 recorded deed.

[69] Emmerson Covel may also have been a member of the family of "James Covel, Junr" who is listed along with one "Noah Levings" on the cover page of *A Record of the Methodist Episcopal Church Brooklyn Long Island New York March 2, 1831* in which the above-mentioned ledger entries concerning Emma's parents' active roles in Wesleyan Methodist church affairs were found. Sarah's marriage to a congregation member would have been strongly encouraged by her parents.

[70] Kings County Surrogate's Court Probated Wills L 7 p. 159; paper copy also in NYC Municipal Archives Accession No. 88-66 from 31 Chambers St.; see also Wills Vol. 2: Commissioner of Records Kings County: Municipal Archives Accession No. 88-107.

[71] George D. Cunningham first appears as independent from his father in Brooklyn Village directories in Spooner's 1823 volume at 29 Front Street; he is also listed in the 1824 edition at that address as a distiller. The 29 Front St. address, as well as the others listed *infra*, is located in the immediate vicinity of where the Manhattan and Brooklyn Bridges cross the Brooklyn shore of the East River. Although much of the street grid of the area has been disrupted by

bridge and other construction noted above, nonetheless Gold, Washington, Water, Main and Front Streets, all mentioned below as business locations, survive in the neighborhood, albeit in sometimes truncated form, lying in the same beds today as they did in the early nineteenth century. The next year's edition of Spooner's Directory shows George at 34 Front Street, together with William Cunningham (his brother or father), and a separate listing for a Cunningham's distillery at 57 Front Street. In 1826, the Cunninghams remained at the 34 and 57 Front Street addresses, and a first appearance in Brooklyn directories was made by one William Cornell, as an inspector of spirits at 13 Front St. Cornell was to play an unfortunate role fifteen years later in a chain of events that ultimately led to George Cunningham's financial ruin. By 1829 William Cunningham, Sr. had moved to 38 Front Street, and the Cunningham distillery to 61 Front Street; significant address changes then occur over several years. George D. Cunningham is listed in the 1834-5 editions of Spooner's Directory as Alderman of the Second Ward of the newly incorporated City of Brooklyn.

[72] *George D. Cunningham vs. William Cornell,* Chancery Court, New York County, Index # BM 2197-C.

[73] Distillery swill was commonly sold in bulk to dairymen as a cheaper alternative to pasturing their herds. In an 1840-1 Brooklyn directory, Thomas D. Williams' dairy advertised the sale of milk from pasture-grazed cows as being healthier than that taken from animals fed on "still-slops."

[74] A transcription of the Police Committee's report to the Common Council is contained in the *Brooklyn Eagle & Kings County Democrat,* February 22, 1842, p. 2, col. 4. Despite the Common Council's refusal to act, Cunningham and Harris were subsequently indicted by the Grand Jury and convicted of public nuisance for having run their swill lines across Front Street; whether the court's sentence was ever carried out is unclear, as exceptions to the decision were taken up to the Kings County Supreme Court. See *Brooklyn Daily Eagle,* June 10, 1844, p. 2, col. 4, and October 19, 1844, p. 2, col. 5.

[75] The reason for appointment of a guardian for William does not appear in the available Surrogate's Court records.

[76] William Cunningham, Sr.'s will is transcribed in Liber 9, Pages 18 et. seq. in the Kings County Surrogate's Court Records, and the 1837 Guardianship proceedings involving his son William, Jr. are noted in the Records indices in Bonds Liber 1, Page 52, and Liber 2, Page 39, and in Letters Liber 2, Page 150 and Liber 3, Page 37. The texts of these Guardianship references are missing.

[77] For a thorough discussion of women's lives in early and mid-nineteenth century New York, see Christine Stansell, *City of Women,* New York: Alfred A. Knopf, Inc., 1986. Stansell's work explains the framework in which Emma Hempstead grew to maturity, the choices facing her at many points in her adolescent and adult life, and also provides a thoughtful feminist political framework in which to consider the rhetoric of the prosecution at Emma's 1857 murder trial.

[78] David Thomas Valentine, *Manual of the Corporation of the City of New York,* D.T. Valentine, New York: 1857, p. 480 and I.N. Phelps Stokes, *The Iconography of Manhattan Island, 1498-1909,* Robert H. Dodd, New York: 1928, v. 3, p. 702, as quoted in *Historic Designation Report for The East 17th Street/Irving Place Historic*

District, Gale Harris, Jay Shockley, Kerry Ehlinger, Glenn Modica, and Marjorie Pearson for The New York City Landmarks Preservation Commission, New York: 1998, p. 11, n. 3.

[79] Carole Klein, *Gramercy Park An American Bloomsbury*, Boston: Houghton Mifflin Company, 1987, pp. 16, 18, 41 and 43.

[80] 26 Irving Place was the southernmost of four row houses, which stood on the southeast corner of 16th Street and Irving Place shown on Perris's 1855 block and lot map of the area at NYPL. The site of the houses is occupied today by a large loft building, 30 Irving Place, constructed early in the twentieth century. Several Greek Revival-style row houses still standing on the East 17th Street portions of the District date from the 1830s and 1840s. Their basic red brick construction with brownstone detail is in all likelihood representative of the design of 26 Irving Place. The surviving Italianate-style houses on the blocks with facades of plain brownstone date from 1853-5, after George and Emma Cunningham departed the neighborhood. For a complete discussion of the development of the neighborhood and its importance in the social fabric of mid-century New York, see *Historic Designation Report, infra*. pp. 3–18.

[81] Perris's 1855 block and lot map at the NYPL shows the church at a site on the south side of East 15th Street on a lot numbered 63-75, between Third Avenue and Irving Place. The site forms a portion of the lot on which the headquarters of the Consolidated Edison Company of New York stand today. Rev. Snodgrass's son, George Vail Snodgrass, was later to figure prominently in the legal proceedings surrounding the murder of Harvey Burdell. Emma took George Vail in as a boarder at 31 Bond Street in November 1856. Rev. Snodgrass apparently moved out of New York City in 1849 or 1850 (no reference to him in Doggett's exists after the 1849-50 edition). He traveled from his home in Goshen, New York to testify in the Surrogate's Court proceedings maintained by Emma to wrest control of Harvey Burdell's estate from the court-appointed administrator. The Reverend testified as to having arranged his young son's tenancy at 31 Bond Street in the year before Harvey Burdell was murdered.

[82] *The Second Presbyterian Church of Brooklyn Session Minutes 1831-66* [ms coll of Presbyterian Historical Society, Philadelphia, PA.] contain the following entries at p. 35: "At a meeting of the Session held at the house of the Pastor on Thursday evening 21st March 1833, . . . The following persons presented their Certificates which being found to be in order they were thereupon admitted into membership with this Church viz. <u>Wm Cunningham</u> from the Presbyterian Church in Rutgers Street New York." Why William, Sr. remained a member of a downtown Manhattan congregation while presumably living across the river is unexplained. [*n.b.* Extant today in New York City on West 73rd Street is the Rutgers Presbyterian Church, the present incarnation of this congregation. The Rutgers Street building during the years 1809-41 was a frame structure at the corner of Henry and Rutgers Streets. A replacement stone edifice was erected on the site in 1841. The Presbyterian congregation departed in 1863. Today the Roman Catholic parish church of St. Teresa occupies the structure.

William Cunningham was an initial subscriber to the building fund of the First Presbyterian Church of Brooklyn in 1822. Disputes among the parishioners delayed the construction of the church. Meanwhile a Second Presbyterian Church was organized in 1831, and an edifice erected in 1834. When Emma's father-in-law William joined the Second Presbyterian congregation, its services were still being held at Classical Hall in Adams Street near Concord Street in Brooklyn. After William Cunningham Sr. joined the new congregation, a structure on Clinton Street near Fulton Street, of "Grecian architecture of brick construction" was dedicated May 4, 1834. See *Inventory of the Church Archives in New York City - The Presbyterian Church*, The Historical Records Survey, Works Projects Administration, New York: 1940. The cited *Sessions Minutes* also contain, at p. 219: " Tues evg April 22d. 1845 Session met this evening. Present Rev.d Dr. Spencer moder. Elders Morris, Alexander, Corning, Baylis, & Clarke. Absent Elders Mr. Farlan. Opened with prayer. Minutes of last meeting were read & approved. On motion resolved that the following list of persons who have died in communion with this Church from its organization up to this date be entered on the Sessions Book ... [includes:] William Cunningham . . ."

Margaret Cunningham was active in Presbyterian Church activities long before her marriage to William Harris. Her role as an educator is established in the *Brooklyn First Presbyterian Church Sunday School Directors' minutes 1824-31* (Presbyterian Historical Society collections, Philadelphia, PA). She was elected a director of the Sunday school association in 1826. A report the same year describes the vigor with which Margaret pursued her duties, as well as the daily fear of the onset of fatal diseases in which parishioners lived in the unsanitary Brooklyn Village. The document notes the addition of twelve teachers in the past year, making a total of nineteen. Other notable achievements during this year of Margaret Cunningham's stewardship included "28 Bibles and 66 Testaments distributed as premiums and 2,179 chapters have been committed to memory by the school during the past year. In addition to this there have been 755 'Sunday School Magazines' distributed to such children as have found and recited four texts of scripture to prove the monthly scripture question." The report also ascribes a decrease in juvenile offenses in the Village in part due to Sunday school growth. Minutes from the Sunday school association in 1830 indicate that Margaret Cunningham had by then ended her tenure as female superintendent, although she remained a director of her congregation's school.

Some years later, Margaret's marriage is noted: *Marriage Register of the Second Presbyterian Church Brooklyn NY 1833-58*, (Presbyterian Historical Society collections, Philadelphia, PA). " January 17, 1839 William M. Harris of Richmond and Margaret Ann Cunningham of Brooklyn [No.] 139"

[83] "Brooklyn NY Second Presbyterian Church Members 1839-75" [probably actually the Spencer Memorial Church records: Melancton W. Jacobus is listed as minister in this ledger 9/15/1839-10/26/1851, but the WPA Methodist Church records Guide states that he was pastor of Spencer Memorial during the relevant period, not of Second Presbyterian] See Presbyterian Historical Society, Philadelphia, PA cat V/F/MI46 B79: " Page of Record 144: Mrs. Emma A Cunningham received as a member Sept 23, 1846 from Fifteenth St. Pres Ch in NY City dismissed 1854; George D. Cunningham admitted May 13, 1849 by Profession – dismissal due to death in 1854 page of record 180." The father of Harvey Burdell's sister in-law Margaret Burdell joined the same Presbyterian

congregation during the intervening years between his Margaret's separation from Harvey's older brother John Burdell, and Emma and George Cunningham's return to Brooklyn from Irving Place: William Alburtis is listed in the same ledgers as a member "received Feb 22, 1842 from the Second Assoc Ref. Church in NYC with his wife Sarah."

[84] Emma is named as a defendant on account of being his wife in one such action: see *Edward Denham vs. George D. Cunningham*, Chancery Court, New York County, Index D CH 257, judgment dated April 14, 1848; also *The President, Managers of the Delaware and Hudson Canal Co. vs. George D. Cunningham, William M. Harris et al*, County Chancery Court, New York, Index # INC BM7D, filed 9/26/1845, and *Charles T. Cromwell vs. George D. Cunningham, Emma Cunningham et al*, Chancery Court, New York County, Index # BM 2018C, filed 8/31/1846. These cases all involved properties in Kings County in which George Cunningham held an interest, directly or indirectly. Another foreclosure occurred in 1843 concerning property in Monroe County, New York: *Jas. G. King vs. George D. Cunningham*, Chancery Court, New York County, Index DCHK27, filed 7/22/1843.

Cunningham had been the defendant in numerous suits brought against him by creditors at the end of the 1840s which resulted in Kings County Sheriff Daniel Van Voorhees' seizure and sale of Cunningham's property on the north side of Front Street, just east of Main Street at "public vendue at the Franklin House No. 15 Fulton Street in the City of Brooklyn" in the summer of 1850. Late in the previous year, George and Emma joined Emma's sisters Cordelia and Anna, as well as an additional married couple, in selling for $2,000 above an existing $800 mortgage, a 2,750 square-foot lot on the north side of Front Street, east of Gold Street.

[85] Beginning in 1830, Louis Godey published his eponymous guide to fashion and etiquette. His *Lady's Book*, edited for many years by Sarah Hale, quickly became the authoritative instruction manual and arbiter of style for women aspiring to middle-class status and more. The magazine ceased publication in 1898. See http://www.uvm.edu/~hag/godey/glbpub.html.

[86] Pessen, *op. cit.* p 202-3.

[87] See *Hearne's Directories* for the years 1847-1853. The Nassau Fire Insurance Company of Brooklyn was initially capitalized at $150,000 when formed in 1852. Harris was one of 35 original members of the Board of Directors, which included prominent Brooklyn businessmen such as Abiel A. Low (creator of the Low family shipping fortune, and father of Seth Low, the future mayor of both Brooklyn and New York City, and President of Columbia College. By the fourth anniversary of its formation, Harris presided over an entity that had almost $6,000,000 of policy risk outstanding. Its assets consisted primarily of bonds and mortgages. The average return to its investors during its first four years of existence was 14% per annum. See "Act of incorporation: charter and by-laws of the Nassau Fire Insurance Company of Brooklyn", I. van Anden, Brooklyn: 1852 [NYPL] and "Special report of the insurance commissioners appointed by the Comptroller to examine into the conditions and affairs of the fire insurance companies in the cities of New York and Brooklyn, 1856" C. Van Benthuysen, printer to the legislature; Albany: 1857 [NYPL]. Another indication of the Harris family's middle-class status is the fact that Margaret Harris

acquired a house at 51 Sands Street in April,1858, for the sum of $4,000. A $3,000 mortgage on the 27 ft. 6 in. wide by 100 ft. deep lot was repaid the following September. It is unclear if the initial acquisition price included assumption of this mortgage balance.

[88] Commencing in early December 1849, George's sister Eliza Cunningham, acting as sole executor of her father's estate, advertised in the *Brooklyn Daily Eagle* an auction sale of the family distillery. The property had been under a 21-year lease to George since 1835, which was still in force at the time of their father's execution of his will in April, 1842. Although the lease rents were placed in trust by the testator for the benefit of his three daughters and certain grandchildren, his executors were empowered to sell the distillery, in which case the proceeds were to be turned over to George. No express provision was made in the will to place any of such proceeds in trust for the named beneficiaries. For reasons which are unclear, Eliza Cunningham took it upon herself to sell the distillery property, probably after George's departure for California, and perhaps unbeknownst to him. Her efforts may have been aborted: by a sheriff's judgment execution sale in July, 1850, George Cunningham lost title to a parcel of over half an acre located at 61 Front Street, west of Main Street, the legal description of which in the sheriff's deed is quite similar to the property described in Eliza Cunningham's auction notice. The parcel sold by the Sheriff Daniel Van Voorhis in July, 1850, was seized by him a result of debt collection efforts by various of George Cunningham's creditors. The sheriff's sale would, in all likelihood, have wiped out the distillery leasehold, and any proceeds were probably paid only to George's creditors, thus cutting off Margaret Cunningham Harris' (and her sisters') annuities. See deed recorded in Kings County Register's Office in Liber 221, Page 283 on July 6, 1850: Daniel Van Voorhis, Sheriff as grantor to Stephen C. Williams as grantee in execution of judgments obtained by various creditors of George D. Cunningham.

[89] A G.D. Cunningham left California to return to New York via Panama on the *Oregon,* sailing from San Francisco harbor on or about June 1, 1850. See California Genealogy Index Departure Number 55877 from p. 3 of the June 1, 1850 issue of *Alta California,* San Francisco.

[90] George Cunningham's residence is listed in *Hearne's Directories* for Brooklyn as being at 107 Jay Street in the 1847-8, 1848-9, and 1849-50 editions. He is unlisted in the 1850-1, 1851-2 and 1852-3 editions, but is shown in the 1853-4 edition at "4th Pl. nr. Clinton" as he is in the 1854-5 Smith directory of Brooklyn. The records of the Brooklyn City Register do not list him as owner of 107 Jay Street during any of these or adjacent years. The 1850 U.S. Census shows George, Emma and their five children living in the 16th Ward on Manhattan's lower west side.

Title records indicate that George and Emma Cunningham never held a recorded deed to the last home they shared through early 1854. It is more likely that the couple rented the modest row house on 4th Place in South Brooklyn or inhabited part of it as a new multifamily dwelling, constructed speculatively. Real estate developers had drained the swampy land at the head of Bompjes Creek on Gowanus Bay when the the Gowanus Canal was first channeled during the previous decade. The draining of the neighboring wetland areas of South Brooklyn traversed by Red Hook Lane, in which mill ponds adjacent to the mouth of Gowanus Creek and Bompjes Hook and other creeks surrounding Gerritsen's and Remsen's Islands were situated, created the neighborhood ultimately named Carroll Gardens, in honor of Declaration of Independence signatory and Revolutionary War General Charles Carroll. [See "Map of the City of Brooklyn and Village of Williamsburgh, Compiled, Lithographed and Published by Richard Butt, Surveyor", 1846; NYPL Ford Collection].

Perris's 1855 maps of the four blocks radiating from the intersection of 4th Place and Clinton Street show only 34 houses, all set back from the curb in "front garden" design that still prevails in the neighborhood. The balance of the blocks was vacant at the time of Perris's mapping with the exception of a "Florist Garden" on the northeast corner of 4th Place and Henry Street. Brooklyn Register's Office records do not show Cunningham as titleholder of any of the parcels on the four possible blocks on which the house stood in which his funeral was conducted. These blocks of Fourth Place are filled today with the three and four story brownstone and brick-front homes that were first being erected in the area during the years surrounding George and Emma's residence there. Although the exact address is unclear, the home is almost certainly one of the extant structures on the blocks.

[91] *Frank Leslie's Illustrated Newspaper,* New York: Vol. III, No. 63, February 21, 1857, p. 192 col. 1.

[92] *Brooklyn Daily Eagle,* February 3, 1857, p. 2 col. 1. The *Tribune's* account of George Cunningham's end differed materially: "Cunningham's fortune having become impaired, he emigrated to California to better his position. Her returned about the year 1853, with what success is not definitely known. He domiciled with Miss Hempstead when he came back, and one morning, about three years ago, he was found dead in his bed. It was known that he drank considerably, and the cause of his decease was therefore evident. Congestion of the brain was the general verdict, and the correctness of the conclusion can hardly be disputed, whatever may be said to the contrary. The idea of exhuming the body after so long a time has elapsed, with the view to ascertaining the cause of death, is all nonsense; no trace could now be detected. Every circumstance goes to show that Cunningham died from natural causes." See *New York Tribune,* February 5, 1857, p. 5, col. 5.

[93] *Brooklyn Daily Eagle,* February 4, 1857, p. 2 col. 3. Cunningham's death notice in the *Eagle* published June 3, 1854 recites his demise "after a lingering and painful illness

[94] George Cunningham's name does not appear in the membership records of the various Presbyterian churches in Brooklyn of which his father, mother, and sister Margaret were members in earlier years. Apparently he did not join Emma in her attendance at Rev. Snodgrass's services near Irving Place, as his name does not appear alongside hers in the roll book of Manhattan's Fifteenth Street Presbyterian Church for the years in question. See: "Brooklyn NY Second Presbyterian Church Members 1839-75" [probably actually the Spencer Memorial Church records: Melancton W. Jacobus is listed as minister in this ledger 9/15/39-10/26/51, but the WPA Methodist Church records Guide states that he was pastor of Spencer Memorial during the relevant period, not of Second Presbyterian] See Presbyterian Historical Society, Philadelphia, PA cat V/F/MI46 B79: "Page of Record 144: Mrs. Emma A Cunningham received as a member Sept 23, 1846 from Fifteenth St. Pres Ch

in NY City dismissed 1854; George D. Cunningham admitted May 13, 1849 by Profession – dismissal due to death in 1854 page of record 180. Note also "Brooklyn N.Y First Presbyterian Church Sessions Records 1838-1859" Cat. No. V/MI46/B79fs. Page 3 in the alphabetical listings of members in this volume shows "Geo. D. Cunningham [admitted in]1849 - died 1854, and at page 180: "at the close of divine service on Sabbath 13 May 1849 Session was convened at the Church, present Rev. M.W. Jacobus Moderator, with Elders Hinsdale, Ledyard, Van Dayne & Sampson when <u>Mr. George D. Cunningham</u> was received to the Church Communion having professed a change of heart" [the front page of this volume is titled *Sessional Records of the First Presbyterian Church*, but again note that Jacobus was pastor of Spencer Memorial in 1849].

The document, witnessed by William J. Hoppin of 378 Fourth St. in Manhattan, George Hargan of 121 Elm St., also of Manhattan, and Horace H. Laddin of Elizabethtown, New Jersey, is the simplest imaginable, appointing Emma executrix and sole legatee. Probate of George's will was accepted on November 21, 1854 in Kings County Surrogate's Court. The probate instruments are pro forma, and devoid of controversy. Kings County Surrogate's Court Will Liber 16 P. 343. See also probate instruments in NYC Municipal Archives Accession No. 88-66; see also Wills Vol. 2: Commissioner of Records Kings County: Municipal Archives Accession No. 88-107

[95] Even a $10,000 inheritance would not have sustained Emma and her children for long. Assuming investment of the money at 5% per annum, the income from the estate would not have paid for more than the rental of a modestly comfortable house in Brooklyn or Manhattan at the prevailing prices. Contemporary classified advertisements in the *New York Herald* provide only one of many abundant sources of prices for real estate, as well as a sense of the cost of furnishings, daily sustenance, school fees, transportation, medical and dental care, clothing, and all of the other necessities of a middle class life to which Emma had become accustomed. Expenditures for these items would have depleted her capital rapidly.

[96] Laddin lived at 196 West 20th St. in Manhattan by 1857, and at the time maintained a place of business downtown at 63 Water Street. See New York County District Attorney Indictment Records: *People (A. Oakley Hall, District Attorney) vs. Emma Augusta Cunningham*: February 1857. Laddin's affidavit is included in these handwritten documents.

[97] The alternatives to a quick and successful resolution of their fate through Emma's remarriage were grim for mother and children alike, particularly so for Emma's daughters. Employment for wages was not a feasible means for Emma to support her offspring. In mid-century New York, unmarried women with no significant family financial support faced a severely limited number of respectable choices in order to support themselves and their children. None of the possibilities offered more than the most meager of livelihoods. At its all-too-common worst, women in the lowest economic strata were forced with their young daughters into lives of prostitution and its attendant miseries. This widespread phenomenon in mid-nineteenth century New York must have haunted Emma Cunningham as she struggled to maintain her equilibrium during the summer and fall of 1854.

[98] Despite references to his existence in the press at Burdell's death, the author

has been unable to locate Dr. Longfellow in contemporary Manhattan directories, nor in the archives of the New York County Medical Society.

Emma Cunningham was also acquainted with Dr. Oliver Wellington, a prominent advocate of the "water cure," who maintained a residential treatment center on 12th Street and University Place during the mid-1850s, and to whom Emma brought one of her daughters for treatment in those years.

[99] Only two months after George's death, Emma Cunningham invested most of her late husband's estate in a house and lot on West 46th Street in Manhattan. She liquidated this $7,000 investment in August, 1857, under duress, after her trial on murder charges in the death of Dr. Burdell. Emma lost approximately 30% of her investment. See deeds recorded in NY County Register's Office: L. 676, P. 46 (recorded September 2, 1854) and L. 733, P. 559 (recorded August 25, 1857).

According to at least one account published after Burdell's murder, Emma was in the habit of visiting conveniently situated Saratoga relatives while searching for a new mate. As the *Utica Telegraph* reported: *"She is a very fine-looking woman, and to judge from her conversation, is given to conquests of the heart. She, it was said, was engaged to be married to a widower of this city, but he broke off the match and married another."* See *Utica Telegraph*, [n.d.] as transcribed in the *New York Tribune*, 2/7/57 p.7.

In the litigation concerning Harvey Burdell's estate that proceeded apace in 1857, evidence from a relative of Whitehall Hyde was offered concerning letters allegedly received by Mr. Hyde from Emma purportedly negating her claim of having married Dr. Burdell in the Fall of 1856. Samuel Tilden, Esq. represented the Burdell blood relatives in the lawsuit, and relevant affidavits are contained in Tilden's legal files for the Burdell matter which are held in the manuscript collections of the New York Public Library.

[100] Miss Van Ness' testimony is transcribed in the May 9, 1857 edition of the *New York Tribune* on p. 11.

[101] During the course of Surrogate's Court proceedings held to decide on Emma's claim to Harvey Burdell's estate, an Elizabethport, NJ cordage manufacturer, James C. Fairbanks, told the court of the many visits in 1855 made to the village by Dr. Burdell in the company of Emma Cunningham, and of the dentist's conversations with him about Emma's wealth and intention to invest in local real estate with Burdell. See the *New York Tribune*, June 16, 1857, p. 7, col. 4. Fairbanks supplied building materials to Burdell for the repair of sidewalks around houses that the doctor owned in the New Jersey village, and when the bills went unpaid, he filed mechanics' liens against the properties that were asserted in the administration of Burdell's estate.

[102] By the beginning of 1857, the cost of many popular photographic processes was available to persons of very modest incomes. For between 20 to 50 cents, an ambrotype could be had in New York City. See *New York Herald*, January 5, 1857, p. 5, col. 3.

[103] Howe's Caverns remains popular today as a regional tourist attraction in the northern Catskill Mountains.

[104] The school's 1855 catalogue offered a curriculum surprisingly consonant with the display advertisement's puffing. Not only were fine and musical arts

offered; the students' regimen also included mathematics, botany, chemistry, physics, astronomy, anatomy physiology, theology, moral science, English grammar and composition, Latin, French and "Butler's Analogy." Although four and six young ladies, respectively, formed the graduating classes of the seminary in its first two years of operation, the matriculants in 1855 for the four-year program numbered 116, hailing virtually entirely from the greater Saratoga/Albany, New York region. This rapid growth in enrollment accompanied the sale of the seminary to a new proprietor. Abolitionist Reverend Luther F. Beecher, D.D., second cousin to the famous Great Divine of Brooklyn's Plymouth Church, the Rev. Henry Ward Beecher, purchased the seminary operations at the end of the 1854-55 academic year. Luther Beecher had already successfully led campaigns for new church buildings as pastor of Albany's First Baptist Church during his tenure there from 1849-1853, and in Saratoga Springs as pastor of the First Baptist Church, where his pulpit continued from 1854 through 1860. Reverend Beecher was apparently skilled at building fund development, and promptly upon his acquisition of Carter's Female Seminary, he secured the necessary funds to erect a new building on the site, (extant today), renaming the operation "Temple Grove Seminary." Emerson Carter remained a principal in the operation of the school. The new name of the seminary derived from unrealized plans of another local religious group, which had contemplated the erection of a worship edifice among a grove of trees on the site. Luther Beecher's prominent role in Saratoga's religious affairs made him an important person with whom to become acquainted for the many individuals wishing to put their days and evenings in Saratoga to optimal social use.

Visitors to Saratoga today can stand on the northeastern corner of Congress Hall Park and look directly into the windows of the structure across the street that once housed the Saratoga Female Seminary. The building, now occupied as a private apartment house, served for many years as a principal building on the original campus of Skidmore College. That institution moved to a newly built campus north of Saratoga Village during the 1960s.

[105] See William L. Stone; *Saratoga Springs: Being a Complete Guide to the Mineral Springs, Hotels, Drives and All Points of Interest Around and In the Immediate Vicinity of This Celebrated Watering Place. Views Taken on the Spot by William Gellatly*, T. Nelson & Sons, 137 Grand Street, New York: 1866. For contemporary and slightly later nineteenth century stereoscopic views of Congress Hall Park and Congress Spring pavilion, see NYPL collection of Stereographic Images of Small Town America http://digital.nypl.org/stereoviews/.

[106] *Frank Leslie's Illustrated Newspaper*, August 27, 1859, p 198, col. 1.

[107] *The Daily Saratogian*, July 11, 1856.

[108] Nathaniel Parker Willis, *American Scenery; or Land, lake and river illustrations of transatlantic nature*, London: G.Virtue, 1840.

[109] *The Daily Saratogian* issue of July 15, 1856, skewered both fashion pretensions and the slavery of both men and women to the custom of the season:

The Fashion at Saratoga*: There unhappy old bachelor, and there, poor, purse-ridden, hen-pecked Benedict, don't be alarmed. We are not about to tell you how many yards of silk should comprise 'my lady's' skirt, and what should be the figure or the size of her taffeta; the particular qualities of her morning robe, her noon negligee, or* her evening promenade dress. All these points you will find set forth, in mathematical order, with plates, in Frank Leslie's Ladies Gazette–price six and a quarter cents. We only intend to give a passing word of notice to the appearance of the fashionable world in Saratoga at the present time; for say what you will, we adhere to the theory Saratoga is a miniature world by itself. It has,- at least at this season of the year, - its peoples, its nationalities, its classes, its grades, and each of them is as exclusively distinct from the other as if it existed in another hemisphere.

In Saratoga, if you calculate to amount to anything, if you wish to attract the merest passing notice of the busy throng; if, in short, you would not be an absolute nonentity among the Kings and Queens of display, you must submit yourself an absolute and uncomplaining slave to the arbitration of Fashion. Comfort, pleasure, personal preference, convenience, propriety, – everything, in short, which may be supposed to appertain to the independence of the human race divine, must be sacrificed to this Absolutism. To murmur against this tyranny, or to refuse to submit to the decrees which it imposes, is to exclude yourself from the world of gayety and frivolity - to make yourself a nobody.

Fashion is fickle as well as tyrannous – We well remember when she had the female sex promenading the street with ridiculously prominent bustles, disproportionate in shape, and far from modest in appearance. Now we find the prominence transferred, the order reversed and a far more ridiculous dominance of display after the fashion of that made by good old Queen Anne of England. "Eugenie skirts" have taken the place of the "tournament" and we presume they will next be succeeded by an abandonment of both, and a return to Quaker wrapper of Penn's period. Such are the inconsistencies of the Dame.

A full dress in the morning is decidedly out of order in Saratoga. If a lady wishes to promenade before the scorching summer sun has wheeled his chariot high up in the heavens, she must do so in a loose negligee, wrapper, or gown, with no shawl or bonnet, a uniform which would almost justify an imputation upon modesty in the drawing room, and one which certainly is wholly out of place in the open street. And so the poor things go shivering along, perhaps with bare arms, and uncovered head, thro' the chill morning air, and with the heavy dews rising all about them, - - nervously gulp down their portion of spring water, and then hasten home to the enjoyment of a choice dose of the chills, or perhaps a thorough compound of fever and ague. Day after day the same routine is followed, and the same sufferings experienced, and the poor victims bear them uncomplainingly, for fashion decrees it.

By-and-by the sun grows hot, and the air is mucky, and all out-door unpleasant and disagreeable. Then the devotee of Fashion must don her silks and satins, cast a cashmere over her shoulders, have her auburn or raven locks erected into pyramids in the latest French style, with jewels and diamonds interwoven, and then, with but a light gauze veil to protect her from the scorching rays which shoot down from above, off for the second display upon the streets. She returns, with bounding brain and aching head; but what of that? it is fashionable, and she must follow the decrees of the tyrant.

As evening draws her mantle over the world, as the air becomes cool and delicious, as the breezes sweep gently through the air, on with the broad wide bloomer _____, the heavy skirts, on with all the ____ of dress and discomfort, and then, if you like, off for a walk, or a dance in the parlor of the hotel. And then, when worn out, almost weary of life, sick of the monotonous routine which you are compelled to *undergo, totter to bed, and get a moiety of slumber, to prepare you for another similar course on the morrow.*

Such is the out-side fashionable life of one sex at a fashionable watering place.

[blanks represent smudges in microfilm text]

[110] Notwithstanding her wealth and lengthy ownership of a beautiful manor home in New York City's Washington Heights, Madame Jumel experienced in Saratoga the same ostracism among the most privileged circles that she had borne for decades in New York, among whispers of the questionable circumstances surrounding her initial acquaintance and subsequent marriage to her first husband, the wealthy French merchant Stephen Jumel. Madame Jumel's brief second marriage to Aaron Burr in the early 1830s did little to improve her fortune among the Saratoga elite. Jumel's revenge was that typical of and frequently realized in America: she acquired a massive property on Lake Avenue and out of spite, set about constructing one of the largest showplaces in town.

[111] *The Daily Saratogian,* June 27, 1856.

[112] Burdell's role in the Webster Fire Insurance Company is documented in the *Brooklyn Daily Eagle,* April 7, 1855, p. 2 col. 5.

[113] See "EDITORIAL. Murder of Dr. Burdell" at p. 285 *et. seq.* of the December, 1857 issue of the *New York Dental Recorder.*

[114] Genealogical data obtained from Jefferson County, New York libraries and a descendant of Harvey's nephew Galen Burdell also state that Harvey and his four brothers were the sons of Polly Cunningham Burdell and a Presbyterian farmer named John Burdell. John Burdell and Polly Cunningham lived on a farm near Sackett's Harbor in Jefferson County. Before John's untimely death, the couple also lived in a farmhouse located where the Baggs Hotel stood in Utica, New York. According to these accounts, the couple eventually sold the Utica area farm and moved to the Herkimer County village of German Flats.

Other news articles published at the time of his death state that Harvey Burdell moved with one or both of his parents to Sackett's Harbor, New York on the southeastern shore of Lake Ontario during or immediately after the War of 1812. According to one account, Harvey's parents were separated, whether by his father's death or for other reasons, during this time, and Harvey's father died when he was a only a few years old. The confusion of the 1857 journalism is compounded by the information in the 1810 U.S. census data, the ledgers of which list a "Wm Burdell" in the German Flatts [sic] community of Herkimer County, [Herkimer County p. 410 of US census ledgers for New York State] with 3 males under 10 years old, 1 male 26-45 and no other household members. Harvey Burdell's father may have moved to Sackett's Harbor with some but not all of his offspring, and/or without his wife, for a variety of reasons, including the fact that Sackett's Harbor was the scene of considerable military activity during the War of 1812. No other relevant Burdell census data from the two counties exists.

Charmaine Burdell Veronda, great-granddaughter of Harvey Burdell's nephew, Galen Burdell, provided the author with family recollections and genealogical society worksheets that support both William and John as putative fathers of Harvey Burdell. Corroborative material of a similar nature is located in a Burdell family genealogical file at Flower Memorial Library in Watertown, NY. No primary archival sources completely validate either conclusion.

[115] All of Polly's offspring were interpled in litigation instituted by Emma Cunningham concerning the disposition of Harvey Burdell's sizeable estate after his murder in 1857.

[116] See Crisfield Johnson, *History of Oswego County*, Philadelphia: L.H. Everts & Co., 1877, Chap. XXXI, p. 118; also *New York Courier*, February 8, 1857, p.5.

[117] *New York Tribune*, February 5, 1857, pp. 5-6.

[118] The other prestigious medical degree-granting institution of the 1820s and 1830s in Philadelphia was the University of Pennsylvania Medical School. The Burdell brothers are absent from its list of degree recipients, as well as from any contemporary lists of graduates of The Medical Department of Pennsylvania College, Philadelphia College of Medicine, Franklin Medical College, Penn Medical University, Eclectic Medical College of Philadelphia, American University of Philadelphia, and the Philadelphia University of Medicine and Surgery. See: Harold J. Abrahams, *Extinct Medical Schools of Nineteenth Century Philadelphia*, Philadelphia: University of Pennsylvania Press: 1966.

The minutes of the Committee on Admissions of the New York Academy of Medicine of 1848 (ms collections of The New York Academy of Medicine) state that Harvey Burdell applied for admission to the Academy as a graduate of the Jefferson Medical College. His prevarication apparently went undetected: membership was denied him on the sole basis that the Academy, after holding hearings initiated as a result of Burdell's novel application, had instituted a policy excluding from membership individuals whose practice was limited to the then still disrespectable profession of dentistry.

Harvey Burdell was admitted in 1835 to the New York County Medical Society based upon his alleged status as a graduate of the Medical College of Tennessee (See Members of the New York County Medical Society From Its Organization 1806-1861: ms. Collections of the New York Academy of Medicine). The Tennessee school became part of the University of Nashville after Harvey Burdell moved to New York City. No mention of his graduation during the relevant years appears in the catalog of graduates of the University of Nashville and its predecessor schools. (See *Catalogue of officers and graduates of the University of Nashville with an appendix, containing sundry historical notices, etc.*, A. Nelson & Co., printers, Nashville: 1850 [Tennessee State Library].) Whether or not either of the Burdell brothers actually resided in Philadelphia during their medical training is also open to question. No mention of John or Harvey Burdell appears in the various Philadelphia City Directories for the years 1825, 1828-31, and 1833 available at The Pennsylvania Historical Society. However, none of this is dispositive as to the brothers' presence or absence in that city during those years. Young students with no financial resources and no trade would not likely be listed in the directories of citizens in common use at the time. Such directories were primarily oriented to listings of males involved in trades, crafts and other profitable employment.

[119] Harvey and John Burdell, *Observations on The Structure, Physiology, Anatomy and Diseases of the Teeth, In Two Parts*, New York: Gould and Newman, 1838.

[120] By 1857, several processes had been developed for the numbing of areas where dental work was performed, providing an imperfect but still worthwhile means of mitigating the torture of dentistry for some patients. Early that year,

one of Harvey Burdell's Bond Street neighbors, dentist E. Wilson, advertised the availability in his office at 27 Bond Street of a novel process, using an apparatus patented by Dr. J.B. Branch of Galena, Illinois. See *New York Herald,* January 5, 1857, p. 3, col. 5, January 18, 1857, p. 7, col. 6, and January 21, 1857, p. 3, col. 4.

[121] Ibid. p. vii. The summary by the Burdell brothers of the woeful state of dentistry in America from these same pages further explains the climate in which their practice thrived:

"Information on the subject of the preservation of the teeth should be more extensively diffused throughout the community; but in this country, where the treatment of the diseases of the teeth is confined principally to unprofessional persons, the licensed practitioner considers it out of his province to interfere, or even to study the subject, so as to impart to others useful knowledge."

"Dental quacks and impostors succeed better in filling decayed teeth than in the other branches of the profession. The reason of this is obvious from the fact, that almost any substance will remain, for a short time in the orifice of a decayed tooth; and previous to the discovery of the deception, and the non-utility of their pastes and succedaneums, they pocket the reward of their vile deception, and walk away."

"Extracting teeth requires as much care, skill, and ability for its judicious and safe performance, as do those operations in surgery to which is attached a much higher degree of importance. The pain of the operation is much diminished by judicious and proper application of the instrument.

"A use of the turnkey, among scientific dentists of the present day is superseded by the forceps, and except among physicians and 'old-fashioned dentists' the turnkey instrument is seldom employed.

"It has been stated that fatal consequences have resulted from removing, or attempting to remove, decayed teeth with a turnkey. It is impossible, however, for any danger to arise, even under the most disadvantageous circumstances, in using the forceps. The awkward and careless manner in which not a few 'pullers' take hold of the tooth, and wrench it from the jaw, reckless of consequences and the sensibilities of the patient, deserves execration."

[122] The preface to the material Harvey Burdell quoted from his Parisian source adds further color to the energy with which he was infused by daily contact with many of his female clients:

To illustrate this fact, the following picture is drawn by Mr. Pleasants, in a work written by him and dedicated, with permission, to Dr. Valentine Mott. [Mott was one of the most prominent and respected physicians in New York in the early and mid-nineteenth century].

'If the sculptor, the painter, or the poet, ' says Mr. Pleasants, ' would invest the production of his genius with those forms of horror [from] which humanity shudders and recoils, he perfectly comprehends the art of giving to his allegorical personages an array of teeth, black with tartar, mutilated with gangrene, broken by violence, or wrested by distortion. Should Envy present herself in the group, her parted lips would disclose but a single fang. Should Malice approach to persecute his victim, his teeth would be turned away as if by the violence of his passion. Thus the wrinkled witch, the smoky gipsy, [sic] the fortune-telling hag, and the freebooter of the seas, would lose the proper expression of their distinctive characters if supplied with perfect, regular and beautiful sets of teeth.

'On the other hand, the skilful artist, who would exhibit the amiable and worthy passions in all their loveliness and attraction, bestows untiringly therein the exhibition of perfect arches of teeth, white as monumental alabaster, and regular as the crystal columns in the Palace of Odin, inhabited by the virgins of the Valhallah. If he exhibit beauty in her smiles, a colonnade of pearls contribute to the enchantment; if he show us Love, with music on her lips, the emblematic purity of her teeth must lend its tributary charm. Thus the ideal Venus of the polished Greeks, as well as the living Beauty in the hamlet of Circassia, would cease to please on the discovery of sensible defect in these important organs.'

A scientific medical writer of Paris thus concludes, in subscribing the influence of the teeth over the other attractions of the face.

[123] John and Margaret lived together at 69 Chambers Street during the early days of their marriage. The house was one of five contiguous brick buildings fronting on the north side of Chambers Street just east of Broadway, acquired by James McCall in March, 1833 as part of an assemblage that included his acquisition two months later of contiguous Broadway frontage from Margaret's father William. Although there is no definitive evidence that John Burdell occupied 69 Chambers Street before William Alburtis conveyed his adjacent property to McCall, it is likely that John was nonetheless acquainted with his future wife's father before the sale: John is listed as living at 69 Chambers Street in Longworth's New York Directories for the two years prior to his 1836 marriage to Margaret. The house stood only two blocks distant from another structure owned and occupied by Alburtis at 22 Duane Street. John and Margaret's bedroom faced Broadway itself, indicating that this house was the westernmost of the five mentioned in title records. [See conveyance recorded in NY City Register's Office L 435 / P 354, dated March 28, 1843]. McCall sold the entire assemblage to merchant A.T. Stewart in November 1847, where the buyer built the still extant structure, a marble-fronted retail emporium. Stewart operated his department store at the site for many years until his move uptown to the easterly block front of Broadway between Ninth and Tenth Streets. The structure at 280 Broadway, which Stewart built on the site of John Burdell's home, was occupied by the *New York Sun* from approximately 1911 to 1950. New York City municipal offices have filled the building in recent decades. A recent addition to the structure of several stories, though part of a fortunate restoration of the entire exterior façade, significantly alters the scale and grace of the original building.

Before the construction at the turn of the twentieth century of architect John R. Thomas' Hall of Records at the northwest corner of present-day Centre and Chambers Streets (today, the Surrogate's Court building), and prior to the reconfiguring of the adjacent northerly street grid into the sites of present-day Foley Square, and the New York City Municipal Building, Duane Street curved in a southeasterly direction through its intersection with Centre Street, crossed Reade Street, and jogged through an intersection with Chambers Street before terminating at Rose Street. Construction projects for the Brooklyn Bridge approaches, portions of Foley Square, and the Municipal Building, each eliminated parts of this Duane Street curve. 22 Duane Street occupied a parcel just west of the Duane and Chambers Streets intersection, only a few yards from Harvey Burdell's first office at 21 Chambers Street premises, as well as his marital home at 69 Chambers Street. Today's Surrogate's

Court building sits on a plot which includes the site of Harvey Burdell's first office at 21 Chambers Street, and is bounded on the west by one block of Elk Street. This block was renamed from and is the sole remnant of Elm Street, in which lying-in rooms above a lager beer saloon played a dramatic role in Emma Cunningham's public disparagement at the end of the Burdell saga.

[124] See the article in *New York Tribune*, February 3, 1857, p 5, col. 5, which reports as fact Harvey Burdell's well-developed taste for wine and women as well as his frequent patronage of houses of pleasure. The deceased's distaste for matrimony and his fear of sharing control of his wealth with a woman is also detailed in the colorful article.

[125] An enumeration of the personal property in the house is contained in a chattel finance document dated March 28, 1843 executed by John Burdell. The document, which is recorded in the New York City Register's Office in Liber 435 Page 354, was part of an unfortunate chapter in John Burdell's life in the early 1840s detailed *infra*.

[126] John Burdell is listed as the only New York City agent for Gove's *Health Journal and Advocate of Physiological Reform*, published in Boston and Worcester in 1840-1841. The October 21, 1840 issue, at p. 99, notes that subscribers in New York City have complained that they are not getting their issues of the biweekly paper, and that it must be the fault of the post office; all copies intended for distribution in New York City will now be sent to John Burdell of 69 Chambers Street for subscribers to retrieve. John's bookshelves at 69 Chambers Street contained 17 volumes of *"Graham's Journal"* when a lease was entered into between him and Thomas Gunning for the house in 1843. See n. 21 and 22 *infra*.

[127] See New York *Aurora* August 31, 1831, p. 2. The entries in Doggett's 1844-5 Directory of New York support this story: John and Harvey Burdell are listed as both occupying space in Harvey's home at 362 Broadway.

[128] The divorce case is filed under Index No. BM 2663 B – 1846 Chancery Court records: Old Records Division NY County Clerk's Office. See also Henry Lauren Clinton, op. cit., p. 159. Pierrepont retained co-counsel (apparently one A. McArthur, Esq., whose name appears on the pleadings as Margaret's attorney of record in the matter), paying him out of Pierrepont's own pocket.

[129] A trip to the West Indies at the time in question and John's stay on a local plantation are corroborated by an account thereof included by John in Part Two of *Observations on The Structure, Physiology, Anatomy and Diseases of the Teeth, In Two Parts* (supra).

[130] See conveyance recorded in NY City Register's Office L 435 / P 354, dated March 28, 1843.

[131] 2 Union Place was located on the northeast corner of 14th Street and Union Place. Union Place was the name employed at the time by city officials for the several blocks of Fourth Avenue that border the eastern edge of Union Square Park.

[132] Two affidavits form part of the litigation file in the divorce proceeding, both from former employees of John Burdell attesting to his skill as a dentist and valuing his practice at $6,000 annually. By order filed June 22, 1847, Vice

Chancellor Lewis Sandisford awarded temporary support to Margaret Burdell in such amount as might be determined by a Special Master in Chancery, together with custody of her three surviving children, all *pendente lite.*

The enmity between William and Harvey over their brother John's and sister-in-law Margaret's affairs continued, and Emma Cunningham was ultimately drawn into the fray. In 1855, Harvey anonymously acquired Pierrepont's judgment against William Burdell. In a chain of several desperate acts seeking to do her lover's bidding and cement her relationship with him, Emma Cunningham accepted an assignment of the judgment on behalf of Harvey Burdell so he could secretly torment his brother. The documentation of the 1855 transaction was to play a prominent role during the coroner's inquest into Harvey Burdell's death as well as Emma's trial for his murder.

[133] Curiously, Gunning's name, as well as that of John Burdell, appear nowhere in the conveyancing records in New York County regarding 69 Chambers Street other than in the pledge of personal property cited *infra.* The possibility exists that Gunning became a lessee of the fee title, and then sublet to his master. John Burdell himself occupied the property years before Gunning moved in, perhaps also as a lessee.

[134] *Thomas B. Gunning vs. John Burdell,* Supreme Court, New York County, Index No. 1844 – 233;

Judgment Record filed July 9, 1844

[135] *Harvey Burdell vs. Thomas B. Gunning,* Supreme Court, New York County, Index No. PL-1844-B 669

[136] *Burdell vs. Burdell,* Supreme Court, New York County, Index No. PL 1848-B # 212 – complaint filed 2/9/48

[137] See *New York Tribune,* February 3, 1857 p. 5-6. Whether Gunning actually served time at Sing Sing is questionable: The New York State Archives in Albany contain two sets of relevant documents, one a handwritten ledger of admissions to Sing Sing for the period 1842-1852 [Index B0143-98 Vol. 1 @V168/3] and the other a typeset ledger of inmates discharged from Sing Sing, Clinton and Auburn State Penitentiaries for the years 1848-1852 [Index B0043-7B v. 1-3]. Prior years of the second set of documents are missing from the State Archives. None of the cited documents contain any mention of Thomas Gunning.

[138] Burdell paid $15,500 for the land and building to The East River Insurance Company for its deed dated May 1, 1852. See New York County Register's Office Conveyancing Records Liber 602 Page 668, recorded June 30, 1852. When Burdell actually moved is a matter of speculation. Trow's 1852-3 Directory lists him as already residing at 31 Bond Street, while Rodes' edition for the same period shows him remaining that year at 362 Broadway. Both publishers' 1853-4 editions show him at 31 Bond Street.

Gunning rented 53 Bond Street from Catherine B. Livingston on May 1, 1848, for a term of four years at an annual rent of $685. The transaction is documented in a memorandum of lease recorded in New York County Register's Office June 11, 1849 in L 491, at p. 421. Gunning had the right to cause Livingston to erect a back house or "tea room" on the westerly side of the lot, but only in a manner which would not block the light admitted to the house through the parlor windows. "Tea rooms" or back porches were a common feature of New York row houses in the 1840s and 1850s. Floor plans and photographs of several configurations of these architectural details are shown in Charles Lockwood, *Bricks and Brownstones*, Abbeville Press, New York: 1972 at pp. 68-9. The new building was to cost not more than $1000, and be not less than two stories in height, with an entrance leading to it from the front hall of the original house. Additional rent equal to a 10% return on the cost of construction of the new extension was to be paid, and the lease was automatically extended to a total of ten years upon exercise of this option.

[139] These ledgers can be inspected in the Old Records Division of the New York County Clerk's Office.

[140] The NY State census of 1855, although arranged on a dwelling-by-dwelling basis, contains no index cross-referencing street addresses to the census takers' idiosyncratic system of dwelling numbers. The 2nd E.D. of the 15th Ward contained the block upon which 31 and 53 Bond Street both stood.

[141] Strangely enough, the 1855 State census also lists in the same Ward and E.D. in Dwelling 243 a "R. Burdell dentist age 35" as a boarder, born in Herkimer County, having resided 20 years in New York City, in the brick house valued at $15,000 principally occupied by 28-year-old salesman H.L. Hart, who was born in Connecticut and had by then resided in New York City for five years. Dwelling 243 could have been 31 Bond, or 2 Bond Street, a house Harvey Burdell owned down the block. The identity of this "boarder" is a mystery; the age given is nine years younger than that of Harvey Burdell at the time, and the listing of the individual as a boarder is inconsistent with his status as owner of the two properties.

[142] Surrogate Bradford was to play a decisive role in the Burdell-Cunningham affair seven years hence when he ruled on the legitimacy of Emma Cunningham's inheritance claim to Harvey Burdell's estate based upon Emma's claim of marriage to Burdell in October 1856. See Records of the New York County Surrogate, L. 100 p. 61 *et seq.*

[143] Apparently by this time John Burdell had been successful in wresting custody of his minor children from his wife, Margaret. The file in the divorce litigation is incomplete, and no final decree of divorce or permanent custody order survives. Surrogate Bradford's probate decision on John's will does mention the existence of John's widow.

[144] *New York Herald*, February 5, 1857, p. 8, col. 3.

[145] Some of the allegations in the *Herald's* article can be corroborated through court documents and other sources cited above. The mix of news reporting and editorial comment in much of the cited journalism was commonplace in the nineteenth century.

[146] Harvey Burdell moved to 310 Broadway in 1841 or 1842, and the following year to 362 Broadway. The divorce complaint was filed in November of 1846.

[147] What arises from this account is a pastiche of possibilities, centered on John Burdell's professional and sexual gullibility, and the possibility of his encirclement during the 1840s by three predators: Thomas Gunning and his brothers William and Harvey. The *Herald's* story of a fraudulent mortgage granted by

John to Harvey is corroborated by a lawsuit brought by William Burdell against Harvey after John's death, itself predicated upon a lien allegedly held by William on John's personal property. Perhaps the forgery prosecution and civil theft suits involving Harvey Burdell and Thomas Gunning resulted in the restoration to John of the personal property that was taken from him in the "Mrs. Crane" incident and which was "leased" back to him by the recorded 1843 "lease" of personal property at 69 Chambers Street mentioned above.

[148] E.S. Pierrepont was a member of a distinguished Brooklyn family. The family gravesite occupies a prominent location in Brooklyn's Green-Wood Cemetery where the earliest graves are contained within an ornate brownstone open-air faux Gothic chapel at the crest of a beautifully wooded knoll. William Burdell's counsel went on to become Judge of the New York Superior Court, US District Attorney, Attorney General of the United States and Minister Plenipotentiary to the Court of St. James. See Clinton, op. cit., p. 317.

[149] Court of Common Pleas, New York County, Index no. 1855-70.

[150] *Galen Burdell vs. William Cullen Bryant*, Supreme Court, New York County, Index No. PL 1848-B #325, complaint filed July 19, 1848. See also, *New York Post* April 1, 1848 p. 2 col. 3. Doggett's New York Directory for 1847-8 shows Galen Burdell as a dentist located at 364 Broadway "*ent. On Franklin*", immediately adjacent to Harvey Burdell's home and office at 362 Broadway. The only extant records in the New York City Buildings Department relating to the structure that now stands at this address on the corner of Franklin Street are dated November, 1902, and concern the alteration of a five-story brick building then approximately 25 feet wide along its Broadway frontage and built almost 90 feet deep on the lot. The five story and basement structure was 57 feet tall at the time, with spruce floor beams and support columns. Beyond this evidence, the vintage of the extant structure is unclear, although its architectural design is consistent with the building techniques and materials utilized in similar structures standing in the neighborhood in the late 1840s.

[151] 1847-8 is the only year that Galen appears in New York City or Brooklyn directories within the decade. Galen was born in 1828; his siblings Harvey, Asahiel, William, Louisa and Adaline Burdell, were the children of Harvey Burdell's brother James and his wife Sila Lamon. [n.b.: John's and Harvey's mother, Polly Cunningham Burdell, married a relative of her daughter-in-law, Sila, one James Lamon, after the death of (or her divorce from) John's and Harvey's father.] Galen Burdell moved to San Francisco as a '49er. Rather than digging holes in the surrounding hills, the dentist limited his involvement with gold metal to drilling and filling prospectors' teeth at his office at 205 Clay Street. The records of Society of California Pioneers list Galen's arrival date as August 22, 1849. With the 30-fold increase in population that occurred in San Francisco during the two years after the nearby discovery of gold, and the departure for the gold-fields of the substantial majority of men engaged in virtually all trades and professions, Galen likely seized the opportunity to build a secure future through the practice of his trade in that booming city. A succinct overview of the havoc endemic in the economic infrastructure of San Francisco is presented in Peter J. Blodgett, *Land of Golden Dreams: California in the Gold Rush Decade, 1848-1858*, Huntington Library, San Marino, CA: 1999, pp. 28 and 121.

In yet another ironic twist, after her flight to California from the East coast following Harvey Burdell's death, Emma Cunningham would come to envy her would-be nephew, Galen Burdell, in his sexual and economic achievements. One might think the two were related by blood, given the means by which Galen achieved wealth and fame in mid- and late nineteenth century Marin County. Galen arrived in California in 1849 after a vacation trip from New York City to Brazil, and a tour of duty as a ship's surgeon. His practice of dentistry in the San Francisco area lasted thirteen years. Having achieved some financial success through his invention of a mass-marketed tooth powder, he married 17-year-old Mary Black, the only child of Marin rancher James Black and Black's first wife, Maria Agustina, in 1863. Galen's betrothal to the young heiress would have been envied by Emma Cunningham, who may also have arrived on the West Coast by the time of Galen's nuptials. Galen's father-in-law, James Black, had been the second wealthiest individual in Marin County as recently as 1854. (See the 1854 Marin County tax assessment roll for real and personal property transcribed on the Roots.com web site at http://www.cagenweb.com/marin/1854assessmt.html#B). After her father consented to her marriage to a man twice her age, Galen's wife was given 950 acres of Marin County ranchland outright.

Matters took a turn for the worse, for Mary and Galen, when her mother died under anesthetic in Galen Burdell's dentistry chair on February 23, 1864. James Black then turned violently against his son-in-law, and after Black's 1866 remarriage to the wealthy widow Maria Loreto Pacheco, he disinherited his daughter and son-in-law. Accounts of Black's behavior during the years after the death of his first wife describe a life of drunkenness and emotional instability. His revised will made it clear that since he had already deeded Marin County's Olompali Ranch to his daughter, she would not share in the inheritance of the balance of his massive estate. When Black passed away in 1870, Mary sued to have the will overturned. After three sensational trials, a jury accepted her contentions of paternal drunkenness and the undue influence of Maria Pacheco in Mary's disinheritance; Galen and Mary then became beneficiaries of thousands of acres of prime Marin County real estate and a substantial amount of cash. The couple went on to become noted horticulturalists, cattle ranchers and members of elite Marin County Society during the later decades of the nineteenth century. A descendant of Galen and Mary Burdell finally sold the Olompali Ranch in 1943. Before being acquired in the 1970s by the State of California as part of the Olompali State Park, the property was owned by a "businessman turned-Hippie-leader Donald C. McCoy" whose ranch house tenants during the mid-1960s included rock musicians Janis Joplin and The Grateful Dead.

The Burdell family has left its mark in the area: Mount Burdell forms a prominent geographic feature in the Novato/Petaluma area in California. The county also includes Burdell Island, a Burdell earthquake fault line and a Burdell School in Novato. See Jack Mason, *Early Marin*, House of Printing, Petaluma, CA.: 1971; also "Olompali Park Filled With History" in *The Coastal Post*, Marin County, CA: September 1997.

[152] See *Margaret Burdell v. John Woodhead et al*, Superior Court of New York County Index Nos. 1851-36 and 297-A, and deed dated February 25, 1851 from Margaret Burdell to Edward H. Alburtis recorded the same day in the New York County Register's Office in Liber 563, P. 508.

Margaret died intestate in November 1876. Her daughter Emily was granted letters of administration for Margaret's estate, citing its value as less than $1,400.

[153] Grace Church was erected in 1846 on a site at the northeast corner of those two streets. The house of worship remains in much the same condition today as it appeared on the day of Burdell's funeral, both inside and out. James Renwick's success in competing for the commission to design the lacy, Gothic-inspired structure led to his winning commissions for the design of Romanesque-styled St. Bartholomew's Episcopal Church, still standing on the east side of Park Avenue between 51st and 52nd Streets, and the extant second home of St. Patrick's Cathedral at Fifth Avenue and 49th Street. Today, the dignified reception room of the Grace Church rectory at 802 Broadway is adorned with a grand oil portrait of Reverend Taylor, as well as a full frontal view of the Church from Broadway in 1857, exactly as the excited crowds would have seen it on the morning of February 5. The congregation's records are still stored at the rectory adjoining the sanctuary building. No individual having a surname "Burdell" is mentioned in the membership ledgers. The February 5, 1846 entry in the diary of prominent citizen and one-time New York Mayor Phillip Hone's details the exorbitant pew rents and reordering of society attendant upon the 1846 consecration of the new house of worship. See *The Hone and Strong Diaries of Old Manhattan,* edited by Louis Auchincloss, Abbeville Press, New York: 1989; pp. 108-110.

[154] *New York Herald,* February 5, 1857, p. 8, col. 1.

[155] Ibid.

[156] Together with Laurel Hill in Philadelphia and Mount Auburn in Cambridge, Massachusetts, Green-Wood was one of the first "rural" cemeteries in the United States, where abundant space and beautiful grounds could accommodate sizeable family burial plots and outsize funereal sculpture. Over the years, Green-wood became the final resting place for many of the rich and famous, as well as New York's general populace. Green-Wood lies atop the Gowanus Hills, an important site in American history for decades prior to its conversion to cemetery use. With an unobstructed view in all directions, the hills overlooked the rural Brooklyn of colonial times, spreading out south and east from free-flowing Gowanus Creek and adjacent wetlands, which, in turn, emptied into upper New York Harbor at Bompjes Hook. The high ground was the scene of the Battle of Brooklyn, a critical confrontation in the early days of the Revolutionary War. George Washington retreated with his troops from this promontory, traveling across the East River under the cloak of an evening fog. After the Revolutionary War, the land continued to form part of large rural holdings of a few Dutch farming families into the early nineteenth century. In neighboring New York City, a population explosion took place during the same decades as maritime trade burgeoned, and the city replaced Philadelphia and Boston as the center of American trade. The real estate needs of the growing city led to the adoption by a commission of city officials of a far-reaching street grid plan. The gradual implementation of this plan interacted with the rapacity of real estate developers and the abandonment of gravesites by mobile urban families, resulting in the demolition of many churchyard burying grounds in Manhattan. Unfortunate and sudden dis-interments and reburials

in undesirable locations were commonplace as sites in Manhattan and the oldest sections of Brooklyn were excavated, new streets and building lots created, and all traces of sacred ground erased from the landscape. Frequent epidemics of yellow fever, cholera and other contagious diseases during the first third of the century in both Manhattan and Brooklyn also placed an enormous strain on available burial facilities.

Green-Wood Cemetery was incorporated as a joint stock company in April 1838, as a non-denominational public burial facility. New York City legislators enacted an ordinance effective May 1, 1851, prohibiting burials in Manhattan south of 87th Street, thus assuring Green-Wood a steady stream of customers. See Stiles, op. cit., p. 261. See also "White Man's Newspaper," New York: May 1851 issue; collections of AAS.

In addition to Augustus Saint Gaudens, the work of Stanford White, Patrizio Piatti, Karl Muller, Robert Launitz, and Henry Kirke Brown are represented within its enclosures. The main gates were designed by Richard Upjohn, architect of Trinity Church's extant 1846 edifice at Wall Street and Broadway in Manhattan.

A comprehensive history of the cemetery together with the histories of 250 famous, infamous, and unknown individuals buried there is contained in Jeffrey I. Richman's lavishly illustrated *Brooklyn's Green-Wood Cemetery: New York's Buried Treasure*, The Cemetery, Brooklyn: 1998.

[157] Dimis' mother, Katherine [nee Cunningham] Hubbard was Harvey and William Burdell's aunt on their mother Polly's side The author has been unable to find any evidence that Dimis' mother and aunt were related by blood to Emma Hempstead Cunningham's first husband, George Cunningham. 1850 Census records for the town of Henderson in Jefferson County, New York merely list Katherine's place of birth as New York State. Katherine and Polly Cunningham were two of ten children of John and Rebecca Cunningham, who resided in upstate New York in the late eighteenth century. By contrast, George Cunningham's father, William Cunningham, Sr., immigrated to Brooklyn from Scotland in the same period. See Stiles, op cit., Vol. II, pp. 93.

[158] A Mrs. Jones had preceded Emma Cunningham as boardinghouse operator of 31 Bond until May 1, 1856; Emma lived at the house and was Mrs. Jones' boarder until Burdell was convinced to turn the lease over to Emma. Likewise, when William and Dimis Vorce arrived in New York, they took a boarding room together from Mrs. Jones, until Vorce fled. See the testimony of Hannah Conlan at Emma's murder trial 6 Parker's Criminal Reports, p. 414.

[159] *Dimis Vorce by Emma Augusta Cunningham, her next friend vs. William H. Vorce,* Supreme Court NY County complaint filed 11/16/1855 (NY County Clerk Old. Ref. # 1855 V-99 PL-B).

[160] The text of the complaint literally states that the couple has no children "now living," implying that they had lost one or more children under unknown circumstances in previous years.

Vorce was among the many individuals who were suggested to the authorities as possibly responsible for Burdell's death. According to the *Tribune*, Coroner Connery received a letter on February 9 from Dr. Ervin Spicer, of Sackett's Harbor, NY, asserting Burdell's role in procuring a divorce for Dimis

Hubbard from her husband on the grounds of adultery "in consequence of which interference Mr. Vorse [sic] feels the utmost bitterness toward Dr. Burdell, who it is alleged, swore to certain facts during the pending of the suit; also that he employed a respectable physician to examine into the matter and testify before the referee in the case, [perhaps as to the legitimacy of the plaintiff's allegations of having contracted a venereal disease from the defendant] and on the representations of Dr. Burdell that divorce was granted – Mr. Vorse being then exceedingly poor and unable to defend himself in the suit. Under these circumstances this Mr. Vorse has expressed to several persons the most bitter and hostile feelings towards Dr. Burdell, and may have been driven to thus avenge his supposed injuries." Spicer had been acquainted with Burdell for a number of years, and had agreed with him to enter into a dentistry partnership during the later part of 1856. There is no evidence that Connery or District Attorney Hall pursued the allegations concerning Vorce's possible complicity in Harvey Burdell's death.

[161] Emma Cunningham was required to sign a bond for costs in connection with the matter, *Vorce vs. Vorce*, heard before Referee Wm. T. Horne. After the case was decided in Dimis's favor, Burdell paid the plaintiff's legal bill of $45, and the bond was discharged. See the *New York Tribune*, June 18, 1857, p. 3, col. 4.

[162] See Coroner's jury testimony of Alexander Frazer, transcribed in the *Herald*, February 5, 1857, p. 1, and that of Mrs. Dennison, transcribed in the *Herald*, February 6, 1857, p. 1. Although Frazer identifies William Burdell as the brother living with Dimis at Mrs. Graham's boarding house at 910 Broadway, Mrs. Dennison does not identify the brother by name; one of the witnesses at Emma's murder trial identified the brother in question as Louis Burdell, also a resident of New York at the time, by all accounts. The Bancroft House is listed in *Trow's 1855-6 Directory* at 906 Broadway, not at all in the 1856-7 edition, and once again the following year at 904 Broadway. A "Jane M. Graham, Boarding" entry appears in the middle of these three years at 910 Broadway, and not at all in the last year. The only other female entry in the three years bearing that surname and listed as a boardinghouse operator is for "Jane A. Graham" listed at both 78 Spring Street and 46 West Washington Street in the 1857-8 edition of *Trow's*.

[163] Harvey Burdell maintained an intimate relationship with Dimis, at least via correspondence, after she moved out of 31 Bond. His letters to his young cousin advising her of the progress of his campaign to rid his home of Emma Cunningham were introduced in evidence in the litigation in Surrogate's Court ensuing in March 1857 over the validity of Emma Cunningham's supposed marriage to Burdell. See *Cunningham vs. Burdell*, 6 Bradford's Reports, 489-90.

[164] Some years after Burdell's death, Blaisdell and John Eckel, who at some point became partners with Blaisdell in the liquor business, were convicted of non-payment of Federal liquor taxes. No mention is made in the journalism of 1857 of Eckel being part of Blaisdell's enterprise. Burdell's death spawned a number of strange relationships, and it seems that the two found occasion after the death of their mutual acquaintance to develop a business partnership. After conviction on the charges, Eckel died while incarcerated in the Federal penitentiary in Albany, NY.

[165] Blaisdell's testimony is transcribed in the *Herald* on Febraury 7, 1857 on p. 1.

[166] Dimis Hubbard's testimony is transcribed in the *Herald* on February 7, 1857 on p. 1. This settlement document was apparently discovered by the coroner's jury and disclosed to the press only on February 8. First mention of it is made in the *Herald* on the following day.

[167] Emma's younger daughter, Helen Cunningham, later testified that Cox offered Burdell $500 the day before the dentist met his death if Burdell would provide testimony favorable to Cox's divorce case against his wife. See transcription of testimony of Helen Cunningham in the *Herald,* February 9, 1857, p. 2, col. 2.

[168] Cox's and Stansbury's testimony is transcribed in the *Herald* on Febraury 7, 1857 on p. 1. Blaisdell returned to the stand on February 7, and his testimony from that day is transcribed in the *Herald* on February 8, 1857 on p. 5.

[169] See Conlan's testimony from her second appearance in front of the Coroner's jury, transcribed in the *Herald* February 6, 1857, p. 1. Blaisdell testified as to this appointment in his appearance on the stand for a third time on February 9; his testimony for that day was transcribed in the next day's *Herald.*

[170] All of the testimony of Margaret Cunningham and her younger sister Helen [misspelled "Ellen"] is transcribed in the New York *Herald,* February 7, 1857, p.1, with Helen's second session on the stand reported in the issue of February 9, 1857.

[171] Harvey Burdell's co-director at the Artizan's Bank, Alexander Frazer, introduced Emma Cunningham to Reverend Luther Beecher in the later part of June 1856 in Saratoga Springs. According to Beecher's testimony during the Surrogate's Court proceedings which disposed of Emma's claim to Harvey Burdell's estate, Margaret Augusta was enrolled in Beecher's Temple Grove Seminary that fall, and arrangements were made to enroll Helen for the winter term. See the *New York Tribune,* June 17, 1857, p. 7, col. 6.

[172] Dr. Wellington's water-cure establishment was located at 34 East Twelfth Street, and was part of a network of similar clinics maintained by practitioners of a medical treatment then in vogue among the devotees of the Grahamite philosophy espoused by John Burdell. The therapy administered to patients in Wellington's clinics in New York and Orange, New Jersey may not have been limited to hydropathy; visitor Bronson Alcott corresponded with an acquaintance in the 1850s after his visit to a Wellington clinic, and claimed that the treatments included therapeutic sexual activities, administered by the doctor to his female patients, and by female medical assistants to the clinic's male patients. See Helen Deese, "'My Life . . . reads to me like a Romance' – *The Journals of Caroline Healey Dall,* the Masachusetts Historical Review, Vol. 3, 2001. Professor Deese's article examines the diary of a well-educated Bostson woman who was a friend of Bronson Alcott's. The entry in her diary for March 26, 1857 quoted in this article provides the cited information, and is repeated in *Daughter of Boston: The Extraordinary Diary of a Nineteenth-Century Woman,* edited by Professor Deese, Beacon Press, Boston: 2005.

[173] The boys' testimony is transcribed in the *Herald,* February 8, 1857, p. 5.

[174] Cristadoro's and Wilson's testimony is transcribed in the *Herald* on February 6 and 7, 1857, respectively, and one example of the shop's advertisement appears in the *Herald* on January 5, 1857, p. 5, col. 3. Despite the movement of fashionable hotels uptown to the Broadway Entertainment District, the Astor House, which stood on the west side of Broadway by City Hall Park since its construction in the mid-1830s, remained a desirable hostelry well into the third quarter of the nineteenth century. It was finally demolished in 1913 to accommodate subway construction.

[175] In his memoirs, Henry Lauren Clinton recalled that several individuals informed him that they attended high-stakes games with Burdell on the evening before his death, and that Burdell walked out with considerable winnings. See Henry Lauren Clinton, op.cit, p. 118.

[176] See article in the *New York Herald*, February 12, 1857, p. 1.

[177] Neither the *Times* nor the *Tribune* published a Sunday edition at that time.

[178] N.b. The total number of copies is extraordinary when one considers the fact that Manhattan's population at the time was approximately 550,000, including a highly percentage of individuals who were illiterate, at least in the English language, and that the *Herald* competed with many other significant metropolitan dailies for readership.

[179] The scene outside the paper's offices and printing plant is described in the *New York Herald*, February 16, 1857, p. 2, col. 4.

[180] For the full text of the editorial see *Ibid.* p. 4, cols. 2-3.

[181] See *The Hone and Strong Diaries of Old Manhattan*, edited by Louis Auchincloss, Abbeville Press, New York: 1989; pp. 168-9. The other reference in Strong's diary to the Burdell matter is serendipitous, even in a city as small as New York, which at the time had approximately 500,000 residents. On February 4, 1857, as the news of the proceedings of the Coroner's jury filled the New York papers, Strong wrote: *"The chief subject of discourse, excluding all others nearly is the Burdell murder . . . and the extravagancies and indecencies of that ignorant blackguard the Coroner, Connery, who is conducting from day to day a broad farce called an inquest as afterpiece to the tragedy . . . I had quite forgotten Burdell. He was frequently in the office a year or fifteen months ago, and used to pay my father interest on a mortgage held by the Lloyd estate . . ."*
Auchincloss notes that Strong had a distinguished colonial ancestry (George's grandfather had been a captain in the Continental Army), and his family belonged to the same inner circle of New York Society as the Astors, Schermerhorns, Stuyvesants, Lenoxes, Brevoorts, and Howlands. Strong's law practice was conducted within the interwoven social, commercial and academic circles that were infused with self-propagating success for so many decades. His marriage to Ellen Ruggles, daughter of Gramercy Park developer Samuel B. Ruggles (and relative of Henry Ruggles who was buried in 1857 on the south side of Elm Avenue immediately across from the Cunningham family plot where Emma Cunningham rests today) is recounted in Strong's diary. The account is replete with references to his spouse that are patronizing, while at the same time filled with adulation of sanctified marriage and spousal obligations. Strong condemns the intemperance and whoring so commonplace even among his so-called genteel peers. Members of "polite" and "established" soci-

ety made no secret of their patronage of brothels, many of them located in the Broadway Entertainment District, although the more perspicacious gentlemen maintained a studied public posture of respectable morality. See Auchincloss, *op. cit.*, p. 123, and Timothy J. Gilfoyle, *City of Eros – New York City, Prostitution, and the Commercialization of Sex, 1790-1920*, W.W. Norton and Co.: New York, 1992. pp. 102-5.

[182] For a comprehensive history and analysis of the events and social framework of America in 1857 with particular attention paid to local the New York City economy, see Kenneth M. Stampp, *America In 1857: A Nation on the Brink*, Oxford University Press, New York: 1990, pp. 24-30.

[183] *New York Herald*, January 1, 1857, p.3, col. 6.

[184] *New York Herald*, January 1, 1857, p. 6, col. 4.

[185] *New York Herald*, January 11, 1857, p. 4, col. 4.

[186] Gustavus Myers, *The History of Tammany Hall*, Boni & Liveright: New York: 1917, p. 151. Myers recounts Wood's history as a bar room brawler, and his currying favor with "the petty criminals of the Five Points, the boisterous roughs of the river edge, and the swarms of immigrants, as well as with the peaceable and industrious mechanics and laborers; and he even won a following among businessmen. All these he marshaled systematically in the Tammany organization. Politics was his science, and the 'fixing' of primaries his specialty; in this case he was without peer." Wood's biographer describes his subject as an attractive man, six feet tall and slender; handsome with keen blue eyes and regular features. His first mayoral campaign was marked by repeated accusations of having participated in several commercial frauds; one had led to his indictment in 1851 for having allegedly defrauded Edward Marvine in a partnership relating to shipping certain merchandise to California. Wood escaped prosecution through the friendly Recorder's decision that the indictment had been brought a hair's breadth too late. The three-year statute of limitations had expired one day prior to the grand jurors' finding of probable cause, despite their conclusion that "the said Fernando Wood of the First Ward of the City of New York in the County of New York aforesaid Merchant being a person of an evil disposition, ill name fame and dishonest conversation" had schemed to steal from his partner "to maintain his idle and profligate course of life . . ." The record of Wood's indictment obtained by the Republican District Attorney Nathaniel Bowditch Blunt (under whose supervision A. Oakey Hall worked for years before the latter's election to chief prosecutor in New York County) can be found in the files in the New York Municipal Archives' District Attorney Archives for New York County for November 7, 1851. The indictment plagued Wood for years: the true bill of "obtaining Money by False Pretenses" was not quashed until December 20, 1857. A colorful account of Wood's career spread over three columns in the pages of the none-too friendly *New York Tribune* on September 6, 1857, in which the history of the Marvine affair was detailed. Although Wood's victimized partner, who came from Auburn, NY, shared the same surname with the Dutch Reformed Minister who allegedly married Emma Cunningham and Harvey Burdell, the author has found no evidence of a family relationship. Rev. Uriah Marvine was a native of Albany, NY, and likely resided in New York City for only a few years of his adult life. See VandenBerge, *op. cit.*

[187] Wood's career is also chronicled in Eric Homberger, *Scenes from the Life of A City – Corruption and Conscience in Old New York*, Yale University Press, New Haven: 1994 at p. 151.

[188] See Homberger, op. cit. pp. 151-2.

[189] Homberger, op. cit. p. 252.

[190] Mayor Wood's proposal was formalized in a statement made to the City's Board of Aldermen on February 18, 1857. See *New York Herald*, February 19, 1857, p. 8, col. 1-2.

The concept of a great public park in mid-Manhattan had been under discussion for years by the time of Burdell's death. The interests of competing groups of property owners, eager to enhance the value of their City lots by siting a new greensward adjacent to their holdings, drove much of the political debate. The legislature formally selected the winning boundary proposal during April, 1857, defeating the competing idea of locating the Park in a forested area adjacent to the East River in the vicinity of present-day East 69th to East 74th Streets, then known as "Jones Wood." Interspersed with the *Tribune's* coverage of the Cunningham-Burdell case through the year are articles reporting on the creation of the new Central Park Commission, the selection of Gilbert Viele as Chief Engineer, the public advertisement announcing the design competition for the Park itself, and the public auction of 350 lots at the losing Jones Wood site "in a state of nature, covered by timber." See esp. issues of April 13 and 20, June 18, July 1, September 2 and October 29. Homberger, op. cit., pp. 254-9 and 292-3 furnishes a succinct summary of the history of the Park's creation, while Witold Rybczynski's *A Clearing in the Distance, - Frederick Law Olmsted and America in the Nineteenth Century*, Scribner, New York: 1999, provides a detailed account of the master architect's involvement in the project in addition to an enlightening account of the overall process of creating the crown jewel of Manhattan's public green spaces.

[191] *New York Herald,* January 5, 1857, p. 5, col. 2. The Astor Place riot began near its Opera House, as local nativist gangs objected violently to performances by famed British actor William Charles Macready.

[192] A thorough analysis of the emergence of this urban culture in America is presented in Karen Halttunen, *Confidence Men and Painted Women – A Study of Middle Class Culture in America 1830-1870*, Yale University Press, New Haven: 1982. Among other examples, the author cites the emerging popularity of negotiable commercial paper and the anonymity of urban trade as elements optimizing the growth of swindling. Agrarian life, with its immobility and commercial tangibility, provided narrower opportunities for fraud in pre-industrial America. A plethora of changes in American society provided fertile soil for the development of cultural ideals centering on the art of the swindle: displaced populations, the deterioration of traditional religious organizations, the explosion of immigration to the United States, and the transfer of electoral control in urban political systems from its nativist and frequently upper-middle-class and upper-class guardians to foreign-born political clubs, all played significant role in creating behavioral role models imitated in many ways by Harvey Burdell and Emma Cunningham, both in their professional lives and sexual behavior. See Halttunen, *op. cit.*, pp. 7, 11-13, 23, 27-8, 32, 191-2 and 209-10.

[193] As one indication, the annual residential mobility rate in Boston between 1830 and 1857 averaged

85.5 per cent; see Halttunen, *op. cit.* p. 35.

[194] After more than a decade of militancy, a compromise overturning the centuries-long British legal rule of *feme covert* was effectively reached in 1860 between feminist leaders in New York State and its legislature. The temporary resolution is summarized in Edwin G. Burrows and Mike Wallace, op. cit., at p. 820:

"Progress came only when feminists trimmed their demands to seek, as the New York Times *delicately put it, the 'legal protection and fair play to which women are justly entitled' while abandoning 'the claims to a share of political power which the extreme advocates of Women's Rights are fond of advancing.' Finally, in May 1860, the legislature accepted a bill drafted by Susan B. Anthony that permitted a wife to own property acquired by 'trade, business, labor or services,' to be the joint guardian of her children, and to bring legal actions in her own name (and to be sued as well)."*

[195] *New York Herald,* January 10, 1857, p. 8, col. 1.

[196] *New York Tribune,* June 2, 1857, p. 3, col. 5.

[197] The transformation of gender politics during the first half of the nineteenth century in the American working-class society into which Emma Hempstead Cunningham was born is explicated and documented in Christine Stansell, *City of Women – Sex and Class in New York 1789-1860,* Alfred A Knopf, Inc., New York: 1986.

[198] The impact of immigration on urban politics in the United States, particularly in New York City, is the focus of Chapter XIV *"The Foreign Vote"* in Robert Ernst's definitive work, *Immigrant Life in New York City 1825-1863,* Syracuse University Press: 1994.

Myers, op. cit., provides a colorful introduction to mid-nineteenth century balloting practices in the City at p. 154:

The primaries were attended by 'gangs' more rowdy and corrupt than ever; Whig ward committees often sold over to Tammany, and Whig votes, bought or traded, swelled the ballot boxes at the Wigwam [Tammany Hall Democratic Party] primaries. Nearly every saloon was the headquarters of a 'gang' whose energies and votes could be bought. In Tammany Hall an independent Democrat dare not speak unless he had previously made terms with the controlling factions, according to a relatively fixed tariff of rates. The primaries of both parties had become so scandalously corrupt as to command no respect.

For other pungent descriptions of the state of electoral politics in 1857 both in New York City and on a national level taken from the writings of Ralph Waldo Emerson, the editorial columns of *Harper's Weekly,* and other sources, see Kenneth Stampp, *America in 1857 – A Nation on the Brink,* Oxford University Press, New York: 1990, pp. 24-30. Stampp's work also provides a comprehensive view of the national socio-cultural background of the Burdell-Cunningham tragedy.

[199] See G. Myers, *op. cit.,* pp. 154-5:

The discoveries of gold in California and Australia created in all classes a feverish desire for wealth. Vessel after vessel was arriving in the harbor with millions of dollars' worth of gold dust. Newspapers and magazines were filled with glowing

accounts of how poor men became rich in a dazzlingly short period. The desire for wealth became a mania, and seized upon all callings. The effect was a still further lowering of the public tone; standards were generally lost sight of, and all means of 'getting ahead' came to be considered legitimate. Politicians, trafficking in nominations and political influence, found it a most auspicious time.

This condition was intensified by the influx of the hordes of immigrants driven by famine and oppression from Ireland, Germany, and other European countries. From over 129,000 arriving at the port of New York in 1847, the number increased to 189,000 in 1848, 220,000 in 1849, 212,000 in 1850, 289,000 in 1851 and 300,000 in 1852. Some of these sought homes in other States, but a large portion remained in the city. Though many of these were thrift and honest, numbers were ignorant and vicious, and the pauper and criminal classes of the metropolis grew larger than ever. The sharper-witted among them soon mended their poverty by making a livelihood of politics. To them political rights meant the obtaining of money or the receiving of jobs under the city, State or national government, in return for the marshaling of voters at the polls. . .

[200] Both Luther and Edward Beecher were cousins of the famous Brooklyn cleric, the Rev. Henry Ward Beecher and the abolitionist author Harriet Beecher Stowe. Blodgett, op. cit., p. 33.

[201] Examples of the media's role in the incitement of "gold fever," religious and social attempts to quell the migration west, and the social circumstances and decision-making processes of individuals and families whose fathers and sons departed for the gold fields, are contained in Blodgett, *op. cit.*, esp. pp. 11, 28,-33, 48, 119-21, and 127-29. A lucid analysis of the role of individuals such as Galen Burdell and Cunningham and their peers in the entire movement west as well as a fascinating history and modern perspective on the mid-century greed that drove the '49ers is contained in Brian Roberts, *American Alchemy: The California Gold Rush and Middle-Class Culture*, University of North Carolina Press, Chapel Hill, NC: 2000. see esp. pp. 32, 37-42, 46, 54-5, 182 and 194-5. See also, Edwin G. Burrows and Mike Wallace, *op. cit.*, pp. 651-7 for a recounting of the contemporaneous local New York City events and effects of the Gold Rush.

[202] Charles Dickens, *American Notes and Pictures from Italy*, London: Oxford University Press: 1957, p. 245-6. Of these two works, *American Notes* appeared earlier, and was first published in 1842.

[203] See *New York Herald*, January 11, 1857, p. 4, col. 4.

[204] Bull was a celebrated Norwegian violinist of the mid-19th century. Although the quoted text implies that he was the proprietor of a restaurant or other place of public entertainment, neither his daughter's memoirs nor contemporary directories of New York City indicate his involvement in such activities. *See Ole Bull, a memoir by Sara C. Bull; with Ole Bull's 'Violin notes,' and Dr. A. B. Crosby's 'Anatomy of the violinist,'* Houghton, Mifflin and Company, Boston: 1883.

[205] The quoted material appears on pp. 224-7 of the recent edition of Foster's work edited by Stuart Blumin, entitled *New York by Gas-Light*, originally published in 1850 [University of California Press, Berkeley, CA: 1990]. Blumin offers the following picture of the pre-eminent position of New York in national and regional affairs in his Introduction to Foster's series of sketches of life in the city at pp. 7-8:

In 1850 New York's port was by far the biggest and busiest in the nation, with respect both to freight and to the human cargo of foreign immigrants, Wall Street was the center of banking and finance, and the city's merchants were a dominant force in the organization of inland commerce. It is perhaps less well known that New York was the leading industrial center in the United States, and that it was already establishing itself as the arbiter of national taste in such things as theatrical production and fashionable clothing . . .The New York post office also handled more than 60 percent of the letters and 75 percent of the newspapers mailed between the United States and foreign countries . . .The external influence of the new metropolis was most keenly felt within its immediate vicinity, especially by those people who visited the city. It is impossible to measure the number of people who came to New York on temporary journeys of business or pleasure, but it was certainly very large. Small-town and country storekeepers did not order goods by mail in those days, but made semi-annual visits to New York wholesalers to select their stock. They were joined by businessman of many other sorts, by increasing numbers of tourists, and by visitors to family members and friends who had migrated from surrounding farms and towns to the big city. These visitors availed themselves of, and quickened the demand for, hotels, restaurants, theaters, pleasure gardens, museums, dry goods palaces, specialty shops and all other ones (including the illicit ones described in New York By Gas-Light) that made New York so exciting, and so different from smaller places.

[206] De Tocqueville, *Democracy in America*, 1:3, 2:144-7.

[207] Halttunen's discourse is contained in her work on the changing public view of murder in the nineteenth century as represented through popular media, *Murder Most Foul*, Harvard University Press, Cambridge, Mass.: 1998, pp 189-91. The material in quotations marks referring to "autophobic sexuality" is taken from T. Walker Herbert, *Dearest Beloved: the Hawthornes and the Making of the Middle-Class Family*, University of California Press, Berkeley: 1993, p. 143.

[208] An extensive discussion of the mid-nineteenth century ideals of sentimentalism between the sexes and its interrelation with American commercial behavior is contained in Halttunen, *Confidence Men and Painted Women*; see esp. pp. 192 and 209-10. The cult of domesticity that swept through America in the same decades is chronicled in Stansell's *City of Women*.

[209] Stansell, op. cit., p. 19.

[210] For a discussion and images of the history of Bond Street's development as a premier residential location in Manhattan during the first half of the nineteenth century, see Charles Lockwood, op. cit, pp. 40-9; see also at pp. 72-3 in that work an 1866 photographic image of the northeast corner of Great Jones Street and Lafayette Place. The corner is one block north of the corner of Lafayette Place and Bond Street. 31 Bond Street was located a few paces from the corner. The photograph, although not precisely contemporary with the Burdell tragedy, fully conveys the pleasant appearance of the immediate environs immediately after the Civil War. The extant house at 26 Bond Street presents a facade quite similar to that of 31 Bond Street in 1857.

Titles to houses on the block where 31 Bond Street stood indicate the presence in the early nineteenth century of prominent New York families, among them Lorillards (whose snuff factory stood until 1855 on a nearby Wooster Street block), Chesebroughs, Roosevelts, and Rhinelanders, as well as those of Henry Brevoort, Hamilton Fish and Joseph Bowne.

In 1834, Samuel Ruggles, the developer of Gramercy Park, moved his family to a Bond Street home, departing not long thereafter for a home on the more fashionable Union Place. Ruggles developed several lots on this latter thoroughfare, then moving on to the planning and development of the better-known Gramercy Park project.

[211] The glittering *richesse* of the shop windows and salons on Broadway also diverted the middle and upper class public's attention from the horribly unhealthy living conditions prevailing only a few blocks away in the poorest residential areas of the city. Brutally brief life expectancies dominated the consciousness of rich and poor alike amidst the unfettered materialism of the era. The unbridled commercial and sexual swindlery so well-admired and thoroughly practiced among the population could be understood as an entirely human response to the prevailing uncertainty of life and death.

City Inspector Dr. D.B. Reid described a horrendous physical environment in his report on public health conditions in Manhattan for the year ending December 31, 1857, barely eleven months after Burdell's death. The city (consisting then of only Manhattan island) contained approximately 550,000 residents in 1857. Dr. Reid reported the death that year of 23,333 of these individuals, of whom 2,553 expired in public institutions such as the Alms-House on Blackwell's Island, Bellevue and city Hospitals, the city Prisons, the Randall's Island Nursery Hospital, the Ward's Island Emigration Hospital, and the separate Small-pox Hospital on Blackwell's Island. Among the overall count of mortality, 20,195 deaths were reported by Dr. Reid to have been caused by diseases such as consumption, "marasmus," "convulsions," cholera, scarlet fever, "inflammation of the lungs," small pox and "teething," all ranked high in numerical incidence. The remaining several thousand fatalities occurred as a result of "external causes," two-thirds of which were "Premature Birth" and "Still-Born." Only 63 deaths were labeled "Killed or Murdered" in this entire year. Despite the level of street crime documented in Strong's diary and elsewhere, murder itself was relatively rare: Burdell's murder was, in fact, the only one reported by the Health Inspector to have occurred during the entire month of January 1857. See *Annual Report of the City Inspector of the City of New York for the Year Ending December 31, 1857*, Chas. W. Baker, Printer, 29 Beekman Street, New York: 1858, p.7-11.

[212] Gilfoyle, op. cit., Table VII, p. 121.

[213] Gilfoyle, *op. cit.* Table IV, p. 126.

[214] Gilfoyle, *op. cit.*, p. 125.

[215] Gilfoyle, *op. cit.*, p. 152.

[216] Constructed in 1854, the Lafarge House was later known for many years as the Broadway Central Hotel. On January 6, 1872, on the hotel's grandiose lobby staircase, Edward S. "Ned" Stokes fatally shot financier Jim Fisk as a result of Fisk's alienation of the affections of Stokes' lover, the famed actress Helen "Josie" Mansfield. Although the Hotel maintained an important place in the world of elegant New York hostelries through the end of the nineteenth century, it slid ever downward through the 1900s, and ended its days as a residence for indigent New Yorkers as well as home to one of the pioneer barrooms frequented by bohemian downtown New Yorkers in the early 1970s. The structure collapsed on August 3, 1973 with a thunderous roar and the loss of several

lives. See *New York Times,* August 4, 1973, 1:3. The St. Denis survives today as an office building on the southwest corner of Broadway and Eleventh Street.

[217] The selection of entrees on an 1856 Lafarge House dinner menu is presented in adjacent Francophone and Anglophone columns, ranging from "Forms of Rice, garnished with Brains, poulette sauce" to *"Macaroni, a la Napolitaine."* Various pickles and relishes, with *"Cole Slaugh"* accompany game selections and roasts of "Mongrel Geese, apple sauce." Dining room service was available most of the day: breakfast was served from 7 to 11 A.M., Lunch from 1 P.M. to 3 P.M., *"Dinner at 5; Tea at 7; Supper from 9 to 11."* Those wishing to dine in a private setting could avail themselves of complete room service. The restaurant menu collection of the New-York Historical Society contains hundreds of contemporary menus from New York and other urban hostelries and restaurants. The quoted items for the Lafarge House are from its menu for December 12, 1856, and the confections are presented in a menu for the 66th Anniversary Dinner of the St. George Society held at Niblo's on April 23, 1852. For a comprehensive contemporaneous description of the hotels and restaurants in Bond Street area, see *Putnam's Monthly,* Vol. III, No. XVI, April, 1853 in its 1853 series *"New York Daguerreotyped,* pp. 359-68.

[218] Carl Schurz, *The reminiscences of Carl Schurz ... illustrated with portraits and original drawings,* New York: The McClure Company, 1907-8, 3 volumes; Vol. 2, p. 5.

[219] Burdell's custom of dining at the Lafarge House after he left Emma Cunningham's boarding table is mentioned in the Surrogate's Court decision regarding Emma Cunningham's claim to have been his widow. See *Cunningham vs. Burdell,* 4 Bradford's Reports, 361. The proprietors of the two hostelries both testified at the murder trial. See 6 Parker's Criminal Reports 477 and 489. The Metropolitan Hotel opened in 1852, and was located at 580-2 Broadway, on the east side of the avenue between Prince and Crosby Streets. Its ownership was controlled by one of William Marcy Tweed's sons in the early 1870s. Tweed *pere* invested some $600,000 in the refurbishing of the hotel in support of his son's investment. The structure was physically contiguous to the famed performance venue, Niblo's Garden. It was demolished in 1895, and loft buildings stand on the site today. See NYHS Hotel Files-Quinn Collection Metropolitan Hotel folder. For Tweed's involvement, see Myers, *op. cit.* p. 246.

[220] See article from the *Hotel Mail* March 28, 1885, transcribed in NYHS Hotel Files-Quinn Collection Metropolitan Hotel folder.. The balance of this article also corroborates Tweed's involvement in the Hotel in later years: "The Lelands were too lavish and openhanded. They did not know the value of money, and so did not become the millionaires they might have been. A.T. Stewart finally bought the property and refused to renew the lease of the Lelands, and they were succeeded by Tweed and Barfield, the former the son of Boss Tweed, in 1871 . . ."

The March 17, 1895 *Tribune* article reported: "In the days when Wm. M. Tweed, Sr. held the city by the throat with vice-like grips the hotel was the scene of many a disgraceful debauch, and if its walls could speak, they could tell many a tale of rascality concocted within them. . ."

[221] The story of Jewett's murder and a comprehensive depiction of the social and historical context are contained in Patricia Cline Cohen, *The Murder of Helen Jewett,* Alfred A. Knopf, Inc., New York: 1998. Cohen locates the 41

Thomas Street structure as being on the south side of Thomas Street, three blocks west of Broadway, and three blocks north of Chambers Street, in an area filled with similar establishments. At the time of Burdell's murder, the area west of City Hall still contained many brothels, but the social classes to which they catered were in general lower than those which patronized similar businesses in the Bond Street area.

222 Also remarkable is the fact that the Jewett murder occurred during a tide of financial speculation that led only a few months later to the Panic of 1837; Burdell was murdered during the peak of the next cycle of fraud and avarice that resulted in the Panic of 1857.

223 See Gilfoyle, *op. cit.* pp. 97-99.

224 Gilfoyle, Ibid.

225 Gilfoyle, *op.cit.*, pp 29-33.

226 In addition to the rumors and testimony printed by the *New York Herald* during the Coroner's inquest, and George Thompson's depiction of Burdell as a well-known gambler in a contemporary novella, the decedent's intermingling with the criminal classes in the neighborhood and his penchant for games of chance are described in Russell Crouse's collection of true New York City crime stories, *Murder Won't Out,* Doubleday and Doran, Garden City, New York: 1932, and in a story published in the *Herald* on June 22, 1890, p. 8.

227 Thompson was a prolific author of pulp novellas and risqué vignettes published in newspapers in the 1850s popular among the sporting class of urban males. Much like today, authors like Thompson turned their immediate attention to any noteworthy crime of the day, generating faintly disguised fictionalizations of gruesome urban tales for an audience of urbanites and rural dwellers hungry for vivid depictions of light and shadow in the nation's metropolises. A copy of the newsprint pamphlet entitled *The Mysteries of Bond Street; or the Seraglios of Upper Tendom* is located in the American Antiquarian Society's collections in Worcester, MA. The author's name is not printed on the pamphlet, although a penciled note exists on the cover page of the document: "George Thompson". Attribution of the work is instead specified as *By the Author of Anna Mowbray, Bridal Chamber, Kate Montrose, La Tour de Nesle, Amorous Adventures of Lola Montes, Marie de Clairville, Confessions of a Sofa, &c., &c.* Thompson is virtually certainly the author of the Bond Street tale, as many of the cited works were serialized in a prurient New York newspaper entitled "Venus Miscellany" to which Thompson was a frequent contributor. The style of *The Mysteries of Bond Street* is archetypical Thompson work. A thorough analysis of Thompson's career and his importance in mid-nineteenth century American literature is contained in an edition of three of his novellas: George Thompson, *Venus in Boston and Other Tales of Nineteenth-Century City Life,* University of Massachusetts Press, Amherst and Boston: 2002, edited by David S. Reynolds and Kimberly Gladman.

228 An immensely readable and colorful account of public accommodations, streets scene and various daytime and nighttime activities of New Yorkers, centered particularly on the Broadway Entertainment District is contained in Stuart Blumin's edition of George Foster's mid-century writings. See *New York by Gas-Light and Other Urban Sketches,* George Foster, Edited by Stuart Blumin, University of California Press, Berkeley, CA: 1990.

[229] N.b.: a community with a variant spelling of the same name sits on the shores of one of New York's Finger Lakes.

[230] See *New York Herald*, February 21, 1857, p. 1, col. 1. It seems strange that none of the many witnesses at the Coroner's inquest who testified about the events of September and October, 1856, made any mention of the presence of Dr. Spicer in 31 Bond Street. His presence in the house was corroborated by letters written by Harvey Burdell to Dimis Hubbard during the fall of 1856, introduced in evidence during the Surrogate's Court proceeding regarding control of Harvey Burdell's estate that ensued after completion of the inquest. Long after Dimis had moved out of 31 Bond Street, her older cousin continued to see her and correspond with her about his troubles with Emma Cunningham. A few days after the breach of promise and slander lawsuits were settled and after Burdell's alleged marriage to Emma, he wrote to Dimis: "I think I should not have had any trouble with Mrs. Cunningham, if it had not been for Spicer, who joined in her attempt to injure me; but all trouble is now at an end, I think; she is a designing, scheming, and artful woman; all her designs were to get me to marry her; but***[she] has failed." See *Cunningham vs. Burdell*, 6 Bradford's Reports, p. 489.

[231] Chatfield had served as Attorney General of New York State and was prominent in New York City politics and municipal affairs prior to the litigation between Emma and Harvey. See Henry Lauren Clinton, op. cit., p. 11. Thayer had also boarded at 31 Bond Street during the summer of 1856, according to testimony offered by Emma's cook, Hannah Conlan, during Emma's murder trial. See *The People vs. Cunningham*, 6 Parker's Criminal Reports 416.

[232] Clinton's career as an attorney spanned more than four decades. After his involvement in the Burdell case, he acted as special prosecutor in the most famous municipal corruption trial in New York City history: the graft conviction of William Marcy "Boss" Tweed, in 1873. Among the other notable defendants who suffered attack by Clinton in the last half of the nineteenth century were Mayor William Havemeyer, Tammany functionary Richard Croker, and, in a notable re-match, Mayor A. Oakey Hall, who was elected to run the City under Tweed's tutelage at the end of the Tweed Ring's hegemony. Clinton's account of his involvement in the Burdell-Cunningham case is described on pp. 1-314 of his *Celebrated Trials*.

[233] Seven years senior in age to Henry Clinton, Samuel Tilden practiced law in New York City since 1841 in partnership with the politically prominent Andrew Green. By the time of the Burdell affair, Tilden had already developed one of the most successful practices in the City. Fifteen years after their initial confrontation as adversaries in the Burdell hearings, Clinton and Tilden joined forces in another case that dominated the nation's attention: Tilden had taken his place as a political force in the City by the early 1870s, masterminding the downfall of the Tweed Ring and its designated Mayor, A. Oakey Hall, with Henry Lauren Clinton acting as chief prosecutor. As a result, Tilden was elected Governor of New York in 1874, and was nominated by the Democrats to run for President two years later. Despite his defeat by Rutherford B. Hayes, Samuel Tilden remained powerful in urban and national politics until his death in 1886. His voluminous library was bequeathed as one of the core collections of the New York Public Library. The legal files from Tilden's most famous cases

are comprised within his private papers stored in the manuscript collections of NYPL and include voluminous amounts of transcribed testimony offered in the Surrogate's Court case as well as Tilden's original handwritten notes of the investigation he conducted as to the *bona fides* of his clients' claim. Visitors today to the National Arts Club at 15 Gramercy Park South can still appreciate the magnificence of his final residence on the south side of the Park. See *The Encyclopedia of New York City*, Yale University Press, New Haven: 1995, p. 1184.

[234] Clinton's statement is contained in the first part of the Surrogate's decision in the case, *Cunningham vs. Burdell*, 6 Bradford's Reports 354.

[235] Connery's employment history is contained in his testimony given in Emma Cunningham's murder trial. See *New York Tribune*, May 8, 1857, p. 5, col. 5.

Many respectable citizens joined in Clinton's petition. See *New York Tribune*, February 28, 1857, p. 7. The controversy arising a few weeks later over an inflated bill submitted by the undertaker appointed by Connery to handle Burdell's funeral could not have helped the Coroner's defense; the invoice for 50 carriages at $6 apiece plus a new suit for the decedent at a cost of $60 was quickly withdrawn and resubmitted at a substantially reduced figure. See *New York Tribune*, March 12, 1857, p.6.

[236] See *New York Tribune*, March 18, 1857, p. 7, col. 3.

[237] *New York Tribune*, March 25, 1857, p. 7, cols. 5-6.

[238] See *Ibid.*, April 28, 1857, p. 7, col. 2, and May 21, 1857, p. 7, col. 2. Connery is mentioned as holding office in various articles published in the *New York Times* through late January 1859; thereafter his name disappears from the paper. D.H. Valentine's *Manual of The Corporation of the City of New-York* for 1862 does not list him as a member of the New York County Coroner's Office, nor as holding any municipal office.

[239] *New York Tribune*, May 1, 1857, p. 5, col. 2-3.

[240] See *New York Tribune*, April 21, 1857, p. 7, cols. 4-5.

[241] After Emma Cunningham's trial for murder ended, Mayor Wood was imprisoned briefly in mid-June due to his failure to cooperate in the changes. The Surrogate's Court proceedings involving Emma Cunningham's claim of being Harvey Burdell's widow were also disrupted on June 17th as the *Tribune* reported the next day: *"At 12 o'clock the Court adjourned for half an hour to allow Judge Dean [Emma's co-counsel] to go and assist the Mayor in his calamities."*

With nativist-immigrant street-corner conflicts always ready to ignite, and the change in police staffing having upset a major source of income in several powder-keg wards, riots broke out at the start of July in lower Manhattan, and several lives were lost. By the end of the month, Mayor Wood was defeated, and control of the force was vested in the new Albany-governed body, one supposedly free from the corrupt patronage of municipal politics.

Accounts of the creation of and battles over control of New York's police force can be found in Edwin G. Burrows and Mike Wallace, *op. cit.*, at pp. 638, and 838-41; also in Stampp, *op. cit.*, pp. 208-12, and Myers, *op. cit.* 185-6. Contemporary newspaper coverage is exemplified in the 1857 articles and editorials in the *New York Tribune* of April 1 and 23, June 3, 15, and 18, and the especially colorful reporting of the judicial decision upholding Albany's action on July 3 and subsequent days' accounts of the July 4 riots.

242 The notice of trial is published in the *New York Tribune* on Monday May 4, 1857, p. 7, col. 2.

243 Dr. Francis' testimony is quoted in *The People vs. Emma Augusta Cunningham, otherwise called Burdell*, 6 Parker's Criminal Reports 400.

244 *New York Tribune*, May 7, 1857, p. 7, col. 2.

245 Dean's objections to the admissibility of Conlan's testimony about the alleged abortion included the following explication of Hall's master plan, one which was to be repeated in various forms through the presentation of the defense's case: *"If this testimony is sought to be introduced to prove a motive for the murder of Dr. Burdell, it is incompetent; and if for that purpose, does it follow that, because Dr. Burdell may have committed an abortion upon the person of the defendant, that she in turn, a year and a half afterward, committed a murder upon his person? Is it not rather a part of the plan of this prosecution to blacken the character of this lady, not by evidence of the fact of an abortion, but by evidence of the loosest kind as to declarations. My friend has hunted through all the classics to find some parallel or name to bring before this Court, and we believe that he forgot but Medea."* See New York *Tribune*, May 6, 1857, p. 7, col. 2.

246 6 Parker's Criminal Reports 414.

247 Much of the testimony at trial as well as Justice Davies' charge to the jury are reported in 6 Parker's Criminal Reports 398-629; Conlan's defense of her sobriety is found on p. 427.

248 *New York Tribune*, May 7, 1857, p. 5, col. 5.

249 See New York Tribune, *May 8, 1857*, p. 5, col. 5.

250 Clinton's opening address is reported in the *New York Tribune* on May 8, 1857, pp. 6-8.

251 Throughout the many months of litigation before both criminal and civil tribunals, Clinton repeatedly emphasized the authorities' failure to pursue leads and theories inculpating persons other than his client in Burdell's death. Despite resolutions introduced before the City Council, no reward was offered for the capture of Burdell's killer until the start of June, whereupon the *Tribune* declared, "At this late date, the offer is almost worthless." See the *New York Tribune*, June 2, 1857, p. 4, col. 2. Assertions of culpability made to Coroner Connery by Burdell's enemy William Vorce (who had been divorced by Dimis Hubbard with her cousin Harvey's assistance) were ignored.

252 The final day's testimony is transcribed in the *New York Tribune*, May 9, 1857.

253 The account of the last trial day is taken from the *New York Herald*, May 10, 1857, pp. 1 and 8.

254 *The New York Herald*, May 10, 1857, p. 1, col. 4.

255 Ibid.

256 6 Parker's Criminal Reports 629.

257 *New York Tribune*, May 11, 1857, p. 7, col.3.

258 Eckel's case was severed after Emma Cunningham's acquittal; the trial in front of Justice Davies in May was only of Emma Cunningham. See *New York Tribune*, May 11, 1857, p. 7, cols. 3-4.

[259] *New York Tribune*, May 11, 1857, p. 4, col. 2.

[260] Edwards' closing summation is transcribed in 4 Bradford's Reports 395-430.

[261] See 4 Bradford's Reports 454. Dean's speech is also transcribed in the *New York Tribune*, February 3, 1857, p. 8, col.1.

[262] In addition to the transcriptions of the testimony and legal documents forming part of the fraud case that appeared in the New York daily newspapers, the pulp journalism industry of the day quickly generated pamphlets to provide a graphic supplement to the public's imagination and the newspapers' lurid prose. See, e.g. from the collection of the New-York Historical Society, *Fictitious Heiress of Dr. Burdell – Confessions of the Accoucher – Bold Game of Mrs. Cunningham,* Boston: 1857 [publisher unknown]. Hall's "bogus-baby" case indictment file is available as part of the official records of the New York County District Attorney's Office under the September 10, 1857 indictment date, available in microfilm form at the New York City Municipal Archives at 31 Chambers Street.

[263] The initial news article of this episode, published August 5, 1857 in the *New York Times* quotes the following section from the contemporary *New York Revised Statutes*: "*Every person who shall fraudulently produce an infant, pretending it to have been born of parents whose child would be entitled to inherit a share of any personal estate, or to inherit real estate with the intent of intercepting the inheritance of any such real estate, or the distribution of any such personal property from any person lawfully entitled thereto, shall, upon conviction, be punished by imprisonment in a State Prison not exceeding ten years.*"

[264] Clinton, *op. cit.*, pp 252-3. A thorough and fascinating discussion of the impact of the Gold Rush in middle-class eastern society is presented in Brian Roberts, *op. cit.*

[265] The quoted material is taken from the *Times'* reporting on August 5, 1857 and is reprinted in Clinton, *op. cit.* p. 253. The house at 190 Elm Street was located just north of Broome Street. Elm Street, a north-south throroughfare, ran north from Reade Street in the bed of present day Lafayette Street. The freight depots of the New York & New Haven Railroad and the New York and Harlem line filled the block bounded by Elm, Centre, Franklin and White Streets in 1857, where today stand the New York City Civil Court and a small park. Elm Street also ran alongside the rear of the Tombs, whose notorious faux-Egyptian main portal opened onto Centre Street just south of the rail freight depots' entrance. The Demotic Tombs and their infamous gallows courtyard stood on the opposite side of Centre Street from the present-day incarnation of the jailhouse.. Elm Street's course continued north past the New York City Arsenal at the northwest corner of White Street, the headquarters of the Board of Education at the northwest corner of Grand Street, and Metropolitan Police headquarters at the southwest corner of Elm and Broome Streets, all the way to the site of today's Cleveland Square. Other than these institutional structures, and Ward School 24 on the its west side between Leonard and Franklin Streets, Elm Street was filled with small low-rise buildings, punctuated with an occasional distillery or mahogany yard. A palimpsest of Elm Street remains visible to the lower Manhattan pedestrian near the end of Lafayette Street in Foley Square: a single short block named Elk Street runs along the west side of the Surrogate's Court building today between Chambers

and Reade Streets. Only the final letter in the street name was changed from the predecessor "Elm Street" when the remnant of the street was renamed in 1940. The Abstract of Title Book for Block 153 located in the New York County Register's Office contains a copy of a letter also recorded in Liber 4040 cp 135, recorded 1/2/40, issued by the New York City Department of Taxes and Assessments memorializing the name change.

[266] *Trow's 1857 New York Directory* lists Abraham Oakley Hall as residing at 107 Madison Avenue. Dr. De La Montagnie's separate account mentions his enlisting *"A medical gentleman, who does not wish his name to appear,"* having consented *"for the fun of the thing, to act as the [California] widow, lying in bed with a nightcap on, and doing the dismal groaning."* See *Fictitious Heiress of Dr. Burdell – Confessions of the Accoucher – Bold Game of Mrs. Cunningham,* Boston: 1857 [publisher unknown], p. 12 [NYHS].

[267] Horse-drawn cars were employed on the Fourth Avenue Railroad that Emma used that evening.

[268] (It was between midnight and 1:00 A.M. according to De La Montagnie's affidavit)

[269] Lunar caustic was the contemporary common name for silver nitrate. Dr. De La Montagnie's affidavit filed with the district attorney's indictment papers describes his marking the two-day-old infant and having *"tied about the umbilical cord a minute edging of a pocket handkerchief."*

[270] See *New York Tribune,* August 14, 1857, p. 7, col. 3.

[271] The court's decision is transcribed in the *New York Tribune,* August 25, 1857, pp.6-7. See

Clinton, *op. cit.* p 279.

[272] "Villikins and His Dinah" was popularized on stage and in cheaply produced pamphlets; n.b. the advertisement in the *New York Tribune,* April 1, 1857, p. 1, col. 2:

"VILLIKINS AND HIS DINAH – Will be ready on the 20th April, A new Comic Publication CALLED PHUN FOTOGRAFT which will contain between FOUR HUNDERD AND FIVE HUNDRED COMIC CUTS, AMONG THEM THE VILLIKINS AND HIS DINAH SERIES, Alone worth the price of this book. Sold by all dealers. Address, Ross & Tousey, NO. 121 Nassau –st., N.Y."

[273] The quoted display advertisement appeared in the *New York Herald* on September 11.

After attaining enormous notoriety in the early 1850s from his sponsorship of Jenny Lind's tour of America, his long career of developing the American Museum, and his presidency of the ill-fated Crystal Palace enterprise in midtown Manhattan, Barnum thereafter resided principally at his sumptuous manor, "Iranistan" in Bridgeport, Connecticut, making it the headquarters of his wide-spread and usually highly successful business enterprises. Unfortunately, the master showman made one astoundingly poor investment in a local manufacturing enterprise, the Jerome Clock Company, personally guaranteeing large amounts of corporate debt. His endorsement of those notes forced Barnum into insolvency in January, 1856. To protect one of his most precious assets, Barnum took the precaution in July 1855 of transferring the American Museum leasehold to his manager John Greenwood, Jr., who immediately conveyed the leasehold to Barnum's wife, Charity.

For years, P.T. Barnum pursued a program of dogged negotiation with his creditors, buying back the problematic notes in many transactions after arduous negotiations, and meanwhile generating as much profit as possible from the Museum and whatever other assets he could keep out of harm's way. The process of dealing with his creditors even resulted in his incarceration during the bogus baby scandal. See *New York Tribune*, September 3, 1857, p. 6, col.4.

The definitive modern biography of P.T. Barnum provides a colorful description of New York during the decades in which Emma Cunningham and Harvey Burdell reached maturity. See A.H. Saxon, *P.T. Barnum: The Legend and the Man*, Columbia University Press, New York: 1989.

[274] The popularity of Barnum's exhibition was immense, although theater critics bemoaned the use of the American Museum's stage for such lowbrow entertainment. George C.D. Odell's comprehensive history of New York City theater recalled the show in all it glory: *"And who or what in the name of drama – thinks the reader – held the stage in mid-August? No less a personage than the bogus 'Burdell' baby, so important a figure in the mysterious Bond Street murder, which in 1857 was the all absorbing topic of conversation. The real mother (Mrs. Anderson) and a photograph (by Meade Bros.) of Mrs. Cunningham, on trial for the crime, were further objects of interest for the gaping crowd. No wonder Thespis wheeled his cart from the hall! Yet I should state that the embroidered baby's dress provided by Mrs. Cunningham for the 'bogus infant' was an added feature of the show. Surely the reader will let me drop the curtain on this morbid exhibition."* George C.D. Odell, *Annals of the New York Stage*, Columbia University Press, New York: 1927-49, Vol. VI, pp. 567-8.

[275] Summaries of the onset of the panic are detailed in Burroughs and Wallace, op. cit. pp. 842-851, and in Stampp, *op. cit.*, pp. 217-238. Particularly fascinating parts of the *New York Tribune*'s coverage of the events, much of it detailing the heartrending scenes of poverty among working-class men and women that quickly ensued that autumn, can be found in its issues of August 26 and 28, September 1, 25, 26, 28, and 30, October 1, 2, 3, 13, 14, 20 and 26.

[276] *New York Tribune*, September 30, 1857, p. 4, col.2.

[277] Greeley's organ pleaded with Americans to stay put, regardless of their own destitution: *"We learn that from all quarters of the country mechanics are thronging to New-York in search of employment,"* intoned the *Tribune*. *"This is folly, for which they are likely to suffer. Business of every sort is stagnant here, as it is everywhere else. Manufactories and workshops are either closed or more than supplied with hands already. There is not a job to be done which has not already at hand twice the number of workmen required to complete it. Keep away from the city, then! Stay where you are known, and where you can struggle through the impending want of Winter with at least some friends and acquaintances to help you, or give you an occasional cheering word. Don't come here to swell the vast array of idleness and suffering which three months hence, will appeal to the citizens of New-York for charity."*

The *Tribune* explained to its readers the fragility of daily existence in an economy that had grown to depend on regional transportation systems to provide foodstuffs formerly available locally: *"In addition to the other causes of distress which exist in the metropolis, we are likely to have for the coming Winter scarcity and* high prices of bread. The crop of wheat is a bountiful one, but there are no means of getting it to New York. The canals are comparatively idle, because the derangement of the exchanges renders it impossible to send forward the breadstuffs, without which the Eastern cities must suffer a virtual famine, with plenty at their doors . . . What then will those do who depend on their daily labor for their daily food, and who, owing to the pressure, are thrown out of employment? It must be a Winter of terrible and wide-spread suffering."

See *New York Tribune*, October 1, 1857, p. 4, col. 6.

[278] Emma Cunningham acquired the 25 ft. by 100 ft. lot on the north side of West Forty-sixth Street between Sixth and Seventh Avenues for $7,000 from Mary William Turner, by deed recorded in the New York County Register's Office on September 2, 1854 in Liber 676 Page 46. She sold the lot for $5,000 and conveyed the property to acquaintance George Wilts by a deed recorded in the same office on August 25, 1857 in Liber 733 Page 559. Catherine and George Wilt had been acquainted with Emma Cunningham for many years; the couple, who resided at 43 Second Avenue in Manhattan, had attended Emma at the "birth" of the bogus baby on August 3, 1857. The conveyance was also noted in the New York Tribune, August 26, 1857, p. 7, col. 3, with the paper noting that Emma had signed the deed *"in a crooked and tremulous hand as Emma A. Burdell. It is said that she has also disposed of some valuable property in New-Jersey, to one of her counsels."*

Hannah Conlan's suit against Emma Cunningham was reported in the *New York Tribune*, September 5, 1857, p, 7, col. 6, September 30, 1857, p. 7, col. 5, and October 9, 1857, p. 7, col. 4.

[279] Emma's departure from 31 Bond was also hastened by the substitution of Harvey's brother, William Burdell, as administrator of Harvey's estate on October 1, 1857. See Liber 65 Page 123 - Bond Book 79, New York County Surrogates Court records. Emma's residence in Ohio is reported in *Harper's Weekly,* June 19, 1858, p. 391

[280] *Harper's Weekly*, December 25, 1858, p. 822.

[281] *Harper's Weekly*, April 9, 1859, p. 230.

[282] The *Gazette's* sometime questionable reputation for factual accuracy may in this case be strengthened by contemporary newspaper coverage. The *Brooklyn Daily Eagle* of April 4, 1863, p. 3, col. 1 contains an article without a reporter's byline (the lack of which was customary at the time) repeating many of the details reported in the *Gazette's* stories. It remains a possibility that the two publications shared a single author for their stories. The *Eagle's* coverage makes a much stronger statement about the existence of an acquaintance among Symonds, Burdell, and Emma Cunningham. See *National Police Gazette*, "The Princeton murder : the Burdell mystery unravelled! : confessions of Charles Lewis, alias Symonds," : 1863 [NYHS call no. 6534.P9N5]; also "Life and adventures of George W. Symonds, the Burdell murderer / by Peter Thomson, official reporter of Special Sessions: 1863 [NYHS call no. HV 6248.T48L72]

[283] *The Trenton State Gazette and Republican* provided extensive coverage of the Princeton murder and Symonds' incarceration, trial, and execution, in many issues dating between November 15, 1862 and April 4, 1863. The last of these issues describes the convict as a frequent gambler and well acquainted with

Burdell and Emma Cunningham. Burdell is said to have won $6000 in a faro game on the night he was murdered; the article claims that the cash was not recovered when police searched 31 Bond Street. One might infer that Symonds had some role in its disappearance.

[284] Various birthplaces in the southern New Hampshire and northeastern Massachusetts are ascribed to Symonds in contemporary accounts. The Templeton, MA Town Clerk has no record of the birth of an individual during the second two decades of the nineteenth century bearing any of the names said to have been employed by Symonds.

[285] The Sixth Avenue bakery is the only one found in contemporary business directories under Symonds' name or any of his many aliases mentioned in *The Police Gazette*. See Doggett's 1844-5 Directory of New York.

[286] Symonds' criminal records for this period are contained in the Boston Municipal Court Records, January-February, 1845, pp 209-213 and the Commitment Register for Charlestown State Prison, Volume 11, Entry Number 3859, both maintained by the Massachusetts Supreme Judicial Court Archives and Preservation Office in Boston.

[287] Many of the details of Symonds' presence in the Hudson, New York area are verifiable through primary archival sources. Parmenter and Van Antwerp's 1852 Hudson City Directory, Hudson: 1851, lists "Geo. Simonds, Confectioner and Charles Paul, baker at 106 Warren Street (home 108 Warren Street." This mention of Simonds is potentially problematic: the individual who spelled his name "Symonds" was jailed in Charlestown from 1845-50, and could have gone on to the crime spree in upstate New York in the early 1850s; however, a "George Simmons als. Simonds" is listed in the ledger of inmates as discharged from Sing Sing prison, Mount Pleasant [a/k/a Ossining or Sing Sing] New York, on August 12, 1848, having served a two-year sentence for grand larceny. The Sing Sing prisoner was a native of England, born in 1823, and a pastry cook by trade, standing only 5 ft. 3 1/2 in.; he could also have pursued a crim-inal career in Hudson at the time in question, but could not have been the same person as the Boston prisoner. See List of Convicts Discharged by Expiration of Sentence or Pardon, Sing Sing Prison, 1848 [Index B0043-7B] New York State Archives, Albany, NY.

[288] Contemporary records perhaps more reliable than the *Police Gazette* corrob-orate its story: the *1852-3 Directory of the City of Hudson,* William B. Stoddard, Hudson: 1852 lists George W. Symonds and the Franklin House at 5 Fleet St. in Hudson. The property was located on the north side of Fleet Street, direct-ly across from a small public park named Franklin Square. Fleet Street itself consisted of two short blocks immediately east of the tracks of the Hudson River Railroad, running from Water Street to South Front Street and bisected on the north by Rock Alley. Fleet Street is shown on the 1871 G.H. Beers Survey Maps of Hudson; it was obliterated from the street grid of Hudson in an urban renewal plan effected during the early 1970s. The Hudson River Railroad's pas-senger depot, which provided service to New York City and other downstate communities, stood near Fleet Street, as well as the passenger and freight depots of the Hudson and Boston Railroad. Both rail lines exist today. The for-mer provides Amtrak passenger service, and the latter carries freight as part of the Conrail system. The site of the Hudson River railroad depot in Symonds'

day is still in use; the depot has been renovated to resemble its late nineteenth century appearance. Meanwhile, Rock Alley and Fleet Street have been obliterated by the construction of a low-income housing project, Hudson Terrace, but the majority of the surrounding street grid and a number of structures dating from the mid- and early nineteenth century survive to this day, many in a condition that shows their venerability. One need only take a brief moment to gaze above curb-level at the weathered clapboard siding and graceful cornices facing Allen, Union, Partition and Warren Streets to imagine the town's appearance as Symonds prowled about looking for new opportunities.

Fleet Street stood in the middle of the famed waterfront area of Hudson, the economic importance of which had already declined somewhat by 1852 due to the growth of rail travel and the efficiency of freight shipments by rail as opposed to river-borne vessels. Hudson's storied days as a center of the Hudson River whaling fleet with its attendant sperm-oil manufactories were by then virtually over. The economy bustled nonetheless, except for intermittent national and regional financial depressions, as the never elegant waterfront area evolved in mid-century, mixing heavy industry and its accessory uses with residential abodes and places of entertainment and refreshment.

A search of the land records in Columbia County also offers information consistent with the *Police Gazette*'s story of the leasing of The Franklin Hotel to George Symonds by a woman uninterested in day-to-day operations. Title to the property had been vested in a couple, Harry D. and Rebekah C. Humphrey since at least February 1, 1845, when they mortgaged it to a third party. No subsequent transfers appear to have taken place until an assignee of that mortgage, one Henry Miller, foreclosed and took title to the property in September, 1866, thereafter selling it to a third party (See Deed Liber 27 p 651; mortgage Liber TT p. 206). Harry Humphrey apparently did not survive his wife, and one finds Rebekah Humphrey listed in *Parmenter's 1851 Hudson Directory* as a widow boarding at the Mansion House (Cornelius H. Miller, Prop.) at 172 Warren Street.

[289] Many medical witnesses at the Coroner's inquest into Harvey Burdell's death insisted that the murderer was left-handed.

[290] Accounts of the fire at the Franklin House and Symonds' arrest and conviction can be read in *The Kinderhook (N.Y.) Sentinel*'s issues of December 9, 1852, January 20, 1853, April 21, 1853, and October 27, 1853. Although many minutes of the Common Council of the City of Hudson, NY survive, the volume covering the period of the Franklin House fire and Symonds' prosecution is unfortunately not among those remaining in the City of Hudson's records room.

[291] The "lady at a hotel on Union Square" refers to an incident described in the first of the *Police Gazette*'s articles about a confidence game practiced by Symonds on an unwitting female victim in New York.

[292] The Bancroft House was located at 910 Broadway.

[293] The murder of Princeton jeweler James Rowland and Symonds' conviction are retold in John Freylinghuysen Hageman, *History of Princeton and its Institutions*, J. B. Lippincott & Co., Philadelphia: 1879, pp. 320-6, 417 and 431.

[294] The *New York Herald*, June 22, 1890, p. 8.

[295] According to the article, Emma Cunningham also supposedly visited 105 Wooster Street during the winter of 1856-7 in her quest to track down Harvey Burdell's many infidelities. The structure was a three story brick house set in a three-building group on the west side of Wooster Street between Spring and Prince Streets. Each of the three lots measured 20 feet wide and 100 feet deep; the houses all had a depth of 44 feet. During the two decades prior to Harvey Burdell's death, title to No. 105 passed from grocer Andrew Bowden to a factory owners James Murray and Abraham Ellis, with an interest being conveyed at one time to Ellis and Murray in 1840 by Daniel Ullman as Master in Chancery. Sixteen years later Ullman would board with Emma Cunningham at 31 Bond Street; he was called as a witness at the coroner's inquest investigating Harvey Burdell's death. The Bowden family re-acquired the house in 1842, retaining it until 1853 when it was sold to a group of Boston investors. Andrew H. Fiske, a prominent Boston attorney, George Morey, also a member of the bar, and Franklin Haven, president of Boston's Merchants State Bank, paid almost $31,000 for the house that year. Fiske, who had owned other property on First Avenue in New York earlier in the decade, later acquired his partners' interests in the house, which was assessed at $5,000 in 1858-9. The author has found no evidence that any of the three men who owned 105 Wooster Street between 1853 and 1858 were directly involved in the brothel trade in New York or Boston. Large amounts of personal property were frequently owned and reported as taxable by madams of successful brothels in New York of the day, but a search of the property address in the Manhattan Tax Assessment records from the Municipal Archives for the 1850s shows no taxpayer who reported holding significant personal property as also stating 105 Wooster Street to be his or her address. Although other nearby structures were used in the 1850s for purposes as diverse as a Jewish synagogue at 110-16 Wooster, and the Lorillard tobacco factory at 73-83 Wooster, the house at 105 Wooster stood squarely in the middle of the Broadway Entertainment District's red-light section. Houses at Nos. 49 and 51 Wooster were listed in an 1853 directory of brothels, and the surrounding blocks of Greene, Mercer, Crosby, and Laurens Streets (Laurens is known today as West Broadway) were filled with houses of assignation and larger brothels. See Gilfoyle, op. cit., pp. 33 and 317, and H.D. Eastman, *Fast Man's Directory and Lover's Guide to the Ladies of Fashion and Houses of Pleasure in New York and Other Large Cities,* New York: 1853 [NYPL microfilm] The *Herald* reported the house as still standing in 1890, with the basement devoted to a "human hair manufactory." The structure was demolished in the early part of the twentieth century to make way for the extant loft building on a site that encompasses the 105 Wooster Street lot as well as several adjoining parcels.

[296] Identity theft and the use of numerous aliases were commonplace in mid-nineteenth century America, not only by criminals, but also by those merely attempting to evade creditors. It is unclear whether, when and why Symonds would have selected the Lefferts name as an alias other than as one of many possible schemes to defraud innocent victims of their wealth. Lewis T. Lefferts is listed in Trow's 1857 New York City directory residing at the Wooster Street address and engaged in the "fancy goods" business at 641 Broadway, near Houston Street. Lefferts, who is similarly listed for several succeeding years, was likely descended from Pieter and Femmetje Hagewout, who emigrated to the New Amsterdam colony from Holland in 1660; the Lefferts name, which has been given to a major thoroughfare in New York City and many structures

throughout the area, derived from the marriage into the Hagewout family of Nicholas Lefferts in 1746. Lewis Lefferts died in March 1910, and was at the time a resident of the Mount Morris Park area in Central Harlem in Manhattan. See L.M.A. Haughwout, *Genealogy of the Lefferts-Haughwout Family*, Wright Press, New York: 1903. [NYGB Society Library and NYPL].

[297] The *Brooklyn Daily Eagle*, in its April 28, 1866 issue, also briefly noted the supposed confession of one Mr. Golden to the Burdell murder. Golden claimed that he had been hired by Emma Cunningham to do the deed. Golden was supposedly carrying on an affair with Emma's daughter Augusta before the murder and was challenged by the distraught mother to help remedy an untenable situation. The *Eagle* reported yet another confession to the crime on February 17, 1869, this time made by one Charles Jefferds. The confessor claimed to have been sexually involved with Emma Cunningham at the time of Burdell's death, and to have volunteered to despatch the dentist after hearing of Emma's displeasure with Burdell.

[298] This slaughterhouse district remained virtually intact until the post-World War II clearing of the multi-block site and its replacement with the extant United Nations headquarters. The author's two-part article about the district, entitled *Dressed to Kill*, appear on his New York City history blog at http://new-york-wanderer.blogspot.com/2006/10/dressed-to-kill-part-1.html

[299] The pleadings in this case are found in the Old Records Division of the New York County Clerks Office: *John J. Eckel vs. Commissioners of the Board of Health for the Metropolitan Sanitary District of the State of New York*, New York County Court of Common Pleas Index No. 1867-316.

[300] See *Brooklyn Daily Eagle*, January 23, 1869, p. 2, col. 2, December 7, 1869, p. 4, col. 1, December 13, 1869, p. 3, col. 1, April 1, 1872, p. 2, col. 2, and September 20, 1890, p. 4, col. 4.

[301] New York's best known and oldest Episcopal parish supplemented its jam-packed Wall Street churchyard with the construction in the 1840s of uptown burial grounds.

[302] One of Harvey Burdell's properties in Elizabethport was located at the corner of Second and Marshall Streets, and consisted of two houses and four vacant lots. Although the New York County Surrogate's Court files contain little if any information on the disposition of Burdell's estate, some information can be pieced together from real estate records and other Court archives both in New York and New Jersey. Among these are the pleading files from the New York County Clerk's Old Records Division for New York County Supreme Court in the cases of George D. Bulen and Alice his Wife, Plaintiffs, agst. William Burdell and Mary Elizabeth, his wife, Louis Burdell and Adeline Louisa, his wife, et al Index No. GA 61-1860, and The New York Life Insurance and Trust Company, Trustees for the children of J. Grant Jackson and his late wife Frances. B. Jackson against William Burdell, Administrator of &c., of Harvey Burdell, et al GA 496-1858. Among the New Jersey deeds of interest are one from James Burdell to Asahiel and William B. Burdell, Jr., acknowledged March 9, 1859, and recorded in Liber 4 at Page 369 in the Union County, New Jersey County Clerk's Office. Deeds filed in New York County pertaining to the estate administration include those recorded October 16, 1857, in Liber 737 Page 561 (and a related agreement filed November 3, 1857) which concern

William Burdell's obtaining an administrator's bond on the endorsement of Edward Stone, and James Burdell's deeds to his relatives and a third party of his interest in his deceased brother Harvey's assets recorded April 27, 1858, in Liber 756 Page 263, and on October 14, 1858 in Liber 769 Page 58. Both of James' deeds were executed in Ohio, but the earlier one, which conveys rights to an unrelated grantee, was executed by William Burdell "as attorney for James Burdell" for reasons unknown. The documents pertaining to the Edward Stone/William Burdell transaction also make mention of a deed of property to Harvey Burdell in Elizabethport, New Jersey. This conveyance was made from James Augns and his wife to Harvey Burdell, and was recorded June 9, 1855, in Liber 211 at page 165. The instrument predates the 1856 creation of Union County, and thus its recording sequence information probably pertains to the contemporary indexing system of Essex County, from which the new county was thereafter formed. Burdell's property in Elizabethport also included a waterfront parcel at the corner of Bond and Front Streets, alongside the Arthur Kill.

[303] See, e.g., the report of Emma Cunningham and two of her daughters arriving in San Francisco noted in the *Brooklyn Daily Eagle*, May 21, 1860, p. 2, col. 2.

[304] See Harry Laurenz Wells, *History of Nevada County*, Thompson & West, Oakland, CA: 1880, p. 234.

[305] Census and voter registration records for Bloomfield Township and surrounding Nevada County indicate that William Ellis Williams was 4 years younger than reported in the 1870 U.S. Census and contain no information indicating that he was married to Emma Cunningham. However, the obituary for a William Williams published in the Morning Call on September 7, 1883 is consistent with Emma Cunningham Williams' return to New York the following year.

[306] *New York Times*, November 25, 1884, p. 5, col. 2.

[307] *New York Times*, September 17, 1887, p. 5, col. 4.

INDEX

SET IN BASKERVILLE
AND ENGRAVER'S ROMAN TYPES.
DESIGNED BY JERRY KELLY.